SPORT STARS

In a culture obsessed with celebrity, sportsmen and women are some of the highest profile figures. We are fascinated by sport stars' lifestyles, love lives and earning power. *Sport Stars* investigates the nature of contemporary sporting celebrity, examining stars' often turbulent relationships with the media, and with the sporting establishment.

Through a series of case studies of sporting stars, including Diego Maradona, Michael Jordan, Venus Williams and David Beckham, contributors examine the cultural, political, economic and technological forces which combine to produce sporting celebrity, and consider the ways in which these most public of individuals inform and influence private experience.

David L. Andrews is an Associate Professor of Sport and Cultural Studies in the Department of Kinesiology at the University of Maryland at College Park, and a Senior Visiting Research Fellow at De Montfort University, Bedford. **Steven J. Jackson** is Senior Lecturer in Sport and Leisure Studies in the School of Physical Education at the University of Otago, New Zealand.

D0217619

SPORT STARS

The cultural politics of sporting celebrity

Edited by
David L. Andrews and
Steven J. Jackson

London and New York

First published 2001
by Routledge
11 New Fetter Lane, London EC4P 4EE

Simultaneously published in the USA and Canada
by Routledge
29 West 35th Street, New York, NY 10001

Routledge is an imprint of the Taylor & Francis Group

© 2001 David L. Andrews and Steven J. Jackson for selection and editorial material;
individual contributors their contribution

Typeset in Galliard by Taylor & Francis Books Ltd
Printed and bound in Great Britain by MPG Books Ltd, Bodmin

All rights reserved. No part of this book may be reprinted or
reproduced or utilized in any form or by any electronic,
mechanical, or other means, now known or hereafter
invented, including photocopying and recording, or in any
information storage or retrieval system, without permission in
writing from the publishers.

British Library Cataloguing in Publication Data
A catalogue record for this book is available from the British Library

Library of Congress Cataloging in Publication Data
Sport stars: the cultural politics of sporting celebrity/edited by David L. Andrews and
Steven J. Jackson
Includes bibliographical references and index.
1. Sports–Social aspects. 2. Athletes–Social conditions. 3. Mass media and sports. 4.
Fame–Social aspects. 5. Celebrities. I. Andrews, David L. II. Jackson, Steven J.

GV706.5 .S77   2001
306.4'83–dc21   2001031655

ISBN 0–415–22118–8 (hbk)
ISBN 0–415–22119–6 (pbk)

CONTENTS

CONTENTS

CONTRIBUTORS

David L. Andrews is an Associate Professor of Sport and Cultural Studies in the Department of Kinesiology at the University of Maryland at College Park, and a Senior Visiting Research Fellow at De Montfort University, Bedford. He is an associate editor of the *Journal of Sport and Social Issues,* and has published on a variety of topics related to the critical analysis of sport as an aspect of contemporary commercial culture.

Eduardo P. Archetti is Professor of Social Anthropology at the University of Oslo. He has written extensively on society and culture in Argentina and Ecuador. His most recent books are *Guinea Pigs. Food, Symbol and Conflict of Knowledge in Ecuador* (1997) and *Masculinities: Football, Polo and the Tango in Argentina* (1999), and he is the editor of *Exploring the Written. Anthropology and the Multiplicity of Writing* (1994). Archetti is currently editor of *Social Anthropology* and chair-person of the Department of Social Anthropology at the University of Oslo.

John Bale is Professor of Sports Geography at Keele University, UK. He is a pioneer in the geographical study of sport. Among his books are *Sports Geography* (1989), *Sport, Space and the City* (1993), *Landscapes of Modern Sports* (1994) and (with Joe Sang), *Kenyan Running* (1996). He has been a visiting Professor at the University of Jyväskylä, Finland and a visiting Fellow at the Centre for Olympic Studies at the University of Western Ontario, Canada. His most recent research has focused on European colonial representation of African athleticism.

Hilary Beckles is Professor of Economic History, Director of the Centre for Cricket Research, and Pro-Vice Chancellor for Undergraduate Studies at the University of the West Indies, based at the Mona Campus in Jamaica. He is author of several books on Caribbean slavery. He recently published a two-volume study on West Indies cricket entitled *The Development of West Indies Cricket: Vol. 1, The age of nationalism; Vol. 2, The age of globalisation* (Pluto Press/UWI Press, 2000). He has edited a number of collections on the socio-cultural history of West Indies cricket. *Liberation Cricket: West Indies Cricket Culture* (Manchester University Press, 1998), was edited with Brian

Stoddart. He also teaches a course at the university entitled 'A Social History of West Indies Cricket, 1790 to present'.

Toni Bruce is a Senior Lecturer in Leisure Studies at the University of Waikato, Hamilton, New Zealand. Her research focuses on the areas of race and gender especially in relation to the sports media. She has also been exploring writing forms that cross the boundary of ethnographic research and fiction. Her research has appeared in various journals including the *Sociology of Sport Journal*, *Journal of Sport and Social Issues* and the *International Review for the Sociology of Sport*.

Ben Carrington teaches sociology and cultural studies at the University of Brighton.

C.L. Cole is Associate Professor of Kinesiology, Sociology, and Women's Studies at the University of Illinois, Urbana-Champaign. She is editor of the *Journal of Sport and Social Issues,* co-editor with Michael Messner of SUNY's book series "Sport, Culture and Social Relations", on the editorial board of *Cultural Studies, Critical Methodology* and the advisory board of *GLQ*. She is currently completing a book on embodied deviance, sport, and national identity in post-WWII America.

Peter Corrigan was educated at Trinity College, Dublin, obtaining BA and PhD degrees in Sociology. He currently teaches Sociology at the University of New England, Armidale, Australia, having also worked at universities in Britain, France and Pakistan. He has published on the sociology of consumption, and is currently working on projects around the meanings of domestic objects and shopping in Pakistan, death, beauty, cybersociety and political discourse.

Michael Gerrard completed undergraduate and postgraduate degrees at the University of Aberdeen. In 1991, he graduated with an MA (Honours, 1st class, summa cum laude) in Cultural History. His doctoral thesis, awarded in 1998, was on religious identity in the North-East of Scotland. He is currently employed as a tutor in Sociology at the University of Aberdeen.

Michael D. Giardina is a doctoral candidate in the Department of Kinesiology and Criticism and Interpretive Theory at the University of Illinois at Urbana-Champaign. His doctoral dissertation focuses on transnational identity, celebrity subjectivity, and global sport from a postmodern cultural studies perspective. Other research interests include experimenting with a variety of interpretive ethnographic methods in cultural studies and communications

Richard Giulianotti is currently a lecturer in Sociology at the University of Aberdeen. He is the author of *Football: A Sociology of the Global Game* (Polity, 1999); and co-editor of *Football, Violence and Social Identity* (Routledge, 1994), *Game without Frontiers* (Arena/Gower, 1994), *Entering the Field* (Berg, 1997), *Football Cultures and Identities* (Macmillan, 1999), and *Football Culture: Local Conflicts, Global Visions* (Frank Cass, in press). He is a reviews editor on the journal *Culture, Sport and Society*. He met Paul Gascoigne briefly at a celebrity function in London in March 1996.

Christopher Hallinan is a Senior Lecturer with the Centre for Rehabilitation, Exercise and Sport Science and the School of Human Movement Recreation and Performance at Victoria University in Melbourne, Australia. He teaches Sociology of Sport and Sport in Australian Society and is a member of the International Sport Sociology Association and the Australian Sociological Association. His research interests are within the politics of ethnic, racial and national identites, youth studies, and ethnographic research methods. He is, with John Hughson, editor of the forthcoming volume *Sporting Tales: Ethnographic Fieldwork Experiences*.

Hajime Hirai is an associate professor at the Faculty of Education, Shiga University, Japan, teaching courses such as sociology of sport, and sports industries. His main interest is the comparative analysis of sport in different cultural and social settings, in particular in the Asia and Pacific region. He did his undergraduate course at Keio University, Japan, and graduate programs at Iowa State University, USA and Hitotsubashi University, Japan. He was a Fulbright Junior Fellow at Pennsylvania State University from 1992 to 1993.

Steven J. Jackson is a Senior Lecturer in the School of Physical Education, University of Otago, New Zealand where he teaches courses in Sport, Media and Culture and Sociology of Sport. His research interests include globalization, national identity, sport media and sports advertising. A member of the editorial board of the *Sociology of Sport*, Steve has published in various journals including: the *Sociology of Sport, International Review for the Sociology of Sport, Journal of Sport and Social Issues*, and *Culture, Sport and Society*. He is currently co-editing (with David Andrews) another volume titled: *Sport, Culture and Advertising*.

Kyle W. Kusz is currently a lecturer on the socio-cultural study of sport at Northern Illinois University and a doctoral candidate at the University of Illinois, Urbana-Champaign. His research focuses on critically interrogating the conjunctural politics of representations of whiteness in American sport, film, and popular culture.

Mélisse Lafrance is a doctoral candidate at the University of Oxford. Her research interests relate to contemporary theories of sexual embodiment and bodily topography. Her work has been published in *Signs: A Feminist Journal of Women in Culture and Politics* and in edited collections published by Northeastern University Press and the State University of New York Press. She is the co-author of *Disruptive Divas: Critical and Analytical Essays on Feminism, Identity and Popular Music* (Routledge, in press).

Mary G. McDonald is associate professor in the Department of Physical Education, Health and Sport Studies and an affiliate with the Women's Studies program at Miami University in Oxford, Ohio, USA. Her scholarship focuses on feminist and cultural studies of sport, the media, and popular culture, and explores power relations as constituted along the axes of race, class, gender and sexuality. Her research has appeared in several journals including the *Sociology of Sport, American Studies* and the *International Review for the Sociology of Sport*. She is co-editor with Susan Birrell of *Reading Sport: Critical Essays on Power and Representation* (Northeastern University Press, 2000), an anthology that ties particular highly publicized sporting events and personalities to larger cultural, economic and political realms.

Geneviève Rail completed her doctoral studies at the University of Illinois and currently teaches in sociology of sport and health at the University of Ottawa's School of Human Kinetics and Institute of Women Studies. Her research interests are related to issues of gender and sexuality and their representational modalities in sport and other cultural domains. She has published, both in French and in English, in a variety of journals focussing on sport and/or health. She edited an anthology entitled *Sport and Postmodern Times* (SUNY Press, 1998).

Nancy E. Spencer is Assistant Professor in the School of Human Movement, Sport, and Leisure Studies at Bowling Green State University in Ohio. She called lines for the famed Billie Jean King *vs* Bobby Riggs match, played and taught tennis professionally, and later received her Ph.D. from the University of Illinois at Urbana-Champaign. Her research focuses on the making of celebrity in professional women's tennis. She has written articles in the *Journal of Sport and Social Issues*, and the *Sociology of Sport Journal*.

Garry Whannel is a Professor of Media Cultures at the University of Luton, and was previously a Co-Director of the Centre for Sports Development Research at Roehampton Institute, London. The chapter on Beckham is based upon research for Garry Whannel's forthcoming book *Media Sports Stars: Masculinities and Moralities* (Routledge). He has published extensively in the fields of sport and leisure studies, and cultural studies, and has edited books on the Olympic Games, the World Cup, television studies, and leisure cultures. He is the author of *Fields in Vision, Blowing the Whistle*, and co-author (with Alan Tomlinson and John Home) of *Understanding Sport*.

INTRODUCTION

Sport celebrities, public culture, and private experience

David L. Andrews and Steven J. Jackson

To speak of a culture of celebrity nowadays is nearly to commit a redundancy.

(Gitlin, 1998, p. 81)

Stars represent typical ways of behaving, feeling and thinking in contemporary society, ways that have been socially, culturally, historically constructed.

(Dyer, 1986, p. 18)

Its drama, its personalities and its worldwide appeal mean sport is the new Hollywood.

(Bell and Campbell, 1999, p. 22)

Raymond Williams' invaluable glossary of cultural terms *Keywords: A Vocabulary of Culture and Society*, although compiled as recently as 1976, does not include a definition of the word "celebrity". Such an omission would be unthinkable had Williams been writing now – at the beginning of the twenty-first century, since celebrity has become a primary product and process underpinning what David Rowe has termed late capitalism's "culturalization of economics" (1999, p. 70).

According to Marshall (1997), the contemporary celebrity is an embodiment of the twinned discourses of late modernity: neo-liberal democracy and consumer capitalism. Indeed, Western liberal democracy represents a political system preoccupied with "the personal, the intimate, and the individual" (ibid., p. xiii); incorporates an equally solipsistic regime of economic (re)production (consumer capitalism); both of which are nurtured by the supreme technology of hyper-individualization (commercial television).

From the outpourings of the commercial media, whom Braudy (1997, p. 550) refers to as the "arbiters of celebrity," we are, at least superficially, privy to a wealth of information that encourages us to develop a sense of familiarity, intrigue, and sometimes obsession with celebrity figures. While the celebrity is usually a complete stranger, and someone we are never likely to meet, nor ever truly know, the virtual intimacy created between celebrity and audience often

1

has very real effects on the manner in which individuals negotiate the experience of their everyday lives. So, as well as being a consequential force within late capitalist Western liberal economies, celebrities are significant public entities responsible for structuring meaning, crystallizing ideologies, and offering contextually grounded maps for private individuals as they navigate contemporary conditions of existence (Marshall, 1997).

To be sure, celebrity is a notoriously difficult concept to define. In his seminal discussion, Daniel Boorstin made a distinction between the celebrity and the hero:

> *The celebrity is a person who is known for his well-knownness* ... The hero was distinguished by his achievement; the celebrity by his image or trademark. The hero created himself; the celebrity is created by the media. The hero is a big man [sic]; the celebrity is a big name.
>
> (1992, pp. 57, 61)

Further refining the notion of celebrity, Monaco (1978) developed a useful hierarchy of celebrityhood sub-divided into: heroes (figures whose actual achievements garnered positive notoriety); stars (individuals who actively cultivate public interest in their own personifications); and quasars (people unwillingly sucked into what Wernick (1991) described as the vortex of promotion). Within this project, we adhere to Marshall's (1997) understanding of celebrity as a descriptor incorporating various forms of public individuality (the hero, star, famous, leader, renowned, notorious) existent and operational within popular culture. The necessary dynamism of the celebrity complex means that individuals can, and frequently do, oscillate between these celebrity categories: there are countless examples of heroic figures (whose performances, achievements, cultural currency and economic value have waned) who consciously embroil themselves in the star system, and subsequently slide into a less flattering notoriety, having been singled out for tabloid treatment by the more sensationalist and exploitative tentacles of the popular media. For instance, the tumultuous celebrity odysseys of a number of the sporting figures discussed in later chapters (i.e. Dennis Rodman, David Beckham, Diego Maradona), vividly illustrate the fluidity and instability of contemporary celebrityhood.

Although our focus is on the contemporary sport celebrity, it is important to note that the public individual, in all its various guises, is certainly not a recent cultural innovation. Aspects of celebrityhood are discernible among the remnants of the most ancient civilizations. For instance, the god-kings of ancient Egypt had their very beings monumentalized through the medium of the built environment, while the Egyptian masses toiled in historical anonymity. More recently, in sixteenth-century Europe the aristocracy had their imaged likenesses captured for posterity by the professional portrait painters that roamed the continent in search of commissions (McCracken, 1988). What is new about contemporary culture is the scale and scope with which variously celebrated individuals infuse and inform every facet of everyday existence. At least partially, this can be attributed to the spread and sophistication of mass media technology over the past four centuries. The successive emergence of formal portraiture, printed engraving, the newspaper, photography, cinema, radio, television, and most recently the Internet, has brought with it a progressive expansion and intensification of human imagery within the cultural realm (Braudy, 1997). In the post-World War II era television revolutionized visual culture, providing heretofore unimagined depictions of the famous and the infamous, the celebrated and the obscure. This prompted Andy Warhol's sardonic prophesy that: "In the future everyone will be famous for 15 minutes." As we enter the twenty-first century, to some degree Warhol's prophesy has been superseded. A web page and digital camera are all that are required to provide instantaneous and continuous public access to even the most mundane lives (*Jennicam* being one of the earliest and most notorious of these celebrity start-ups). The anointing (or perhaps more accurately *celebration*) of anyone possessing the merest semblance of public visibility, regardless of its derivation or societal import, has led to what Braudy described as the "democratization of fame" (1997, pp. 548–9). Yet, while democratized and diluted, there continues to exist a hierarchy of celebrityhood, measured in terms of cultural penetration and endurance.

The highly personalized topography of today's media culture has its roots in the early twentieth century, even though the incipient visual technologies of the time (particularly the silent film and nickelodeon) initially promoted the novelty of the new media without any reference to the actors involved (Gamson, 1994). However, actors in the early cinema did not remain anonymous for long. In response to the audience's evident predilection for particular players, filmmakers soon recognized the commercial benefits derived from producing films that were as much vehicles for specific performers, as they were cinematic narratives in their own right: thus, the Hollywood star system was born (deCordova, 1991). The accompanying appearance of the cinema newsreel also provided a forum for the general public to develop more intimate, visually informed, relationships with an array of public personalities (royalty, politicians, labor leaders, religious figures, athletes, singers, as well as actors), many of whom had previously been distinctly vague figures within the popular imagination. The production of mass-mediated public individuals during the course of the twentieth century was ever more accelerated with the rapid dissemination of television during the 1950s. Within a remarkably short space of time, television ownership reached critical mass and usurped the newspaper, radio, and cinema, as the most influential medium of mass communication. Invoking McLuhan's somewhat clichéd, but still insightful, notion that "the medium is the message" (McLuhan, 1964), television sprang forth as a mass medium whose focus on readily identifiable human figures – with whom an audience is encouraged to develop a *faux* intimacy – increased the physiognomic vocabulary, and expectancy, of the general audience. As Giulianotti noted, "The role of the media in promoting stardom and celebrity status is critical and reciprocal for the biggest medium of all" (1999, p. 118).

With the dominance of the individualizing production aesthetic of the new "television culture" (Fiske, 1987), the identification, nurturing, exposition, celebration, and/or castigation of public individuals became a core constituent of the popular media universe: "everyone is involved in either producing or consuming celebrities. Through TV advertisements, restaurant openings, charity balls, trade shows, and sports events, our lives are celebrity saturated" (Rein *et al.*, 1997, p. x). Within this context, diverse arenas such as politics, religion, commerce, the judiciary, sport, and virtually all other forms of entertainment, have cultivated their own celebrity economies. As a consequence, social institutions, practices, and issues are principally represented to, and understood within, the popular imagination through the actions of celebrated individuals.

Contemporary celebrity culture's constitutive link with consumer capitalism is most visibly evidenced by the dual role occupied by celebrities as both products (the preponderance of celebrity-driven media and commodities) and processes (the pre-eminence of celebrity endorsement) within the dominant, symbolically propelled, regime of capital accumulation underpinning the late capitalist economy (Jameson, 1991; Marshall, 1997). Although at one point in time the emergence of celebrity figures was a haphazard and arbitrary voyage of discovery, today the process is considerably more proactive in its focus on the cultivation of potential celebrities. Indeed, the celebrity industry (the institutions and individuals responsible for the manufacturing of celebrity identities) has evolved into a multi-faceted, integrated, and highly rationalized phenomenon through which "people can be manufactured into, and marketed as, celebrities in any field" (Rein *et al.*, 1997, p. 5). The premeditated nature of contemporary celebrity is outlined in Rein *et al.*'s descriptive explication of the celebrity industry: *High Visibility: The Making and Marketing of Professionals into Celebrities*. Rein *et al.* identify eight interrelated industries which contribute to the manufacturing of celebrity: the representation industry; the endorsement industry; the publicity industry; the communication industry; the entertainment industry; the coaching industry; the legal industry; and the appearance industry. The optimum goal of this celebrity-making process is for the individual, and his/her representatives, to harmoniously orchestrate the various industrial facets of cultural production, and thereby foster a consistent and highly visible celebrity identity.

Despite synergistic ties that blur the boundaries between the various armatures of the culture industries, it would be erroneous to assume that many of them do not still possess a considerable degree of autonomy. In this regard the celebrity is very much "a negotiated terrain of significance" (Marshall, 1997, p. 47). The various facets of the new media complex (network, cable, and satellite television; cinema; radio; newspapers; magazines; and websites, etc.) interface in

4

varied, and variable, ways (ranging from the collusive, through the parasitic, to the antithetic) to substantiate the necessarily intertextual demeanor of contemporary celebrityhood. Significantly, the inability to control the manner in which many mass media channels choose to represent celebrities frequently results in the circulation of conflicting messages. These often contradict the intended imaged persona as scripted by the more collusive components of the celebrity manufacturing process. Similarly, even the most carefully laid plans of cultural producers are frequently derailed by the unscripted, unpredictable, and often scandalous, exploits of celebrities *in process*. Such behaviors range from the trivial (a failure to fulfill contractual obligations with a corporate sponsor) to the consequential (drug use, violent or sexual assault), of which the latter can fatally undermine even the most culturally and commercially entrenched celebrity persona.

As with any cultural product, there is also no guarantee that celebrities will be consumed in the manner intended by those orchestrating the manufacturing process. Audiences are far from homogeneous entities, and consumers habitually display contrasting expressions of celebrity appropriation according to the cultural, political, and economic contingencies of their social location (Hall, 1980; Johnson, 1987). Given their contested nature, those within the celebrity industry seek to manufacture celebrity identities which acknowledge, and seek to engage, the perceived sensibilities of the audience(s) in question. As such, celebrities are crafted as contextually sensitive points of cultural negotiation, between those controlling the dominant modes and mechanisms of cultural production, and their perceptions of the audience's practices of cultural reception. The celebrity is thus, at any given conjuncture, a *potentially* potent "representative subjectivity" (source of cultural identification) pertaining to the "collective configurations" (social class, gender, sexuality, race, ethnicity, age, nationality) through which individuals fashion their very existence (Marshall, 1997, pp. xi, xii).

Despite its contemporaneous importance, only relatively recently – arguably since the cultural turn initiated in the social sciences during the 1970s – has the academic community taken a concerted interest in critically analyzing the celebrity phenomenon (cf. Dyer, 1979, 1986; Gamson, 1994; Gledhill, 1991; Marshall, 1997; Schwichtenberg, 1993; Smith, 1993). While there has been at least some recognition of the cultural significance of celebrities within the realms of music, film, art, or politics, the ubiquitous and expansive economy of sport celebrities which invades our daily lives has not generated the same degree of interest among critical cultural commentators (for recent exceptions to this neglect see (Altimore, 1999; Baker and Boyd, 1997; Birrell and McDonald, 2000; Cole and Hribar, 1995; Holt *et al.*, 1996; King, 1993; Rowe, 1994; Vande Berg, 1998) and especially (Whannel, 1992; 1998; 1999; 2000). Thus, and as formulaic a rationale for this project as it may sound, a comprehensive and critical study of sporting celebrities is nonetheless long overdue.

According to many observers, the era of the modern sport celebrity began with William Randolph Hearst's establishing of the first newspaper sport section within *The New York Journal* in 1895. This popular initiative soon spawned imitations in numerous national settings, and provided a mechanism and forum for the transformation of notable athletes into nationally celebrated figures: a process of familiarization which – given the public's voracious interest in gaining a more intimate knowledge of their nascent sport stars – evolved as an effective means of increasing newspaper circulation. Hence, figures such as the English cricketer W.G. Grace, the Welsh Rugby union player Gwyn Nicholls, and the American jockey Tod Sloan, all sprang to national prominence around this time, and could be considered among the first modern sport celebrities (see Dizikes, 2000; Rae, 1999; Williams, 1991). The next stage in the evolution of the sport celebrity can be traced to the mid-1920s, and is exemplified by the popularizing of Harold "Red" Grange, the University of Illinois and Chicago Bear running back. Perhaps most significant in this process was the influence of the legendary sports journalist, Grantland Rice, and his newsreel reporting competitors, who mythologized Grange's pyrrhic exploits to the estimated 60 million Americans then visiting movie houses each week (Carroll, 1999; Harper, 1994; 1999). As Rader (1983, p. 11) noted, Grange was one of a coterie of skillfully promoted sporting figures at this time (others included Babe Ruth, Jack Dempsey, Bobby Jones, and Bill Tilden) elevated to the status of popular "compensatory" heroes, through their imaged personas which helped assuage public anxieties pertaining to the "passing of the traditional dream of success, the erosion of Victorian values and feelings of powerlessness."

Grange was able to financially capitalize upon his great popularity as the "Galloping Ghost" by hawking his iconic identity to corporations within America's burgeoning consumer economy. However, his contemporary, the legendary baseball player George Herman "Babe" Ruth, most successfully translated astounding on-field performances into lucrative off-field appearance and sponsorship contracts. Ruth's larger-than-life persona (both on and off the baseball diamond) lent itself to the lionizing sensibilities of the newspaper and newsreel coverage of the time, to the extent that Ruthian became an adjective used to describe individual success, heroism, and style (Susman, 1984). The popular media rendered Ruth an "idol of consumption" (Lowenthal, 1961) by keying on his celebrated gluttony and extravagance, thus articulating a populist vision of what Americans could and should expect from their burgeoning consumer culture. Ruth possessed an unrivalled:

> capacity to project multiple images of brute power, the natural unin-hibited man and the fulfillment of the American success dream. Ruth was living proof that the lone individual could still rise from mean, vulgar beginnings to fame and fortune, to a position of public recogni-tion equalled by few men in American history.
>
> (Rader, 1983, p. 12)

Given his populist aura, a myriad of commercial entities sought to secure Ruth's services as a spokesperson for their products, and he became the prototypical sport celebrity endorser: a figure and role that possess continued relevance to today's $324 billion global sport industry (Meeks, 1997), as evidenced by the fact that sport celebrity endorsers were present in 11 percent of all television advertisements in 1995, receiving more than $1 billion dollars from US companies for their services (Dyson and Turco, 1998).

The nature and influence of the sport celebrity were elevated to a considerably higher plane in the post-World War II era with the advent of a postmodern "civilization of the image" (Kearney, 1989), instantiated by the widespread adoption of televisual communications technology. Television's innate predilection for human intimacy, coupled with live sport's telegenic qualities (the drama of the uncertain outcome played out by a cast of definable characters), secured sport's place in the schedule during the early years of network television, and bred a new generation of television sport heroes such as Arnold Palmer, Mickey Mantle, and Joe Namath. In the intervening decades, the ever more collusive relationship between television and sport profoundly influenced the tenor of popular sport culture, such that sport is now "basically media-driven celebrity entertainment" (Pierce, 1995, p. 185). Sports are customarily structured, marketed, mediated, and experienced, as contests between identifiable individuals (or groups of individuals) with whom the audience is expected to possess (or develop) some kind of affective attachment. As Whannel (1998, p. 23) has identified, "Sport is presented largely in terms of stars and narratives: the media narrativises the events of sport, transforming them into stories with stars and characters; heroes and villains." Or, in Lusted's (1991, p. 251) terms, if "Personalities are central to the institution of television", they are even more central to the institution and era of televized sport.

Given the centrality of noteworthy individuals to the constitution and experience of contemporary sport culture, it is little wonder that a thriving sport celebrity industry has come to the fore. Headed by such mega-agencies as IMG, Octagon, and SFX, the manufacturing of sport celebrities has become a highly systematized, almost McDonaldized (Ritzer, 1998) process. The postmodern disposition toward the blurring of institutional boundaries has meant the spheres within which sport celebrities operate as cultural and economic agents have broadened beyond those of the playing field and the corporate endorsement. Indeed, the "sports superstar ... has sufficient prominence ... to spin off into the wider realm of popular entertainment" (Rowe, 1995, pp. 117–18), and is liable to appear in commercial settings ranging from ghosted autobiographies, to television situation comedies, talk shows, mainstream movies, popular music recordings, animated video games, and websites. So, within today's multi-layered "promotional culture" (Wernick, 1991), the sport celebrity is effectively a multi-textual and multi-platform promotional entity.

Without question sporting celebrity possesses numerous qualities that distinguish it from the imaged embodiments of other cultural realms. On a positive note, as a celebrity domain there are certain tangible benefits derived from sport's historically configured social positioning and implicit structure. First, when positioned against other celebrity formations (within which inherited wealth and status frequently play an important role), sport is considered to be fundamentally meritocratic. Sport celebrity then becomes the assumed corollary of performative excellence:

> The cultural illusion is fostered that, one day, the "ordinary but special" individual consumer may realize his or her unique qualities, and join the ever-changing pantheon of celebrities. Sport has a particularly potent role to play within this ideological formation.
>
> (Giulianotti, 1999, pp. 118–19)

In true neo-liberal fashion, the ascent to sport celebrityhood is habitually reduced to individual qualities such as innate talent, dedication, and good fortune, thus positioning the sport star as a deserved benefactor of his/her devotion to succeed within the popular imaginary. Second, sport is a uniquely valued cultural practice: "Only sports has the nation, and sometimes the world, watching the same thing at the same time, and if you have a message, that's a potent messenger" (Singer, 1998, quoted in Rowe, 1999, p. 74). Although by no means guaranteed, sport figures are likely to possess a heightened presence and affection within popular consciousness, making the transition to potent celebrityhood that much easier. Third, in the cinematic and popular music industries, individual performers routinely adopt fictive identities within their primary performative realms (e.g. films and music videos). Conversely, in sport, there is a perception that spectators/viewers are confronted with *real* individuals participating in unpredictable contests. Hence, the seeming visceral, dramatic immediacy of the sport practice provides the sport celebrity with an important veneer of authenticity, that sets him or her apart from celebrities drawn from other, more explicitly manufactured, cultural realms.

More problematically, sport also incorporates a host of idiosyncratic instabilities that can impact upon the process of celebrity manufacture. For instance in most – but not all – cases, sport celebrities emerge and endure due to continued excellence within their respective fields of endeavor. This represents an added layer of instability for those managing sport celebrity, since carefully scripted and heavily invested imaged personas can potentially be compromised by declines in performative function, or even individual failures on the field of play. In addition, off-the-field indiscretions can also play a role in undermining the personal narrative associated with a particular sport celebrity (the classic example being O.J. Simpson, see Johnson and Roediger, 1997).

Of course there are plentiful examples of where, sometimes catastrophic, failures in competition have been used as part of a (re)imaged identity, thus demonstrating the damage limitation potential of the postmodern celebrity industry. This was evidenced with the lauded decathlete, Dan O'Brien's failure to qualify for the 1992 Barcelona Summer Olympic Games, which prompted a humorous new direction for the $25 million Dan v Dave (Johnson) Reebok campaign. In a similar vein, the perhaps less renowned Stuart Pearce, Chris Waddle, and Gareth Southgate – all responsible for missing vital penalty kicks for England in major football tournaments – subsequently appeared in a series of Pizza Hut commercials. There are even rare examples of where sustained sporting incompetence has proved the basis for an individual's notoriety. The classic example of this is the British ski-jumper, Eddie "the Eagle" Edwards, whose daring exploits – for one so athletically limited – at the 1988 Calgary Winter Olympic Games garnered him worldwide notoriety. Similarly, but to perhaps less commercial effect, Eric Moussambani and Paula Barila competed for Equatorial Guinea in swimming at the 2000 Sydney Summer Olympic Games, despite their evident inexperience in the water. The duo became instant global celebrities as the world's media somewhat patronizingly, and wholly hypocritically, lionized them for demonstrating the true Olympic spirit in an age of cynical commercialism.

In summation, this anthology comprises a collection of essays that – both individually and in unison – acknowledge the complex and varied roles that contemporary sport celebrities occupy as athletic laborers, entertainers, marketable commodities, role models, and political figures, within an increasingly global cultural economy. As such, the anthology provides a unique insight into what Rowe (1999) described as the "unruly trinity" of commercial sport, the entertainment media, and late capitalist culture. To that end, this anthology is underpinned by the notion of the sport celebrity as a product of commercial culture, imbued with symbolic values, which seek to stimulate desire and identification among the consuming populace.

In explicating the social significance of sport celebrities as culturally and politically resonant entities, the progressive intellectual project implicit within this anthology seeks to counter the economic fetishism and blind populism frequently associated with celebrity consumption. This anthology thus could thus be considered a corroborative response to McDonald and Birrell's call to critical interpretive arms:

> We advocate focusing on a particular incident or celebrity as the site for exploring the complex interrelated and fluid character of power relations as they are constituted along the axes of ability, class, gender, and nationality. Each cultural incident offers a unique site for understanding specific articulations of power ... Thus these analyses traverse the boundaries between lived experience, knowledge production, and political practices.
>
> (1999, p. 284)

Evidently, the various contributors to this book are united in their concern with the power of celebrity (Marshall, 1997) and how particular, contextually grounded, subjectivities are articulated on, and through, individual sport stars. Differently put, this entire project is premised on the notion of sport celebrities as contextually informed discursive subjectivities, or "Emblematic individuals" (Braudy, 1997, p. 601), that act as "channeling" devices for the "negotiation of cultural space and position for the entire culture" (Marshall, 1997, p. 49). As representative subjectivities (ibid.), contemporary sport celebrities function as contextually negotiated "embodiments of the social categories in which people are placed and through which they have to make sense of their lives" (Dyer, 1986, p. 18). So, the chapters within this collection examine their chosen sport celebrities as manufactured elements of *public culture*, that consciously make visible individual personalities and practices in ways that seek to engage and inform *private experience*.

The sixteen analyses comprising this anthology excavate the often submerged politics of sport celebrity that contribute to the normalization of particular meanings, identities, and experiences within various national cultures (i.e. the UK, the USA, Canada, Pakistan, Australia, Japan, the West Indies, and Argentina). However, whether implicitly or explicitly, all the chapters herein demonstrate the national resonance of sport celebrities. Yet, the complexity of celebrity identities means that the sport figures under scrutiny are constituted by, and contribute to the constitution of, multiple representative subject positions: although grounded in the national context, sport celebrities almost unavoidably mobilize other collective configurations (Marshall, 1997, p. xii). This fact has consequential ramifications for the structure of this anthology. In many ways it would be neater if celebrities were singular entities, since then the chapters could be grouped into distinct sections each focused on a specific identity category (i.e. class, gender, sexuality, race, ethnicity, or nation). The inherent plurality of sport celebrityhood renders this stratagem wholly artificial and inadequate. Of course, each chapter can be read as a distinct entity, in and of itself. However, we have attempted to sequence the chapters in accordance to the logic and instances of celebrity multiplicity and affinity. For this reason, the following chapter summaries take on added importance, since they indicate the continuities – and indeed discontinuities – between the respective sport celebrities that prompted the precise ordering of the chapters.

In a book concerned with contemporary sport celebrityhood it would be difficult for the opening chapter to be focused on anyone other than American basketball star, Michael Jordan. So, in Chapter 1, Mary McDonald and David Andrews identify Jordan as the quintessential late capitalist sport celebrity. This charge is attributed to the influence of major corporations (particularly Nike) in the intertextual fabrication of his public persona in accordance with the pervasive American ideals of rugged individualism and personal perseverance. McDonald and Andrews' discussion points to the complex racial politics mobilized by Jordan's articulation as a seductive All (African) American hero. However, they also outline how his mediated identity evokes contextually specific gender and familial discourses through which Jordan, the *family man*, came to embody what could be described as a compassionate masculinity. This subject positioning further facilitated his American hero status, by positioning him in stark relief against the more stereotypically pejorative representations of African American manhood that continue to flourish within the American popular media. Finally, the authors broaden the context of their analysis to illustrate the contrasting ways in which Jordan's unself-consciously *American* celebrity has been received within diverse national cultural settings.

In Chapter 2, Mélisse Lafrance and Geneviève Rail encounter a sport celebrity, American basketball player Dennis Rodman, considered by many to be the anti-Jordan. Their analysis actually unearths numerous similarities between Rodman and Jordan, particularly in terms of the way their – differentially represented – black bodies both contribute to reinforcing dominant racial discourses. The authors demonstrate how Rodman's exaggerated presentation of self, as a transgressive being, belies the inherent limits of his potential as a culturally and politically subversive agent. Rodman's promotional persona actually legitimates mainstream (white, masculinist, heterosexist) American fears and fantasies relating to expressions of race, gender, and sexuality. Lafrance and Rail charge that Rodman effectively perpetuates racist – yet widely held – notions pertaining to the pathological black family, and the deviant, hyper-sexual, and animalistic black male. As such, Rodman's commercial appropriation by numerous multinational corporations is highly understandable, since his very celebrity – despite its subversive veneer – actually reinscribes many of the questionable conventions underpinning consumer capitalism.

The first two chapters tackle sport celebrities with contrasting, yet similar, relations to dominant discourses of black American masculinity. In Chapter 3, Kyle Kusz identifies how the shifting generational categorization "Generation X" – the derogatory early 1990s' narrative used to personify the perceived crisis of white, American, masculine youth – has framed American tennis star Andre Agassi's protean imaged identity. The author illustrates how Agassi's celebrity identity went from being the embodied emblem of the "Generation X" slacker discourse, to contributing toward its neutered reinvention. In the early phases of his celebrity career, Agassi was portrayed as displaying a poor work ethic, being lazy, and lacking sufficient personal will: all deficiencies characteristic of the slacker. Agassi's subsequent hard-earned victories on the tennis court problematized his slacker identity, and prompted the mass mediation of a new Agassi who exuded more traditionally valorized personal traits such as hard work, achievement, and determination. Thus, Kusz explicates how Agassi, the one-time cultural rebel, ultimately contributed to the reinscription and normalizing of expressly more conservative renditions of white American masculinity, just as "Generation X" discourse became re-articulated around notions of equally docile and productive bodies.

Like Agassi, golf phenomenon Tiger Woods' commodified celebrity is closely connected to a perceived crisis in American culture. In Chapter 4 C.L. Cole and David Andrews elucidate how Woods' public image has evolved in response to the widely felt fears and anxieties related to the anticipation of a post-white American future. Through the voluminous popular discourse of "Tigermania," Woods has been lauded as a brazenly multi-cultural being, whose very presence seemingly assuages the racial inequities of America's past–future, and the multi-racial crisis of its future–present. Woods, the authors contend, thus corroborates the regressive anti-affirmative action and white victim masculinity ideologies, both of which disavow the enduring influence of race-based discrimination. Hence, Woods has become a seductive agent in the dissemination of a post-Civil Rights American mythology that serves to confirm, rather than confound, the white cultural dominance upon which the nation was founded.

Following on from the discussion of Woods, in Chapter 5, Nancy Spencer considers tennis starlet Venus Williams, another American athlete apparently breaking down the barriers of racial exclusion in what was once an exclusively white sport. Despite Williams' very presence providing a compelling veneer of racial tolerance within the tennis world, the author identifies how coded racist references continue to punctuate the media's narrativizing of Williams' rise to tennis prominence. These troubling allusions to race were first engaged when the popular media sought to explain Williams' emergence; a narrative which remains anchored in ghetto discourse, despite the actuality of Williams' experience. Subsequently, through Williams' focused on-court demeanor, deemed unpalatable by many, she assumed the burden of representing the African American populace *in toto*. Williams' very presence within the upper echelons of professional tennis roused wider cultural fears and anxieties about affirmative action policies – and their effects on the racial reconstitution of traditionally white cultural spaces – which manifest themselves in a pernicious vein of aggressive reportage within the mainstream media. Spencer even asserts that the media's more positive recent representation of her celebrity persona, in the light of a string of outstanding performances, posits her like Jordan, and Woods, as a figure whose success effectively obscures the racism that continues to hinder the life chances of people of color in the United States.

Shifting the discussion to a different national cultural context, Ben Carrington, in Chapter 6, dissects footballer Ian Wright's mediated persona within the context of multicultural Britain. In charting Wright's career in the media spotlight, from player to talk show presenter, the discussion attributes his widespread popularity to his expression of an enduring and confident affiliation with his working-class background. Wright's demonstrative association with the British cultural mainstream results in a spectacle which both sanctions his racial Othering, while simultaneously allowing an equally unapologetic form of black expressive behavior. Ultimately, Carrington is critical of the tentative shift towards the version of black Englishness that Wright has come to represent, largely because this postmodern blackness has submitted itself to the neutering governmentality of consumer culture. While advancing an image of "black coolness" tied to a resistant black politics, as a commercial entity Wright effectively aestheticizes black radicalism by appropriating it as an accoutrement to his individual and masculinist style. In the end, Carrington suggests, Wright actually serves to depoliticize the very same black radicalism which he superficially endorses, and thus contributes to the evacuation of the political context of black culture in general, and black sport culture in particular, as a potentially transformative sphere.

In Chapter 7, Richard Giulianotti and Michael Gerrard focus on football maverick Paul Gascoigne, another icon of 1990s' British football culture. Gascoigne's career has encompassed periods of wildly inspirational and imaginative play, and equally creative recreation pursuits, both of which greatly endeared him to the general populace. However, as the authors indicate, although such exploits may have contributed to the commercial reinvention of English football during the decade, and bolstered some of the less palatable, masculinist elements of English nationalism, the "Gazza" mythology cannot be reduced to these external forces. Rather, Giulianotti and Gerrard attribute his longevity and presence within the popular imaginary to Gascoigne's affective appeal as an expressive and excessive individual (both on and off the field). They even construe the assaults on his wife to be genuinely uncontrolled behaviors, that nonetheless align with the rest of his unpredictable persona. In true postmodern vein, Gascoigne's celebrity identity shuns meta-narrativizing into a neat category of representative subjectivity, as he inhabits a panoply of discontinuous discourses that provide the Baudrillardian masses with no coherence or meaning, just delight in the depthless exuberance of the playful aesthete.

Staying with English football, in Chapter 8 Garry Whannel portrays David Beckham as a self-referentially and intertextually constructed celebrity. The popular media is cited as turning Beckham's career into a *de facto* masculine morality play, within which he has sequentially been celebrated for his early playing promise; feminized and emasculated for failing to follow masculine aesthetic conventions; pilloried for indiscretions on the field; humiliated for his allegedly questionable intellect; and redeemed due to his continued playing excellence routinely tied to his maturation, and thereby remasculination, as a "family man." Beckham and his wife Victoria Adams (aka Posh Spice), are subsequently identified as figures trapped in a self-generating vortex of publicity primarily focused on their varied displays of conspicuous consumption. As such, the popular media seem more interested in Beckham's status as an idol of personal consumption, rather than his role as an outstanding footballer. As Whannel notes, due to the blurring of the boundaries between lifestyle and career, between private and public domains, Beckham is decentered from his primary performative domain, and emerges as the archetypal postmodern sport celebrity known as much for his well-knownness as for any concrete sporting achievement.

Although Beckham commands a significant presence within English popular culture, he is not a figure who has been elevated to the status of a national icon: someone inhabiting a special and protected position within the national imaginary.

The same cannot be said for footballer Diego Maradona whose status as a national hero in Argentina is interrogated by Eduardo Archetti in Chapter 9. The author notes that Maradona's meaning and influence, as with any heroic sports figure, can only be understood within the cultural context in which he/she operates. In Maradona's case, his nomadic football career has seen him engage local, national, and supra-national constituencies. However, Archetti is primarily concerned with Maradona's relationship to discourses of Argentinian football identity and style. This masculine national rhetoric is spatialized through the *potrero* (the small areas of either rural or urban wasteland on which impromptu games are played) and personified by the *pibe* (a young player responsible for developing an effortless, individualistic, and undisciplined, or *criollo*, style of play). Archetti identifies how the social stereotype of the *pibe* has reached its apotheosis in the form of Maradona, whose triumphs and tragedies, strengths and failings, have secured him a mythical position within the Argentinian popular imaginary. As such, the Maradona mythology is inextricably related to a system of national cultural differences, through which Argentinian identity continues to be spatialized, imagined, and experienced.

Archetti demonstrates how the various crises in Maradona's career came to be understood through an evocative figuration of Argentinian national identity, thereby underscoring his national iconic status. Conversely, in Chapter 10, Steven Jackson relates how a crisis of Canadian national identity in the late 1980s shaped the popular representation and perception of ice hockey great Wayne Gretzky's exploits at this time, both on and off the ice. In 1988 Canada was gripped by an economic and cultural panic related to the impending signing of the Free Trade Agreement (FTA) with the United States. To many, the FTA represented the latest expression of American cultural and economic colonization, and brought questions related to the future of Canadian culture, identity, and sovereignty to the fore. Within the context of this threat of Americanization, Gretzky, the "All-Canadian" hero, did the unthinkable. Twice. Not only did he marry an American (the actress Janet Jones), he was also subsequently traded from the Edmonton Oilers to an American franchise (the Los Angeles Kings). Jackson documents how, given Gretzky's footing as a national emblem, his marriage and trade came to be understood through the contemporaneous discourse of national crisis. Moreover, he illustrates how highly visible sport celebrities are necessarily implicated in a dialectic interplay with the national cultural context in which they are immersed.

In Chapter 11, Hajime Hirai explores the career of Japanese baseball player Hideo Nomo, another migrant athlete whose relocation to the United States became a point of cultural contention within his native land. In 1995, Nomo was released from his contract with the Kintetsu Buffaloes, and was free to sign with the Los Angeles Dodgers. Nomo's move to the United States, and initial successes, stirred debate within Japan reflecting broadly held values of aspiration and achievement, as well as more circumspect consideration of the ramifications of the global mobility he had come to represent. The author demonstrates how Nomo's decline and subsequent revival were similarly articulated according to the behests of contemporary cultural discourses, specifically those focused on the trials and tribulations of workers within a post-industrial Japan wracked by economic insecurity. Within this context, Nomo was lauded in Japan for being a determined figure who overcame hardship to succeed at his chosen profession. Hirai goes on to show Nomo's ascribed stature as a global celebrity represents a source of national pride for the Japanese populace, despite his stated indifference to himself being more than a regular baseball player.

Furthering the discussion of sport stars' mobility across national boundaries, in Chapter 12, Michael Giardina focuses on tennis player Martina Hingis as an exemplar of transnational celebrityhood. Born in the Czech Republic (then Czechoslovakia), raised in Switzerland, now largely domiciled in the United States, but fully involved in the global women's professional tennis circuit, Hingis' life has indeed been an exercise in border crossing. More than her physical migrations, and propelled by machinations of global corporate capitalism, the symbolic elements of Hingis' celebrity have traversed the globe to significant effect. Unlike most of the sport celebrities discussed in this anthology, Hingis' promotional persona operates in different settings within which she projects equally divergent meanings. This is attributable to the eminent malleability of her mediated image, in terms of its ability to appeal to highly localized cultural meanings and desires. Giardina demonstrates that, as a flexible citizen, Hingis is able to project caricatured embodiments of Swiss, European, and American values dependent on the context of consumption. Consequently, her transnational positioning and appeal render Hingis a highly productive and prophetic instrument of the ascendant global capitalist order.

In Chapter 13, John Bale introduces a more explicitly politicized domain of celebrityhood, to varying degrees removed from the realm and influence of corporate capitalism: that of the postcolonial athlete. To that end, he focuses on Kenyan middle distance runners, Nyandika Maiyoro and Kipchoge Keino, whose careers spanned the 1950s to early 1960s and 1960s to early 1970s respectively. The author identifies Maiyoro and Keino to be among the first postcolonial athletes, not because their actions encompassed intentional political resistance against a colonizing power or its legacy, rather because their very presence and performances transgressed conventional, Western, ways of writing and thinking about the black body. Bale ponders the manner in which the Occidental gaze came to represent Maiyoro's, and particularly Keino's, outstanding achievements on the world stage. He identifies a peculiar ambivalence within the popular media discourses that enveloped these athletes, characterized by tropes of surveillance, appropriation, idealization, and negation. Hence, as colonized athletes represented by the rhetoric of the colonizer, Maiyoro and Keino offered discursive subjectivities that both assuaged post-imperial angst, as they provided inspiration for the athletes of post-independence Africa.

Moving on to a more contemporary postcolonial athlete, and certainly one with a more explicit political agenda, in Chapter 14, Peter Corrigan explores the career of Pakistani cricketer Imran Khan. Born into Pakistan's highly educated elite, Khan's move into national politics was wholly predictable. This was particularly true since his cricket career had provided him with a rigorous apprenticeship, and considerable popular presence, within the public domain. Corrigan analyses the manner in which Khan represented himself, and his ideas, to the Pakistani populace in a number of texts: autobiographies; travel books; and interviews. Through these texts, Khan legitimized himself as a political leader by delineating his noble line of descent (positioning himself as the embodied intersection of two ancient and noble families). On numerous occasions within his writings, Khan appropriated the differentiation and solidarity he experienced within the colonially and racially implicated international cricket order, as interpretive vehicles for framing his empirically grounded political philosophy. Thus, he outlined his strident championing of the impoverished and underserved within Pakistan, and his commitment to the interwoven institutions of Pakistan nationhood and Islam. Khan's transformation from postcolonial athlete to postcolonial politician was undoubtedly eased due to his highly visible cricketing persona. Indeed, as Corrigan concludes, such were the national, class, and familial expectations of him, it is doubtful whether he would have been able to avoid his move into public service.

Excavating the more troubling aspects of postcoloniality within the age of global capitalism, in Chapter 15, Hilary Beckles contemplates the contradictory figure of West Indian cricketer Brian Lara. As his record attests, Lara is one of the greatest batsmen the world of cricket has ever seen. Nevertheless, he is by no means widely revered within the West Indies. Indeed, in a time when the nation's cricketing performances have dramatically slumped, Lara serves to deeply divide public opinion with regard to his impact upon West Indian cricket. To many, he is an arrogant and egocentric individual whose achievements are motivated by the desire for personal gain. As such he simply cannot be thought of among the inventory of historic West Indian cricketing icons, whose exploits and images served to provide a collective bond to the formative West Indian state. To others, Lara is an iconic figure whose entrepreneurial attainments point to the possibility of West Indian success within the contemporary global corporate economy. As Beckles indicates, Lara's ability to cleave public opinion can only be understood within the context of the broader debate pertaining to the various crises facing postcolonial West Indies. For, in the age of globalization, West Indian cultural, economic, and political union appears in tatters, dissected by the disaggregating influence of global financial agencies more interested in regional exploitation than national integration. Lara's very being is thus negatively judged by many according to the dictates of an earlier, more optimistic and contained, stage in the evolution of the postcolonial nation. When, in actuality, he perhaps points to a more expansive vision of West Indian possibility and engagement with the global economy.

Finally, in Chapter 16, Toni Bruce and Christopher Hallinan portray a more superficially cohesive postcolonial figure, in the guise of Australian track star Cathy Freeman. Over the past decade Freeman, who is of Aboriginal descent, has been celebrated as the new face of Australia by the nation's popular media. Freeman's status as an evocative national icon was forever confirmed with her victory in the 400m at the 2000 Sydney Olympic Games: a happening which seemingly captured the attention, and harnessed the emotion, of the entire nation. Australia's anointing of Freeman – the Aboriginal Other – would indicate a degree of reconciliation and accord between the Indigenous inhabitants and the successive waves of non-Indigenous immigrants, whose uneasy combination constitutes the Australian populace. Certainly, and immeasurably influenced by Freeman's cultural exploits and presence, postcolonial Australia's national identity would appear considerably more ethnically inclusive, and diverse, than its colonial predecessor. However, the postcolonial experience may be considerably different. Despite the nationalistic euphoria that enveloped Freeman, and the political possibilities of the Australian hybridity that she could potentially represent, Bruce and Hallinan pinpoint the pitfalls associated with the superficial embracing of people of color. Specifically, they identify the perils of self-congratulatorily celebrating Freeman as evidence of the disappearance of structurally based racial inequality, when in actuality the oppression of Indigenous peoples continues largely unchecked.

Bibliography

Altimore, M. (1999) "Gentleman athlete": Joe DiMaggio and the celebration and submergence of ethnicity. *International Review for the Sociology of Sport*, 34(4), 359–68.

Baker, A. and Boyd, T. (eds) (1997) *Out of Bounds: Sports, Media, and the Politics of Identity*. Bloomington, IA: Indiana University Press.

Bell, E. and Campbell, D. (1999: May 23) For the love of money. *The Observer*, p. 22.

Birrell, S. and McDonald, M.G. (eds) (2000) *Reading Sport: Critical Essays on Power and Representation*. Boston: Northeastern University Press.

Boorstin, D.J. (1992) *The Image: A Guide to Pseudo-events in America*. New York: Random House.

Braudy, L. (1997) *The Frenzy of Renown: Fame and its History*. New York: Vintage.

Carroll, J.M. (1999). *Red Grange and the Rise of Modern Football*. Urbana, IL: University of Illinois.

Cole, C.L. and Hribar, A.S. (1995) Celebrity feminism: *Nike Style* – post-Fordism, transcendence, and consumer power. *Sociology of Sport Journal*, 12 (4), 347–69.

deCordova, R. (1991) The emergence of the star system in America. In C. Gledhill (ed.), *Stardom: Industry of Desire* (pp. 17–29). London: Routledge.

Dizikes, J. (2000) *Yankee Doodle Dandy: The Life and Times of Tod Sloan*. New Haven, CT: Yale University Press.

Dyer, R. (1979) *Stars*. London: BFI Publishing.

—— (1986) *Heavenly Bodies: Film Stars and Society*. London: Macmillan.

Dyson, A. and Turco, D. (1998) The state of celebrity endorsement in sport. *The Cyber-Journal of Sport Marketing*. http://www.cjsm.com/Vol2/dyson.htm.

Fiske, J. (1987) *Television Culture*. London: Routledge.

Gamson, J. (1994) *Claims to Fame: Celebrity in Contemporary America*. Berkeley, CA: University of California Press.

Gitlin, T. (1998) The culture of celebrity. *Dissent*, (Summer), 81–4.

Giulianotti, R. (1999) *Football: A Sociology of the Global Game*. Cambridge: Polity Press.

Gledhill, C. (1991) *Stardom: Industry of Desire*. London: Routledge.

Hall, S. (1980) Encoding/decoding. In S. Hall (ed.), *Culture, Media, Language* (pp. 128–38). London: Hutchinson.

Harper, W.A. (1994) *Grantland Rice and his Heroes: The Sportswriter as Mythmaker in the 1920s*. Knoxville: University of Tennessee Press.

—— (1999) *How You Played the Game: The Life of Grantland Rice*. Columbia: University of Missouri Press.

Holt, R., Mangan, J.A. and Lanfranchi, P. (eds) (1996) *European Heroes: Myth, Identity, Sport*. London: Frank Cass.

Jameson, F. (1991) *Postmodernism, or, the Cultural Logic of Late Capitalism*. Durham, NC: Duke University Press.

Johnson, L. and Roediger, D. (1997) "Hertz, don't it?" Becoming colorless and staying black in the crossover of O.J. Simpson. In T. Morrison and C. Brodsky Lacour (eds), *Birth of a Nation'hood: Gaze, Script, and Spectacle in the O.J. Simpson Case* (pp. 197–239). New York: Pantheon Books.

Johnson, R. (1987) What is cultural studies anyway? *Social Text*, 6 (1), 38–79.

Kearney, R. (1989) *The Wake of the Imagination: Toward a Postmodern Culture*. Minneapolis, MN: University of Minnesota Press.

King, S. (1993) The politics of the body and the body politic: Magic Johnson and the ideology of AIDS. *Sociology of Sport Journal*, 10 (3), 270–85.

Lowenthal, L. (1961) *Literature, Popular Culture and Society*. Englewood Cliffs, New Jersey: Prentice-Hall.

Lusted, D. (1991) The glut of the personality. In C. Gledhill (ed.), *Stardom: Industry of Desire* (pp. 251–8). London: Routledge.

McCracken, G. (1988) *Culture and Consumption: New Approaches to the Symbolic Character of Consumer Goods*. Bloomington: Indiana University Press.

McDonald, M.G. and Birrell, S. (1999) Reading sport critically: a methodology for interrogating power. *Sociology of Sport Journal*, 16 (4), 283–300.

McLuhan, M. (1964) *Understanding Media: The Extensions of Man*. New York: Mentor.

Marshall, P.D. (1997) *Celebrity and Power: Fame in Contemporary Culture*. Minneapolis, MN: University of Minnesota Press.

Meeks, A. (1997) An estimate of the size and supported economic activity of the sports industry in the United States. *Sport Marketing Quarterly*, 6 (4), 15–21.

Monaco, J. (1978) Celebration. In J. Monaco (ed.), *Celebrity*. New York: Delta.

Pierce, C.P. (1995). Master of the universe. *GQ*, April, 180–7.

Rader, B.G. (1983) Compensatory sport heroes: Ruth, Grange and Dempsey. *Journal of Popular Culture*, 16 (4), 11–22.

Rae, S. (1999) *W.G. Grace: A Life*. London: Faber & Faber.

Rein, I., Kotler, P. and Stoller, M. (1997) *High Visibility: The Making and Marketing of Professionals into Celebrities*. Chicago: NTC Business Books.

Ritzer, G. (1998) *The McDonaldization Thesis: Explorations and Extensions*. London: Sage.

Rowe, D. (1994) Accommodating bodies: celebrity, sexuality, and "tragic magic." *Journal of Sport and Social Issues*, 18 (1), 6–26.

—— (1995) *Popular Cultures: Rock Music, Sport and the Politics of Pleasure*. London: Sage.

—— (1999) *Sport, Culture and the Media: The Unruly Trinity*. Buckingham: Open University Press.

Schwichtenberg, C. (ed.) (1993) *The Madonna Connection: Representational Politics, Subcultural Identities and Cultural Theory*. Boulder, CO: Westview Press.

Singer, T. (1998) Not-so-remote-control. *Sport*, March, 36.

Smith, P. (1993) *Clint Eastwood: A Cultural Production*. Minneapolis, MN: University of Minnesota Press.

Susman, W.I. (1984) *Culture as History: The Transformation of American Society in the Twentieth Century*. New York: Pantheon Books.

Vande Berg, L.R. (1998) The sports hero meets mediated celebrityhood. In L.A. Wenner (ed.), *Mediasport* (pp. 134–53). London: Routledge.

Wernick, A. (1991) *Promotional Culture: Advertising, Ideology and Symbolic Expression*. London: Sage.

Whannel, G. (1992) *Fields in Vision: Television Sport and Cultural Transformation*. London: Routledge.

—— (1998) Individual stars and collective identities in media sport. In M. Roche (ed.), *Sport, Popular Culture and Identity* (vol. 5, pp. 23–36). Aachen: Meyer & Meyer Verlag.

—— (1999) Sport stars, narrativisation and masculinities. *Leisure Studies*, 18 (3), 249–65.

—— (2000) Stars in whose eyes? *Index on Censorship*, 29 (4).

Williams, G. (1991) *1905 and All That: Essays on Rugby Football, Sport and Welsh Society*. Llandysul: Gomer Press.

Williams, R. (1976) *Keywords: A Vocabulary of Culture and Society*. London: Collins.

1

MICHAEL JORDAN

Corporate sport and postmodern celebrityhood

Mary G. McDonald and David L. Andrews

In a contemporary Western culture excessively saturated with media images of celebrity, no American athlete, perhaps no American has been more incessantly promoted than Michael Jordan. Jordan's seeming ubiquitous global fame is in part built upon a dual career as a distinguished basketball player and as a celebrity endorser. Yet, in many ways Jordan's reach goes beyond his individual status as he serves as the prototypical sport celebrity, whose US and global marketing conquests have provoked debate, admiration and emulation. Besides leading the Chicago Bulls to six National Basketball Association (NBA) championships and earning five league Most Valuable Player trophies, Jordan has also pitched such diverse products as Nike sneakers, Hanes underwear, MCI long-distance telephone service, Ball Park Franks hotdogs, Bijan cologne, McDonald's hamburgers and Rayovac batteries. This visibility as an athlete-endorser has translated into considerable capital accumulation. In 1998, Jordan reportedly earned $45 million in endorsements ($16 million of it from Nike), a sum far greater than the $34 million salary he earned that same year for playing basketball (Einstein, 1999). In his over 15-year relationship with Nike, Jordan-related product sales have reportedly surpassed the $3 billion mark. His *Space Jam* movie is said to have garnered more than a half-billion dollars in box office and video sales. And one year after signing Jordan in 1991 and encouraging consumers to "be like Mike," Gatorade's annual revenues climbed from $681 million to over $1 billion. Gatorade's 1998 revenues were approximately $1.5 billion, giving the company an 80 percent share of the sports nutritional-drink market (Armstrong, 1999).

Although Jordan has now retired from professional sport for the third time (twice from the NBA and once from minor league baseball), the commodification of the Jordan persona has hardly abated. Jordan's hyperreal image continues to circulate around the globe, reaching such diverse spaces as California shopping malls, the streets of Poland, and among the diverse nations that house the Black Diaspora (Andrews *et al.*, 1996). Indeed, Michael Jordan has become a brand unto himself, serving as a significant example of America's transnational commodity culture, what Kellner (1995, p. 5) calls an "export to the entire world." In a global culture increasingly dominated by the exchange

20

of commodity signs, that is mediated objects, practices and personalities, Jordan is but one of numerous forged images engaging in "sign wars" (Goldman and Papson, 1996) seeking increased profitability for a variety of transnational and US corporations. Jordan's celebrity sign is also incredibly malleable, highly mobile and the carrier of shifting, but important cultural meanings. His status continues to be hyperbolically promoted, as evidenced by a recent ad campaign in which marketing research supposedly discovered that "a photograph of the back of Jordan's bald head is better recognized (at least in California shopping malls) than the faces of Bill Clinton, Newt Gingrich and Jesus Christ" (cited in Ahrens, 1999, p. C01). And a short while ago when Nike launched a new Jordan Inc. division, Steve Miller, the president of the new unit, unabashedly proclaimed: "We have the most recognized person in the world ... His appeal transcends sports, gender, race and age. We think that appeal is going to continue into the future" (cited in Friedman, 1999, p. 3).

In contrast to this exaggerated statement of Jordan's transcendence, this chapter places into crisis the shallow affective elation that characterizes the articulation and consumption of Michael Jordan's image, by making visible the economic and political implications of wanting to *be like Mike*. Grounded in cultural studies, post-structuralist, and postmodern theories, this chapter provides multiple contextually specific interpretations of this most visible celebrity sign, arguing that the prototypical Jordan persona, while incredibly mobile and malleable, has material effects in shaping people's everyday relations, experiences, and identities. Rather than transcending gender, race, class, sexuality and nationality, in this chapter we demonstrate the ways in which Jordan's hyperreal image is embedded in a postmodern global media culture awash with endless chains of politically and emotionally meaningful signifiers related to a complex, shifting matrix of social inequalities. By offering this chapter as an alternative account we seek to disrupt the bodily inequities and systems of differentiation which circulate and are remade through the historically specific intertextual discourses of the popular print, electronic and advertising media.

In excavating the political significance of Michael Jordan, we first make discernible the ways in which Nike has helped to mobilize particular emotional and affective investments through Jordan's hyperreal image. We argue that there is considerable evidence to suggest that Jordan's African American heritage engages particular desires and identities (see Andrews, 1996; Andrews, 1998; Cole and Andrews, 1996; Cole, 1996 #2925; McDonald, 1996), and we discuss these in relationship to contemporary US race relations. Within the context of post-Reagan America, Jordan also serves as a particular type of masculine hard body, one that promotes conservative family values and advances the agenda of the New Right. And finally we engage "International Jordan" to illuminate the process of globalization while interrogating the reception of Jordan as an American icon within diverse global spaces including those of New Zealand, Poland and Black Britain. Through Jordan we note the

21

global–local nexus as it pertains to the transnational manifestations of American sporting and celebrity commodities. Our aim in providing critical multi-contextual understandings of Michael Jordan is to encourage people to interrogate their own engagement with commodity and celebrity cultures as a process necessary to bringing about cultural change.

The corporate body: imagining Jordan's postmodern celebrity

If there is one analogy repeatedly linked to Michael Jordan, it is the allusion (and illusion) of flight. As the now well-told creation story goes, under the auspices of the Los Angeles advertising agency Chiat/Day Nike first created the "Air Jordan" celebrity persona in hopes of challenging corporate rivals Converse and Reebok's economic hold on athletic shoe sales. One of the first commercials of the 1985 campaign for the signature Air Jordan line was titled "Jordan Flight" and featured Jordan executing a slam-dunk on an urban basketball court to the sound of jet engines revving to take off at an increasingly higher pitch. The commercial concluded by asking, "who said man was not meant to fly?" This clever commercial marks Michael Jordan's identity (re)constituted as Air Jordan, "the Nike guy who could fly" (Katz, 1994, p. 7). This depiction of Jordan as a rugged individual, an athlete whose basketball athleticism suggests an uncanny ability to remain suspended in air, as if in flight, provided a financial boon for the Air Jordan brand, which grossed $130 million in its first year (Strasser and Becklund, 1991, p. 3) while helping to elevate Nike to the status of an American corporate icon. Coke quickly followed Nike's lead, employing intertextually resonant meanings in commercials depicting Jordan in space silhouetted against the moon, leaping for a bottle of Coke. In both cases the metaphor of flight is used to link Jordan's sign value with the enduring American ideologies of competitive individualism (Andrews, 1998).

Against these uncritical characterizations of orbit and of flight, we offer another suggestion of swift passages and motions as particularly useful in contextualizing and criticizing corporate sport's creation of and investment in "Air Jordan's" postmodern celebrityhood. As a culturally created persona, Jordan's mediated identity has been inscribed with multiple cultural and commodified meanings, none of which are essential or fixed; rather, the Jordan persona as a commodity sign must be understood as fluid, complex, and contradictory. Jordan's hyperreal celebrity image is, therefore, a highly mobile sign that displays a lack of uniformity as well as a lack of permanent value (Andrews, 1996). Borrowing from Stuart Hall (1983) we might say that there are no necessary correspondences, or for that matter non-correspondences, between meanings and cultural symbols like Jordan. In this way Jordan's ever changing image is unpredictable and thus signals "the absence of guarantees, the inability to know in advance the historical significance of particular practices" (Grossberg, 1986, p. 64).

Given this fluidity and uncertainty, it is misleading to view Jordan as merely an outstanding basketball player and marketing icon whose accomplishments universally speak for themselves. Nor should Jordan be seen as the sole author of the shifting cultural meanings connected to his image. Given these insights it is further ill advised to suggest any inevitability about Jordan's prominence, as Jordan's agent David Falk seems to suggest in proclaiming: "No one ever tried to invent Michael Jordan. We didn't try to create something in 1984; it just evolved. When you try to create that, the public sees through it, and they think it's insincere" (cited in Murphy, 1999, p. 1). Contrary to Falk's claims of autonomy, authenticity and genuineness, as an elastic and empty sign (see Gilroy, 1991), there has been considerable ideological work in transforming Jordan into a signifier in the first place. Moreover, conjunctionally specific representations of Jordan not only do ideological work, but also seek to secure affective investments in mobilizing specific forms of power and authority (Andrews, 1998). Because it is impossible to separate the affective from the ideological, used here affective suggests an economy of intense, energetic and emotional response to and involvement in mediated ideological narratives which are increasingly, but not always, communicated through the electronic media (ibid.). Thus popular cultural sites are invested not only with powerful ideologies but with divergent moods, energies and intensities that anchor people "in particular experiences, practices, identities, meanings and pleasures" (Grossberg, 1992, p. 82).

Frequently, ideological and affective articulations of commodity signs attempt to rally consent for dominant alliances and their worldviews. In a hyperreal media-saturated culture, power is exercised through the means of representation, as those who have greatest access to the media set particular agendas while having the ability to frame what counts as real and significant. Given this insight, it is not surprising then that Nike has built Jordan's image in accordance with the dominant structure of the feelings that are continuously affectively rearticulated in relationship to American consumer culture, including those of the American Dream, rugged individualism and the value of personal perseverance (Andrews, 1998). For example, one commercial features a pensive Michael Jordan dramatically assuring us of the value of hard work and dedication:

> I've missed more than 9,000 shots in my career. I've lost almost 300 games. Twenty-six times I've been trusted to take the game-winning shot, and missed. I've failed over and over again in my life. That's why I succeed.
>
> (cited in Base, 1997, p. 20)

The basketball star's ability to mobilize similar sentimentality is such that Phillip Knight, CEO of Nike calls Jordan "the ultimate Just Do It athlete," restating Nike's famous individualistic slogan (cited in Einstein, 1999 p. B1). Under the direction of agent David Falk, Jordan's status as corporate spokesperson has consistently involved promoting an image of All-American affability not only for Nike and the NBA, but for numerous other corporations. Thus Jordan now exists within an economically lucrative intertextual scenario in which each Jordan commercial helps to promote the other commodity signs in a considerable promotional arsenal (Andrews, 1998).

With considerable capital already invested in Jordan, attention has been increasingly applied to remaking a fresh emotionally salient persona for Jordan. For example, Nike CEO Phil Knight justifies the creation of the Nike brand Jordan subdivision as:

> I think that when people say his career is over, I would limit it to his basketball career. He's very bright, he's very competitive and when he decides to take out some of his competitive instincts on the business world, look out!
>
> (cited in Einstein, 1999, p. B1)

This new image of CEO Jordan projects the ex-player dominating in the corporate world, and accumulating material success. According to Bob Dorfman, who rates the marketability of sports stars for the advertising agency Foote, Cone and Belding in San Francisco, Jordan is "such a super-human talent that everybody aspires to his level of performance ... Everybody wants to be that good and have that much success" (cited in Einstein, 1999, p. B1). The Jordan brand has spawned a plethora of Jordan "wannabes," a pool of aspiring young athletes/celebrities/commodity signs who now wear and endorse the Jordan brand. Jordan athletes include shortstop Derek Jeter of New York Yankees, Randy Moss, wide receiver for the Minnesota Vikings and boxer Roy Jones Jr. Additionally, six NBA athletes: the Charlotte Hornet's Eddie Jones, Vin Baker of the Seattle Sonics, Michael Finley of the Dallas Mavericks, Ray Allen of the Milwaukee Bucks, Mike Bibby of the Vancouver Grizzlies and Cleveland's Derek Anderson are all aligned with the Jordan logo (McKinney and Romero, 1999).

In the late 1990s Jordan's CEO persona as a tough competitor in the business world has been made to serve as an antidote to a badly bruised Nike public image. Activism over Nike's deplorable international labor practices, low wages and poor working conditions in certain nations where Nike shoes are produced has tarnished the carefully cultivated Nike persona. Knight downplays any sense of responsibility for the company's poor labor record, arguing that the firm has been unfairly made the "poster boy for the global economy" (cited in Lofton, 1998, p. 1). While denying responsibility, Nike has responded to public pressure with modest initiatives including the removal of toxins in international factories. Given this context, the elevation of the Jordan brand above the oversaturated tarnished Nike swoosh logo represents an attempt to exploit the affective economy surrounding Jordan to deflect attention away from Nike's lack of commitment to responsible labor politics.

Sign language: Michael Jordan as a floating racial signifier

Within this complex array of signs and hypersignification, it is crucial to note that Michael Jordan also serves as a "free floating" *racial* signifier representing a complex fluid process that both engages with and disengages from an economy of signifiers related to stereotypical and ideological depictions of Black masculinity. For example, before entering the NBA and prior to his relationship with Nike, during his collegiate career the popular media had already begun linking Jordan with lingering codes of natural athleticism thus recapturing the mind–body dualism that has dominated popular racial discourses (Andrews, 1996). This discourse of extraordinary athleticism relies upon common sense assumptions of an innate Black physicality, a racist characterization once used to justify the institution of slavery and Social Darwinist constructions of White supremacy. This narrative of alleged naturalness clearly displays aspects of the racialized history out of which Michael Jordan, the celebrity sign, was initially constructed. When Jordan helped lead the US team to the 1984 Olympic gold medal in Los Angeles, he was described within similar pseudo-scientific logic as someone who was "seemingly born to dunk" (ibid.). This narrative of innate physicality has been rearticulated throughout Jordan's successful basketball career and undoubtedly has helped fuel the allegedly natural "Air Jordan" persona. Jordan's repeatedly valorized sporting body thus serves as a highly visible signifier of racial Otherness (ibid.).

Given this depiction, it is also necessary to stress a post-structuralist contention that cultural meanings are also contingent upon the shifting, over-lapping territory of popular culture within particular historical, geographic, and political contexts. Within the context of contemporary America Michael Jordan has been repeatedly fashioned by Nike, the NBA, other corporate sponsors, and the media in accordance with the forceful imperatives of late twentieth-century capitalism, popular racial ideologies, and often within a reactionary post-Reaganite cultural agenda (Andrews, 1996). Indeed, the rise of Jordan's basketball career parallels the ascent of the era of Reagan and of post-Reagan America, unique historical moments characterized by the implementation of regressive economic and cultural policies in which conservative values held sway in the USA. Repeatedly throughout the 1980s and 1990s members of the New Right argued that the excessive liberal policies of the 1960s and 1970s had placed the United States in a moral and economic downturn. In making this argument conservatives engaged in populist affective politics while mobilizing popular sentiment, taste, and culture. In doing so, Reaganism became an affec-tivity-oriented struggle in which popular culture led politics. Throughout his presidential campaign, and during his tenure as President, much of Reagan's popularity was attributed to his capacity for turning the political into gut-level issues (Schneider, 1990). The aim of the new conservatism was to restore US national pride by encouraging the public to care passionately about strategic aspects of their everyday lives. So while seeking minimal state intervention in social policies, and a strong national defense, conservatives linked a roll-back in progressive policy initiatives as necessary to the resurrection of presumed traditional American values such as hard work, personal responsibility, and sacrifice (Reeves and Campbell, 1994). The 1980s saw the elevation of new policies and practices that suggested gender and racial politics assaulted the basic American notion of "liberty for all" just as the tenets of affirmative action were rolled back and a New Right rhetoric emerged complete with accusations of "reverse discrimination." Notable among the material consequences of this rhetoric has been the slashing of social welfare programs by both conservatives and liberals and the attempts by the New Right to translate social and political inequities related to unemployment, urban decay, violence and drug abuse into problems of individual pathology and deviance.

Reeves and Campbell (1994, p. 3) argue that the New Right's attempt to moralize and individualize larger social ills, seen most clearly in the "war on drugs campaign" actually masked a series of cultural and structural concerns: "the economic devastation of deindustrialization, aggravated White–Black tensions in the electorate and, ultimately helped to solidify middle class support for policies that favored the rich over the poor." By nationalizing bodies, that is equating particular bodies with desirable characteristics and other bodies with deviance and decay, Reaganism helped to define signifiers of national import and mobilize racist sentiments (Jeffords, 1994; Andrews, 1996). Deviant bodies were inevitably of color and/or female. Yet as a highly visible, talented male athlete with an affable persona, Jordan quickly countered this trend and was signified as a one of the desirable hard bodies – strong, assertive and successful. These hard bodies were affectively and effectively held out by the New Right as exemplary in contrast to the soft bodies allegedly linked to welfare dependency, crime and drug abuse. In this racist characterization, Jordan was portrayed as the moral obverse of the masses of African Americans vilified by the New Right for allegedly lacking the (new) right stuff.

By embodying the neo-liberal economics, neo-conservative politics, and moralistic cultural traditionalism of the New Right, the Nike-initiated Jordan narrative celebrated Reaganism's racist vision of a color-blind American society. Within this mythical realm, personal perseverance was cast as the primary determinant of individual success and the socially inscribed experiences and identities associated with racism and exploitation were viewed as irrelevant remnants of the past. In true Reaganite fashion, Jordan's humility, inner drive, personal responsibility, and moral righteousness were widely praised. Through subsequent creative associations (see Andrews, 1998) with McDonald's, Coca-Cola (later Gatorade), Chevrolet, and Wheaties – all significant "All-American" corporate icons – Jordan was cast in numerous public spaces as a "spectacular talent, well-spoken, attractive, accessible" with "old-time values" (David Falk, quoted in Kirkpatrick, 1987, p. 93). For instance, early in his career, Jordan appeared in a McDonald's commercial spouting a message of personal responsibility and rugged individualism while following then first lady Nancy Reagan's mandate to "Just Say No to Drugs." In this commercial a pensive Jordan pleads: "So don't blow it, don't do drugs. If you're doing it, stop it. Get some help. McDonald's wants you to give yourself a chance, a chance to find out the wonderful things you really can be. And so do I." This particular clip positions Jordan as an upright individual, wholesome, trustworthy and concerned, a "hard body" capable of personal restraint in resisting temptation. Jordan's willingness to recount his own aversion to drug use is key to signifying his own apparent moral worth. Furthermore, this wholesome charisma is made to stand in stark contrast to the undisciplined, presumably drug-infected Black urban bodies demonized by the New Right. Within the context of a conservative agenda, Jordan stands apart from the demonizing stereotypical characterizations of black masculinity as criminal and violent. Jordan is thus aligned with other African American stars of this era such as Bill Cosby, Whoopi Goldberg, and Oprah Winfrey whose high-profile success stories further condemned the struggling African American masses for lacking the personal resolution which, according to Reaganism's doctrine of rugged individualism and color-blind bigotry, was all that was required to achieve in American society (Reeves and Campbell, 1994; Andrews, 1996; McDonald, 1996).

In further demonstration of the malleability of Jordan's image in particular and of commodity signs in general, one needs only to look at the shifting contexts when Jordan's All-American persona was remolded in ways that fit with soft-bodied depictions of Black masculinity as deviant. This is particularly the case in media reports of Jordan's gambling activities. In light of these allegations in the early 1990s, the figure of Jordan as someone who transcended race, was displaced by the incessant media accusations that suggested Jordan was obsessed with gambling. For example, Dave Anderson's intentionally provocative story "Jordan's Atlantic City Caper" (1993, p. 11), speculated that the "best player in basketball history" let down his teammates and coaches during the playoffs by gambling until 2.30 a.m. (an hour later refuted by a variety of sources, including Jordan) linking Jordan to a deviant lifestyle. The intense scrutiny concerning Jordan's gambling habits only intensified upon the release of Richard Esquinas' (1993) book, *Michael and Me: Our Gambling Addiction ... My Cry for Help*. While Jordan was able to use his already well-cultivated All-American persona to deflect attention away from allegations of large gambling debts, the gambling narrative became violently re-activated after the murder of his father in August 1993. Upon the discovery of James Jordan's body members of the press alluded to a link between the father's murder and his son's gambling which implied that the murder was a pay-back for Michael Jordan's gambling debts (Dobie, 1994). Media speculation related to Jordan's allegedly deviant (racial) identity slowed with the arrest of James Jordan's alleged murderers. Subsequent coverage of the grieving son helped to revitalize Michael Jordan's All-American sign value.

A few good men: Jordan, family values and (post-)Reaganite hard bodies

To explore Jordan solely in relationship to contemporary racial meanings would produce an incomplete analysis. Indeed, Jordan's sign value is also repetitively constructed in accordance with particular discourses related to gender. In a consumer culture that continuously celebrates masculine achievements in movies, films and other popular forms, advertisers, commentators and the media also excessively and romantically laud Jordan's basketball skills. The celebration of Jordan's playing ability has at times been taken to the point of deification. Indeed, early in his career when he scored 63 points in a play-off game against the Boston Celtics, rival Larry Bird remarked: "That's God disguised as Michael Jordan." "Jesus in Nikes" is how Jason Williams of the New York Nets once described Jordan. Author David Halberstam has been particularly hyperbolic in glorifying Jordan's play as

> brilliant, balletic, and, of course, fierce. He possessed in the highest proportions all the requisite qualities for greatness; in addition, it was as if some geneticist had injected a magical solution for supercompetitiveness into his DNA, and he came to represent, more than any athlete of recent years, the invincible man, someone who simply refused to be defeated.
>
> (Halberstam, 1999, p. 417)

Similar uncritical celebrations depict his basketball skills as "pure genius" (ibid., p. 9).

This canonization is hardly new, as sport has long been tied to the glorification of masculinity and male bodies. Think back to those US sport heroes of yesteryear, including Babe Ruth, Mickey Mantel and Joe Namath – whose accomplishments were, in the popular press and in private conversations, often equated with heroism, courageousness and cultural significance. This intense focus on Jordan's body represents one more example of America's continued obsession with the physical capabilities of the male body. Despite women's continued presence in sport, dominant constructions of athletic masculinity help to construct sport as a male preserve, a site where, regardless of their backgrounds, men are encouraged to (mis)identify the physicality of male athletes as a sign of male social superiority (Messner, 1988).

Given this repetitive veneration of male sport stars, it is hardly surprising former Chicago Bulls Head Coach Doug Collins admiringly suggests (with much macho bravado) that while on the basketball court Jordan "wants to cut your heart out ... and then show it to you" (cited in Halberstam, 1999). Yet, when read across the conservative tenor of the times, representations of Jordan's competitive zeal and powerful slam-dunks suggest a larger than life, mythic masculinity prevalent in contemporary Hollywood blockbuster movies (McDonald, 1996). Like Sylvester Stallone as Rambo and

28

Arnold Schwarzenegger as the Terminator, Jordan signifies a particular type of masculine hard body – strong, competitive and brave. During the Reagan–Bush era, the iconic hard body proved to be the movie figure Rambo, a White heterosexual male who battles military ineptitude, abandonment, and extreme governmental excess (Jeffords, 1994).

Yet just as he is celebrated for being the embodiment of mythic masculinity as forceful, talented and assertive on the court, so too is Jordan represented as an affable and approachable athlete away from the game. Indeed, in commercial endorsements, the popular press and in public spaces Jordan's sign value is frequently attached to that of children and members of his family. This framing is significant suggesting a kinder, gentler masculinity and helps explain why an African American athlete can garner mainstream attention without excessive White cultural unease (McDonald, 1996). Throughout his playing career Jordan's handlers have been careful to connect his macho athletic persona to the court while Jordan continuously evokes his family's concern and support as the cornerstones of his personal and athletic successes. Agent David Falk has been active in selling this image, once noting that Jordan's parents "James and Doloris [sic], had been very, very close to their children, had great family values – they were disciplined, respectful, pretty much color-blind" (cited in Gates, 1998, p. 52). When announcing his second retirement from the NBA Jordan tells the international media:

> Unfortunately, my mother, my family, brothers and sisters, could not be here. But as you see me, you see them. My father, my mother and certainly my brothers and sisters. They are here, through me, and they, along with myself, say thank you for taking me in and showing me the respect and gratitude you have shown me over the years I have been here.
>
> (cited in Lazenby, 1999, p. 5)

Michael Jordan's persona as a dedicated family man helped to link the NBA with an idealized wholesome image while diffusing lingering impressions of masculine force, stereotypes of Black hypersexuality and deviance (McDonald, 1996). The picture of familial happiness has been a consistent portrait of Jordan throughout the years and Jordan's own parents Deloris and James have been featured in commercials, which now include Jordan's wife Juanita Jordan. The image of an idealized Jordan family portrait has been so widely repeated and reported, that this vision of harmony has been able to withstand recent charges from Jordan's sister, Deloris, that father James was emotionally abusive during their childhood. Deloris' picture of a family subject to patriarchal rule has been effectively countered by the habitual characterization of the Jordan family as a site for the transmission of serenity and acceptance. This, for example, is the vision painted by Jordan in explaining, to talk show host Larry King, his wife Juanita's role in a Bijan cologne campaign:

Mr. Bijan invited my wife to get involved with it, and she graciously accepted it, because she felt my life was taking a different turn. And although basketball is not a part of that, you know, my private life is – it includes her as well as my kids. And she can explain that and explore that a little bit better than, you know, anyone else, I think, that is even closer to me. And her participation gives a more simple side to Michael Jordan other than just basketball. And I was very surprised, yet very happy that she chose to be a part of it. And I guess she doesn't really truly want to come out of her shell or her closet in terms of being exploited or being, you know, promoted because I think she truly enjoys her private life. But this time I felt – or she felt that she wanted to be a part of this whole campaign to help illustrate, you know, what Michael Jordan is all about other than just basketball.

(cited in King, 1999)

This portrait of Jordan is an enticing image of Black masculinity, suggesting family intimacy coupled with an affable, even sensitive new age man. In an era notable for racist assaults on Black masculinity as deviant and criminal, Jordan's commodity sign suggests an incredible athlete and a dedicated family man thus inviting "desire without evoking dread" (Jackson, 1994, p. 49).

There are numerous images of Michael Jordan advocating for the family. October 1, 1996 saw the dedication of "Jordan Institute for Families" at the University of North Carolina, which came about because Michael Jordan apparently believes "that everything that can be done should be done to preserve the family" (Jordan Institute for Families, 1998). In another advertisement for Ball Park Franks, Jordan appears with his wife Juanita and a small child who appears to be one of his sons. The headline proclaims: "Enjoy Ball Park Franks, Fat Free Classics, and kid-size Fun Franks, all with the delicious Ball Park taste that your family values." This slogan again links Jordan to one of the most ubiquitous images of recent times: an idealized harmonious vision of family life complete with the ever present family values. The explicit link to family values suggests that Jordan participates in a highly salient, affective and ideological realm related to the nuclear family. Indeed, most recently in the United States, the nuclear family's alleged decline continues to be used as the scapegoat for New Right moral panics over welfare dependency, drug addiction, and "sexual promiscuity" (Stacey, 1996). The family values rhetoric has been deployed by conservatives and liberals alike to prevent sex education programs in public schools, the distribution of condoms, the integration of gays into the military and access to abortion. Furthermore, the simplistic celebration of the nuclear family continues to be used by members of the New Right to demonize poor single women with children who are simultaneously blamed both for their own poverty and the perceived collapse of national morality. Rather than look critically at the gendered division of labor and institutional racism, the intense focus on the alleged naturalness of the nuclear family with the stay at home mother and breadwinner father renders invisible a series of political and economic issues that have a huge impact on the poor. Ideologies related to gender and (hetero)sexuality play a crucial role in demonizing the poor, suggesting that irresponsible poor women dominate and control indigent men, both of whom refuse to or cannot curtail excessive sexual impulses (Thomas, 1998).

Repeated images of the Jordan family offer the moral obverse of the most vilified image of single female-headed households. The Jordans offer an enticing vision of Black success and consumer comfort countering the suggestion that Black families are inherently pathological. Still, the Jordan family bliss is built upon traditional gender expectations that middle-class people have long been expected to abide by. In this way images of Michael Jordan represent him as the ultimate family breadwinner, providing consumer comfort for his family with numerous cars, vacations and a luxurious home. Read against the demonization of single motherhood, this enticing vision of Jordan familial bliss participates in and bolsters a conservative project related to US families.

International Jordan: global contexts and commodity sign cultures

Michael Jordan's commodity sign has never been entirely contained within the borders of the United States. As Nike and the NBA sought to increase profitability by expanding into international markets, so too has Jordan's image traversed national boundaries. Jordan is thus one of many American commodity signs including those of Nike, the NBA, Coke and McDonald's, that circulate around the globe and are especially promoted via US and transnational media conglomerates. In an increasingly global, indeed an increasingly Americanized world, numerous nations are engaging in an on-going process of accessing American commodity signs in local contexts.

The reception of Jordan in a variety of local national contexts suggests a complex process that cannot simply be reduced to a unidirectional conceptualization of American commodity imperialism (Andrews et al., 1996). Rather, Jordan's reception in such diverse spaces and contexts as contemporary New Zealand, Poland and Black Britain suggests that local cultures contain fluid meanings and consist of "relational space constituted only in and through its relation to the global" (Robins, 1991, p. 35). Thus a critical analysis of American commodity signs such as Jordan illuminates transnational influences on local cultures, revealing that these meanings are contingent on their reception within an array of diverse national contexts. For example, the presence of Jordan and the NBA within the New Zealand popular imaginary is suggestive of the increasing centrality of American iconography as essentially different and unique from local artifacts (Jackson and Andrews, 1996). Despite noticeable resistance, Jordan's generally positive reception in Poland serves as another example of a long-time Polish fascination with America, a fascination height-ened after the collapse of communist rule in the country. In Britain, to many Blacks, the success of Jordan represents not simply that of an American athlete, but that of a Black athlete symbolically countering the ideologies and practices of White supremacy (Andrews *et al.*, 1996).

In New Zealand, the dominant meanings attached to the NBA and Jordan suggest glamour, wealth, and overt commercialism. Thus Michael Jordan is a signifier of America and American difference in New Zealand in ways that are similar to Hollywood movies. Yet Jordan's American difference in relationship to New Zealand culture has also served to distinguish and energize multiple local sporting cultures. Thus the very same global forces that have caused the proliferation of American commodity signs in post-colonial New Zealand have also enabled more localized sports, such as rugby union and rugby league, to become commercially viable as signifiers of "New Zealandness," and to be exported worldwide (Andrews *et al.*, 1996).

For many Poles who once lived under a communist regime, signifiers of Americana such as Michael Jordan provide another set of complicated culture meanings. With the collapse of communism in 1989 came the development of a Polish consumer culture and an increased proliferation of American commodity signs. In the midst of this cultural, political, and economic transition the United States remained closely aligned with an ideology of liberation through individual pleasure seeking. Against this depiction, debates raged in the Polish parliament related to the degradation of Polish culture through the crass consumerism and hedonism of American capitalism. Despite this opposition, increasingly people in Poland, and especially the young, look to define themselves in relationship to an enticing picture of American consumer culture populated with compelling images connecting American commodity signs with personal freedom and the pursuit of leisure. Thus images of Jordan suggesting American individualism, freedom and competition contrast sharply with the mundane concerns of everyday post-communist Polish life (Andrews *et al.*, 1996).

Within a post-colonial Black British context, the reception of Jordan suggests the necessity of adopting more than a simple "national" framework and instead invites a movement toward an investigation of transnational spaces. Jordan thus must be conceived of as one of many Black sports celebrities embraced within the Black Diaspora. In attempting to extend the "existing formulations of the Diaspora idea," Paul Gilroy (1996, p. 22) has suggested engaging the Black Atlantic as "a deterritorialised, multiplex and anti-national basis for the affinity or 'identity of passions' between diverse black populations" (ibid., p. 18). Thus Jordan is but one of numerous Black male sport stars whose image has traveled across and among nations but whose significance as a symbol of Black achievement transcends national borders. In the context of White supremacy, and white hegemony, Jordan serves as a resistant cultural figure (Andrews *et al.*, 1996).

Given these insights, any discussion of Michael Jordan's significance must take into account particular local and transnational contexts. While there is no doubt of the political and cultural power connected with capitalist expansion, it is impossible to look at this process as a simple act of US homogenization. Indeed, as the examples from Black Britain, Poland and New Zealand demonstrate, American commodity signs like Michael Jordan are never uniformly received within diverse histories and geographies. Thus while Jordan is clearly a part of a global world notable for the circulation of signifiers of Americanness, these transnational corporate representations mean very different things, to different people, in different geographical spaces and historical contexts (Andrews *et al.*, 1996).

Concluding thoughts on Jordan, sport celebrityhood and cultural criticism

Throughout this chapter we have argued that Michael Jordan does not occupy a stable and uniform place within diverse and complex popular cultures. In short, Jordan has and will continue to mean different things, to different people, in different cultural contexts within diverse historical moments. Yet, while it is important to recognize and accentuate the multiple, competing meanings of celebrity sport stars such as Michael Jordan, it is also necessary to interrogate the ways in which athletic celebrities are imbedded in complex matrixes of power. Practices, ideas, images, signs and knowledges that constitute the Jordan phenomenon have been organized to produce and reproduce certain interests, thus careful scrutiny is needed to reveal who benefits when a particular spin or version of Jordan is promulgated, accepted and naturalized as "the way things are." The goal of this and indeed any critical analysis of postmodern celebrityhood must be to develop the types of knowledge that encourage critical engagement with mediated discourses in order to explicate what might have been obscured and dismissed by hegemonic forces (McDonald and Birrell, 1999).

This engagement with Michael Jordan's promotional ubiquity has sought to create an alternative account, to problematize the desire of merely wanting to *be like Mike* by revealing affective and ideological underpinnings of the Jordan phenomenon. Indeed despite shifting representations, the dominant construction of Jordan's hyperreal image represents a preferred vision of Black masculinity, an identity, against which all *others* are measured. While offering the possibility of resistant appropriation, too often the harsh realities and entrenched global, racial and gender inequalities are conveniently obscured by the Jordan hyper-mythology. In offering cultural criticism of the Jordan phenomenon, our goal has been to expose what might first appear as harmless personal investments to advance a critique that discloses how power and privilege are produced through sport celebrities. Our hope is that as people discern the political stakes at play in postmodern culture and sport celebrityhood that they work toward collective opposition and cultural change.

33

Bibliography

Andrews, D.L. (1996) The fact(s) of Michael Jordan's blackness: excavating a floating racial signifier. *Sociology of Sport Journal*, 13 (2), 125–58.

—— (1998) Excavating Michael Jordan: notes on a critical pedagogy of sporting representation. In G. Rail (ed.), *Sport and Postmodern Times* (pp. 185–220). Albany, NY: State University of New York Press.

Andrews, D.L., Carrington, B., Jackson, S.J. and Mazur, Z. (1996) Jordanscapes: a preliminary analysis of the global popular. *Sociology of Sport Journal*, 13 (4), 428–57.

Armstrong, J. (1999) Retired "Airness" still sells. *Denver Post*, July 25, p. C13.

Ahrens, F. (1999) Follow the bouncing ball; for Michael Jordan, an infinity of possibilities. *The Washington Post*, January 13, p. C01.

Base, B. (1997) Nike speaks in tongues to psychographic targets. *Strategy*, 20, September 29.

Cole, C.L. (1996) American Jordan: P.L.A.Y., consensus, and punishment. *Sociology of Sport Journal*, 13 (4), 366–97.

Cole, C.L. and Andrews, D. L. (1996) "Look–it's NBA ShowTime!": visions of race in the popular imaginary. In N.K. Denzin (ed.) *Cultural Studies: A Research Volume* (vol. 1, pp. 141–81).

Dobie, K. (1994) Murder by the roadside in Robeson County. *Vibe*, February, 72–8.

Einstein, D. (1999) Jordan's life off the basketball court. *The San Francisco Chronicle*, January 14, p. B1.

Esquinas, R. (1993) *Michael and Me: Our Gambling Addiction ... My Cry for Help.* San Diego, CA: Athletic Guidance Center Publishing.

Friedman, W. (1999) Jordan the star athlete retires, Jordan the brand comes to life. *Advertising Age*, 3, January 18, p. 3.

Gates, H.L. (1998) Net worth: how the greatest player in the history of basketball became the greatest brand in the history of sports. *The New Yorker*, June 1, pp. 48–61.

Gilroy, P. (1991) '*There Ain't No Black in the Union Jack': The Cultural Politics of Race and Nation.* Chicago: University of Chicago Press.

—— (1996) Route work: the black Atlantic and the politics of exile. In I. Chambers and L. Curti (eds), *The Post-colonial Question: Common Skies, Divided Horizons*, (pp. 17–29). London: Routledge.

Grossberg, L. (1986) On postmodernism and articulation: an interview with Stuart Hall. *Journal of Communication Inquiry*, 10 (2), 45–75.

—— (1992) *We Gotta Get Out of this Place: Popular Conservatism and Postmodern Culture.* London: Routledge.

Halberstam, D. (1999) *Playing for Keeps: Michael Jordan and the World He Made.* New York: Random House.

Hall, S. (1983) The problem of ideology: Marxism without guarantees. In B. Matthews (ed.), *Marx 100 Years On* (pp. 57–86). London: Lawrence & Wishart.

Jackson, P. (1994) Black male: advertising and the cultural politics of masculinity. *Gender, Place and Culture*, 1 (1), 49–59.

Jackson, S.J. and Andrews, D.L. (1996) Excavating the (trans)National Basketball Association: locating the global/local nexus of America's world and the world's America. *Australian Journal for American Studies*, 15 (1), 57–64.

Jeffords, S. (1994) *Hard Bodies: Hollywood Masculinity in the Reagan Era.* New Brunswick, NJ: Rutgers University Press.

Jordan Institute for Families: http://ssw.unc.edu/Jif/aboutIns.htm

Katz, D. (1994) *Just Do It: The Nike Spirit in the Corporate World*. New York: Random House.

Kellner, D. (1995) *Media Culture: Cultural Studies, Identity and Politics Between the Modern and the Postmodern*. London: Routledge.

King, L. (1999) Michael Jordan still plays to win. *CNN Larry King Live*, June 14.

Kirkpatrick, C. (1987) In an orbit all his own. *Sports Illustrated*, November 9, 82–98.

Lazenby, R. (1999) A heartfelt departure. In M. Morris (ed.), *Michael Jordan: The Ultimate Career Tribute, 1984–1998* (pp. 4–14). Bannockburn, IL: H & S Media.

Lofton, D. (1998) Nike unveils new products, plans during Memphis, Tenn. meeting. *The Commercial Appeal*, 1, September 24.

McDonald, M.G. (1996) Michael Jordan's family values: marketing, meaning, and post-Reagan America. *Sociology of Sport Journal*, 13 (4), 344–65.

McDonald, M.G. and Birrell, S. (1999) Reading sport critically: a methodology for interrogating power. *Sociology of Sport Journal*, 16 (4), 283–300.

McKinney, M. and Romero, E. (1999) Jordan brand to install concept shops in NY, Chicago. *Business and Industry*, 29 (46), 2.

Messner, M. (1988) Sport and male domination: the female athlete as contested terrain. *Sport Sociology Journal*, 5, 197–211.

Murphy, M. (1999) Michael Jordan: end of an era. *The Houston Chronicle*, 1, January 14.

Reeves, J.L. and Campbell, R. (1994) *Cracked Coverage: Television News, the Anticocaine Crusade, and the Reagan Legacy*. Durham, NC: Duke University Press.

Robins, K. (1990) Global local times. In J. Anderson and M. Ricci (eds), *Society and Social Science: A Reader* (pp. 196–205). Milton Keynes: Open University.

—— (1991) Tradition and translation: national culture in its global context. In J. Corner and S. Harvey (eds), *Enterprise and Heritage: Cross-currents of National Culture* (pp. 21–44). London: Routledge.

Schacter, E. (1999) Jesus in Nikes. *National Review*. February 22, 47–50.

Schneider, W. (1990) The in-box president. *Atlantic Monthly*, January, 34–43.

Solnik, C. and Lee, G. (1998) Nike fights back: Denies swoosh talk, plays up Jordan. *Footwear News*, 54 (39), 1, September 28.

Stacey, J. (1996) *In the Name of the Family: Rethinking Family Values in the Postmodern Age*. Boston: Beacon Press.

Strasser, J.B. and Becklund, L. (1991) *Swoosh: The Unauthorized Story of Nike, and the Men Who Played There*. New York: Harcourt Brace Jovanovich.

Thomas, G.S. (1998) *The United States of Suburbia: How the Suburbs took Control of America and What They Plan to Do with It*. New York: Prometheus Books.

Thomas, L.M. (1998) Moral deference. In C. Willett (ed.), *Theorizing Multiculturalism: A Guide to the Current Debate* (pp. 359–81). Oxford: Blackwell.

Thomas, S. (1998) Race, gender and welfare reform: the antinatalist response. *Journal of Black Studies*, 28 (4), 419–46.

2

EXCURSIONS INTO OTHERNESS

Understanding Dennis Rodman and the limits of subversive agency

Mélisse Lafrance and Geneviève Rail

American basketball star Dennis Rodman's multitudinous personas and unpredictable interaction with television media have been frequently characterized as disruptive and counter-cultural. Indeed, according to many observers, Rodman has radically defied normative convention and redefined representations of gender, race, and desire within the American cultural imaginary (Barrett, 1997; Jefferson, 1997; Johnson, 1996; McDonald and Aikens, 1996). Even after having considered those elements of Rodman's productions that might challenge cultural norms, we have concluded that his extraordinary spectacular enactments consolidate dominant fantasies of race, gender and desire, and are therefore only problematically subversive. Indeed, our previous examinations (Lafrance and Rail, 1997, 1998) of existing literature as well as Rodman's most important promotional strategies have shown that understanding Rodman's self-presentations as vitally disruptive elicits serious theoretical and conceptual dilemmas.

As regards the first dilemma, we have highlighted the paradox encountered by observers attempting to make sense of the Rodman craze: that is, Rodman's persona appears to be predicated on the exploitation and reproduction of dominant norms and codes while being recognized as rebellious and intelligently non-conformist. We have addressed this contradiction and discussed how the apparently incongruous constituents of Rodman's success at once effloresce and limit his subversive agency. Rodman's enactments of "marketable difference" (Kellner, 1996, p. 459) destabilize the American semiotic by mainstreaming superficial aesthetic transgressions, but his mobilization of white masculinist and heterosexist fantasies reinforces dominant discourses of race, gender and sexuality.

Second, we focused on Rodman's performances of drag and the limits of his subjective agency. Contrary to McDonald and Aikens (1996) and Barrett (1997), who interpreted the Rodman phenomenon as a disruptive force *vis-à-vis* regimes of gender and sexuality, we found Rodman's cross-dressing to have little disruptive effect. In fact, we argued that construing Rodman as disruptive

36

to dominant gender codes was problematic on three counts: (a) Rodman's cross-dressing strategies rely on heteronormative formulations of gender and thus exploit and confirm male supremacist formulations of femininity; (b) Rodman's comportment, whether in or out of drag, is frequently aggressive, sexist or sexually violent, and therefore reproduces dominant modalities of masculinity; and (c) Rodman's cross-dressing does not confuse perceptions of his sex/gender identity and therefore has little implication for the maintenance and resulting privilege of his dominant masculine persona.

Finally, we have assessed Rodman's behavior as it relates to the (popular and academic) discursive fields of sexual difference and AIDS. So far, a number of cultural observers have contended that Rodman, by discussing his homoerotic fantasies, dying the AIDS red ribbon into his hair, publicizing his visits to gay bars, and defending the rights of transsexuals and transvestites, is effectively queering mainstream audiences, however temporarily (Barrett, 1997; Jefferson, 1996; Johnson, 1996; McDonald and Aikens, 1996). Although we are not in complete disagreement with such assertions, we have considered the subversive potential of Rodman's sexual persona within the context of related acts and comments as well as Rodman's stake in their representation. Our analysis allowed us to identify a number of discontinuities that permit Rodman to benefit from the publicity and popular exoticization of queer chic while success-fully courting a primarily heterosexual male reader/viewership. Coupled with the overwhelmingly heteromasculine tone of his books and interviews, we have argued that such discontinuities "[invite] status quo readers to imagine that they too can consume images of difference, participate in the sexual practices depicted, and yet remain untouched – unchanged" (hooks, 1994, p. 15).

The present chapter builds on earlier writings (Lafrance and Rail, 1997, 1998) and further elucidates the cultural and economic logics both underlying and sustaining the Rodman sensation. Having assessed the subversive potential of Rodman's spectacles of difference (i.e., cross-dressing, homoerotic acts and disclosures, "queer" self-marking), we now endeavour to understand how representations of Rodman's aggressive, hyper-masculine sexuality are mediated by his blackness and whether they reinforce the demonization of the "failed" black family, the commodification of black struggle, the exoticization of the black sporting body, and the mythification of black physicality. We end the chapter with a number of reflections on Rodman as "corporate warrior"[1] and on the limits of subversion-through-consumption.

Recovery, transformation and transcendence: Rodman, the failed black family and the American Dream[2]

> A lot of times you'll hear somebody ask an NBA player what he'd be doing if he wasn't getting paid to play basketball. The answer they get pretty often is: Dead or in jail. Most of us are from shitty backgrounds: projects, ghettos, no money, no father, no hope ... I

37

didn't have a male role model in my life until I got to college and
started getting my shit together.

(Dennis Rodman)

Cole (1996) and Cole and King (1998) have maintained that the success of the
black athlete both generates and affirms national fantasies of meritocracy and
fluid social mobility while pathologizing the alleged failure of black America.
We contend that Rodman's depiction as an African-American man who transcended his ascribed situation to finally attain a life of fame and material wealth,
articulates at least two national fantasy discourses: (a) the failed black family;
and (b) America as an open economic system.

Both Rodman and the media that represent him emphasize his fatherlessness
in the projects and, subsequently, the white middle-class nuclear family that
adopted him when he went off to college. An overwhelming number of articles,
in fact, dedicate at least one passage to Rodman's friendship with, and surrogate
adoption by, the Rich family after he leaves the projects. His biography is re-
written to appear as though it was only Rodman's inauguration into this white
nuclear family that allowed him to excel in his sporting endeavors.
Simultaneously, Rodman's biological mother, the struggles she encountered
raising and supporting a family of four, and her contribution to his career are
effaced.

Rodman's success has also been used to confirm sport as the protector of
black masculinity, a discourse contingent on dominant formulations of the failed
black family. For instance, Rodman has declared, "I grew up in a house of
women ... I thought when I was growing up that I was going to be gay," and
this notorious declaration has been frequently mobilized by the mainstream
press to narrate the perverse implications of absent black masculine role models.
Moreover, the considerable media attention attributed to this declaration shows
the extent to which Rodman's move to a white, middle-class nuclear family and
involvement in professional sports have been interpreted as events that have
saved him from emasculation. In this context, sporting activities become
narrated as essential to African-American communities; they compensate for the
homosocial bonding and paternal role modeling portrayed as inaccessible in
black America (Cole, 1996; Cole and King, 1998).

Rodman's books and interviews host lengthy ruminations on the virtues of
American society, the most important of which pertains to every individual's
right and ability to better his or her economic situation. In the aforementioned
publications, Rodman offers himself up as proof of American society as an open
system wherein individuals, regardless of race, class, gender or sexuality, are
empowered to transcend their ascribed identities and forge new lives for themselves. Like Barrett (1997), we posit that Rodman's recurring narratives of
economic recovery and transcendence, as well as his emphasis on hard work and
merit-based achievement, position him as an affirmation of American "rags-to-
riches" fantasies. Consider the following citations from *Walk on the Wild Side*:

Some of my friends think I'm the second coming of Elvis, and I must admit there are some similarities between me and the King. Like Elvis, I'm a southern boy who lifted himself out of a poor upbringing and hit the big-time. When I was growing up in the projects and things seemed bleak, I always looked at Elvis as proof that anyone with the right combination of flair, talent, drive, and luck can become important in America.

(1997, p. 26)

I wouldn't be a strict parent, and I'd make it easy for [my daughter] to appreciate things. But I'd want her to appreciate the value of hard work, because the best way to get your priorities in order is to work for what you get. You've got to work, work, work, work, work, work, work, work. That's what I did, and I've appreciated what it's got me – I still do.

(ibid., p. 224)

We conclude, therefore, that the subversive potential of Rodman's utterances relating to the destitution of American inner-city life is undermined, if not annuled, by his meritocratic formulations. Rodman's apparent hostility towards political explanations of social inequality also ratify dominant depoliticized conceptions of national socioeconomic processes. Silver's interview with Rodman reveals this hostility:

There is a fatalistic side to Rodman, but he's more of a '90s dissident than a '60s insurgent. He thinks anything political is *crap* and has adopted a younger generation's everything-is-screwed-up-beyond-repair resignation. He is drunk on his own ability to do whatever he wants, a rebel without a boss.

(1995, p. 23; emphasis added)

The Dallas-based consulting firm Sports Marketing Group confirms this assertion, positing: "The under-29s see him as a rebel with a cause. They appreciate his values. *He doesn't play politics*, he says what he thinks and feels" (Hirsley and DeSimone, 1996, p. 3; emphasis added). In fact, Rodman tends to eschew most explanations of social inequality that posit systemic relations of white domination.[3] Instead, Rodman tends to adopt relativistic positions on questions of race and class:

This is coming from somebody who doesn't see skin color. I'm color neutral. I'm black, but my friends joke about me being a 'white' black man. Most of my close friends are white, and I go out with white women. I don't think about color. I try to go beyond that. The problem is, some people won't let you go beyond it. If you're black and a high-profile athlete, you're all of a sudden under pressure to be a spokesman for the race ... Sometimes I think: Fuck the race and the people, I'm going to be honest with myself. That way people – no matter what color – can make their own judgments about me. Everyone has a different experience. Everyone has a different story. When it comes to race, my experiences are different than anybody else's.

(Rodman, 1996, pp. 166–7)

It is our belief, then, that Rodman has triumphed with mainstream audiences partly because he allows whites to abdicate responsibility for their direct or indirect roles in the reproduction of unequal social relations while simultaneously fulfilling national fantasies of the failed black family and meritocracy.

Good black/bad black: Dennis Rodman and binary conceptions of racial Others

[O]n the whole, I believe that [Michael] Jordan is positioned in media culture as the "good black," especially against the aggressiveness and visual transgressions of teammate Dennis Rodman, who with his bleached and undisciplined hair, earring, fancy clothes, and regularly rebellious behavior represents the "bad" black figure.

(Kellner, 1996)

Beausoleil (1994) argues that dominant culture formulates simple, monolithic and often binary conceptions of racial Others in order to justify their socio-cultural subordination. This contention, it could be argued, is confirmed through considerations of Rodman's popular representation. Indeed, when contrasted with representations of Michael Jordan – who is constructed as the zenith of "good" blackness – Dennis Rodman is an unmistakable embodiment of "bad" blackness. For Barrett, Rodman's badness renders him incongruous and therefore disruptive to the highly regulated rectitude of the NBA:

This logic is given the shorthand of "family values" and is deeply implicated in the economic fortunes of the NBA, corporate culture, and the powerful representations they underwrite. An enormous financial return for the NBA depends on the winsome introduction of (primarily African-American) 'young guys' into what US culture insists on regulating as demure domestic wards. Rodman's unusual appearance and cynicism, on the other hand, interrogate these presumptions. They query the NBA's economic/entertainment monopoly, [and] the equally suspect monopoly of moral/ethical discourse in the US.

(1997, p. 109)

Unlike Barrett, we posit that although Rodman's aggressive refusal of NBA role-model culture and family values subscription may trouble select dominant discourses undergirding professional basketball, his unruly behavior is not culturally and/or economically unproductive. On the one hand, Rodman's badness is culturally productive as it becomes reformulated to satisfy white fantasies of black savagery and to further mark black (sporting) bodies as deviant. On the other hand, we contend that Rodman's badness is economically productive in that the NBA benefits enormously from Rodman's spectacles. Such benefits have been discussed by sports journalist Wayne Scanlan. As regards the economic productivity of Rodman's badness, Scanlan observes:

> The scariest notion to reckon with is that the celebrated antics of ... Rodman have become a financial necessity to major-league sport and the media that present it and cover it. Jim Bouton [suggested that] sports have learned from the John McEnroe example in tennis. Tantrums raise profiles, sell tickets and even attract sponsors.
>
> (1997, p. 1)

Hence, Rodman's appeal to sports fans of the NBA is not irrational, as Barrett (1997) maintains. In fact, we would argue that Rodman's success is entirely logical in that it implies both the consolidation of dominant discursive regimes and the proliferation of NBA economic fortunes. Moreover, Rodman's "badness," especially when contraposed with Jordan's "goodness," facilitates mainstream media's dichotomized good/bad representations of black men. Black men are thus locked into a profoundly stereotypical representational politics that denies and even disavows the complexities of their cultural situation and the pluralistic nature of the subject positions they currently inhabit.

"Getting a bit of the other": Dennis Rodman and black male sexuality

In earlier writings (Lafrance and Rail, 1997, 1998), we have assessed the subversive potential of Rodman's seemingly counter-cultural spectacles of difference (i.e., cross-dressing, homoerotic acts and disclosures, "queer" self-marking). We have not, however, discussed how these spectacles of difference and their representation in the American cultural imaginary relate to Rodman's blackness. Here, we consider Rodman's blackness in an attempt to evaluate why his sexuality appears to be a palpable object of popular fascination. Using his success as a yardstick, we show that representations of Rodman's aggressive, hyper-masculine sexuality are always already mediated by his blackness. In so doing, we also show that these representations are redeployed in order to articulate white supremacist fantasies of savage, phallocentred, and sexually predacious black men.

41

Rodman as postmodern savage: blackness, phallocentrism and sexuality

> I have this fantasy that I can live my life like a tiger in the jungle –
> eating whatever I want, having sex whenever I want, and roaming
> around butt naked, wild and free .... It sounds difficult and
> complicated, but it doesn't have to be.
>
> (Dennis Rodman)

The front and back covers of Rodman's most recent effort, *Walk on the Wild Side* (1997), see him in animal-like poses. On his hands and knees, Rodman is naked, adorned with brown, orange and yellow paint, and covered with black horizontal stripes. One is most likely supposed to gather that Rodman is, in these pictures, a tiger or another wild animal of sorts. Fragments of these pictures recur on most pages of the book. Despite its almost unspeakable repetition and contradiction, *Walk on the Wild Side* is characterized by several themes. Of particular pertinence to this section are two predominant leitmotifs: his physicality and his sexuality. Rodman's lengthy discussions of both his body and his sexuality are couched in gratuitous and voyeuristic terms, often consisting of lists and summaries detailing his rawest and most unconventional sexual encounters. These narratives are inevitably framed by Rodman's uncontrollable sexual urges and his basic willingness to entertain sexual relations in any situation.

Walk on the Wild Side is also characterized by detailed autobiographical descriptions of Rodman's penis. In fact, these penis narratives seem to have at least two recurring themes. On the one hand, Rodman's penis is always described as enormous and, most importantly, black. Consider, for instance, Rodman's observation that intolerant individuals "beat on [him] for being an uppity N-word who loves to show his big black dong to white women" (1997, p. 240). On the other hand, his penis is often represented in threatening and intimidating terms. Consider, for example, Rodman's description of his meeting with Cindy Crawford at an MTV function: "The highlight was when I put on a G-String. Her mouth got all wide and she looked totally amazed when she saw my big bulge. I told her, 'don't worry – there's a monster in my pants'" (ibid., p. 140).

According to hooks (1992), phallic obsessions are particularly acute in certain facets of black male culture. hooks attributes this especially high frequency to white supremacist logics that seek to divert black men from resistance struggle while preoccupying them with banal and depoliticized questions of genital anatomy. She problematizes the implications of black men, like Rodman, who embrace a phallocentric orientation:

> Should we not suspect the contemporary commodification of blackness orchestrated by whites that once again tells black men not only to focus on their penis but to make this focus their all consuming passion?

Such confused men have little time or insight for resistance struggle.
Should we not suspect representations of black men ... where the black
male describes himself as "hung like a horse" as though the size of his
penis defines who he is? ... How many black men will have to die
before black folks are willing to look at the link between the contemporary plight of black men and their continued allegiance to patriarchy
and phallocentrism?

(1992, p. 112; emphasis added)

Indeed, those who read Rodman's books are likely left with the impression that
Rodman resembles nothing short of a sexually irrational black man whose enormous penis and visceral instincts are directed at and satisfied by apprehensive
white women. Rodman, then, presents himself as primitively hyper-sexual,
phallic identified and racially threatening. We suggest that the aforementioned
formulation of Rodman's sexual identity is met with overwhelming commercial
success in the popular realm, precisely because it articulates specific white
supremacist fantasies of black male sexuality. Historical and cultural contextual-
izations of Rodman and dominant representations of his sexuality confirm our
position. White American culture's complicated interest in black sexuality, and
indeed blackness in general, can be traced back to the settlement of the New
World (Morrison, 1992). For Morrison, young America was a country:

in which there was a resident population, already black, upon which
the imagination could play; through which historical, moral, metaphys-
ical and social fears, problems and dichotomies could be articulated.
The slave population, it could be and was assumed, offered itself up as
surrogate selves for meditation on problems of human freedom, its
lure and its elusiveness. This black population was available for medita-
tions on terror – the terror of ... internal aggression, evil, sin, greed.

(ibid., pp. 37–8)

The elaboration of American identity was thus achieved through not only white
culture's suppression of Africanism "deployed as rawness and savagery" (ibid., p.
44), but also through its highly invested and profoundly troubled engagement
with the African Other. This engagement produced, in literary and filmic imagi-
nations, the African Other as the savage, the rapist, and /or the criminal (Davis,
1984; hooks, 1992, 1994; Morrison, 1992; Snead, 1994). That is, the African
Other was materialized through all of the fictive personages with which whites
could not and would not allow themselves to personally identify. Such cultural
and historical displacements, resulting in the mythification of African Otherness,
allowed and continue to allow dominant groups to consume various modalities
of difference (i.e., racial, ethnic, sexual), experience pleasure from the consumption of such difference, and maintain white supremacist relations. hooks
discusses the problematic nature of white longing for contact with the Other:

43

To make oneself vulnerable to the seduction of difference, to seek an encounter with the Other, does not require that one relinquish forever one's mainstream positionality. When race and ethnicity become commodified as resources for pleasure, the culture of specific groups, as well as the bodies of individuals, can be seen as constituting an alternative playground where members of dominating races, genders, sexual practices affirm their power-over in intimate relations with the Other.

(1992, p. 23)

White Americans have long been living out fantasies of the Other through the consumption of black literary and filmic images. According to Snead (1994), this consumption is reflective of a cultural moment in which images of blackness are actively implicated in the reinscription of dominant norms and codes. We contend that the American mass consumption of Rodman's black physicality and sexuality should be understood in similar terms – something connotative of a crisis in white cultural identity and reinscriptive of dominant regimes of race, ethnicity and sexuality. We next consider some particularly acute articulations of white culture's fantasies of the Other's racially coded sexuality, while situating Rodman within this cultural history.

Unbearable blackness: Rodman's savagery and the resurgence of the racially coded monster

In Western culture, the literary and historical tendency to identify blacks with ape-like creatures is quite clear and has been well-documented. A willed misreading of Linnaean classification and Darwinian evolution helped buttress an older European conception (tracing from as early as the 16th Century) that blacks and apes, kindred denizens of the "jungle," are phylogenetically closer and sexually more compatible than blacks and whites.

(Snead, 1994)

This masculinist preserve of the NBA is further complicated by the stereotypical association that equates people of color with sensuality and physicality. Thus, perceptions of hypersexuality and eroticism persist as powerful racist undercurrents within the consumer culture and the commodified space of the NBA.

(McDonald, 1996)

We have already delineated the underlying elements of dominant culture's deployment of blackness as rawness and savagery. In so doing, we have worked towards elucidating the constituents of Rodman's success with white audiences. To solidify such elucidations, we suggest a comparison of mainstream cultural engagements with two seemingly distinct spectacles of blackness: Dennis Rodman and King Kong. We maintain the pertinence of considering Dennis Rodman and King Kong concomitantly for two reasons: (a) both are spectacles evincing hyper-aggressive black savagery; and (b) there has been a resurgence of like-natured, and arguably racially coded, ape spectacles in late twentieth-century America – an epoch, it should be noted, that coincides with Rodman's successes.

We argue that Rodman's successes must be understood within the context of a cultural imaginary increasingly strewn by awe-inspiring representations of animalistic blackness. This popular cultural resurgence of anthropomorphic ape images has been materialized by profitable Hollywood remakes of classics such as *Mighty Joe Young* (a *King Kong* sequel) and *Godzilla*, as well as by television commercials depicting apes wrapping Christmas presents (Fido Cellular Telephones), stealing credit cards (Visa Credit), intimidating white women in pantyhose (Leggs Hosiery), watching movies (Blockbuster Video), offering Valentine Day flowers (Rogers Cantel Inc., AT&T Corp.) and observing circus events (Subway Submarine Sandwiches). This resurgence has also been evidenced by an uncommonly significant amount of news coverage pertaining to anthropomorphic ape events.[4] No matter the manifestation, the recent and undeniable resurrection of anthropomorphic ape representations in late twentieth-century America might be interpreted as white culture's attempt to discharge, through popular forms, its increased frustration and resentment toward people of color.

Dennis Rodman is an interesting individual to consider within this analytical context as he is quite obviously not an ape. His voluntary and involuntary representation as a primitive, aggressive, oversexed black man, however, tends to situate him in a semiotic economy shared by other alleged black savages like King Kong. *King Kong*, the movie, is especially worthy of deliberation in this instance due to its "blatant linkage of the idea of the black with that of the monster" (Snead, 1994, p. 7). Although the Hollywood mobilization of monstrosity is complex in and of itself, many posit that the monster functions as a figurative release of repressed sexual desires that would otherwise threaten social stability and reigning discursive regimes (e.g., Snead, 1994; Wood, 1979). Snead remarks: "The Hollywood monster film allows, among other things, a safe outlet of such sexual desires in a surrogate form, and a vicarious experience – pleasurable and horrific – of the chaos that such a release would bring about in reality" (1994, p. 7). Bearing in mind that Rodman is represented, and indeed represents himself, as a primitive, aggressive, irrational, hyper-sexual, exceedingly "well-hung" black man who dates predominantly white women, consider Snead's recapitulation of *King Kong*'s effects:

> The figure of King Kong would allow the white male to vent a variety
> of repressed sexual fantasies: the hidden desire of seeing himself as an
> omnipotent, phallic black male; the desire to abduct the white woman;

or the combined fantasy: to abduct a white woman in the disguise of a phallic black male.

(ibid., p. 24)

It could be argued that mainstream viewers, presumably white and male, might extort from representations of Rodman similar pleasures as those extorted from engagements with King Kong, as both spectacles allow viewers to fantasize about formidable physical prowess, menacing black phallic masculinity, and misogynistic sexual domination. Indeed, both King Kong and Rodman allow white male audiences to consume signs of racial and sexual difference for plea-sure-related purposes while, almost paradoxically, rearticulating white supremacist fantasies of black savagery, hyper-sexuality and deviance. It could be argued, then, that a mainstream spectator's engagement with Rodman's persona, as well as the effects produced by such an engagement, are character-ized by affective displacements similar to those produced by the popular consumption of animalistic blackness in other mediatized forms. These events must therefore be understood as highly problematic representations of black masculinity.

Rodman as corporate warrior: the limits of subversion-through-consumption

The claim that Rodman is a destabilizing cultural force can finally be evaluated on the basis of his economic location. We argue that because Rodman's alleged subversive praxis is inherently accomplished through consumption, its subver-sive potential and overall disruptive effects are seriously constrained. We contend that Rodman's persona is a cultural sensation precisely because it works within and reinforces what queer theorist Jeffrey Escoffier calls "the regimes of the normal" (1994, p. 135). Spectators therefore enjoy Rodman-the-spectacle unproblematically as it allows them to engage with acceptable and marketable forms of difference while residing unchallenged and unchanged (hooks, 1994). Indeed, a cursory glance at his financial profile reveals that the kinds of differ-ence for which Rodman is reputed are most certainly marketable and might even be, as Stuart Hall writes, "a kind of difference that doesn't make a differ-ence of any kind" (1992, p. 23). A brief look at Rodman's economic affiliations sheds light on our skepticism.

Since he first started eliciting substantive media and fan responses, Rodman has made considerable commercial inroads. In the last few years, Rodman has signed contracts with Nike, Pizza Pizza, Converse, Kodak, McDonald's, Oakleys, Victoria's Secret, Mistic Beverages, a national hotel chain, several clothing store chains, multinational computer companies, and has negotiated with Walt Disney Productions and Warner Brothers for the film rights to his book *Bad As I Wanna Be*. On top of Rodman's multimillion dollars salary, in 1996 his business manager was already expecting a yearly off-the-court income of over $10 million (Armour, 1996a, 1996b; Barboza, 1996a, 1996b; Hirsley and DeSimone; 1996; Johnson, K.C., 1996).

One has to question the fundamentals of Rodman's subversive potential when over ten multinational corporations are involved in his alleged subversion. Most importantly, one has to query Rodman's allegiances to multinational corporations such as Kodak, McDonald's and Disney – multinationals renowned for their collusion with dominant discursive regimes of race, ethnicity, gender and sexuality. Surely if these conventional corporations are willing to "risk" their reputations on Rodman, it is precisely because there is very little substantive risk involved. As Kodak's chief marketing officer Carl E. Gustin exemplifies: "We did a background check on Rodman and determined that his brand of naughty is benign ... Rodman is just comically naughty or cartoon naughty – a curious caricature of badness" (cited in Barboza, 1996a, p. D8).

Not only do the corporate think-tanks of popular culture consider Rodman's "counter-cultural" behavior innocuous, but they have and will continue to successfully mark such behavior as pathological. Susan Gianinno, general manager at Thompson New York, the ad agency in charge of Kodak's contract, openly declares: "We're using him [Rodman] *and all he represents* as a foil. The contradistinction between Rodman as the ostensible bad boy seemed an excellent contrast with the goodness and wholesomeness of Kodak" (cited in Barboza, 1996a, p. D8; emphasis added).

Hence, positing that subversive potential can be realized through consumptive patterns is problematic. Bordo reminds us that "consumer capitalism depends on the continual production of novelty, of fresh images to stimulate desire, [frequently dropping] into marginalized neighborhoods in order to find them" (1993, p. 25). By the very fact that alleged "novelty" or "subversion" is being "produced" for consumption requires that such "difference" be rendered (pleasantly) intelligible to mainstream audiences. Thus, if all representations formulated through consumer capitalism must in one way or another become normalized, then we must seriously doubt the subversive potential of any cultural icon whose image relies on male/heteronormative/white supremacist capitalist market forces. Since consumer capitalism requires a constant flow of new colonies and since consumption is by nature unstable granted its dependence on market forces, one cannot expect any consumer craze to last – even if it happens to be one with "subversive style."

Conclusion

As previously stated, the far from negligible success of Rodman's persona indicates that mainstream audiences exact a peculiar pleasure from Rodman's communications. We propose that Rodman's success with mainstream audiences is most astutely attributed to dominant culture's desire to make contact with the Other (and to live out its fantasies of savagery, hypersexuality and deviance through the consumption of black male sporting bodies), and not to its willingness to embrace progressive socio-cultural change. Despite a few evanescent moments of significant disruption, we have shown that Rodman, even in the midst of his alleged transgressions, maintains and reinscribes dominant modalities of masculinity, phallocentrism, heteronormativity, white supremacy and consumer capitalism.

Notes

1   See Varda Burstyn's (1999) discussion of professional athletes as "corporate warriors" ready to fight in the interests of the "sport nexus" and its dominant discursive regimes of race, ethnicity, gender and sexuality.

2   The title of this section was inspired by Cole and King's observation that:

> NBA superstars were created through and provided fertile ground for narratives of limited scope that emphasized recovery, transformation, transcendence, and utopic social visions ... Indeed, the complex marketing network that territorialized the NBA's celebrity zone privileged seemingly incontrovertible evidence of self-improvement, self-reliance, self-determination, and "choice" as it simultaneously produced an apparently endless supply of morality and cautionary tales.
>
> (1998, p. 52)

3   Rodman has, at times, made astute observations concerning racism on the basketball court and in American society. In *Bad As I Wanna Be*, Rodman states that Larry Bird was "way overrated ... because he's white. You never hear about a black player being the greatest" (1996, p. 162). Similarly, in *Walk on the Wild Side*, Rodman proclaims:

> The black culture still hasn't recovered from slavery. You can see it in the poverty, the crime, and amount of single-parent families. When you take a proud group of people and whip them and rape them and humiliate them to the point of torture, it's not something they can easily shake off. White people should understand that, but a lot of them don't, and this is still a very racist country.
>
> (1997, p. 233)

The trouble is, however, that the resistant value of such race consciousness gets lost, as it were, amidst his carnival of remarks accusing blacks of equally pernicious racism (see Rodman 1996, 1997). In this context, Rodman's comments about "white racism" appear to be just as culturally important, and indeed, just as culturally productive, as "black racism." In this sense, the relativistic nature of Rodman's race consciousness "allows American [middle-class] audiences to recognize themselves as compassionate and ethical subjects in 1990s America" (Cole and King, 1998, p. 54), without forcing them to acknowledge their own implication in systems of oppression.

4   This observation, it should be noted, is not based on a rigorous content analysis of mainstream news coverage. It is based merely on the authors' daily engagements with popular cultural forms such as the televised news, newspapers and magazines. These engagements have resulted in the authors' conclusion that anthropomorphic ape spectacles seem to preoccupy mediatized space with significant frequency. We contend here that ape-centered media narratives often displace moral and cultural panics related to black cultures onto the apes in question. For example, consider the following two headlines that appeared in *The Ottawa Citizen* in early 1999: in "'Sick gorilla' threatens economy," Beauchesne argues that the recovering Canadian economy is in danger of being knocked back down by the Brazilian economic crisis

(represented as the "sick gorilla"); and in "AIDS virus came from chimps," Clover and Highfield report that scientists have discovered that the AIDS virus originated in a sub-species of chimpanzee in the central African rainforest. These examples solidify our assertion that, in this *fin-de-millennium*, "Apes are in the news again" (Disraeli, 1998, p. A1).

Bibliography

Armour, T. (1996a) "Nearly broke, Rodman rebounds." *The Chicago Tribune*, May. [Online]. Available: http://www.chicago.tribune.com/sports/bulls/belndr/bsrchive/rodbroke.htm

—— (1996b) "The Enigma." *The Chicago Tribune*, March. [Online]. Available: http://www. chicago.tribune.com/sports/bulls/belndr/bsrchive/rodman7.htm.

Barboza, D. (1996a) "A star athlete goes from naughty to nice, hoping to earn a Kodak Advantix camera for Christmas." *The New York Times*, December 19, p. D8.

—— (1996b) "To build basketball sneaker sales, Converse tries a novel double team: Dr. J and Dennis Rodman." *The New York Times*, March 26, p. D3.

Barrett, L. (1997) "Black men in the mix: Badboys, heroes, sequins and Dennis Rodman." *Callaloo*, 20(1), 106–26.

Beauchesne, E. (1999) "'Sick gorilla' threatens economy." *The Ottawa Citizen*, January 16, p. D1.

Beausoleil, N. (1994) "Make-up in everyday life: an inquiry into the practices of urban American women of diverse backgrounds." In N. Sault (ed.), *Many Mirrors: Body Image and Social Relations* (pp. 33–57). New Brunswick, NJ: Rutgers.

Bordo, S. (1993) *Unbearable Weight: Feminism, Western Culture, and the Body*. Los Angeles: University of California Press.

—— (1993a) "Critically queer." *GLQ: A Journal of Lesbian and Gay Studies*, 1(1), 17–32.

—— (1993b) *Bodies That Matter*. New York: Routledge.

Burstyn, V. (1999) *The Rites of Men: Manhood, Politics, and the Culture of Sport*. Toronto: University of Toronto Press.

Clover, C. and Highfield, R. (1999) "AIDS virus came from chimps." *The Ottawa Citizen*, February 1, p. B1.

Cole, C.L. (1996) "American Jordan: P.L.A.Y., consensus, and punishment." *Sociology of Sport Journal*, 13(4), 366–98.

Cole, C.L. and King, S. (1998) "Representing black masculinity and urban possibilities: Racism, realism and Hoop Dreams." In G. Rail (ed.), *Sport and Postmodern Times* (pp. 49–86). Albany, NY: State University of New York Press.

Davis, A. (1984) "Rape, racism, and the myth of the Black rapist." In A. Jaggar and P. Rothenberg (eds.), *Feminist Frameworks: Alternative Accounts of the Relations between Women and Men* (2nd edn, pp. 428–31). New York: McGraw-Hill.

Disraeli, B. (1998) "Return to the planet of the apes." *The Ottawa Citizen*, January 21, p. A1.

Doty, A. (1993) *Making Things Perfectly Queer: Interpreting Mass Culture*. Minneapolis: University of Minnesota Press.

Escoffier, J. (1994) "Under the sign of the queer." *Found Object*, Fall, p. 135.

Hall, S. (1992) "What is this 'black' in black popular culture?" In G. Dent (ed.), *Black Popular Culture* (pp. 21–33). Seattle, WA: Bay Press.

Hirsley, M. and DeSimone, B. (1996) "Worm's world: mainstream clamors for Rodman's next move." *The Chicago Tribune*, May 4. [Online]. Available: http://www.chicago.tribune.com/sports/ bulls/belndr/bsrchive/rod04.htm

hooks, b. (1992) *Black Looks: Race and Representation*. Toronto: Between the Lines Press.

—— (1994) "Power to the pussy: we don't wannabe dicks in drag." In *Outlaw Culture* (pp. 9–25). New York: Routledge.

Jefferson, M. (1997) "Dennis Rodman, bad boy as man of the moment." *The New York Times*, January 30, pp. C13, C20.

Johnson, K.C. (1996) "How much is this man worth: Rodman's popularity and bank balance soar." *The Chicago Tribune*, May. Available: http://www.chicago.tribune.com /sports/bulls/ belndr/bsrchive/rodman05.htm#top

Johnson, S. (1996) "Trash talk." *The Chicago Tribune*, December. [Online]. Available: http://www.chicago.tribune.com/sports/bulls/belndr/bsrchive/rod61205.htm

Kellner, D. (1996) "Sports, media culture and race – some reflections on Michael Jordan." *Sociology of Sport Journal*, 13(4), 458–68.

Lafrance, M. (1998) "Colonizing the feminine: Nike's intersections of postfeminism and hyperconsumption." In G. Rail (ed.), *Sport and Postmodern Times* (pp. 117–39). Albany: State University of New York Press.

Lafrance, M. and Rail, G. (1997) "Gender crossing in the context of mad capitalism: Dennis Rodman and Madonna as cultural imposters." Paper presented at the annual conference of the North American Society for the Sociology of Sport, Toronto, Ontario, Canada, November.

—— (1998) "Dennis Rodman – cultural imposter – paper doll: dragging down Dennis Rodman as drag queen." *Borderlines*, 46, 8–11.

—— (in press) "As bad as he says he is?" Interrogating Dennis Rodman's subversive potential. In S. Birrell and M. McDonald (eds.) *Reading Sport Critically: Essays on Power and Representation*. Evanston, IL: Northeastern University Press.

McDonald, M. (1996) "Michael Jordan's family values: marketing, meaning and post-Reagan America." *Sociology of Sport Journal*, 13(4), 344–66.

McDonald, M. and Aikens, E. (1996) "Damn is he funny: Dennis Rodman and the queer politics of (ms.) representation." Paper presented at the annual conference of the North American Society for the Sociology of Sport, Birmingham, Alabama, November.

Morrison, T. (1992) *Playing in the Dark: Whiteness and the Literary Imagination*. New York: Vintage.

Rodman, D. (1996) *Bad As I Wanna Be*. New York: Dell.

—— (1997) *Walk on the Wild Side*. New York: Dell.

Silver, M. (1996) "The Spurs' no-holds-barred forward gives new meaning to the running game." *Sports Illustrated*, December, pp. 20–8.

Snead, J. (1994) *White Screens, Black Images: Hollywood from the Dark Side*. New York: Routledge.

Wood, R. (1979) *The American Nightmare: Essays on the Horror Film*. Toronto: Festival of Festivals.

3

ANDRE AGASSI AND GENERATION X

Reading white masculinity in 1990s' America[1]

Kyle W. Kusz

Introduction

In his examination of the meanings expressed through the "white guy" identities of Bruce Springsteen and Axl Rose, Pfeil (1995) argues that although the sweaty and writhing bodies of these two rockers (celebrities) could not seem to be more "true" or self-evident when one first looks at them (on television or in a magazine), how we come to see and make sense of their bodies/identities is a much more complex process. His study of Springsteen's and Rose's white male rock star bodies makes visible the myriad of invisible codes, conventions, and discourses (both categorical and conjunctural) which frame our popular understanding of their identities. In this chapter, I use Pfeil's critical analytical method to illuminate the codes, conventions, and discourses which implicitly organize the seemingly self-evident "true" identity of American tennis player, Andre Agassi. I contend that Agassi's celebrity is not all self-evident nor is it neatly explainable through references to his "charisma" (Dyer, 1991) or his extraordinary athletic talents on the tennis court. Instead, I argue that to properly make sense of Andre Agassi's mediated identity one must be cognizant of how it has been constituted through the meanings and logics of the Generation X discourse – a discourse about a new generation of coming-of-age Americans which was produced in the early 1990s. So, in this chapter, I will show how the meanings articulated with Agassi at any given moment have always been constituted by, and constitutive of, the codes, meanings, and logics produced in and through the Generation X discourse at that particular moment in 1990s' America.

In order to perform an analysis of the various ways in which Agassi's identity has been represented in the US popular press, I first outline the rather derogatory image of the generation of American youth produced within, what I call, the Generation X discourse. Then, I critique some of the popular and academic discussions of Generation X and briefly sketch a more critical reading of the Generation X discourse which begins to make visible the conjunctural politics through which it was produced, as well as the racial and gender politics of the discourse. In terms of the latter, my attention turns to the way in which the

Generation X discourse has produced a main figure – the slacker – who has been, in mainstream American media culture, almost exclusively coded as white and male. Drawing on Wallach's (1997) work on generational discourses, I argue that the Generation X discourse should be read as a discourse which is implicitly concerned with producing a normative white masculinity which can be articulated as a distinctly American figure. Finally, I examine how Andre Agassi's imaged identity has been constituted in the popular press through the codes, meanings, and logics produced within the Generation X discourse.

Interrogating the Generation X discourse

In order to understand how Andre Agassi has been coded as a Generation X figure and to interrogate the forces which produced, and the politics of, his (white, masculine) Generation X identity, I must first explain what I mean by the "Generation X discourse." In the early 1990s, a discourse was produced which represented a new generation of coming-of-age Americans as a "lost generation, an army of aging Bart Simpsons, possibly armed and dangerous" (Barringer, 1990, quoted in Strauss and Howe, 1991, p. 317). Within this discourse, this new generation was introduced as a "symbol .... of America in decline" (Howe and Strauss, 1993, p. 19). Labeled "Generation X" with the "X" meant to symbolize the purported alienated and confused character of this generation of Americans, this derogatory discourse was widely generated, reproduced, and legitimated throughout American media culture – in magazines, television news programs, newspapers, Hollywood and independent films, and popular music. Together, the knowledges, narratives, codes, logics, power relations, and identities constitute what I identify as the "Generation X discourse."

A *U.S. News & World Report* article provides a quick summary of the rather negative way in which Generation X was characterized in the early 1990s:

> Twentysomethings are a generation in need of a press agent. Their elders think of them (when they think of them at all) as a generation of uppity, flesh-and-blood Bart Simpsons, so poorly educated that they can't find Vietnam on a map or come within 50 years of dating the Civil War. With their MTV-rotted minds and sound-bite attention spans, they are a whiny cohort with the moral compass of street gang Bloods and Crips, a bunch of apathetic slackers who don't vote and couldn't care less.
>
> (Shapiro, 1993, p. 50)

This disparaging construction of the Generation X identity of the new generation of Americans was enthusiastically understood in the United States by almost everyone who did not fit within the category[2] (conservatives, liberals, parents, educators, older generations, academics, and corporate marketers), and even by some young Americans who were said to be members of Generation X, as an accurate representation of the characteristics and sensibility of this new generation of American youth coming of age in the 1990s. For those who did contest the accuracy of this "Generation X" description, they often contended that it was simply a fabrication of the media or merely a hip, new consumer category contrived by American marketers (see Giles, 1994).

These overly simplistic explanations for the creation of Generation X do not adequately explicate how and why this rather belittling characterization of this new generation of Americans came to be produced, widely circulated, and popularly accepted as true in early 1990s' America. In order to develop a more sophisticated explanation of the Generation X discourse – one which recognizes the political character of the discourse – we must situate it within the historical conjuncture in which it was produced and consumed as the "common-sense" way of imagining American youth.

The Generation X discourse was produced at the intersection of widely circulated crisis narratives about disintegrating families, about a nation in decline and at risk (from weakening traditional values and a disintegrating common culture), about a radically changing domestic economy which was widening the gap between the rich and poor and eroding the middle class, and finally, about anxieties over the continued efficacy of the American Dream in the present and future due to these economic and social changes. Although it has gone largely unnoticed, the derogatory portrayal of Generation X was crucially instrumental in constructing and legitimating these conservative-inflected crisis narratives about the American family, the nation, the middle class, and the economic and cultural position of white males in the early 1990s. In addition, each of these crisis narratives have been instrumental within a conservative backlash project which seeks to re-secure the normative and central cultural position of white masculinity in the United States.

For example, contemporary conservative-inflected proclamations of the crisis of the American family and of disintegrating "family values" relied upon (in fact, required) the derogatory characterization of the next generation of American coming-of-age youth produced in and through the Generation X discourse. While the unflattering representation of Generation Xers as a bunch of irresponsible, apathetic and uncaring slackers "choosing" to "slack" in temporary or part-time jobs served as an imaginary solution to the economic anxieties and tensions (what Ehrenreich (1989) has called the "fear of falling")[3] being felt by older members of the white, middle classes who could not comprehend the younger generation's inability to procure modestly well-paid, career-oriented (middle-class) work as the elders once did during their twenties. Characterizing Generation X as a bunch of uneducated and inarticulate slackers who did not acquire, what Hirsch, Jr. (1988) called a basic American cultural literacy, was used to construct national panic narratives about the US global position (economically and politically) relative to Japan and Germany in the late 1980s. Such a pejorative view of the poor academic achievements of Generation Xers was also employed within the discourses of the "culture wars" of the early

1990s to construct multicultural and feminist scholarship as a threat to "traditional" American values and a national common culture (see Sacks and Thiel, 1995). In each of these cases, Xers are offered as embodiments of threatened "traditional American values" represented as being under attack from the irrational, disruptive, and distinctly "un-American" discourses of a host of historically marginalized "others" (feminists, multiculturalists, gays and lesbians). Of course, the "traditional values" under threat are not traditional at all, instead they represent a set of knowledges, social relations, subjectivities which have been employed historically to secure and reproduce the normative and central position of white masculinity. Thus, the unflattering Generation X representation of an imagined "next generation" was mobilized, in various ways, to implicitly demonize feminist and multicultural forces and to proclaim a nostalgic desire to return to "traditional" American values, a proclamation which is part of an implicit project to secure and reproduce the normative and central cultural position of white masculinity in the United States.

Although these are some of the political functions of the Generation X discourse and its negative portrayal of the next American generation, I turn my attention to explaining how the Generation X discourse operates as a technology of white masculinity[4] which first produced and demonized the practices, values, and investments of an "abnormal" youthful white masculinity – the slacker – and then through representations of public figures like Andre Agassi (after 1994) forwarded an image of docile and productive white, middle-class, masculinity (one which is familial, entrepreneurial, and invested in liberalism). My study of the Generation X discourse – specifically, the subjectivities produced within it – is guided by the notion that "scientific and popular modes of representing bodies are never innocent but always tie bodies to larger systems of knowledge production and, indeed, to social and material inequality" (Terry and Urla, 1995, p. 3).[5] Read in this way, the Generation X discourse becomes an important cultural site involved in the struggle over the meanings being articulated with white masculinity in 1990s' America. In order to envision the racial and gender aspects of the Generation X discourse a brief discussion of the knowledges and identities constituted in and through the category of a generation is required.

Interrogating the racial, gender and nationalistic aspects of the Generation X discourse

Strauss and Howe (1991) in their seminal text,[6] *Generations*, which is largely responsible for shaping the generational discourses of the 1990s, subtly reveal the racial and gender politics which implicitly organize the present-day generational discourse:

> we could not always feature a totally representative sample of the
> population. Sometimes, for example, we had to limit the attention

given to women and minorities – either because not as much is known about them or because we wanted to refer to actors and events that most readers would recognize.

(1991, p. 16)

Framed in the guise of a novel and "refreshing historical narrative," a conservative-inflected, generationally-oriented historiography of American history was produced by Strauss and Howe which implicitly privileged the contributions, perspectives, and interests of white men over and against all others (ibid.: back cover). In his study of the cultural and political meanings articulated with generational discourses, Wallach (1997) argues that generational discourses in America, although seeming to be inclusive (in terms of race, class, and gender), have historically been implicitly constituted in and through white, middle-class, masculinity – its perspectives, its interests, and its imagined experiences. Wallach goes on to say that generational discourses have long been implicitly involved in articulating white, middle class, masculinity as a symbol of American national identity (ibid., p. 8). I want to employ Wallach's insights about the function of generational discourses in the United States to argue that the Generation X discourse functions, on at least one level, as a technology concerned with organizing the practices, values, and investments of white, middle-class male youths and their symbolic relation to American national identity. The Generation X discourse initially produced a white masculine figure – the slacker – whose practices, values, and investments were marked as different and abnormal. Through the demonization of the slacker's white masculinity, the invisible but present, even if only in shadow form, normative American white masculinity of the 1990s is produced (Terry and Urla, 1995, p. 5).

Interrogating the Generation X slacker

The Generation X slacker was the main figure produced within the Generation X discourse up until approximately 1994.[7] The slacker was represented as an almost alien and incomprehensible figure who was exclusively coded as white and male. His difference was inscribed onto his body through his grunge clothing, long hairstyle, goatee, and body piercings. Older generations' public derision of the slacker came from its disinvestment in the practices, ideologies, social relations, and affective investments expected of white, middle-class, males living in post-World War II United States. Within this social formation, the proper white masculinity for coming of age white, middle-class, males was to be invested in striving for upward economic mobility, getting married, having children, and securing a comfortable suburban lifestyle. Additionally, this normative white masculinity constructed its identity through the logic of American liberalism. Although these practices and the "normative" white, middle-class masculinity constituted by them are imagined as being transhistorical, it is necessary to point out that they are not transhistorical at all. In fact, they are effects of particular economic, cultural, and political arrangements, namely, a Fordist era of mass production and consumption within an economic boom economy during post-WWII United States (until about 1973).[8] This normative white masculinity was not only encouraged in American society, but was officially subsidized by the US government through legislation such as the Servicemen's Readjustment Bill of 1944 (popularly known as the GI Bill of Rights), the Interstate Highway Act of 1956, and government-sponsored programs which allow federally insured home loans and tax deductions for mortgages (Corber, 1997, p. 7).

By the early 1990s, the specific set of cultural, social, political, and economic forces and conditions of the post-WWII United States which enabled this normative image of white masculinity to be produced were no longer available to twentysomething white males who were coming of age in the early 1990s. By this time, the economic conditions of the United States had shifted away from being organized by a Fordist logic to a post-Fordist logic characterized by the global flight of production from the USA with manufacturing sector jobs being replaced by service economy jobs which had lower pay and less benefits. Americans under the age of 25 were said to have been most severely affected by these changes, with their median income declining by 10.8 percent from 1980 to 1990, while for all other age groups their median income rose by 6.5 percent during the same time period (Shapiro, 1993). These changes in the American economy significantly changed the economic opportunities available to young, coming-of-age, white, middle-class, males, as compared with their generational elders. Consequently, some young white males did not invest in the practices, values, and identifications which constituted this normative white masculinity.

The slacker represents a spectacular white masculinity whose appearance in American media culture during the early 1990s functioned as an embodiment of the practices, values, and identifications which young white males should not invest in.[9] The slacker appears in public culture so that his white masculinity can be marked as abnormal and effectively demonized. So, then, how was the slacker's white masculinity constituted as abnormal and subsequently demonized?

The slacker's abnormality was most often produced through stories of his failure to be a productive working white masculine body. In her book, *The Official Slacker Handbook*, Dunn writes that a "real job" is "anathema to a slacker" (1994, p. 22). The slacker's poor work ethic is frequently conveyed through stories of Xers choosing not to climb the corporate ladder or to opt out of the corporate rat race, with the corporate "ladder" and "rat race" representing shorthand signs of displaying a desire for upward mobility (Martin, 1993). Within these stories, the slacker's unproductive (and abnormal) white male body gains its meaning from its difference from a primary imaginary figure: a modestly upwardly mobile, hard working, family-oriented figure who is usually coded as a Babyboomer. This figure is imagined as a productive (normative) white male figure who shares the economic aspirations of the Yuppie, but is distanced from the Yuppie's excessive narcissism, disinvestment in the family, and materialism.[10] Implicitly revealed through the criticism of the poor work ethic of the slacker are the characteristics of a "normal" and productive white, middle-class masculine body, which, in this case, means being invested in work which has the potential to yield an upwardly mobile economic position.

The abnormality of the slacker's white masculinity is also conveyed through his reluctance to enter into a committed heterosexual relationship which would presumably end in marriage. In the film, *Reality Bites*, goateed and grunge-clothed Troy Dyer (Ethan Hawke) represents the quintessential Generation X slacker. In the film's opening scene, we see Troy leaving a sexy co-ed's apartment after a one-night stand. The purpose of the opening scene is revealed later when Lelaina (Winona Ryder), Troy's best friend and secret love, angrily voices her disappointment in Troy after they had a falling out. Within this scene, Lelaina's critique renders visible the foundations of Troy's slacker identity. The scene goes like this: after not seeing Troy for several weeks, Troy enters Lelaina's apartment, where he has been temporarily staying because he was evicted from his own place. Troy enters with a new girl in tow whose name he cannot remember. After trading some incisive barbs, Lelaina lashes out at Troy for "dicking around with her [meaning this girl who accompanies him] and dicking around with me." Throughout the film Lelaina's implicit role is to act as a disciplinary agent of Troy; here, she emasculates Troy's slacker white masculinity for not being invested in a marriage-oriented, familial life path and for not dedicating himself to a productive career path. The scene reveals how the abnormality of the slacker's white masculinity is not solely constituted in relation to his aversion to being a productive worker, but is also secured through his unwillingness to invest in a heterosexual marriage-directed relationship.

Finally, I want to argue that the abnormality of the Generation X slacker is also produced through his apparent (dis)investment in American liberalism.[11] On the one hand, the slacker's white masculinity is demonized for problematizing the link between white masculinity and liberalism which was secured in post-WWII America. In the economic boom of post-WWII America, economically successful middle-class white men constructed their identities through a liberalist logic which represented their economic success as the sole effect of their hard work, dedication, perseverance, and capable will. American liberalist rhetoric claims that one's will, absent of any structural privileges or constraints, is the sole determining force for whether one is successful or unsuccessful (Flax, 1998). Such stories prevent any thought or discussion of the structural conditions, discussed previously, which significantly enabled (and constrained) the economic prosperity experienced by white males in post-1945 America. Additionally, it does not consider how the institutional structures and arrangements implicitly advantage whites and males. The prosperous economic and social conditions of the post-WWII economic boom enabled a link to be formed between white masculinity and American liberalism which, by the 1990s, became a "naturalized" characteristic of a productive and docile white masculinity. White masculinities which do not reproduce this link are demonized as being abnormal (marked as either incomplete, inadequate, or deficient).

The slacker displayed his apparent disinvestment in American liberalism when he claimed, unlike these older generations of white males (all of whom came of age after World War II), that contemporary economic conditions were unfairly impairing or limiting his economic opportunities. The slacker broke the liberalist code of white masculinity by claiming that his will was limited or constrained by, in this case, radically changing economic conditions which were making it difficult for him to achieve the economic comfort and stability which previous generations of white males, at least since the end of World War II, are imagined as having enjoyed. His claims were problematic for two reasons: first, they had the potential to make visible the historical character of the articulation of white masculinity and American liberalism by calling attention to differences between the economic conditions in the early 1990s and those of the late 1960s and early 1970s; and the slacker's proclamations threatened the identities of older generations of white men by exposing their investment in liberalist narratives. In this light, an article like Martin's (1993) editorial in *Newsweek* where he angrily and resentfully attacks Generation Xers for whining about the poor employment opportunities and wages available to them might be read as Martin's anxious reaction to the way in which the slacker's identity exposes the historical character of the economic, as well as, racial and gender privileges of older generations of white males.

Thus, the Generation X slacker's white masculinity was marked as abnormal because of its poor work ethic, its reluctance to invest in a marriage/family-oriented romantic relationship, and its disinvestment in American liberalism. In variously coded ways, these themes, which were employed to demonize the white masculinity of the slacker, are reproduced through the various representations of Andre Agassi, particularly through the years 1989–93. In the next section, I begin to draw parallels between the white masculinities of Agassi and the Generation X slacker.

Andre Agassi's relation to the Generation X discourse

Although Andre Agassi's connection to Generation X has never been explicitly conveyed, the inextricable link between Agassi and the contemporary attention being given to generations – of which the Generation X discourse is a part – is expressed in several seemingly innocent and inconsequential ways. Agassi has been articulated by Nike as "the talent of his generation" (http://www.nike.com/athletes/Agass_1003/1003_bio). In television adverts, Mountain Dew has represented Agassi as an X-treme athlete – a figure which has been produced in and through the Generation X discourse – and as a fan favorite of two long-haired, flannel-shirted Generation X slackers. Finally, Canon's advertisements for their "Rebel X" camera, which prominently draws upon the sign-values of the "X," further reinforce this implied connection between Agassi and Generation X. That the most explicit links between Agassi and Generation X occur within commercials should not be very surprising considering the prominent role which American marketers have had in creating and reproducing the "Generation X" discourse (see Ritchie, 1995, Walker Smith and Clurman, 1997).

However, in the following sections, I show how the connection between Agassi's varied representations and the creation of the Generation X discourse extends beyond these rather facile and superficial connections. I make visible the themes which organized the popular press articles written on Andre Agassi beginning in the late 1980s and extending throughout the 1990s to demonstrate how Agassi's identity has been constituted by (and, in turn, is constitutive of) the meanings, tropes, and narratives which organize the Generation X discourse, even as the identity of Generation X was significantly rearticulated in 1997.

It should be noted though that Andre Agassi's imaged identity has not by any means been static, essential or coherent across the various texts in which he has been represented. Rather, his identity has been notably dynamic, complex, unstable and even contradictory. It is, in fact, the changes in the meanings articulated to Agassi's imaged identity which are interesting in relation to the discourse about Generation X and his white masculinity. In the rest of this chapter I discuss how Agassi's white masculinity has been constituted in and through meanings and logics produced within the Generation X discourse of the 1990s.

Agassi as Generation X slacker

From 1989 to 1993, Andre Agassi climbed near the top of men's professional tennis finishing each of these years in the top ten. In 1989, Agassi set a circuit record by surpassing $1 million in career earnings after having played in only forty-three matches. During this five year span, Agassi reached four Grand Slam finals on three different playing surfaces (clay, hard courts, and grass) winning just one of these tournaments. Ironically, his only victory came in the one Grand Slam – Wimbledon, played on grass – where many experts wondered whether his explosive back-court game would ever be suited for success. Despite these apparent successes on the tennis court, the stories written about Agassi during this period were largely mean-spirited and, rather than emphasizing his successes, frequently focused on his poor training habits, his "tanking" sets, his lack of an education, his poor sportsmanship, his commodification and celebrification, his apparent disrespect toward tennis' traditions, and his apparent disavowal of his tacit responsibilities associated with being an American professional athlete (see Amdur, 1989; Hirshey, 1989; Jenkins, 1992, 1993; Kirkpatrick, 1989; Lupica, 1990a, 1990b). How does one make sense of the disparaging way in which Agassi's identity was rendered visible during this time period?

In order to make sense of the derogatory character of the press coverage of Agassi, one must consider that the Generation X discourse was being formed in the American culture at the same time – the early 1990s. Amazingly, Agassi's identity, in these articles, parallels, with a remarkable symmetry, the identity of the Generation X slacker produced in the Generation X discourse about the new coming-of-age generation of Americans in the 1990s. It is in and through the codes and meanings constitutive of the Generation X slacker that Agassi's white masculinity was implicitly constituted and vilified.

In 1988 and 1989, Agassi climbed near the top of the men's tennis rankings. His good looks, entertaining playing style, and his extraordinary tennis potential garnered the attention of companies like Nike, Donnay, and Canon who signed him to lucrative multi-million dollar endorsement deals. Agassi became the biggest drawing card of men's professional tennis which allowed him to collect six-figure appearance fees in smaller regional tournaments before he had even reached the tender age of twenty. But, when Agassi failed to reach the number one ranking or to win a Grand Slam final, suspicions about Agassi's work ethic and his apparent contentment with being tennis' biggest name on the marquee, rather than a tennis champion, began to organize the stories written about Agassi in the popular press. The tone of the stories shifted from being largely positive toward Agassi even representing him as the "savior of American tennis" to more negative articles which questioned his competitive desire and motivations. This change in the tone of the articles was even noted in the press, "At first it was confined to pressroom cynicism, but then little digs started showing up in articles: 'peroxide' instead of 'blond,' 'smirk' instead of 'smile'" (Wetzsteon, 1989, p. 62).

Most significantly, Agassi's identity was re-constituted at the beginning of the 1990s from being a hard-working player (Leerhsen, 1988; Sullivan, 1987) to being soundly criticized for his lackadaisical or lackluster on-court efforts and for having very poor training habits. Feature articles about Agassi in *Sports Illustrated* and *Gentlemen's Quarterly* mentioned stories of his practicing for only fifteen minutes before playing an important Davis Cup match (Hirshey, 1989; Kirkpatrick, 1989), or his taking red-eye flights to tournaments, practicing for twenty minutes, if at all, and then playing later that night (Jenkins, 1992). Or, Agassi was portrayed as having an almost uncontrollable and seemingly insatiable appetite for fast food and candy (ibid.). These comments about Agassi's alleged poor work ethic, his laziness, and his seemingly deficient will parallel those characteristics used to constitute the identity of the Generation X slacker. As you recall, the Gen X slacker is constituted by his extreme laziness, his disdain for work of any sort, and his alleged valorization of the "leitmotiv: [that] second place seems just fine" (Gross and Scott, 1990, p. 60). At this time, Agassi was popularly imagined as not making the most of his athletic talents. Agassi's losses in his first three Grand Slam finals (the 1990 US Open and 1990 and 1991 French Opens), matches in which he was favored to win, along with several public and private accusations (by players and reporters) that he frequently "tanked" sets and matches were frequently employed to call into question Agassi's work ethic and his commitment to being a tennis champion. Absent from these stories about Agassi's Grand Slam losses and his tanking sets, was any sense of sympathy for Agassi or effort to emphasize Agassi's accomplishments (having made it to the finals of these Slams). This lack of sympathy toward Agassi, and the way in which these stories questioned Agassi's work ethic, must be understood, at least in part, as an effect of a broader cultural suspicion about the allegedly wayward values and practices of a new generation of Americans (read: young, white, middle-class males) expressed in and through the Generation X discourse. The deficient will of the Generation X slacker is marked by his contentment with his downward economic mobility and with not having to be number one. Agassi's inability to win a Grand Slam in his first three opportunities, coupled with his apparent disdain for performing the requisite work ethic of a professional athlete enabled him to be implicitly coded and popularly understood as the "real" embodiment of the simulated Generation X slacker (Baudrillard, 1983).

Agassi was also represented at this time as naïve and uneducated with writers who seemed to take great enjoyment in poking fun at Agassi's ignorance of global geography and international politics, knowledge which was represented in these stories as rudimentary knowledge which everyone would and should know. For example, Agassi was defined as being poorly educated and ignorant through a story of his not knowing what the word "coup" meant or that Peru (where he was playing) was in the midst of a military coup (Kirkpatrick, 1989). In another, Agassi is chided for not knowing about the Tower of London (Jenkins, 1992). Additionally, Agassi would be represented in ways which suggested that his sense of history extended as far back as the latest television commercial (Collins, 1991). This representation of Agassi as an ignorant young person with a short attention span was undoubtedly framed by a burgeoning broader cultural discourse which asserted that the new coming-of-age generation of Americans were ignorant of basic ideas, values, and knowledge about the United States and the world (Hirsch, Jr. 1988).

In this period, Agassi's public image was also rendered visible through the "Image is everything" promotional campaign of Canon cameras. The advert generated much popular fervor and resentment toward Agassi. I contend that the resentment generated toward Agassi's "Image is everything" identity can be read as a part of the cultural anxiety over Generation Xers' alleged affinity for media culture.[12] The Generation X slacker was popularly imagined as a disaffected youth, whose disaffection was a product of a dysfunctional home and his immersion in a pervasive media culture. The slacker's proclivity for the media, which is said to provide him with a sound-bite attention span and an ignorance of American history, was used to argue that he was disconnected from traditional American norms and values (Kellner, 1995). In these commercials for Canon, Agassi is dressed in vibrant and decidedly un-traditional neon colors, smacking tennis balls in various locations around the world. The final shots of these commercials show a close-up of Agassi enthusiastically proclaiming that "Image is everything." This "Image is everything" phrase was popularly interpreted as being authentically created and espoused by Agassi himself. There was no consideration that Agassi was merely a mouthpiece for a camera company trying to sell its product. The "Image is everything" phrase seemed to reinforce the popular interpretation that Agassi's failures at his first three Grand Slam were the result of his desire to merely be a celebrity rather than a tennis champion. Within the context of the popular anxieties about Generation Xers' mesmerizing affinity for media culture, Agassi's "Image is everything" image became interpreted as further proof of a young white male (of this new generation) whose apparent endorsement of "image" and "style" exemplified his disconnection from traditional norms and invested in a suspect set of values.

One also finds in these early articles written about Agassi, the question: "who is the real Andre Agassi?" repeatedly asked. The question conveys a remarkably similar concern about the new generation's "hazy sense of their own identity" expressed in *Time*'s seminal 1990 article about Generation X (Scott, 1990, p. 57). The confusion over who is the "real" Andre Agassi stems, on one level, from the disparity between the early representations of Agassi (those prior to 1989) and those produced between 1989–93.[13] However, I contend that the confusion expressed in these articles about Agassi can be understood as being indicative of an inherently political struggle to produce, secure, and contain the meanings of Agassi's white masculinity. The disdain for Agassi expressed in the articles written between 1989 and 1994 represent the confusion and anxiety raised by his failure or reluctance to perform the practices and values embodied by a productive and docile white masculinity. Agassi's apparent unwillingness to demonstrate a professional work ethic and his inability to be number one at this time in his fledgling career each were used to symbolize his dis-investment in American liberalism and its logics (hard work, individualism, and meritocracy). Such practices performed by American white males need to be marked as abnormal in order to implicitly establish and maintain the idea of the normative white masculine body. Consequently, the question of who is the "real" Agassi explains more about the cultural expectations of the content of a normative (productive and docile) white masculinity in the 1990s in the United States than it tells us about Agassi. This recurring concern over who is the "real" Andre Agassi indicates how Agassi's appeal – both as an athletic endorser and as the key figure in popularizing tennis to a mass American sporting audience – is rooted in his apparent struggle to be a productive white guy who espouses and embodies those norms and values expected of white men in America at the *fin de siècle*. Our cultural fascination with Agassi exemplifies America's cultural appetite – especially in the mid to late 1990s – for white guys who are struggling to be better men (familial, upwardly mobile, and sensitive).[14] This rationale for the fascination with Agassi is further substantiated, as you will see, by the way in which the press embraced "the new Andre Agassi" after winning his second and third Grand Slam titles (the US Open and Australian Open respectively) in 1994 and 1995.

Andre Agassi as slacker savior

The inflammatory and skeptical tone of the articles describing Agassi in his early years (prior to 1994) would disappear after he returned from career-threatening wrist surgery in the middle of 1993 to become the first unseeded player to win the US Open in 1994. Agassi's second Grand Slam victory was described in the press as signaling the "redemption of Andre Agassi" (Price, 1994). *New York Times* sports columnist Harvey Araton wrote the following about Agassi after he won the 1994 US Open, "he [Agassi] was making a convincing argument for the peaceful coexistence of substance and style" (1994, p. B9). Agassi followed up his amazing win at the 1994 US Open by notching his third Grand Slam title (and second in a row) just a few months later at the 1995 Australian Open. Together these victories marked a turning point in the way in which Agassi's identity would be constituted in the next two years.

Following these victories, no less than four feature articles written on Agassi appeared, not only in sport magazines (*Sports Illustrated, Tennis, Tennis Match*), but also in mainstream magazines and newspapers as well (*Esquire, New York Times Magazine*, and *GQ*). The appearance of these stories of Agassi's "redemption" in these non-sport magazines and newspapers suggests that his reformation was one which transcended the American sports world and resonated with broader cultural concerns and anxieties about the investments and values of young white males within the mid-1990s.

Within these feature stories, America was introduced to "the new Andre Agassi" (Jenkins, 1995). For the first time, the articles about Agassi focused not simply on his tennis career, but significant attention was given to constructing an image of Agassi off the tennis court. These stories of Agassi beyond the tennis court were employed to reinforce the legitimacy of the claim that he had truly developed a new, more positive attitude. The narratives used to construct this "new Andre Agassi" are particularly interesting as they relate to the narratives that had been used to construct the identity of the Generation X slacker in the early 1990s. In these articles, any suggestion that Agassi was lazy, uneducated, instantly gratified by his wealth and sports celebrity status, satisfied with being less than number one, or that he had a deficient will – the characteristics used to define the slacker – were explained away as the result of the frivolity of youth. What is significant about these articles is that the narratives which organized this rearticulation of Agassi's imaged identity distinctly marked him as the antithesis of the Generation X slacker. Agassi's representation as the "new Andre Agassi" was figured through stories of his blossoming romantic relationship with actress and American icon, Brooke Shields; stories of his new corporation, Agassi Enterprises, that he and his childhood friend Perry Rogers formed to manage Agassi's image and his riches; and stories of his hard work and commitment to being an enduring tennis champion. In addition to these main themes, Agassi was also represented as a thoughtful and vulnerable guy who was valorized for displaying a determination to be optimistic about people and his future (see de Jonge, 1995; Higdon, 1994; Jenkins, 1995; Sherill, 1995). These themes – being invested in a marriage-oriented relationship, being upwardly mobile and entrepreneurial, being invested in friends and family, being committed to hard work, and being optimistic rather than cynical – were precisely the practices and attitudes which Generation X slackers lacked or were said to be not investing themselves in. Consequently, I argue that the form and content of this rearticulation of Agassi's identity suggest that he was being conspicuously portrayed as a symbol of a white, male Generation X slacker who was able to elevate himself out of his allegedly self-imposed downward spiral to invest himself in the behaviors, values, and ideological investments which were expected of him as a professional athlete, and as a productive white male. In short, Agassi was constructed as slacker savior. Put another way, the rearticulation of Agassi's white masculinity in the mid-1990s exemplifies the process in which he was constructed and valorized for exemplifying a reformed Generation X slacker.

But the rearticulation of Agassi, and specifically his differentiation from the Generation X slacker, were not by any means simple processes, but were instead complex and seemingly contradictory. At the same time as this barrage of articles about the new Agassi distanced him from the identity of the Generation X slacker, Agassi's commercial images, produced through Mountain Dew's "Extreme Agassi" commercials produced the most explicit links ever produced between Agassi and the Generation X slacker. How can we make sense of this seemingly problematic incongruency between Agassi's new anti-slacker identity produced in the popular press and his commercialized identity being more closely associated with the slacker?

Within a Mountain Dew television advert broadcast during 1994–95, Agassi was displayed as an extreme athlete sky surfing off a helicopter. In the next image, Agassi is shown playing an aggressive, all-out tennis in a Wimbledon-like setting. Next, two inarticulate slacker-like white guys with long-hair, goatees, and flannel shirts (the dominant codings of the slacker) are shown sitting court-side enthusiastically cheering Agassi's every shot. The commercial ends with Agassi sprawled out on the ground, displaying a mouthful of dirt, after having dived after one of his opponent's challenging returns. The commercial consti-tutes Agassi's identity through its difference from the identities of the slackers positioned in the stands. The choice of an action shot (showing Agassi diving after his opponent's shot) enables a comedic moment in the commercial, but it simultaneously constitutes Agassi with the very anti-slacker qualities of being a hard worker and displaying an extraordinary will to be his very best (a sporting metaphor for desiring upward mobility). Thus, Mountain Dew's commercial more closely articulates Agassi with the Generation X slacker, not to assert Agassi's similarity to the slacker, but rather to constitute him as being different from (and superior to) the slacker. The positioning of the slacker figures as enthusiastic fans of this hard-working, strong-willed Agassi also suggests that Agassi is being constituted as an exemplary form of white masculinity which young white male slackers should emulate.

This reconstitution of Agassi's identity in 1994–95 is also significant with respect to Generation X because his rearticulation pre-dates a remarkably similar rearticulation of the identity of Generation X which would be documented by *Time*'s (1997) cover story entitled, "Great Expectations." In this article, *Time* suggests that the initial representation of Generation X as a bunch of slackers was entirely wrong. This egregious error was proclaimed on the magazine's cover – "You called us slackers. You dismissed us as Generation X. Well, move over. We're not what you thought" (Hornblower, 1997: front cover). *Time* asserts that the image of Generation X as a bunch of whining, passive, nihilistic, downwardly mobile, latchkey kids who were fearful of commitment (of marriage) was too premature and not accurate at all. The article exemplifies how, by 1997, the slacker image of Generation X was popularly imagined as an inaccurate stereotype rather than as an accurate reflection of the behaviors, values, and ideological investments of this twentysomething generation. In the place of the slacker image of Generation X, *Time* constructs an image of Generation X which virtually inverts the initial derogatory Generation X slacker image. Citing new and more extensive research, *Time* contended that Generation Xers were ambitious "get-aheads" who were confident, savvy, committed, connected, materialistic, and "crav[ing] success American style" (ibid., p. 58). They were said to be "deeply competitive" and wholeheartedly believing that "competition encourages excellence," as well as, poignantly espousing a "do-it-yourself, no-one-is-going-to-look-out-for-me-but-me spirit" which they purportedly developed from the Reagan and Bush years (ibid., p. 62). The role models of this optimistic and highly motivated image of Generation X were said to be risk-taking enterpreneurs like the technological wunderkind creators of Yahoo! search engine: Jerry Yang, 28, and David Filo, 31 (ibid., p. 62). Finally, Xers were portrayed as putting a stable family at the center of their portrait of the American Dream (which also included affluence, a two-parent family, and a comfortable suburban home) (ibid., p. 68). Through these representations of Generation X, the former anxiety about the values and ideological investments of the next generation which pervaded the earlier discourse about Generation X was defused through a confident tone which assured the reader that Gen Xers (read: white male youths) were invested in and committed to upward mobility, materialism, family, individualism (over and against entitlements and social welfare), and hard work.

The *Time* article is important to my present discussion because it shows how this rearticulation of the identity of Generation X in 1997 parallels the significant reconstitution of Agassi's imaged identity just two years earlier. It seems as if the rearticulation of Agassi's imaged identity in 1994–95 prefigured, in its form and content, the popular rearticulation of Generation X expressed in the

1997 *Time* cover story. I do not mean to suggest that the rearticulation of Agassi's imaged identity in 1994–95 somehow caused the broader rearticulation of Generation X's identity in 1997. Instead, I merely want to show that although Agassi's rearticulated identity in 1994 was consituted in and through some anti-slacker like codes – a change which could problematize my argument, the subsequent broader rearticulation of the identity of Generation X in 1997 demonstrates how Agassi's identity is still inextricably linked with the identity of Generation X. In fact, the timing of the rearticulation of Agassi's identity illustrates the mutually constitutive relationship between the identities of Andre Agassi and Generation X.

Conclusion

In summation, I have pointed out how Andre Agassi's popular significations have been inextricably constituted by (and constitutive of) the various codes and meanings of the Generation X discourse at any particular moment in time even as these codes and meanings have significantly changed during the 1990s. Additionally, I have gestured at the conjuncturally specific racial and gender politics which organize the white male identities of Agassi and the Generation X slacker to show how the Generation X discourse implicitly operates as a technology of white masculinity involved in a process of producing a (productive and docile) normative white masculinity in late 1990s' America. Such work strives to make visible how the seemingly banal and innocent images of our media culture (especially those produced within the space of "sport") are not at all innocent and inconsequential, rather, they are intimately tied to the relations between social power, identity formation, and the reproduction of social and material inequalities.

Notes

1 I would like to thank Syndy Sydnor and Kristin Kane for providing helpful comments on previous drafts of this chapter; Nancy Spencer for many thoughtful discussions about tennis and theory; and Cheryl Cole for her class on Masculinities. My discussions with them have informed my readings of Andre Agassi's Gen X white masculinity.

2 Although the Generation X characterization of American youth of the 1990s was, I think, pervasively accepted as an accurate rendering of 1990s' American youth, it is important to note that the Generation X characterization was contested by many whose birth dates implicated them as Generation Xers. Nonetheless the derogatory, slacker-like image of a new generation of Americans generated in the Generation X discourse was largely accepted within mainstream media culture as an uncontestable truth. In order to contest this image, one would have had to disagree with the crisis narratives about the nation, the American family, the deleterious effects of multiculturalism/political correctness/and feminism. For the most part, most Americans accepted the truth of these crisis narratives which attests to the success of conservative forces in establishing these narratives as uncontestable "truths."

3 These tensions and anxieties of the white middle classes were caused by the significant restructuring of the American labor market since 1973 – the elimination of
manufacturing, middle-management, and professional entry level positions which
were replaced by lower paying jobs with lesser or no benefits in the service economy
(see Harvey, 1990; Weis *et al.*, 1997; Wellman, 1997) – which only began to significantly affect these classes in the late 1980s and early 1990s (Beaty, 1991).

4 The term "technology of white masculinity" specifies de Laurentis' (1987) term
"technology of gender."

5 Terry and Urla's text (1995) *Deviant Bodies*, from which I take this quote, outlines
an interrogative method which is deeply influenced by post-structuralist ideas, most
notably those of Michel Foucault. Although I do not explicitly or extensively discuss
my method in this chapter, I should note that this project is meant to be guided by
post-structuralist concerns about subjectivity, discourse, the normal/abnormal, and
normalizing power.

6 I identify Strauss and Howe's (1991) book as a "seminal" text in the formation of
Generation X discourse because it was widely read and subsequently used by journalists and other media pundits to produce the many newspaper and magazine articles
about Generation X.

7 Although the Gen X slacker reappears even today in particular cultural sites, he was
the predominant embodiment of Generation X from 1990 to 1994.

8 For discussion of these economic changes, see Harvey (1990) and Lowe (1995).

9 For the purpose of my argument here, my reading of the Generation X slacker tends
to oversimplify his appeal. Although I contend that the increased visibility of the
slacker served first to demonize its deficient characteristics (in terms of the characteristics of a native white masculinity) and then to reconstitute it within the more
normative codes and characteristics of an acceptable white masculinity. It should also
be noted that the slacker was an appealing white masculinity for many young white
males. An infinitely contradictory figure, the slacker, through his refusal to invest in
the characteristics expected of white, middle-class, males, utilized the codes of the
rebellious youth in order to reconstruct a seemingly autonomous and unconstrained
masculinity whose appeal could be related to its ability to provide psychic relief for a
generation of white males feeling the added weight and constraint of not being able
to fit within the desired breadwinner, familial, white middle-class masculinity
expected of them.

10 It is important to note that the "normal" Babyboomer (white) masculinity is not
represented through the Yuppie – as some might think – who is imagined as an
excessive workaholic, highly materialistic and a conspicuous consumer, and anti-
familiar figure, although this "normal" Babyboomer white masculinity does embody
in a watered down version some of his more productive characteristics – namely, his
desire for upward economic stability and his excellent work ethic. I would contend
that like the slacker, the proliferation of the Yuppie in the mid-1980s represented the
demonization of the excesses of this white, middle-class subject – namely, its anti-
familism and its excessive investment in work (to the detriment of family life).

11 My reading of the marking of the Generation X slacker's abnormality through his
apparent disinvestment in American liberalism is informed by Flax's (1998) discussion of white masculinity's investment in American liberalism in the 1990s.

12 To fully understand the motivating forces of the popular resentment directed towards
Agassi for Canon's "Image is everything" campaign one must also consider how the
increasing commodification and astronomically rising salaries of professional athletes
at this time were also forces which produced this popular resentment of Agassi's
representation via Canon's "Image is everything" campaign.

13 In these pre-1989 articles Agassi's identity was constituted mainly through the category of a "teen idol." He was explicitly marked as a distinctly American white

masculinity and celebrated as a productive and docile athlete through the category of an "athletic throwback" (Amdur, 1988; Leerhsen, 1988; Sullivan, 1988).

14 I would argue this appetite is evidenced in the production, and popularity of films such as *Jerry Maguire*, *Good Will Hunting*, and *For the Love of the Game* in late 1990s' America.

Bibliography

Amdur, N. (1989) The real thing?, *World Tennis*, October, 24–8.

Araton, H. (1994) A grungy showman: 'Uh wow! and Cool. *New York Times* (national edition), September 12, p. B9.

Baudrillard, J. (1983) *Simulations*. New York : Semiotext(e).

Beatty, J. (1994) Who speaks for the middle class? *The Atlantic Monthly*, May, 65–78.

Collins, B. (1991) What's it all about Andre? *World Tennis*, March, 22–6.

Corber, R. (1997) *Homosexuality in Cold War America*. Durham, NC: Duke University.

De Jonge, P. (1995) Cocky, foulmouthed champ vs. insecure, born-again champ. Sampras and Agassi on Agassi and Sampras. *The New York Times Magazine*, August 27, 44–9, 60, 68, 72.

DeLauretis, T. (1987) *Technologies of Gender: Essays on Theory, Film, and Fiction*. Bloomington, IN: Indiana University Press.

Dunn, S. (1994) *The Official Slacker Handbook*. New York: Warner Books.

Dyer, R. (1991) Charisma. In C. Gledhill (ed.) *Stardom*. London: Routledge.

Ehrenreich, B. (1989) *Fear of Falling*. New York: Harper Perennial.

Flax, J. (1998) *The American Dream in Black and White*. Ithaca, NY: Cornell University Press.

Giles, J. (1994) Generalizations X. *Newsweek*, June 6, 63–71.

Granger, D. (1996) My winner with Andre. *Gentleman's Quarterly*, 126–31, 178.

Gross, D. and Scott, S. (1990) Proceeding with caution. *Time*, July 16, 56–62.

Harvey, D. (1990) *The Condition of Postmodernity*. Cambridge, MA: Blackwell.

Higdon, D. (1994) Taking care of business. *Tennis*, 32–40.

Hirsch Jr., E.D. (1988) *Cultural Literacy: What Every American Needs to Know*. New York: Vintage Books.

Hirshey, G. (1989) The frosted flake. *Gentleman's Quarterly*, September, 416–21, 492–5.

Hornblower, M. (1997) Great Xpectations. *Time*, June 9, 58–69.

Howe, N. and Strauss, W. (1993) *13th Gen*. New York: Vintage Books.

Jenkins, S. (1992) Image is not everything. *Sports Illustrated*, May 11, 35–7.

—— (1993) Comic strip. *Sports Illustrated*, July 5, 20–3.

Kellner, D. (1995) *Media Culture*. London: Routledge.

Kirkpatrick, C. (1989) Born to serve. *Sports Illustrated*, March 13, 65–74.

Leerhsen, C. (1988) Teenage courtship. *Newsweek*, September 12, 82.

Lowe, D. (1995) *The Body in Late-Capitalist USA*. Durham, NC: Duke University Press.

Lupica, M. (1990a) Tennis without balls. *Esquire*, July, 39–40.

—— (1990b) Here's to the Wieners! *Esquire*, September, 83.

Martin, D. (1993) The whiny generation. *Newsweek*, November 1, 10.

Nike Online web site. Available HTTP: http://www.nike.com/athletes/Agass_1003/1003_bio

Pfeil, F. (1995) *White Guys: Studies in Postmodern Domination and Difference*. London: Verso.

Price, S. (1994) Anarchy and Agassi. *Sports Illustrated*, 30–9.

Ritchie, K. (1995) *Marketing to Generation X*. New York: Lexington Books.

Sacks, D. and Thiel, P. (1995) *The Diversity Myth*. Oakland, CA: The Independent Institute.

Scott, E. (1996) Vantage point. *Tennis Week*, February 8, 6.

Shapiro, J. (1993) Just fix it! *U.S. News & World Report*, February 22, 50–6.

Sherill, M. (1995) Educating Andre. *Esquire*, May, 89–96.

Strauss, W. and Howe, N. (1991) *Generations*. New York: William Morrow and Company, Inc.

Sullivan, R. (1987) The teen dream who could wake up U.S. tennis. *Sports Illustrated*, 22–3.

Tennis Match (1995) Andre Agassi: the metamorphosis of a champion. September–October, 32– 5.

Terry, J. and Urla, J. (1995) *Deviant Bodies*. Bloomington, IN: University of Indiana Press.

Walker Smith, J. and Clurman, A. (1997) *Rocking the Ages: The Yankelovich Report on Generational Marketing*. New York: Harper Business.

Wallach, G. (1997) *Obedient Sons*. Amherst, MA: University of Massachusetts Press.

Weis, L., Proweller, A. and Centrie, C. (1997) Re-examining "a moment in history": loss of privilege inside working-class masculinity in the 1990s. In M. Fine *et al.* (eds) *Off White*. New York: Routledge.

Wellman, D. (1997) Minstrel shows, affirmative action talk, and angry white men: marking racial otherness in the 1990s. In R. Frankenburg (ed.) *Displacing Whiteness*. Durham, NC: Duke University Press.

Wetzsteon, R. (1989) I was a teenage U.S. hope. *Sport*, July, 60–3.

4

AMERICA'S NEW SON

Tiger Woods and America's multiculturalism[1]

C.L. Cole and David L. Andrews

Oprah Winfrey: Well, you don't have to know what a birdie or
bogey is to love my guest today. You don't need to understand
par. You don't even have to like golf, because Tiger Woods transcends golf. He is magical and he's mesmerizing. He's just what
our world needs right now, don't you think?

Audience: (*In unison*) Yeah!

Oprah Winfrey: Whoo! Whoo! I call him America's son.
                        (*Oprah Winfrey Show*, April 24, 1997)

Introduction

Typical of her inspiring insights that resonate with mainstream sensibilities, and
which have made her the most influential woman in American entertainment
today, Oprah Winfrey's declaration extends the euphoric public consensus
evidently reached over Tiger Woods (the show was taped soon after Woods'
victory at the 1997 US Masters). Winfrey's proclamation enlists elements
embedded in popular discourses – particularly elements encoded through and
aligned with race, family, and nation – that facilitated and framed Woods' march
into the American consciousness. Invoking the national familial bond, Winfrey
identifies Woods as an "antidote" to the anxieties weighing down America ("the
world") at the end of the century. Although the anxieties remain unnamed,
Woods enters a context defined by the regular fanning of apprehensions about
and celebrations of America's multi-cultural racial future: racially-coded celebrations which deny social problems and promote the idea that America has
achieved its multicultural ideal. At the same time, racially thematized crises
related to sexuality, family, crime, welfare, and moral depravity, normalize the
policing and punishment of already vulnerable populations. This dynamic is
encoded and enacted in the rhetoric of color-blindness which guides, for
example, the argument that America no longer needs race-conscious affirmative
action programs. Ironically, contemporary debates about the role of race and
ethnicity in public policy declare the importance of not being classified by race

while panics regularly surface over the ever impending demotion of the white population from the statistical majority.

Woods, an appointed symbol of national multiracial hybridity, is an element in the stabilizing "narrative of continuity" (Jeffords, 1993) that furnishes Oprah's American audience with a reassuring sense of self. After all, the virtuous Woods was born in a contemporary America defined by affirmations of color-blindness and the close association of, even slippage between, America and the world. The universalism invoked by Winfrey's extended valorization of America's new *son* directs attention to an imagined international–national future–present. In that imagination and in an era of global restructuring, America has assigned itself a privileged and superior moral position.

We contend that Winfrey's rhetorical question and directive, "He's just what our world needs right now, don't you think?", reference dominant ways of thinking about nation, race, and progress which govern American popular cultural politics. Thus, we seek to investigate how the narrative around Woods participates in normalizing and routinizing these ways of thinking. In particular, we consider the relations among a prominent reactionary sensibility and politics (as they are regularly expressed in the related logics of anti-affirmative action and white victim masculinity) and the facilitation of a multinational (upwardly mobile) sporting figure as the prototypical future–present American. In order to begin to "make sense" of the duplicitous optimism invested in the national icon Tiger Woods, we build on Lauren Berlant's (1996) analysis of the state of American citizenship in the last decades of the twentieth century.

Facing America's future

Berlant argues that the contemporary formation of American citizenship pivots around heteronormativity, personal acts, and a national intimacy generated through the mass media. Within this conjuncture, a new sexual politics (expressed and authorized most virulently through the *hyper*mythologized American family) now regularly trades places with and suppresses the experience of economic and political injustice. Moreover, the mass media – with the exception of a slew of populist products aligned with the new moral politics – replaces and demonizes any semblance of public debate and activism.

Central to Berlant's explanation of the new citizenship is the invention and promotion of a series of *new* "faces of America": computer-generated, racially hybridized, *feminine* representations of a future, post-white, American popu-lace. Such simulations have appeared on the covers of *Time* and *Mirabella*, and have even shaped the latest rendition of the Betty Crocker brand embodiment. As Berlant depicts it, these cybergenetic visions of the future, multiracial American citizenry are constituted by an amalgam of racially hybridized phenotypes (skin tone, facial structure, hair, etc.). Such simulations, Berlant argues, are imagined to be civic and commercial solutions to the "problems of immigration, multiculturalism, sexuality, gender, and (trans)national identity that haunt the U.S. in the present tense" (1996, p. 398).

Like Berlant, we contend that despite their progressive appearance, such representations of America's racial future are aligned with a regressive racial politics. This racial politics is embedded in a national familial politics that, by our view, has accompanied and is inseparable from, the crisis of white masculinity (for the campaign to strengthen white masculine privilege routinely escalates the rhetoric of family values). In its most recent version, a prominent masculinity is figured around the popular belief that white men (the future minority) are the new persecuted majority. Moreover, in post-civil rights America, minuscule advances made by women and people of color are imagined as the impediments to white men's access to the means of making their own destinies. In other words, women and people of color are perceived as *the* restraints on white men's realization of the American way of life. In the white male victim imaginary, the American Dream itself has been extinguished ... for white men.

Enter Eldrick "Tiger" Woods, characterized as "a breath of fresh air." Indeed, Wood's cultural significance is inseparable from the figures (explicit and implicit) over and against which he is defined. Woods, a critic for *Business Week* explains, is a breath of fresh air for an American public "tired of trash-talking, spit-hurling, head-butting sports millionaires" (Stodghill, 1997, p. 32). Although race is not explicitly mentioned, Stodghill's reference is clearly to African American professional basketball players who are routinely depicted in the popular media as selfish, insufferable, and morally reprehensible. Woods' cultural significance is further implicated in the politics of post-national familial multiculturalism and mediated intimacy that govern ways of thinking about America's future citizenry:

But times are changing. Interracial marriage and reproduction are on the upswing, and a new generation of post-1960s multiracial children is demanding recognition, not in the margins of society but as a mainstream of their own ... To get a glimpse of its future, look at Eldrick "Tiger" Woods, the golf prodigy. His mother, from Thailand, is half Thai, a quarter Chinese, and a quarter white. His father is half black, a quarter Chinese and a quarter American Indian.

(Page, 1996, pp. 284–5)

It is our contention that Tiger Woods is an extraordinary exemplar of the new American logic. That is, Woods is the masculine extension of the already familiar hybridized American [feminine] face invested in white American culture. As such, he is the latest (but perhaps the first masculinized) rendition of the American supericon: a commercial emblem who makes visible and concrete late modern America's narrative of itself as a post-historical nation of immigrants. Woods thus embodies the imagined ideal of being and *becoming* American which, in its contemporary form, requires proper familial affiliations and

72

becoming the global-American. As a figure embedded in and who renders multiple national narratives comprehensible, it is no wonder Woods appears to be a "universally celebrated" example of "America's son" – the "new commercial stereotype advertising the future of national culture" (Berlant, 1996, p. 417).

In this chapter, our preliminary discussion of the unfolding Tiger Woods phenomenon, we seek to clarify some of the dynamics governing the national euphoria inscribed on Woods. Here, we offer a critical–contextually based reading of the promotional discourses (primarily, but not exclusively, those emanating from Nike Inc.) which contributed to the fabrication of Tiger Woods as a national crisis resolving, *new face* of America. We concentrate on a period defined by his joining the PGA Tour (August 1996) and his winning the US Masters in April 1997. We contend that the commercialized multicultural masculinity advanced through and around Woods is the latest in America's imagined realization of its ideals (agency, equality, responsibility, and freedom) and its imagined trans-formed sense of national self (America has become the world that came to it). Indeed, we argue that the representation of national ideals through the global multiculturalism inscribed on Woods tacitly extends optimistic ways of thinking about the nation (the post-Cold War resurgence of American nationalism) which are constitutive of racism directed at America's non-white populations in general, and the African American population in particular. The multicultural future-present embodied by Tiger Woods is deeply implicated in expressions related to America's declared color-blindness and white male as victim fantasies.

Nike's national *Moment in the Making*

According to the "origin stories" which ostensibly document Woods' rise to national prominence, the American public has long recognized Tiger Woods' exceptionalism. Numerous video-clips of the child-Tiger's accomplishments are sutured together and recirculated to provide evidence of an America collectively anticipating a sporting, cultural, and economic phenomenon in the making. We (the American populace) watch America watching a precocious (in terms of ability) and atypical (in terms of racial difference) child-golfer drawing the attention of the "human interest" popular media. Clips featuring the child-Tiger from television programs such as *The Mike Douglas Show*, *That's Incredible*, and *Eye on L.A.* are recast in ways that position each as a snapshot in the national family album. Images of a playful freedom embodied by the young Woods are accompanied by clips of a comically-impressed Bob Hope, James Stewart, and Mike Douglas. Such images evoke sentimental feelings as they suggest that we have caught a glimpse of the national record of America's white patriarchs previewing and approving the figure of the nation's future.

National intimacy was encoded and enacted through these recontextualized media clips of the child-Woods. Through the trite machinations of the American popular media, Tiger Woods was positioned and confirmed as America's son. Relatedly, Woods' personal achievements were easily translated into national accomplishments. Recollections of his ground-breaking successes on the golf course (most notably winning his first tournament at the age of eight, an unprecedented three US Junior National Championships, three straight US Amateur Tournaments, and appearing in the 1992 Nissan Los Angeles Open as a high school sophomore) corroborate the fantasy of a conflict-free and color-blind America.

Stirred by the aftermath of his record breaking third consecutive victory at the US Amateur Championship and media speculation over his decision to leave the amateur ranks during August of 1996, Woods' popular presence reached a new intensity. Indeed, Woods' immediate future became a focal point of media, and therefore, national attention. His announced decision to enter the PGA Tour was greeted with much enthusiasm by Tim Finchem, the PGA Tour commissioner. Finchem, speaking on ABC's *Nightline* (September 2 1996), defined the characteristics that made Woods a welcome addition into the professional fold:

> I just think that there are three major elements to Tiger Woods. One is his, his, the level of his competitive skills he has demonstrated time and time again. Secondly, he is from a multi-racial ethnic background which makes him unique. And, third is, he has exhibited the poise, and the integrity, and the image, of the kind of players who have performed well on the PGA Tour. And that is the package, and it's a very marketable package.

Finchem's *very marketable package* was taken up, in much the same vein, by the expectant titans of the American sport industry. Mark McCormack's International Management Group (IMG) had so aggressively courted the 15-year-old Woods that they offered his father, Earl Woods, a paid position as "talent scout" for the American Junior Golf Association (whose tournaments his son was then dominating). Upon turning professional, Woods *officially* signed with IMG. He also signed a $40 million five-year sponsorship deal with Nike, which expected that Woods' racial difference *and* prodigious talent would "revolutionize" the public's relation to golf. That is, Nike anticipated that Woods, as a multi-market endorser, would resuscitate their stagnant golf division and, in so doing, significantly bolster the company's overall profits. The success of America's latest revolution, orchestrated around Woods' body and style, would be measured in terms of the diversification and expansion of the market for golf-related products and services both within the United States and abroad.

On Wednesday August 28, 1996, two days after Tiger turned professional and on the eve of the Greater Milwaukee Open, Woods held his first press conference as a PGA Tour player. At the microphone, a seemingly sheepish Woods intoned, "I guess, hello world." The familiar global address simultaneously insinuated the decline of national boundaries and trumpeted the significance of Nike's latest worldly American citizen. The *faux* spontaneity of this carefully scripted sound-byte was made evident when, the next day, Nike launched a print and television advertising campaign featuring Woods, entitled "Hello World." Despite a chain of events intimating Nike's swift and creative response to a national moment in the making, the national moment in the making, was, no doubt, an example of the sort of strategic marketing that placed Nike at the vanguard of contemporary promotional culture (Wernick, 1991).

The "Hello World" television campaign introduced Woods (as he was apparently introducing himself to "the world at large" [Allen, 1996, p. 11C]), by interspersing, and overlaying, the following text between and upon images of his early golfing exploits and recent successes at US Amateur championships:

> Hello world.
> I shot in the 70s when I was 8.
> I shot in the 60s when I was 12.
> I won the US Junior Amateur when I was 15.
> Hello world.
> I played in the Nissan Open when I was 16.
> Hello world.
> I won the US Amateur when I was 18.
> I played in the Masters when I was 19.
> I am the only man to win three consecutive US Amateur titles.
> Hello world.
> There are still courses in the US I am not allowed to play because of
>   the color of my skin.
> Hello world.
> I've heard I am not ready for you.
> Are you ready for me?

Wood's recitation was accompanied by an emotive musical score, whose pseudo-African tones and timbre added to the dramatic – and the familiarly exotic – content of the visual narrative.

As Nike's "Hello World" advertisement reinforced a familiar aesthetic, it seemingly presented a challenge to America by disrupting and violating America's unwritten racist ("no national critique, particularly in terms of racism or sexism") code. By highlighting Woods' energy, skill, and earned successes, and then deliberately confronting America with a "racial dilemma," America's ideals of color-blindness and proper citizenship were – at least apparently – frankly violated and questioned. Moreover, while previous annotations to the burgeoning Woods phenomenon exploited his difference in ways that maintained a non-threatening ambiguity concerning his *precise* racial identity, the "Hello World" campaign flouted such American racial propriety by "determining" his African Americanness. According to Henry Yu, a professor of history and Asian American studies at UCLA, the "Hello World" campaign was

75

evidence of Nike's attempt to *African Americanize* Woods: "To Nike (*at least at this juncture*), he was African American" (Yu, 1996, p. 4M, italics added).

Race carding and white victim masculinity

The abundance of popular counters to the "Hello World" campaign intimate the force accrued by America's color-blind credo and codification of citizenship – the suppression of the specter of racial politics – over the last two decades. Reactionary critiques habitually invoked the rhetoric of "the race card" which had been exceptionally promoted and legitimated through the media's coverage of the O.J. Simpson trial (Higginbotham *et al.*, 1997). As one critic neatly summarized the accusation: "In Tiger's case, the race card was quickly slapped on the table. Dealt face-up and from the bottom of the commercial deck" (Spousta, 1996, p. 1C).

The race card is a primary and explicit expression of the regulatory logic that governs discourses around race in the USA. As an accusatory category, it implies that the introduction of racial divisions is inappropriate and unfair. Moreover, it implies that consciousness of race is itself an obstacle to racial equality. Drawing attention to restrictions based on the color of Woods' skin violates, according to anti-affirmative action logic, America's unquestioned obedience to the doctrines of individualism and meritocracy.

At least from one available point of view, then, "Hello World" relies on the strategy of race carding. From this point of view, it is an expression of the imagined victimization of white males. Other criticisms of the campaign are also symptomatic of this barely submerged anxious white masculinity. That Woods' destiny was not shaped by his talent alone was a popular, repeated, and revealing response:

> It is funny how it works. Part of Woods' appeal is his race. If he were just another blond-haired, blue-eyed golfer, he wouldn't be this overnight marketing phenomenon. He would be just another blond-haired, blue-eyed golfer struggling to finish in the top 125 in earnings to gain exempt status on the PGA Tour.
>
> (Knott, 1996, p. B1)

In his comments about Nike's promotional strategy, noted sports journalist John Feinstein expressed familiar anti-affirmative action rhetoric as he named race as the key dimension of his extraordinary marketability. For Feinstein, Woods was:

> the great black hope for golf ... The fact that Nike is marketing him as a black player, not just as a talented player, but as a black player, tells you that all this money that's being thrown in his direction has as

much to do with the color of his skin and his ability to be a role model as it does with his golf.

(Nightline, September 2, 1996)

While such expressions of resentment are entangled in contemporary white male identity, blame was not directed at Woods. Instead, racial consciousness was seen to be an outgrowth of Nike's opportunistic politics. For example, Spousta names Nike, not Woods, as the player of the race card:

> if any of that made you feel uncomfortable, don't squirm too much ....
> Truth is, Woods never portrayed himself as our social conscious until
> Nike pushed him across that line ... But it's the message that makes
> you wince, not the messenger, and we should embrace and celebrate
> Tiger as a person and a player. Watching him develop into a champion
> should be a great adventure for fans of any color.

(Spousta, 1996, p. 1C)

And, in one of the most revealing moments of displacement, *Advertising Age*'s Rance Crain admonished Nike for Woods' "militant, almost angry stance" (1997, p. 13).

The theme of Nike's mismanagement of Woods' identity is a rhetorical mechanism that sidesteps critical reflection on national racial politics. In addition, it makes Woods a casualty of Nike, and in so doing, disavows the possibility of Woods' political assertiveness. This proclamation of political "lack" locates the virtue of his personal acts through terms which designate Woods as apolitical. By extension, his apolitical, even pre-political classification is crucial to his capacity to signify personal and national "goodness." As Woods is articulated as innocent, pure, virtuous, and victimized, the possibility for multiple consumer desires and identifications are created and mobilized:

> The ad agency argues that Woods approved the ad. Woods, 20, might
> be mature beyond his years, but he still is 20 and perhaps somewhat
> naive in the ways of the world ... Woods has never been inclined to use
> his influence as a bully pulpit on the issue of race and golf. He disdains
> the notion that he is the great black hope. He has never expressed a
> desire to be the best black golfer in history, only the best golfer in
> history ... The world not only is at Woods' feet, it is on his side. Why
> would Nike see fit to embroil him in a senseless, needless controversy
> that threatens to turn some against him, from day one of his career?

(Strege, 1996, p. D10)

In response, Nike reclaimed the critics' charges and announced that it had intentionally fashioned a highly charged advertisement. Jim Small, Nike's director of public relations, embraced the controversy by depicting the conflict

77

as indicative of Nike's success: "The very fact that it made people so uncomfortable shows it did what it was intended to. We hit the nail on the head" (quoted in Custred, 1996, p. 27). But the popular investment in Woods, despite the controversy surrounding the advertisement, suggests that the "Hello World" campaign did not significantly discomfort national consumers. Instead, Nike and Tiger Woods were united in the pursuit of another of America's favorite pastimes – the hailing of American consumers through, what paraphrasing Cornell West (1988) might be called, pragmatic symbols (symbols through which America tells stories about itself).

Although the "Hello World" campaign identified and named racism, it did so through the familiar and acceptable terms of social criticism. Capitalizing on narratives already in place – and particularly narratives that America loves to consume through sport – Woods' entry into professional golf was cast as an event of national magnitude. Consumer identification was invited and secured by cloaking Woods in a swathe of overtly patriotic sentiment: he was vaunted as an emblem of racial progress, a righter of wrongs à la foundational figures such as Jackie Robinson and Arthur Ashe. Indeed, the extraordinary proliferation of allusions to Jackie Robinson surrounding Tiger underscores the sort of pleasures promised to American consumers. Thus, the "Hello World" campaign announced itself as America's quintessential tantalizing tale of racial progress: one that combined race, sport, masculinity, national healing, and proper citizenship. As Woods and Nike crossed the final sporting frontier (a remote sector of a frontier typically conflated with the American way of life and the American Dream), consumers, hailed as compassionate, informed citizens, were invited to recollect mediated national–ethical moments of the past and to participate in a national–familial–ethical moment of the present.

In this way, Tiger Woods became the latest version of a commercialized raced masculinity implicated in political backlash while certifying national transformation, progress, and equality (see Andrews, 1996; Cole, 1996). One commentator pointedly captured the conservative "some of my best friends ..." orientation of Tiger Woods' enthusiastic appropriation by the hearts and minds of the American establishment:

> the core constituency of golf, those "members only" who have managed to make the country club, after the church, the most segregated institution in America, think Tiger will get people off their backs. How can you call golf racist now, you liberal jogger, just look who we invited to tee?
>
> (Lipsyte, 1996, p. 11)

Woods, like Colin Powell, Michael Jordan, and Oprah Winfrey, was thus used by the populist defenders of core American values and ideologies (i.e. those cultural producers operating within the ratings-driven media- and poll-driven centrist politics), as self-evident proof of the existence of a color-blind meritocracy. So, in a time of increasing racial polarization along social and economic lines (cf. Kelley, 1997; Wilson, 1997), Tiger Woods emerged as a popular icon from whom the American populace could derive a sense of intimacy, pride, and reassurance.

To the extent that Woods was perceived to be an activist, it was clearly a nationally sanctioned activism linked to media, family, and consumption. In this case, a familiar dramatic and heroic narrative – in and through which consumers could participate – was fabricated against the backdrop of an exceptional experience. In a national context ostensibly already devoid of racism, Woods and Nike had identified a local and temporary situation of racial discrimination in the private and protected elite space of golf. Moreover, its already given and expeditious resolution to make golf the place of the people (all people, regardless of race or sex, now seemingly had the right to participate in the multiple consumption practices surrounding golf) would be mediated "live." *Under the guise* of public debate and intervention, America's self-congratulatory mood was affirmed. Rather than encouraging critical thought about contemporary national politics and the complexity of racism, the "Hello World" campaign relied on and reproduced a mediated-patriotism. Ironically, racial discrimination, formulated as a holdover from another time, was used to reauthorize the nation's view of itself as beyond race.

America's post-historical *Everyman*

During the Fall of 1996, the media coverage of Tiger Woods reached extraordinary proportions following his victories at the 1996 Las Vegas Invitational and 1996 Walt Disney World/Oldsmobile Classic tournaments. As much as they were interested in his exploits on the golf course, the popular media were obsessively concerned with documenting, and thereby advancing, the "Tigermania" seemingly sweeping the nation. Paradoxically, Tigermania was represented through the dramatically increased viewing and attendance figures for tournaments and blanket media coverage incited by the popular media (Potter, 1997; Stevens and Winheld, 1996; Williams, 1996).

Nike, in a moment symptomatic of the expansion of Woods' celebrity-citizenship, debuted their second Tiger Woods commercial. Nike's Tiger Woods Mk II was revealed to an expectant prime time American public during coverage of IMG's made-for-TV "Skin's Game", which ran on the ABC network over the Thanksgiving Day 1996 weekend. Nike undermined any sparks from the "Hello World" backlash as it capitalized on Woods' accruing cultural capital as the unequivocal embodiment of America's future multicultural citizenry. Capitulating to dominant cultural norms and values in a more banal – and therefore – even more powerful way, Nike contributed to the fabrication of Woods as the latest version of the *new* face of America.

Woods' apparently re-engineered racial image was facilitated via a television commercial entitled "I am Tiger Woods." The 60-second commercial's visual, a mixture of black and white and color images with still, slow, and full motion footage, was accompanied by a musical soundtrack incorporating an understated mix of drum beats and chorus harmonies. The result was a somewhat pious celebration of that which Tiger Woods had come to represent. This process of deification centered on a cast of racially diverse and geographically dispersed children (on golf courses and distinctly urban settings), who collectively embodied Nike's vision of Tiger Woods' essential heterogeneity. Moreover, they signified, by inference, the future American populace.

Borrowing the "I am ..." strategy previously adopted in both Stanley Kubrick's *Spartacus* (1960), and more recently Spike Lee's *Malcolm X* (1992), each strategic child representative proclaimed, with varying degrees of solemnity, "I am Tiger Woods." The golfing Woods is periodically glimpsed as young males and females possessing characteristics stereotypically associated with African Americans, Asian Americans, or European Americans offer invocations of "I am Tiger Woods." The commercial ends with slow motion footage of Woods hitting a drive down the center of a tree-lined fairway. As he reaches the apex of his follow through, "I am Tiger Woods" in white text appears in the bottom center of the frame, followed by Nike's international–national sign, the obligatory swoosh.

Less than three months earlier, the "Hello World" campaign had enabled, despite its immediate displacement, the possibility of reading Woods as an outspoken racial insurgent. Now, Woods was clearly re-articulated into a multicultural figure who, like his young imitators, was framed as the pre-political and post-historical embodied manifestation of contemporary racial politics. Moreover, a significant change is claimed for the golf world: not only have we witnessed an immediate change in personnel but, golf's future will include a significantly different cast of characters. Indeed, through what Yu (1996) depicts as a shift away from Nike's African Americanized representation, Woods, Yu argues, was conclusively cast as "a multicultural godsend to the sport of golf" (ibid., p. 4M). Under the sign of multiculturalism and in America's golfing future, everyone will be included.

It was the emotive appeal of this post-historical multiculturalism that situates Oprah Winfrey's anointing of Woods as "America's son":

Oprah Winfrey: Can we get this straight? What do call yourself? Do you call yourself African American? I know you are – your – father's half black, quarter Chinese, quarter American Indian; your mother's half Thai, quarter Chinese and quarter white. So you are – that's why you are America's son.
Tiger Woods: Yes.
Oprah Winfrey: You are America's son.

(*Oprah Winfrey Show*, April 24, 1997)

80

With Oprah's designation and the ascending understanding of Woods and the nation as multicultural hybrids in the background, Woods lends authenticity to the imaginary moment by listing his multicultural qualifications. Conjuring up America's fantasy continuum (marked by a past in which the world had come to America and a present in which America had become the world), Woods locates himself:

Tiger Woods: Yeah. I guess two things ... is that I guess now that I'm on the Ryder Cup team, which – we get to go over and play in Europe in September – that I won't be representing the United States: I'll be representing the United Nations ... which is a little different ... a little funny thing is, growing up, I came up with this name. I'm a Cablinasian: Ca, Caucasian; bl, black; in, Indian; Asian – Cablinasian.
Oprah Winfrey: That's what you call yourself?
Tiger Woods: Yeah.

(*Oprah Winfrey Show*, April 24, 1997)

Woods, denying any particular allegiance, appeals to a mythic globalization and declares himself a citizen of the world. While he and the apparently complex identity he claims appear to work against the discourse of nationalism, both are very much part of it. Not only does his refined multi-racial category suggest that identity is a factual representation of genetic and cultural heritage, but it, paradoxically, reinforces the notion of the abstract person (detached from time and place) and imagines identity as voluntary (like the identity implanted in the multicultural new face of America). This is not to say that Woods is not implicated in globalization. Indeed, Woods *is* part of the international community, he *is* embedded in multiple connections to multiple places. However, those connections are economic and political, not the innocent invention of a child "growing up." National interests are naturalized through mechanisms that imagine larger global loyalties and current and familiar racial categories obsolete. Like the feminine cultural hybrids manufactured by *Time, Mirabella*, and Betty Crocker, Woods seemingly provides morally sufficient answers to the cultural, economic, and political crises afflicting the contemporary United States and its position in global capitalism.

Affirmative culture in 1990s' America

In this chapter, we have introduced the salient and remarkable assertions about identity, community, and culture made in the name of America through Tiger Woods. Indeed, Woods signifies a post-national order, suggests a transnational coalition of sorts, and is imagined as a global-national antidote. In the USA, a global organic community (an organic community that links the local, national, and global) is visualized through thoroughly nationalist terms. Most distinctively, at the level of nation, Woods is coded as a multicultural sign of color-blindness.

Proclamation of the nation's venture to be color-blind, as Judith Butler explains, "is still to be related to race in a mode of blindness. In other words, race does not fall away from view, it becomes produced as the absent object that structures permissible discourse" (1998, p. 156). Keeping the productive dimensions of discursive constraints in mind, we conclude by underscoring the contradictory effects of the national multicultural myth advertised through Woods. We review how disavowals of racism, apparently principled claims of inclusivity, and declarations of color-blindness, organize the regulatory discourses about race and nation, as they are encoded and enacted around a national event called "Tigermania."

America's responses to Nike's "Hello World" campaign, as we have argued, rely on and reactivate the logic guiding opponents of racial consciousness and affirmative action. Anti-affirmative action sentiment, particularly as it has become entwined with demands for color-blindness, was most recently reinvigorated during the mid-1990s as the media focused national attention on the Board of Regents of the University of California. The UC Regents were among the first to repeal their affirmative action program. Despite the perceptible distance (geographically and conceptually) between public affirmative action debates and America's celebration of Woods, Woods' intelligibility is deeply embedded in the commonplace values expressed in and through opposition to affirmative action. Thus, Woods is a crucial transfer point in the network of resistance to affirmative action. These dynamics are illustrated in the ambivalent representations of Woods as he repeatedly is designated a racial sign of America's radical racial transformation.

As the "Hello World" campaign identified racism as a contemporary problem, the issue of racism was quickly translated into a problem of race consciousness. Evaluated through the restrictions on post-civil rights discourse, the problem was redefined in terms of *how* the category was introduced. By associating Woods with a racial category, Nike is deemed an agent of victimization. According to neo-liberal and conservative post-civil rights logic, Woods is the victim of an ill-conceived marketing strategy which denies him his deserved transcendent position.

Moreover, a logic of reverse discrimination is expressed in another of the popular responses to Woods: "It is funny how it works. Part of Woods' appeal is his race. If he were just another blond-haired, blue-eyed golfer ... he would be just another blond-haired, blue-eyed golfer struggling" (Knott, 1996, p. B1). Such a reactive comment is symptomatic of the historical moment in which white men claim to be unfairly burdened by history. In particular, white male athletes are introduced as the new class of victims who suffer because race (rather than merit and accomplishment) determines value and marketability. Racial preference, presumed to be and presented as a violation of America's moral model (the transcendent figure who bears no marks of history is the effect of the moral model), is advanced as a fundamental issue.

"The national moment in the making" narrative (exemplified by the invitation to consumers to participate by watching "live" as Woods breaks through what is presumably the final racial barrier) seemingly departs from and intervenes in anti-affirmative action sentiments. Yet, both anti-affirmative action arguments and the national moment in the making narrative draw on the same celebrated morals that are the core of national culture. The isolation technique, which reduces racial discrimination in terms of time and space, is crucial to the event's national consumer appeal. Moreover, the already-in-place "hero," a hero encoded as an antidote to an outdated race discrimination that can be fathomed only because it exists in the "remote and elite" golf world, enhances its marketability. National intimacy is further secured as America imagines itself anticipating this hero's arrival for more than a decade. Thus, "the national moment in the making" that consumers experience is not simply a celebration of Tiger's personal accomplishments, but of America's accomplished abolition of golf's elitism. Both the technique of isolation and the mediation of the event establish a national intimacy that allows consumer-citizens to take part in this intimate national event.

Relatedly, Tiger is codified through terms that deny and inscribe, in ways that are specifically anti-African American, racialized Othering. Indeed, the precise terms of opposition through which Tiger is interpreted as "a breath of fresh air" (Stodghill, 1997, p. 32) are telling. The phrase easily recalls the now familiar demonizing representations of generations of African American NBA players whose diverse infractions are routinely translated into a criminalized contempt for authority. And, more often than not, those infractions are taken up as a sign of a collective irresponsible sexuality and consumption. Woods, in this case, is offered as a carefully hued multiracial *response* to what is widely considered to be the primary *source* of the dissolution of the familial and – by extension – the national core culture: the regularly pathologized African American population (cf. Reeves and Campbell, 1994; Scott, 1997; Smith, 1994).

Given the prominence of reproduction and family in the contemporary national politics of intimacy, the declaration of Woods as America's new son is telling. Again, in a historical moment in which African American athletes are routinely characterized as engaging in non-familial sexual relations, Woods is represented as the embodiment of normal, immigrant-familial America. Like the other simulated multicultural figures discussed by Berlant, Woods' very existence sanctions the "disinvestment in many contexts of African-American life in the present tense," and points to a "new citizenship-form that will ensure the political future of the core national culture" (Berlant, 1996, p. 424).

Woods, America's *multicultural* son, is a seductive element in a national image archive figured on the paradoxical claims about the nation. While African American basketball players are regularly charged with violating national core values, Woods has become revered for his cultural heritage and cultural literacy. Aware that earlier promotional incarnations of Tiger Woods' persona had created media and popular interest but not the desired level of commodity consumption, Nike sought to appeal to the "classic" golfer (i.e. middle class and white) whose high levels of disposable income bolstered the golf economy. So, Nike's Tiger Woods strategizing sought to evoke a brand image that was "more Armani than Gap" (Meyers, 1998, p. 2B). This involved the use of more conservative designs and materials for the Tiger Woods apparel collection and, more crucially, it signalled a distinct change in the way Woods was represented within Nike advertising campaigns. This shift is exemplified in the deeply reverential "I am lucky" Nike advertising campaign which followed the "I am Tiger Woods" commercial: "Hogan [Ben Hogan] knows, Snead [Sam Snead] knows, Jack [Jack Nicklaus] knows. I am lucky. Everything I have I owe to golf, and for that I am lucky." This appeal to Woods' position among the litany of golfing greats was indicative of the "revamping" of the "Woods brand" (ibid., p. 1B), in that it highlighted and mobilized another dimension of contemporary cultural dynamics and larger political concerns in America. Its rhetoric, a conservative appeal to tradition, draws a connection between Woods and those who came before him, thus furnishing Woods with a reassuring sporting and national cultural lineage. Unlike popular reactions to rank-and-file NBA players, Woods was thus codified as a multicultural agent who restores virtue to, as he is designated an extension of, America's sporting tradition.

Woods' iconic national sporting pedigree was subsequently underscored by his superlative displays during the 1999 and 2000 PGA seasons. In 1999 Woods won eleven events, including the US PGA Championship (his second major title) to finish top of golf's world rankings and the PGA money list. Even these stellar achievements were surpassed in the 2000 season when Woods won the US Open, the British Open, and the US PGA Championship (three of golf's four major championships), and a total of nine PGA tour events. In the wake of his domination of golf, Woods – everybody's favorite multicultural American – has been rendered a cultural phenomenon, distinguished by his ability to stimulate popular interest (as measured by either the number of spectators at events or television audience ratings figures) rather than incite critical reflection. So this potentially progressive cultural figure has effectively been neutered by the forces of corporate capitalism, such that presently:

> Most of us don't need him to be a savior or a hero or a role model. We simply want the spectacle: Tiger gliding down the fairway, Tiger hitting rainmaker drives, Tiger pummeling his opponents and then putting his arm around them, Tiger hugging his mom. If he turns and winks back at us every once in a while, that will be enough.
>
> (Ratnesar, 2000, p. 66)

The popular spectacle that Tiger Woods has become was evidently enough for Nike which, in September 2000, signed him to a new five-year endorsement contract worth $100 million: Nike effectively paying this exorbitant sum in order to augment their – somewhat faltering – brand identity through a continued association with a suitably benign, yet engaging, face of America's future citizenry that is Tiger Woods.

In the end, this national–multicultural icon's agency is figured through his squeaky clean image, his enormous smile, and his ability (in terms of cultural work) to reproduce the permissible discourse of nation and race. America's Tigermania is, finally, a celebration of cultural literacy, of a national myth, projected onto and relayed through Woods, that reinvigorates, rather than contests, white cultural prestige. Threats of cultural miscegenation, interference with the myth's facile reproduction, are displaced onto racial identities now declared outdated. Thus, the narrative of continuity, Woods' place within the genealogy of white male golfers and his location in the lineage of black athletes, work to enhance what it means to be an "American" in a global-moment, which translates, in the last instance, into augmenting white culture. It is in this sense that Woods is America's new model entrepreneur and citizen.

Note

1   This chapter is a revised and updated version of an article that appeared as Cole and Andrews (2000). It is printed by permission.

Bibliography

Allen, K. (1996) "Advertising blitz to introduce Woods to the world at large." *USA Today*, August 29, p. 11C.

Andrews, D.L. (1996) "The fact(s) of Michael Jordan's blackness: excavating a floating racial signifier." *Sociology of Sport Journal* 13 (2): 125–58.

Berlant, L. (1996) "The face of America and the state of emergency." In C. Nelson and D.P. Gaonkar (eds), *Disciplinarity and Dissent in Cultural Studies* (pp. 397–439). New York: Routledge.

Butler, J. (1998) "An affirmative view." In R. Post and M. Rogin (eds), *Race and Representation: Affirmative Action*. New York: ZONE Books.

Cole, C.L. (1996) "American Jordan: P.L.A.Y., consensus, and punishment." *Sociology of Sport Journal* 13 (4): 366–97.

Cole, C.L. and Andrews, D.L. (2000) "America's new son: Tiger Woods and America's multiculturalism." In N.K. Denzin (ed.), *Cultural Studies: A Research Volume* (Vol. 5, pp. 109–24). Stamford, CT: JAI Press.

Crain, R. (1997) "The unique selling proposition falls prey to ads as entertainment." *Advertising Age*, June 23, p. 13.

Custred, J. (1996) "Swoosh! There it goes: after much debate, Nike pulls controversial Woods spot from TV circulation." *Houston Chronicle*, October 6, p. 27.

Gabriel, J. (1998) *Whitewash: Racialized Politics in the Media*. London: Routledge.

Higginbotham, A.L., François, A.B., and Yueh, L.Y. (1997) "The O.J. Simpson trial: who was 'improperly playing the race card'?" In T. Morrison and C.B. Lacour (eds), *Birth of a Nation'hood: Gaze, Script, and Spectacle in the O.J. Simpson Case*. New York: Pantheon Books.

Jeffords, S. (1993) *Hard Bodies: Hollywood Masculinity in the Reagan Era*. New Brunswick: Rutgers University Press.

Kelley, R.D.G. (1997) *Yo' Mama's Disfunktional!: Fighting the Culture Wars in Urban America*. Boston: Beacon Press.

Knott, T. (1996) "Hello, Nike, and many thanks for telling Tiger's tale to America." *The Washington Times*, September 11, p. B1.

Lipsitz, G. (1998) *The Possessive Investment in Whiteness: How White People Profit from Identity Politics*. Philadelphia: Temple University Press.

Lipsyte, R. (1996) "Woods suits golf's needs perfectly." *New York Times*, September 8, p. 11.

Meyers, B. (1998) "Nike tees up to try again Woods brand gets new look." *USA Today*, September 18, pp. 1B-2B.

Page, C. (1996) *Showing My Color: Impolite Essays on Race and Identity*. New York: HarperCollins.

Potter, J. (1997) "Woods widens game's appeal: role model encourages minorities." *USA Today*, January 15, p. 3C.

Ratnesar, R. (2000) "Changing stripes: Just as with his golf game, Tiger has had to adjust his life to meet the demands of celebrity." *Time*, August 14, pp. 62–6.

Reeves, J.L. and Campbell, R. (1994) *Cracked Coverage: Television News, the Anti-cocaine Crusade, and the Reagan Legacy*. Durham, NC: Duke University Press.

Scott, D.M. (1997) *Contempt and Pity: Social Policy and the Image of the Damaged Black Psyche 1880–1996*. Chapel Hill: The University of North Carolina Press.

Smith, A.M. (1994) *New Right Discourse on Race and Sexuality: Britain, 1968–1990*. Cambridge: Cambridge University Press.

Spousta, T. (1996) "Ready for Tiger, not Nike." *Sarasota Herald-Tribune*, September 11, p. 1C.

Stevens, K. and Winheld, M. (1996) "Fans flocking to catch Tiger at brink of fame." *USA Today*, September 19, p. 16C.

Stodghill, R. (1997) "Tiger, Inc." *Business Week*, April 28, pp. 32–7.

Strege, J. (1996) "Nike in the rough with Tiger's controversial ad." *The Orange County Register*, September 19, p. D10.

Wernick, A. (1991) *Promotional Culture: Advertising, Ideology and Symbolic Expression*. London: Sage.

West, C. (1988) *The American Evasion of Philosophy: A Genealogy of Pragmatism*. Madison, WI: University of Wisconsin Press.

Williams, S. (1996) "Tiger a ratings master, too: his Grand Slam triumph is most-watched TV golf ever." *Daily News*, April 15, p. 87.

Wilson, W.J. (1997) *When Work Disappears: The World of the New Urban Poor*. New York: Vintage Books.

Yu, H. (1996) "Perspective on ethnicity: how Tiger Woods lost his stripes." *Los Angeles Times*, December 2, p. 4M.

5

FROM "CHILD'S PLAY" TO "PARTY CRASHER"

Venus Williams, racism and professional women's tennis

Nancy E. Spencer

In September 1997, Venus Williams advanced to the finals of the US Open to become the first unseeded woman finalist in the Open era of tennis. Despite losing to top-seeded Martina Hingis, Venus' advance to the finals could not have been more perfect if it were scripted. It was "the right moment, according to fate. An African-American teenager with a game blooming just in time for the dedication of the Arthur Ashe Stadium in 1997, the year of Jackie Robinson's remembrance and Tiger Woods' Masters" (Lopresti 1997: 12C). The women's final "drew a near-sellout of 21,566 at the new Arthur Ashe Stadium, and the overseers of the women's tour" could not have been happier (Smith, 1997a, p. 2C). Tennis had seemingly "found its Tiger Woods. Venus Williams, no longer a curiosity or a teen pumped up by hype, emerged as a legitimate claimant to the future of women's tennis" ("Venus rising at Open," 1997, p. 7B).

Amidst the euphoria generated by the arrival of America's newest tennis star, Williams' advance to the final was marred by one ignominious moment during her semifinal match. With the score 4–3 in the second set, Venus and her opponent, Romanian Irina Spirlea, literally bumped into one another as they changed sides. When asked about the bump, Venus claimed not to see Irina, while Spirlea announced that "it happened because 'she thinks she's the f——ing Venus Williams'" (Price, 1997, p. 35). Venus' father/coach, Richard, labeled Spirlea's bump as racially motivated, adding that Irina was "a big, ugly, tall, white turkey" (ibid.).

Whether the unfortunate collision was racially motivated or not, narratives about Venus and her younger sister, Serena, have typically been coded with reference to race. Their father Richard often describes his daughters as "Cinderellas of the Ghetto," noting that they are not fearful of opponents since they are from the ghetto (Jenkins, 1994b). At times, Richard Williams seems to purposely deploy narratives of threat in attempts to evoke fear/intimidation in his daughters' opponents.

In this chapter, I examine how narratives about the celebrated rise of Venus

Williams, coupled with the articulation of the "bump" incident at the 1997 US Open semifinal, reveal discursively constructed evidence of racism in professional women's tennis. Although Serena Williams won her family's first Grand Slam title by capturing the 1999 US Open Women's Singles, the focus of this chapter is on Venus Williams. Certainly, Serena's success and her articulation with Venus as "Sister Act II" inject an intriguing dynamic to explore for future research. However, because coded references to race initially emerged through narratives about Venus, my focus is on the articulation of race as seen through the optic of Venus' rise to fame.

Tennis and race

Like most sports in America, tennis remained largely segregated until 1950. The few facilities and/or opportunities for people of color to play were afforded largely by the American Tennis Association (ATA), founded in 1916 (Collins and Hollander, 1994). During the 1920s, the all-Negro American Tennis Association is credited with producing the achievements of several female tennis players – Lucy Slowe, Anita Gant, and Inez Patterson (Captain, 1991). Undoubtedly, the most famous players to emerge under the auspices of the ATA were Althea Gibson and Arthur Ashe.

Althea Gibson captured five major titles during her career, and is best known for breaking the color barrier in major events by entering the United States National Championships in 1950. She was not the first to enter a United States Lawn Tennis Association (USLTA) tournament, since Dr Reginald Weir, a New York physician, first played in the US Indoor in 1948 (Collins and Hollander, 1994). Despite Weir's entry, obstacles prevented Gibson's subsequent attempts to enter USLTA events. Her efforts were eventually strengthened by the advocacy of Alice Marble, a dominant woman player of the 1930s. In an editorial published in the July 1950 issue of *American Lawn Tennis*, Marble wrote:

> If tennis is a game for ladies and gentlemen, it's also time we acted a little more like gentlepeople and less like sanctimonious hypocrites ...
> If Althea Gibson represents a challenge to the present crop of women players, it's only fair that they should meet that challenge on the courts where tennis is played
>
> (cited in Gibson, 1958, pp. 55–6)

Embarrassed by Marble's editorial, the USLTA accepted Gibson's entry into the 1950 United States National Championships. In her first appearance at Forest Hills, Althea encountered the reigning Wimbledon champion, Louise Brough, in the second round. In a rain-delayed match, Brough ultimately prevailed in three hard-fought sets, 6–1, 3–6, 9–7 (Collins and Hollander, 1994).

Even after her impressive showing at Forest Hills, it was difficult for Gibson to compete, primarily due to lack of financial resources. Clearly, tennis' code of amateurism worked to privilege more affluent players, while players like Althea, who emerged from a poor background in Harlem, lacked the necessary finances. As a result, Gibson often had to rely on donations from more affluent black athletes such as boxer Joe Louis (Gibson, 1958).

In 1957, Gibson finally realized her dream of winning Wimbledon and the United States National Championships. Ironically, she might not have accomplished those feats were it not for intervening political circumstances that prompted the US State Department to organize a promotional tour in 1956. Soon after the killing of Emmett Till in Georgia, when "world opinion of the racial situation in the US was at a low ebb," Gibson (1958, p. 87) was invited to join three other tennis players for a world tour. As a member of the contingency, Althea's expenses were paid to travel, give exhibitions, and play in tournaments. Gibson concluded that she was meant to serve as a race ambassador and was warned by State Department officials that she would undoubtedly "be asked a lot about the Negro's life in the United States" (ibid.).

Although Althea Gibson is regarded as the "Jackie Robinson of tennis" for crossing the color barrier in her sport, she did not relish her role as a race ambassador, according to Bud Collins (O'Hara, 1995). Nor did Althea's entry into the upper echelons of the tennis world lead to widespread integration of the sport, as resulted from the "Jackie Robinson experiment" in baseball. It was not until a decade later that an African American won a major tennis championship. In 1968, during the first year of the Open era of tennis, Arthur Ashe became the only black male ever to win the US Open. The same year, he also captured the US National Amateur – a feat that is unlikely to be duplicated (Collins and Hollander, 1994).

Arthur Ashe emerged at a moment when tennis players could earn a legitimate living from the game and sustained his career over a decade. Beyond center court, Ashe became spokesperson for a variety of causes, including opposition to South African apartheid, the US policy toward Haitians seeking asylum in the United States and, finally, in the battle against AIDs (Ashe, 1993). Even though Ashe enjoyed greater longevity in his tennis career than Gibson, he still felt what he termed the oppression of his race. When asked by a reporter from *People Magazine* if AIDs was the heaviest burden he had to bear, Ashe said it was not, but admitted that being black was the greatest burden he ever had to bear. He described having to live as a minority in America as feeling like an extra weight was tied around him.

Ashe lamented the fact that racism hurt and inconvenienced him infinitely more than AIDS, noting that even as a former Wimbledon champion whose celebrity made him recognizable: "A pall of sadness hangs over my life and the lives of almost all African Americans because of what we as a people have experienced historically in America, and what we as individuals experience each and every day" (1993, p. 127). Although Ashe lived in a time of relative integration, he still felt that he was marked by segregation, and he was forever aware of a shadow of contempt that lay across his identity and sense of self-esteem.

Despite the inspirations of Althea Gibson and Arthur Ashe, few African Americans rose to the upper echelons in professional tennis. No one since Ashe won a Grand Slam event until Serena Williams captured the Women's Singles at the 1999 US Open. Only three other black players – Zina Garrison, Malivai Washington, and Venus Williams – advanced to singles' finals in Grand Slam events during the 1990s; Zina and Malivai lost in the finals of Wimbledon, while Venus lost in the 1997 US Open final.

Malivai's father, William Washington, charges that minorities are not supported in the game by the governing body of tennis. The elder Washington alleges that the USTA has been "flagrantly negligent in addressing the needs of minority competitors" (Flink, 1994, p. 8). Citing "a definite pattern of discrimination," Washington contends that the USTA, ATP Tour and other tennis-related firms "have stifled the development of talented young minorities," including his son Mashiska (Smith, 1998, p. 10C).

Although William Washington's recent charges focus on the USTA's failure to award wild cards into the main draws of major tournaments, he also criticizes the USTA for a failure to provide inner city programs with funds to foster the growth of tennis among minorities. Washington contends that for tennis to be successful among minorities, the USTA must take programs into the inner city. According to Washington:

> You can't go to the country clubs looking for minorities; we are just not there. You can't go to the high tech tennis camps to look for us because we aren't there. You have to come to the inner city and that is where we are.
>
> (Flink, 1994, p. 8)

Even though Venus Williams originally hailed from the inner city environs of Compton, California, she ultimately left that environment for one of those high-tech tennis camps to which Washington referred – Rick Macci's Tennis Academy.

In light of the meager financial support invested in minority player development, perhaps the multi-million dollar Ashe Stadium was meant to ward off allegations that the USTA had not done enough for minorities. The dedication of Ashe Stadium certainly seemed to signal the USTA's desire for a new era of multi-culturalism. At the dedication of the new stadium, Arthur's widow, Jeanne Moutoussamy-Ashe preached about inclusion (Price, 1997), while Venus Williams acknowledged the symbolic importance of Ashe Stadium as well. When reporters pressed her to talk about her father's charge of racism after the infamous bump in her match with Spirlea, Williams said: "I think with this moment in the first year in Arthur Ashe Stadium, it all represents everyone being together, everyone having a chance to play. So I think this is definitely ruining the mood, these questions about racism" (Kirkpatrick, 1997, p. 22). Venus may have dodged questions about racism for the time being, but the issue would remain, given that narratives about her rise to stardom were inflected with race.

Early glimpses of "Planet Venus"

In the late 1980s, media reports had begun to create a positive buzz about a precocious 8-year-old African American tennis player named Venus Williams (Spencer and Cole, 1996). John McEnroe and Pete Sampras were among the elite male players to take notice of Venus when they saw her hitting with McEnroe's former coach, Paul Cohen, in Brentwood, California (Steptoe, 1991). After winning her 17th singles title in less than a year, the Southern California 10-and-under championships, *The New York Times* featured a piece about Venus on the front page of the entire paper. At the age of 10, she was described as "the most hotly pursued preteen in U.S. tennis history" (Steptoe, 1991: 48) – a remarkable statement given that her predecessors included the likes of Jennifer Capriati, Tracy Austin, and Chris Evert.

Amidst the hoopla, Venus Williams was sought after to sign autographs before she could even write in cursive; she was asked to give interviews, to appear in celebrity events, and to play exhibitions around Southern California. Among the perks offered just for showing promise, Venus was showered with free rackets, shoes, and clothes, while agents from sport management firms lobbied to represent her (ibid.). According to her father, Richard, the family had "been offered houses, cars, and millions of dollars by people who wanted Venus' name on endorsement contracts" (ibid., p. 53).

In 1991, before Venus signed an endorsement contract or turned pro, the Williams family moved from Southern California to Haines City, Florida, where Venus and her sister Serena, accepted scholarships to attend Rick Macci's Tennis Academy at the Grenelefe Resort. There, "the basic charge, waived in the case of gifted girls like Venus, was $2,200 a month for room, board, tennis instruction, and transportation to and from local public schools" (Mewshaw, 1993, p. 209). Richard Williams was reportedly enthusiastic about the family atmosphere offered by the Grenelefe community ("Court Report", 1991).

The environs of Grenelefe contrasted sharply to the ghetto of Compton, where Venus and Serena learned to play the game "surrounded by poverty, squalor and gang rumbles" (Kirkpatrick, 1993, p. 48). Their father jokingly referred to the cracked macadam public courts as the "East Compton Hills Country Club" (ibid., p. 49). Yet, Richard was hesitant to leave Compton since he believed that living and practicing amidst the mayhem had made Venus a more tenacious player (Steptoe, 1991). He ultimately decided that the relocation was necessary because the inner city had become too "dangerous" (Drucker, 1994, p. 56).

By 1991, Compton had become perhaps the most familiar signifier of "racially-coded urban America" and all that entailed (Spencer and Cole, 1996). Between 1987 and 1990, especially during Reagan's so-called war on drugs,

Compton had been made the premiere national referent for racially-coded poverty, gangs, drugs, and threat. During 1987, African American gang activity in Compton was routinely featured in the news to explain causes of urban deterioration, community decline, escalating violence, and the need for increased policing. Moreover, as rap became an increasingly pervasive form of popular culture, albeit a racially-coded form associated with violence, the articulation of Compton and black youth was reinforced (ibid.). Mainstream narratives about Venus cultivated this association through reports of an athlete whose practice sessions were "often interrupted by gang confrontations" ("Court Report", 1991, p. 16).

When *Sports Illustrated* described Venus' surroundings in the 1991 article entitled "Child's Play," the description resonated with media consumers:

> It's a cool spring night in Compton, California, a rough-and-tumble community just south of Los Angeles and hard by Watts. Last year the number of murders declined slightly, to 78, but life in the city of 110,000 remains bleak. The median income for a family of four is about $13,000, dangerously near the poverty line. One young man's idea of an entrepreneurial undertaking is the drive-up drug business he has set up near the city tennis courts and playground in East Rancho Dominguez, a Hispanic enclave in Compton.
>
> (Steptoe, 1991, p. 47)

If the dangers of Compton were not conducive to the nurture of a rising tennis star, the environs provided Richard Williams with the *raison d'être* for his business. "Based in Compton, Richard managed Samson Security, a company started to provide on-site security services for construction projects" (Kirkpatrick, 1993, p. 56).

For someone raised in the context of Compton, playing at Wimbledon might seem like a remote dream. However, as Steptoe's article presaged:

> Not far away, inside a small, mint-green house that has been spray painted with black graffiti, a 10-year old girl sleeps, untroubled by the nightmarish things occurring outside her home. She is dreaming of wearing a white dress and playing tennis on the grass courts of Wimbledon.
>
> (1991, p. 47)

As remote as it might have seemed to play at Wimbledon, Richard Williams nurtured that "fairy-tale" hope for his daughters. Only the dream would take a detour through Haines City, Florida.

Upon relocating to Florida, Richard determined that Venus should not turn professional too young, and proclaimed that "any father who allows a 14-year-old to turn pro should be shot" (Doherty, 1995, p. 112). In 1994, at age 15,

Venus made her pro debut at the Bank of the West Classic at the Oakland Coliseum. In her first professional tournament, Venus "caused a sensation when she defeated the world's 59th ranked player, Shaun Stafford, in straight sets and then had second-ranked Arantxa Sanchez-Vicario down a set and a service break before succumbing 2–6, 6–3, 6–0" (Jenkins, 1994b, p. 30). Although Richard Williams had been roundly criticized for his unorthodox methods, Venus' triumphant debut seemed to vindicate him – at least for the time being (ibid.).

In May 1995, after playing in only one tournament, and without a titan sport management company, Venus secured an impressive endorsement contract with Reebok ("In the same old orbit," 1995). Although terms of the deal were not initially disclosed, "sources said it was comparable to the gold strike made by Jennifer Capriati when she turned pro at 14 in 1990 and was more lucrative than the deal Arantxa Sanchez Vicario, the No. 1 player in the world, had with Reebok" ("In the same," 1995, p. 18). McNab (1995) estimated that the multi-year deal with Reebok was worth $12 million, enough to afford "a house in an affluent West Palm Beach resort" where the Williams' family built two tennis courts in their backyard (Leand, 1995, p. 10).

Although her family moved to a more upscale neighborhood, media narratives about Venus continued to reflect her connection to the inner city (read: blackness). At the 1997 US Open, Pentz said that:

> [she] brought youthful joy, exuberance, and yes, blackness, onto our sport's main stage. This was the week that Venus Williams proved she was the real thing. She proved that a black child can emerge from the inner city, schooled not by tennis experts but by her parents, and gain the heights predicted for her.
>
> (1997b, p. 52)

Contradictory messages are conveyed through the coding of inner city narratives in Venus' spectacular rise. Just as Richard Williams evoked fear through employing ghetto tropes, the notion of threat is reflected by statements that tournament officials feared Venus and Serena might make competitive tennis "too much like the NBA." Meanwhile, the emergence of the Williams sisters injected hope into a game perceived to be in crisis.

"Tennis crisis" narratives

A 1994 *Sports Illustrated* cover posed the question: "Is tennis dying?" In the accompanying article on the "Sorry state of tennis," Sally Jenkins noted that "fans are bored, TV ratings are down, equipment sales are soft and most pros seem to be prima donnas who don't care about anything but money" (1994a, p. 78). Subsequent coverage of this "crisis" focused more specifically on the "malaise in the women's game" (Feinstein, 1994, p. 12). Philip Morris Executive Ellen Merlo depicted the so-called *problem* in terms of loss of celebrity: "Billie Jean, Martina and Chris sold the sport as well as selling them-selves. They realized that their obligation went beyond showing up on court and doing a post-match interview. The players today feel that fulfills their obli-gation" (Leand, 1994, p. 16). Merlo suggested that the loss of celebrity was a clear concern and that the solution to this "crisis" was that the WTA needed to be firm in letting players know their responsibilities.

Chris Evert noted similarly that many of the top women players seemed "unapproachable, defensive and isolated" (Jenkins, 1994a, p. 78). If the top players seemed defensive, perhaps there was good reason for them to be since a number of scandals had worn on women's tennis in the early 1990s (Spencer and Cole, 1996). In April 1993, No. 1 ranked Monica Seles was stabbed by an avid Steffi Graf fan who wanted Graf to regain the No. 1 ranking. In that same year, rising star Mary Pierce was forced to obtain a restraining order against her father/coach, Jim Pierce, in order to thwart escalating incidents of abuse. In May 1994, Jennifer Capriati was arrested on charges of possessing marijuana.

If the individual woes of top-ranked players were not enough, women's tennis had lost the compelling rivalry of Martina Navratilova and Chris Evert when Evert retired in 1989. Even though Navratilova maintained her ranking among the top 4 in the world, she too was on the verge of retirement. In the context of this perceived "crisis," Curry Kirkpatrick suggested that the then 13-year-old Venus Williams and 12-year-old Anna Kournikova could become the "Next Great Historic Rivalry" (1993, p. 4). To heighten the intrigue, Kirkpatrick characterized them as less like Evert and Navratilova and more like Saddam Hussein and George Bush. However, even if Williams and Kournikova were to resuscitate the women's game, their entry into professional tennis would have to await the Women's Tennis Association's (WTA) revised age rule guidelines.

Following the arrest of Jennifer Capriati, the WTA had begun to face increasing pressure to restrict entry of its youngest players. As the age for turning professional decreased, there was growing concern among experts that young players would be susceptible to burnout. In 1991, when Capriati emerged on the tennis scene at age 13, she seemed to be destined for super-stardom. Initially, Jennifer fulfilled the promise that afforded her multi-million dollar endorsement contracts (Mewshaw, 1993). She rose to a high ranking of No. 6 in the world and won the 1992 Olympic gold medal in women's singles. However, Capriati's arrest in 1994 produced one more visible sign that the future of women's tennis was facing a "crisis."

Enter Tiger Woods

In 1997, the emergence of golf sensation Tiger Woods enabled the world of professional golf to receive a boost in television ratings for the Master's Golf Championships. Within the tennis world, many lamented the lack of a charis-matic figure to parallel the likes of Woods. Despite the successful results of young tennis stars like World Nos 1 ranked Pete Sampras and Martina Hingis, tennis marketers seemed unable to link their success to the celebrity stature of a Tiger Woods. When Hingis was asked about comparisons to Woods, she replied cockily: "It's all the time. 'Tiger Woods. Tiger Woods. Tiger Woods.' I am better than he is. I've been on top longer. I'm just better" (Preston, 1998, p. 18).

When Venus Williams advanced to the final of the 1997 US Open, it appeared that tennis might have found its "tiger." As Price reported: "suddenly, tennis had a brilliant new talent – witty, intelligent and charismatic – a streetwise child of gang-plagued Compton, California, who could well be sport's next Tiger Woods" (1997, p. 35). Some tennis writers suggested that Venus could outperform Tiger in terms of athletic performance. Scott (1997) argued that although Tiger had won the Masters, he was already 22, while Venus – at 17 – still had five years in which to win major championships. Whatever predictions are realized, the bottom line for Venus is that she promises to improve TV ratings in tennis just as Tiger did for golf. That Venus is described as the "Tiger Woods of tennis" (Aronson, 1999, p. 8) is especially encouraging, given that Woods' marketability in the 1990s is likened to Michael Jordan in the 1980s, with both considered "untouchable when it comes to endorsement power" (Enrico, 1997, p. 8B).

While narratives about Tiger have not typically been connected to the ghetto, the coding of Tiger's (perceived) blackness has been linked to the inner city. In one particular Nike commercial, as inner city (predominantly black) youth proclaim to be Tiger Woods, we understand Nike to be hailing inner city youth, and inviting them to enter a space (i.e., the golf course) where they have previously been unwelcome. Through the figures of Venus and Serena Williams, the articulation of "blackness" now appears in professional women's tennis narratives as well. These narratives seem to evoke what Pentz (1997a, p. 48) describes as a "fear" that if Venus becomes a superstar, tennis might become like the NBA. What does this fear reveal about cultural anxieties? Perhaps one fear stems from concern about what has become of the white athlete – a concern that is linked to cultural anxieties about affirmative action policies. Or perhaps there is a fear that racism will be exposed. Certainly when Venus and Irina bumped into one another during their semi-final match, this was one indication that the specter of racism had already reared its ugly head.

A national dialogue on race

In a year highlighted by celebrations of individual African American athletes, President Clinton launched what he termed an unprecedented conversation about race. On June 14, 1997, the President announced his "Initiative on Race," whose aim was to have a diverse community in which we respect and even celebrate differences, while also embracing our shared values ("Minorities ..."). As a white southerner, Clinton had enjoyed a lifetime of support among blacks and therefore garnered special credibility on an issue that stood as perhaps the rawest wound on the nation's agenda (Kurtz, 1998).

Although 1997 highlighted progress in some arenas, it became evident during the 1990s that race had become a hot-button issue for our nation. Several mediated spectacles highlighted and conceivably exacerbated an apparently growing racial divide. In the early 1990s, the public's conscience was seared by repeated televising of videotaped coverage of Rodney King, a black motorist who was beaten by white police officers. When news of the acquittal of four police officers (tried in connection with his beating) was issued from Simi Valley, three days of rioting erupted in Los Angeles, resulting in 55 deaths, 2,000 injuries, and 1,100 buildings damaged or destroyed ("Riot results," 1997). Several years later, Los Angeles again became the focal point of attention in the O.J. Simpson case. Following Simpson's acquittal in his criminal trial, racial polarization was highlighted by mediated coverage that displayed split-screen images of blacks cheering the non-guilty verdict juxtaposed against whites crying out in disbelief at the decision (Berger, 1999).

Underlying the polarized articulation of these mediated spectacles were issues that threatened to impact large segments of the population. In particular, controversy surrounding affirmative action had become perhaps the most sensitive point of contention. Ironically, or perhaps conveniently for Clinton, opponents of affirmative action were not initially named to the race panel. Clarence Page, one member who favored continuing the policy, criticized Clinton for his reluctance to deal with affirmative action, calling it the most divisive issue along racial lines facing our nation besides crime ("A dialogue ...", 1998). In response, Clinton reiterated his support for affirmative action, noting that he thought test scores were unreliable measures for determining a person's capacity to grow and that society had a vested interest in diversity.

By failing to address affirmative action, Clinton's ambitious and well-meaning race initiative promised little hope of changing a racially-polarized nation where evidence of discrimination persisted. As Clarence Page pointed out, even in 1998, we remained a segregated society, in which blacks and whites lived mostly separate lives. Page credited whatever advances had been made in the workplace over the past thirty years to policies of affirmative action.

Statistics from a 1992 longitudinal study commissioned by the Federal Judicial Center reflected a less hopeful picture. Between 1984 and 1990, the average sentence for blacks rose from 28–49 percent higher than for whites, and the disparity had worsened by 1994. Between 1969 and 1993, the median black family income declined from $22,000 to $21,550, meaning that black family earnings declined from 61 percent to 55 percent of what white families earned during that time period. Black unemployment rates in 1980 and 1993 were twice those of whites, i.e., 14 percent vs. 6 percent (whereas blacks comprised 12.7 percent of the population, they constituted 21 percent of the unemployed). The poverty rate for black families (31 percent) was greater than for whites (9 percent) in 1993, a gap that has remained unchanged in the past twenty-four years (Higginbotham *et al.*, 1997). While these statistics reveal a compelling discrepancy between quality of life among black and white families, this is a reality largely obscured by the media in 1990s' America. As Lipsitz points out, the real racism that confronts millions daily (e.g., broad systematic practices like discrimination in housing, employment and education) remains obscured until or unless a white person "claims to be a victim of 'reverse discrimination'" (1997, p. 25).

A dialogue on race in women's tennis

Three months after Clinton launched a national dialogue on race, a similar conversation began within the space of women's tennis. When Venus Williams and Irina Spirlea bumped into one another in their semifinal match, Mary Carillo and Tim Ryan commented on the incident. In response to Ryan's observation that Irina seemed intent on running into Williams, Carillo explained that this tension had been building for months, adding that some of it was related to race.

After the 1997 US Open final, the September 15, 1997 issue of *Sports Illustrated* featured Venus on the cover with a caption that read: "Party crasher – Venus Williams shakes up tennis." The accompanying article, entitled "Venus envy," included a two-page spread of Venus' red, white and blue beads, and reported that although Hingis and Rafter won their respective singles titles, "the play of Venus Williams was the bigger story, much to her peers' dismay" (Price, 1997, p. 32). Price described Venus' debut at the US Open as a mixed blessing largely because of the issues of race that accompanied her advance to the finals. As Venus proceeded toward an eventual showdown with No. 1-seeded Martina Hingis, the resentment of Williams and her family became increasingly evident among her rivals (ibid.). Players began to complain "publicly about her arrogance, her unfriendly demeanor, her trash-talking" (ibid., p. 35). To exacerbate the situation, Venus' mother, Oracene, intimated that the tour was racist, a suggestion that was further reinforced by her husband, Richard, when he referred to Spirlea's bump as racially motivated. When Mr Williams was asked to elaborate on his charge (on the *Montel Williams Show*), he retracted his earlier allegation and defined racism as "forming an opinion before gathering all the information" (Smith, 1997b, p. 23C). Richard Williams acknowledged that he had not gathered all the information and could have been wrong (ibid.).

Meanwhile, several women players were asked to comment on whether the tour was racist. When top-ranked American Lindsay Davenport was asked about the allegations, she explained that the sentiment toward Venus was not about race. Evans (1997) confirmed Davenport's stance, noting that Zina Garrison, Lori McNeil, Carrie Benjamin and Chanda Rubin were all welcomed onto the Tour in recent years. By contrast, Pentz (1997b) concluded that some of it had to be race-based. Dismissing charges of racism on the basis of such logic obscures more subtle ways in which racism operates in tennis as well as in other spheres of American culture.

The fact remains that Venus' advance to the 1997 US Open final coupled with Serena's capture of the 1999 title were the first for African-American women since Althea Gibson nearly forty years ago. That reality, combined with the scarcity of African-American men and women among the professional ranks belies the notion that tennis has become more inclusive. Further obscured by the emphasis on ghetto-to-US Open final narratives is the reality that Venus and Serena spent much of the past decade in an environment typically afforded to the most privileged. So it is misleading to suggest that the route from ghetto to Grand Slam finals is a direct route. As Rick Macci points out, Venus and Serena worked out with him between 1991 to 1995, "five or six hours a day, six days a week" (1997, p. 12). Certainly, William Washington can appreciate the recent success of Venus and Serena Williams. And yet, he knows that it was not a USTA program that produced the Williams sisters. As in society, the trope of the ghetto bears witness to an inequitable system. If escaping the ghetto changes anything within the structure of society, it is the impression that one can make it on one's own.

Conclusion

In September, 1999, Venus Williams appeared on the cover of *Tennis Match* with the caption: "Time to put up or shut up?" In the accompanying article, Leand (1999) chronicled Venus and Serena Williams' brash claims that they would eventually sweep Grand Slam titles and dominate rankings in women's tennis. Yet, aside from Venus' ascent to the finals of the 1997 US Open, the sisters had managed to capture a disappointing three doubles' titles between them in Grand Slam events. Not surprisingly, tour veterans did not embrace their boasts, as reflected by Steffi Graf, who suggested that "they should prove it first and let their racquets do the talking" (Leand, 1999, p. 47). Shortly thereafter, Serena Williams captured her first Grand Slam singles title by winning the 1999 US Open.

In the year 2000, Venus Williams followed in her younger sister's footsteps to "let her racquet do the talking" as she swept to championship singles victories at Wimbledon, the US Open, and the Summer Olympics at Sydney. In one of tennis' most impressive displays of dominance during the past ten years, Venus extended her "unbeaten string to 32 matches and join(ed) Steffi Graf as the only women to win Wimbledon, the US Open and an Olympic gold medal in the same year" (DuPree, 2000a, p. 4E). In addition, Venus teamed with sister Serena to capture the gold in doubles, becoming "only the second American woman to win two gold medals at the same Olympics, Helen Wills doing it in 1924" (DuPree, 2000b, p. 2F).

The string of victories by Venus seemingly enabled her to live up to the hype, while her presence at the Sydney Olympics endeared her to her peers as well as to the crowds. According to DuPree, "Venus' smile, total involvement with the team and graciousness toward her opponents had virtually every crowd rooting for her and enabled her to at least partially shed an image as arrogant" (2000b, p. 2F). If Venus' storied rise to the heights of her sport makes visible the racism that persists, what then does her newfound acceptance reveal about the future? Perhaps a telephone conversation with President Clinton following her capture of the US Open provides insight.

When President Clinton made the customary congratulatory call following her US Open victory, Venus asked: "Do you think that you could lower my taxes, please, Mr. President?" (Kim and Mravic, 2000, p. 30). Posing that question did more than enable Williams to "seize the moment"; her question acknowledged attainment of higher socioeconomic status. Indeed, her reality reflects what many blacks now experience, as Cose (1999, p. 29) reports that it is "the best time ever to be black in America. Crime is down; jobs and income are up. White kids choose African-Americans as their heroes. But not everyone's celebrating." Certainly, we can appreciate the success of a highly visible few (Michael Jordan, Tiger Woods, and the Williams sisters). And yet, we must remember the reality pointed out by sociologist Elijah Anderson, that many blacks "are worse off than ever" (Cose, 1999, p. 36). If we are to deal with the full spectrum of racism, we cannot allow the success of an elite few to obscure the racism that persists.

Bibliography

"A dialogue on race with President Clinton." (1998) *NewsHour,*, July 9. Online. Available: HTTP: http://www.pbs.org/newshour/bb/race_relations/OneAmerica/transcript.html

Aronson, V. (1999) *Venus Williams.* New York: Chelsea House Publishers.

Ashe, A. (1993) *Days of Grace: A Memoir.* New York: Alfred A. Knopf.

Berger, M. (1999) "America's dialogue on race." *The History Place.* Online. Available: HTTP: http://www.historyplace.com/pointsofview/berger.htm

Bodo, P. (1995) "Race: the hard road to tennis glory." *Tennis* 31 (6), October, 57–60.

Captain, G. (1991) "Enter ladies and gentlemen of color: gender, sport, and the ideal of African American manhood and womanhood during the late nineteenth and early twentieth centuries." *Journal of Sport History,* 18 (1): 81–102.

Collins, B. and Hollander, Z. (eds) (1994) *Bud Collins' Modern Encyclopedia of Tennis.* (2nd edn). Detroit, MI: Visible Ink Press.

Cose, E. (1999) "The good news about Black America." *Newsweek* 133 (23), June 7, pp. 28–40.

"Court Report." (1991) *Tennis Week,* 18 (9), November 28, pp.16–20.

Doherty, D. (1995) "Can we talk, Mr. Williams?" *Tennis,* 30 (9), January, pp. 112.

Drucker, J. (1994) "Venus rising." *Tennis Match,* 2 (4), September–October, pp. 54–57

DuPree, D. (2000a) "Emotions collide for Venus after an 'unbelievable' win." *USA Today,* September 28, p. 4E.

—— (2000b) "Warmer Venus adds doubles gold to singles." *USA Today,* September 29, p. 2F.

Enrico, D. (1997) "For Nike, Tiger Woods ads are stroke of luck." *USA Today*, September 8, p. 8B.

Evans, R. (1997) "Roving eye." *Tennis Week*, 24 (7), September 18, p. 20.

Feinstein, J. (1994) "What would Ted have said?" *Tennis*, 30 (1), May, p. 12–13.

Flink, S. (1994) "Washington's Will vs. USTA's way." *Tennis Week*, 21 (4): 8–10.

—— (1996) "Coming of age." *Tennis Week*, 22 (17): 16, 32–4.

Galenson, D.W. (1995) "Does youth rule? Trends in the ages of American women tennis players, 1960–1992." *Journal of Sport History*, 22 (1): 46–61.

Gibson, A. (1958) *I Always Wanted to Be Somebody*. New York: Harper & Row Publishers.

Hiestand, M. (1997) "Sport counts on USTA center for lift." *USA Today*, August 21, p. 11C.

Higdon, D. (1998) "Williams gets real." *Tennis*, 33 (9), January, pp. 30–1.

Higginbotham, A.L., François, A.B. and Yueh, L.Y. (1997) "The O.J. Simpson trial: *Who was improperly 'Playing the Race Card?'*" In T. Morrison and C. Brodsky Lacour (eds), *Birth of a Nation'hood*. New York: Pantheon Books.

"In the same old orbit" (1995) *Sports Illustrated*, 82(21), May 29, p. 18.

Jenkins, S. (1994) "The sorry state of tennis." *Sports Illustrated*, 80 (18), May 9, 78–86.

—— (1994) "Venus rising." *Sports Illustrated*, 81 (20), November 14, pp. 30, 32.

Kim, A. and Mravic, M. (2000) "Bill calls Venus." *Sports Illustrated*, 93 (11), September 18, p. 30.

Kirkpatrick, C. (1993) "Babies grand." *Tennis*, August, pp. 46–51.

—— (1997) "Whinespotting." *Tennis Week*, 24 (7), September 18, pp. 22–3.

Kurtz, H. (1998) *Spin Cycle – Inside the Clinton Propaganda Machine*, New York: The Free Press.

Leand, A. (1994) "Fixing the foundation. WTA rallies to reinvent itself." *Tennis Week*, 21 (9), November 24, pp. 16–17.

—— (1995) "Wish upon a star." *Tennis Week*, 22 (5), August 17, pp. 10–11, 30–1.

—— (1999) "The Williams: We are family." *Tennis Match*, 7 (5), September, pp. 44–51.

—— (2000) "Survivor: the sequel." *Tennis Week*, 27 (5), September 21, pp. 10–13.

Lipsitz, G. (1997) "The greatest story ever sold: marketing and the O.J. Simpson trial." In T. Morrison and C. Brodsky Lacour (eds), *Birth of a Nation'hood*. New York: Random House.

Lopresti, M. (1997) "Father casts pall on Williams run." *USA Today*, September 9, p. 12C.

Macci, R. (1997) "Venus's blistering backhand." *Tennis*, 33 (8), December, pp. 12–14.

McNab, A. (1995) "The world according to Richard." *Tennis*, 31 (8), December, p. 11.

Mewshaw, M. (1993) *Ladies of the Court*. New York: Crown Publishers, Inc.

"Minorities' Job Bank". Online. Available: HTTP: *http://www.minorities-jb.com/asian/dialogue/asinit.html#top*

O'Hara, J. (Executive Producer) (1995) *A Passion to Play: The African-American Experience*. New York and Los Angeles: American Broadcasting Company, April.

Pentz, L. (1997a) "Righting (writing) wrongs – Part I." *Tennis Week*, 24 (6), September 4, pp. 46–8.

—— (1997b) "Dealing the 'Race Card.' Part II of our investigation." *Tennis Week*, 24 (7), September 18, pp. 26–7, 52.

Preston, M. (1998) "Aces and faults, 1997." *Tennis*, 33 (9), January, pp. 18–23.

Price, S.L. (1997) "Venus envy." *Sports Illustrated*, 87 (11), September 15, pp. 32–7.

"Riot Results" (1997) *Online Focus,* April 28. Online. Available: HTTP: http://www.pbs.org/newshour/bb/race_relations/jan-june97/riot_4:28.html

Scott, E.L. (1997) "Vantage point." *Tennis Week,* 24 (7), September 18, p. 8.

Smith, D. (1997a) "Hingis emerges as US Open's teen queen," *USA Today,* September 8, pp. 1C–2C.

—— (1997b) "Open showing opens floodgate of media requests for Williams." *USA Today,* October 3, p. 23C.

—— (1998) "Discrimination suit planned." *USA Today,* p. 10C.

Spencer, N.E. and Cole, C.L. (1996) "Creating space for Venus: professional women's tennis and family in urban America." Paper presented at the North American Society for the Sociology of Sport, Birmingham, AL, November.

Steptoe, S. (1991) "Child's play." *Sports Illustrated,* 74 (22): 46–54.

"Venus rising at Open." (1997) *The Champaign-Urbana News-Gazette,* September 6, p. B-7.

6

POSTMODERN BLACKNESS AND THE CELEBRITY SPORTS STAR

Ian Wright, "race" and English identity

Ben Carrington

Introduction

In the first decade of the twenty-first century, Ian Wright has become one of the most visible, high profile and popular black celebrities in Britain. Wright has his own weekly national television chat show, regularly appears on television and radio shows as a celebrity guest, as well as occasionally appearing as a football pundit. His popular appeal has not been lost on advertisers – Wright has advertised everything from Nike goods to instant coffee and cooking sauces, to holiday companies and mobile phones. He has also supported many "good causes" and charities gaining him a celebrity status outside of the sports world matched only by fellow footballer David Beckham, whose high media profile arguably has as much to do with his celebrity marriage to pop singer "Posh Spice" as his own star characteristics. Wright's status is such that he had his portrait exhibited in the National Portrait Gallery and was awarded an MBE by the Labour government in the New Years Honours list of 2000. This process of national canonization was complete when Wright appeared on the BBC's *This Is Your Life* to receive "the Red Book" from Michael Aspel. Given this we could be forgiven for forgetting that up until the mid-1980s Wright was an unskilled labourer from south London, playing local league football, with few prospects, no formal education and a criminal record.

This chapter examines this transformation and explores some of the reasons why Ian Wright has achieved the level of acceptance he has, at a time when British society is still struggling to come to terms with its multicultural reality. It has been on the sports field, and more often the football field – where, as Hall notes, "the nation's myths and meanings are fabricated" (1998, p. 43) – where the most significant reconfiguration of Britain's racialized imaginings have taken place. By exploring what we might term "a genealogy of Wright", and by contrasting him to John Barnes' mediated persona, arguably a more successful and talented but less "popular" black footballing celebrity, the chapter traces the delimitations of "race" and nation within British society. The chapter also develops an argument concerning the articulation of "postmodern blackness". It is suggested that within contemporary media culture the meanings inherent

102

within black culture have been divorced from any political connotations. That is, commercial practices within late capitalism have increasingly emptied out the potentially radical elements of black vernacular culture and appropriated these solely in terms of the stylized elements of "cool" that blackness is supposed to connote. I argue that the case study of Ian Wright provides a useful way of mapping these changes as he is perhaps the most visible postmodern black cultural icon in Britain today, and embodies some of the contradictions around the decidedly tentative formation of what we might term a specifically post-colonial black English ethnicity.

The makings of bad bwoy Wright

> I can't say that if it wasn't for football, then I would be doing a prison sentence now, because I pray that wouldn't be the case, but the life I was leading was doing me no favours at all. Driving round south London in cars with no tax, insurance or MOT, flitting in and out of jobs, doing community service: it doesn't take a genius to work out that I wasn't exactly heading anywhere.
>
> (Ian Wright)

Ian Wright was born in Woolwich, south London, in 1963. In a striking parallel with other black sports stars such as Linford Christie and Frank Bruno, Wright was brought up in a strongly matriarchal family environment – "it was my mum who was the driving force behind our family" (1997, p. 34; all following quotes by Wright are taken from his autobiography *Mr. Wright*, unless otherwise cited). Wright's father left his mother and three brothers when he was 4 years old, though he only mentions this in passing in his autobiography and claims he did not miss him. Wright's early life was financially difficult, moving home often, and growing up in various parts of south London's less salubrious suburbs [1].

Wright tells us in his autobiography that he soon began to be seen by teachers as a "troublesome youth" and was put into a special class for disruptive boys. His "street attitude" (1997, p. 38), as he puts it, was perceived by his teachers as a threat to the school's authority and his actions (swearing, smoking in the toilets, playing truant) were met by strict measures – he was frequently caned by the headmaster. Wright argues that school sport functioned as a mechanism which helped to save him from the worse excesses of his behaviour: "football was the one thing that was keeping me in school. If I hadn't had that, then I would have been out of there, big time, and on the street" (ibid., p. 39). Football being cast as the only disciplinary mechanism capable of containing and directing the excesses of Wright's anti-social black masculinity. Given the limited opportunities available to him, Wright invested much of his energies into football as this was the one arena where his social standing and status among his working-class male peers, and to a degree from his teachers, could be assured: "In between fights, suspensions and cannings, I was at least managing to make a name for myself in sport" (ibid., p. 41).

Despite being a promising player he was overlooked by many professional clubs, meaning, initially at least, football failed to offer the young Wright a way out of the "ghetto life" he appeared to be heading for – professional clubs did not think he had the discipline required to "make it". Although in his autobiography Wright fails to explicitly mention the racialized nature of his relationships to the white authority figures he encountered, it is interesting to note how the demeanor of a young, working-class, black male in the late 1970s would have been perceived. The necessity to act in a particular way – to fit in – has often been a key mechanism of control over black youth, requiring them to conform to certain narrowly proscribed ways of acting, talking and behaving – what we might call a form of white govermentality (see Hesse, 1997). Those who do not conform to such mechanisms of surveillance and control are seen to be "disruptive" and often formally excluded from the very social institutions which are supposed to be supporting them – the high rates of expulsion from school for black children deemed beyond the boundaries of the disciplinary logic of the educational state apparatus being one example of this. As Wright notes, "I don't think my face really fitted on the professional scene at that time – I had a look, and the way I talked and acted must have put some of them off, without a doubt" (1997, p. 42). Therefore, unlike most professional footballers, Wright did not follow the traditional route of a football apprenticeship as a precursor to a professional career. [2]

Wright eventually left school at 16 with no educational qualifications, moving from one manual job to another (plastering, building work) engaging in small-time crime, which eventually led to a short custodial sentence in Chelmsford Prison for theft. During this time he also had a number of relationships with the result that he has four sons and a daughter from three different women which has meant that, like his father, he has not had the opportunity to see all his children grow up, something which appears to have been a great regret in his life.

Despite the lack of interest from professional clubs, Wright continued to play football for various sides including a local south London black football team (his autobiography is dedicated to players from this club) before joining a semi-professional team where he was spotted by a Crystal Palace scout. He soon helped Palace get promoted to the top division, established himself as one of the country's leading goal scorers, before moving onto Arsenal where his public profile both on and off the pitch soared. He remains Arsenal's highest ever goal scorer. Yet what is most interesting in this "rags to riches" tale, is the extent to which Wright – whether playing for Crystal Palace, Arsenal, or even England – has been accepted in a way that few black athletes have while maintaining elements of black expressive behaviour that have traditionally meant exclusion from the racialized national imaginary. I would argue that Wright has been able to make this transition from "outsider" to the English imaginary to "insider", largely due to his perceived class location as "one of us" – that is, his class positioning and urban vernacular have usurped any doubts over Wright's racial status so long as he is seen to embrace more populist notions of contemporary English identity, tied as they are to narrow constructions of appropriate masculine performance.

Wright, perhaps more than any other modern black footballer, has strived to be seen as a true, honest, patriotic and committed Englishman almost as if to pre-empt questions over his national allegiance. It is this construction of a guy, "just like us", demonstrating a form of localized patriotism, that confirms Wright's integrity within the masculinist boundaries of English nationhood. As he says at the end of his autobiography:

> I want people to value my opinion and realise that I am always talking from the heart ... This book has been a way of doing that, and all I want is for people to read it and realise that I try to be 100 per cent honest in everything that I've ever done, in football as well as life. I'm no saint, just an ordinary guy who has been privileged to play football for a living.
>
> (1997, p. 224)

From part-time plasterer to prime-time presenter

> I like people I'm interviewing to be themselves. In fact, I'd love to be a guest on my own show.
>
> (Ian Wright)

In an age where footballers have transcended the ladder from local heroes to global media stars, the sense of organic connection and solidarity between players, clubs and fans has clearly been stretched. Wright's ability to convey a sense of "authenticity" and emotional integrity is key to his enduring appeal in an increasingly sanitized and manufactured media culture. After Wright's emotional and tearful appearance on *This Is Your Life* many people commented on how the show had moved them in way unfamiliar to most – even for those who had little knowledge of football or Wright. It was clear that part of the attraction for many white viewers was the voyeuristic gaze into the lifeworld of black expressive behaviour – Wright tearfully embraced his friends such as the singer Maxi Priest, and his fellow football friend Paul Ince – that the programme allowed. *The Observer*'s television critic confessed:

> for the record, this critic cried because during last week's *This Is Your Life* – yes, *that* silly old time-warped, crushingly banal charade, a TV retirement home for old golfers and last-gasp comedians – you got the sense that these people really cared for Wright and that he

was an awful nice guy. And while there was a complete lack of fashionable metropolitan cynicism about the proceedings, there was no
icky sentimentality either – just a big, warm celebration featuring an
awful lot of very un-white, un-middle-class touchy-feeliness.
Suddenly, in living colour, England looked like another country, and
it was good.

(Flett, 2000, p. 16)

This sense of emotive communication is partly achieved as we know that
Wright was "lucky to make it" as a professional footballer and often appears to
still be "in touch" with where he came from, despite his huge personal wealth.
Wright himself is keen to maintain this sense of "connectedness", which has
been important to his popular success, despite his entry into the world of
celebrities. His television chat show, which has included guests such as Elton
John, Will Smith and Denzel Washington, is noticeable for the way in which
the interviews are not "staged" for the camera and appear to show two people
just having a chat in a night-club. The set also involves top London DJs (as
opposed to the traditional "live band") spinning the latest garage and house
tunes in between segments, and who engage in subaltern banter with Wright,
while people dressed as if they are on their way out for a night clubbing,
respond to Wright's call and response-type dialogue. The show, which many
people thought would flop, has been a surprise success. As one journalist
observed:

Initially, a lot of folk scoffed at the idea. True, it was probably the first
chat show to have a host who rarely uttered a complete sentence, but it
proved a winning formula nonetheless. Wright looked relaxed,
disarmed his guests with his raw charm, and wore fetching leather
trousers. The two pilot shows attracted six million viewers – 60 per
cent of them women.

(Lindsey, 1999, p. 7)

Clearly, this "informal style" is itself specifically created by the show's producers
who realized that to package Wright as a professional interviewer would be to
lose his appeal and "natural" spontaneity. The interesting point here is that it
works. How many other national chat show presenters have a shaven head, a
silver-studded earring and a gold tooth? As Lindsey noted, "People love him
because he plays to the gallery just by being full of himself, a fact not lost on
advertisers who've rushed to sign him up" (ibid., p. 7). Wright has managed to
construct an image of black coolness that is capable of appealing to a growing
and knowledgeable consumer-driven youth market, floating between the
increasingly blurred spheres of Premiership football fandom and pop world
celebrity stardom.

106

"Race", nationalism and identity

Playing for England means everything to me.

(Ian Wright)

When, in 1998, the BBC celebrated fifty years of African-Caribbean migration to Britain in the Windrush series, it was the image of Ian Wright (as well as Linford Christie draped in the Union Flag) that was used to epitomize "black Britons' progress in Britain". Unlike other black sports stars, such as Frank Bruno, Wright's entry into the national lexicon of sports heroes has not led to his blackness being questioned by black Britons. This presents an interesting paradox which deserves further exploration as it problematizes simplistic accounts of the exclusivist logic of contemporary cultural racisms.

By the end of his truncated international career, Wright was seen as a footballing hero, particularly after his part in England's 1997 draw against Italy, which secured England's passage to the following year's World Cup Finals in France. Wright was pictured on television screens and in the tabloid press tearfully embracing the then manager Glenn Hoddle, invoking memories of the "Gazza tears" of Italia 1990, which helped to mythologize Paul Gascoigne into the collective national memory. *The Mirror*'s back page carried a colour photograph of a tearful Ian Wright hugging Gascoigne, with the title "The Crying Game: Paul Gascoigne and Ian Wright get emotional after England's epic 0–0 draw in Rome". In a rare image of black domesticity being allowed to frame the narration of Englishness, the front page leader showed a jubilant "England Hero Ian Wright" and his young son Stacey in a full-page colour photograph, under the banner "We'll Conquer the World, Son' (*The Mirror*, Monday, 13 October 1997). Inside Wright revealed:

> It doesn't matter how much of a superstar you are at your club, we are all just part of a team once there are three lions on your shirt ... I'm not ashamed to admit I shed a few tears at the end – but it was an emotional finish to a massive week for English football ... It was one of the greatest moments in my life and certainly my proudest moment in football.
>
> (Walters, 1997, pp. 32–3)

Crying for your country, especially in the circumscribed arena of competitive male team sports, is one of the few socially sanctioned public spaces for the expression of such emotions for men and a powerful way in which you can signify to audiences your unequivocal commitment to "the nation". As one sports journalist recalled:

After England's memorable 0–0 draw in Rome during the autumn of 1997, which sealed qualification for France 98, Wright received the loudest cheer from the section of the crowd I was sitting in, which was full of supporters from many different English clubs. Even when he is on the bench for England, he is the player most often seen leaping out of the dugout to shout encouragement. Fans warm to someone who so clearly wears his heart on his sleeve and cares about the team as much as they do.

(Rampton, 1999, p. 26)

Yet, as with many high profile black athletes who have represented their country in international contests, Wright has still received extensive racial abuse for his troubles, something which appears to have become an almost accepted rite of passage for black athletes in breaking the mono-cultural parameters of British sport – Cyril Regis, one of the first black footballers to represent England, received a bullet in the post with his name on it before his England debut (cited in Back *et al.*, 2001). It is clear that for many black British athletes this paradox of being called upon to represent your country, and simultaneously persecuted for this, strikes deep into the sense of self-identity for those forced to endure this complex and difficult positioning of yearning for identification, yet being denied recognition. For Wright this sense of dislocation was all the more acute as his first England game took place at Millwall's ground in south London, close to where he had lived and whose team he actually supported as a young-ster. Wright painfully recalls:

The first time I pulled on an England shirt should have been one of the proudest days of my life. Instead it was spoilt for me in a terrible way by racism. The great memories I have of that night are overshad-owed by the fact that I was targeted for abuse just because I was black, and the most sickening thing for me was that it happened virtually in my own back yard at Millwall.

(1997, p. 104)

For Wright the thought that racism might be intimately related with nation-alism often seems to be a connection he cannot make. His unproblematic embrace of a particular tabloid-style populist English identity leaves him unable to critique English nationalism itself. As he notes about the above incident, "I can generally handle racial abuse, but this time it hit me hard" (ibid., p. 105). One of the problems with Wright is his inability to fully understand the articula-tions of racism and the problems with dominant versions of contemporary English nationalism, to which he subscribes, which still call into question the position and commitment of black people who are not willing to cry for their country at every given opportunity.

Across the class lines

> I love Ian Wright's chat show; that format suits Wrighty's bubbly
> character. It wouldn't do for me, although people would accept it,
> I'm sure, because I'm black, I can dance, I've got rhythm and I
> can talk like a real Jamaican. But I have had enough stereotyping.
> (John Barnes)

A striking comparison with Wright's thoughts on "race" and nationalism can be
made with John Barnes, arguably the most gifted and talented black footballer
Britain has ever seen. The differences between them, and their differing public
receptions, reveal something of the complex ways in which the configurations of
"race" and nation, mediated via the modalities of class and gender, still powerfully operate to position and exclude black Britons in particular ways. In
contrast to Wright's urban and working-class upbringing in south London,
Barnes was born to a relatively prosperous and middle-class family in Jamaica
(he spent most of his life living in army barracks where his father was an officer
and seems to have had little engagement with Jamaican life outside of this shel-
tered environment). Moving to England, aged 11, and after being spotted
playing football by a local club just north of London, Watford, he became a
professional footballer. Barnes eventually moved to a very successful Liverpool
side in the mid-1980s where his skills earned him player of the year three times
and over seventy England caps. Barnes also became the first black coach of a
professional football club in Scotland when he joined Celtic in 1999 and interestingly actually signed Wright, though he was sacked within a year and Wright
left the following month. Yet despite Barnes' undoubted brilliance, he was
never truly accepted by the British sporting public and given the same degree of
national sporting praise as Wright – despite his footballing ability and being the
most capped black player in English football history, he was not considered
worthy, unlike Wright, of inclusion in the National Portrait Gallery's celebration of over 200 British Sporting Heroes (see Huntington-Whiteley, 1998).[3]

A clear example of the divergence between Wright and Barnes could be seen
during the World Cup held in France in 1998. Barnes, while commentating on
the Jamaica versus Croatia game, waved a Jamaican flag in the television
studios. His co-commentator noted "We traveled in on the mini bus with John
Barnes and the Jamaican fans were greeting him like royalty" (quoted in Back *et
al.*, 2001). The irony of this profound moment of national and racial reconfiguration would not have been lost on Barnes. Namely, that the supporters of
England, for whom he had played all his international career had only ever
jeered his efforts, while black Britons had often perceived Barnes with a degree
of suspicion, yet here he was now transformed into a Jamaican national hero for
a country he had not lived in since a child or even played for, and by the very
same black Britons – now supporting Jamaica – with whom he had felt such a
sense of dislocation. Ian Wright by contrast, when not in the TV studios, was in

the stands draped in the St. George's Cross flag alongside the England fans, and when they played Argentina actually engaging in "banter" with the South American supporters. Yet this "coming out" of the national closet in articulating Barnes' Jamaican identity is a very recent development, and something that remained hidden throughout his playing career. This transformation is in many ways a remarkable shift which undoubtedly has wider political significance in how discourses of "race" and nation, within the context of sport, are perceived.

Despite his, apparent, more political persona, Wright's autobiography is generally a predictable, uninteresting account of his life as a pro with, as I argue later, highly questionable accounts of what constitutes racism, whereas Barnes metamorphosizes from his politically conservative past – he was a supporter of the Conservative Party during Thatcher's reign – to reveal a much more analytical and insightful awareness of the complexities of "race" and nation.[4] In his autobiography Barnes publicly reveals the pressures that have affected him in trying to resolve the double consciousness, as W.E.B. Du Bois termed it, for those blacks in the New World who have had to wrestle with the often conflicting pressures of racial and national identities and identifications. For a high profile public figure, and a black figure in particular, his critique of the dominant ethnic absolutist version of English nationalism is quite exceptional:

> I am fortunate my England career is now complete so I don't have to sound patriotic any more. Nationalism causes so many problems. I hate it ... I loathe the fact that the England team embody and foster nationalism .... Extreme nationalism provokes a non-acceptance of people because they come from somewhere else ... Life is hard enough without being restrained by boundaries or rejected simply for being born in a different country. Nationalism is such a curse on the world. It causes so many wars, so many problems. Boundaries and greed for land have caused the slaughter of countless millions. None of my England team-mates ever questioned patriotism as I did ... Nationalism is an evil part of English society.
>
> (Barnes, 1999, pp. 69–71)

Barnes is not likely to get the England manager's job. Part of the reason for Barnes' understandable angst is that for most of his career he quietly and stoically accepted the abuse he received, and played the part of the unassuming black public figure, yet was still never fully accepted as an English hero. Barnes recounts an incident when a small number of far right nationalists were, amazingly, allowed onto an England flight in the mid-1980s and subjected Barnes (as well as Viv Anderson and Mark Chamberlain) to non-stop vitriolic racial abuse, which none of the players, including his white colleagues, did anything about. But as Barnes sardonically notes, "I suppose it might have been different if Ian Wright had been on the plane" (1999, p. 69). It is not surprising that

Barnes identifies more with Martin Luther King's "intelligent approach" (1999, p. 108) to challenging racism compared to Malcolm X's "militant stance" (ibid.). Barnes' Conservative politics during the 1980s and 1990s, very much similar to that of Frank Bruno, should have enabled his national inclusion, yet his middle-class demeanour and his "strange" accent (neither black working-class nor white middle-class) meant the majority of working-class fans, black and white, questioned his status, while his scepticism towards forms of overt nationalism meant that he could not be accepted by the dominant conservative culture either. As Barnes himself concedes:

> My philosophy is to treat racists with the contempt they deserve, to ignore them or laugh about the situation. Neither of these approaches endear me to the black community, who still call me an Uncle Tom. "John, you hide behind a joke too easily," they chide me. But pandering to the black community by lashing out or labelling opponents racists is simply not me. Revenge does not feature in my psyche, even if an opponent racially taunted me. The black community loves how Ian Wright reacts, the way he flings out a fist or mouths off. That's fine for Ian Wright but not for me. I'm different.
>
> (Barnes, 1999, p. 94)

Barnes, then, presents an interesting counter-example to Wright – indeed, throughout Barnes' autobiography he explicitly compares, but more often contrasts, himself to Wright.[5] Right-wing commentators, and sports journalists in particular, have often used Barnes as an "example" to show other black players how to properly deal with (that means ignore) racism. For example in the aftermath of, the then Manchester United goalkeeper, Peter Schmeichel's alleged racist abuse of Wright during the 1996–97 season – for which Schmeichel was not penalized – the *Daily Mail*'s Jeff Powell wrote:

> Wright, as a role model for every black youngster in the country, seems oblivious to the damage his inflammatory conduct inflicts on his own community. The rational majority of black footballers deal with the racist taunts in a self-controlled manner which dignifies them, shames their would-be tormentors and plays a part in the healing process. This is easy for a white man to say, I hear Wright and his activists cry. So permit brief mention of just one incident. When John Barnes, whose behaviour in this regard is exemplary, came under physical threat on an airport bus from fascist yobs following England on tour of South America, it was two or three of we newspapermen who rallied to his protection. We would do the same again if Wright were the victim.
>
> (Powell, 1997, p. 77)

Though this is a clever piece of rhetoric, distinguishing the "good" and "rational" blacks from those "activists" foolish enough to "follow" the troublesome Wright, thereby shifting attention away from the racist perpetrators to the actions of those victimized, the suggestion that the victims of racism in Britain should rely on the heroic interventions of white *Daily Mail* journalists is a thought too worrying, if not ridiculous, to contemplate – indeed, according to Barnes' account of the same episode few people did anything to stop the abuse.[6] Barnes is someone, who, by his own admission, is aware that he is perceived as an "Uncle Tom" figure – the black personality ready to accede to white demands about the limits to black expressive behaviour, to not appear "too black". In a similar way to Bruno, Barnes often talks about "the black community" in the third person, as though it is something which he is not a part of. In a limited sense this is true of course as he was someone who migrated to England late in life, grew up in predominantly white, middle-class surroundings before entering the hermetically sealed and artificial social world that is professional football, while living a lifestyle far removed from most black Britons. Thus unlike Wright, Barnes finds the self-descriptor Black English or even Black British problematic.

Yet despite his conservative convictions, Barnes is also capable, at times, of a much more nuanced understanding of racism and its pervasiveness than Wright. He talks with emotion and force about the "reality of being a black person in a white country" (1999, p. 101) in a way which the more "political" Wright glosses over. Barnes discusses at length in his autobiography racism's "everyday existence in a white country" (ibid., p. 102), and questions the desire to see black sporting stars as role models, given the paucity of black public figures in other spheres.[7] Barnes also discusses the ways in which film representations distort our understandings of "race" and the ways in which models of beauty are based on implicit and unacknowledged white norms. In criticizing a tabloid poll of the most beautiful people who were universally white, Barnes notes:

> Such embodiments of whiteness represent what the *Mirror* thinks its readers want to look like. But what about the billion Chinese? Or hundreds of millions of blacks? Or Indians? It's so narrow-minded and stereotypical. What does black stand for? Darkness. The contrast is white, Snow White. It's such rubbish.
>
> (ibid., pp. 101–2)

It's almost inconceivable to imagine Wright talking about "embodiments of whiteness" and racialized representation in this, or any other, context.[8]

Barnes also talks of his frustration when he addressed the Oxford Union where he wanted to discuss wider social issues but was only asked about his sporting feats: "I was astounded. I struggled to contain my frustration and irritation as the questions continued in a similar [sporting] vein. I wanted to discuss meatier subjects than football. I do have views beyond sport. It was so depressing" (1999, p. 103). It is clear that Barnes is struggling to come to terms with his own racial and professional identities and the limits society places on both – he is known because he was "that famous black footballer", yet clearly wants to not be constrained by the very identity for which he is known. The paradox, which Barnes seems unwilling to confront, is that it is the very same forms of Conservative ideology – that he himself supported – that allowed a black presence within the British imaginary so long as it stayed within the confines of the culture industries, that prevents black sporting figures from breaking free from the "bantustan of sport" as Sivanandan (1982) has termed it and into the wider socio-political world.

Postmodern blackness and the end of radical politics

> I want to be recognised as someone who never sold out; as someone who made black people proud and was fearless in the same way Malcolm X was.
>
> (Ian Wright)

Ian Wright is one of the few leading black sporting figures willing to talk openly about racial politics in Britain. Wright has argued for the need to locate racism historically and to draw upon the legacy and insights gained from Bob Marley, Martin Luther King and Malcolm X, even going as far as to question King's passive protest style. It is at such moments that Wright appears to fulfil a long-awaited need within British society for a politically-aware black athlete who can use their position and location within the popular cultural field not just for personal financial gain but as a site of intervention, and to draw attention to the continuing prevalence of social inequalities around "race". Indeed, you could be mistaken for believing that Wright believes that a more militant form of black politics is not only viable but necessary. In a direct criticism of King's "pacifism", Wright asserts:

> It's all very well drinking from the cup of peace, but when that cup is being used to smash your head in, why should you turn the other cheek? Malcolm X said we should combat racism by any means neces-sary. That doesn't mean rushing out and shooting the first white guy that comes along, but it does mean using some force.
>
> (1997, p. 109)

I can think of no other mainstream black public figure, sporting or otherwise, who would even venture to talk about the possibilities for more radical and direct forms of political struggle against racism. In 1996, in an interview with the black newspaper *The New Nation*, Wright suggested that a future career in politics was a possible option:

I would not like to be the pen-pushing, stuck-in-an-office-or-umpteen-boring-meetings type of politician, so I guess I am more your community leader type or spokesperson type. I am not saying I want to be the new Malcolm X, but I would like to be the Ian Wright that people will listen to and be inspired by. My priority is to see the black community start caring about itself, unify and stand proud.

(Emmanus, 1996, p. 17)

Yet, on closer inspection, Wright's "leadership" appears unconvincing, and lacking in any understanding of the complexities of racism and social disadvantage. Wright appears to be an outspoken rebel, prepared to embrace genuinely oppositional politics, but only ever does so at the level of rhetoric. He speaks out against racism, but normally only within the sports arena, and rarely extends this critique to forms of racially exclusive nationalism. He is not willing for his black identity to be marginalized for his acceptance, but often fails to transcend the very same racial stereotypes he wants to avoid. At times Wright appears to embrace a radical conceptualization of anti-racist praxis, at other times he promotes a neo-conservative dismissal of anti-racism. He is at one and the same time radical and de-politicized, outspoken but with no agenda, a threat to mono-cultural nationalism, but an uncritical endorser of populist nationalism. These contradictions are nowhere as apparent as when Wright discusses the causes of racism in more depth. When Wright has explained, more precisely, his views he actually ends up endorsing a theory of racism that the political right has fostered for many years. Wright states:

People tell me I'm a role model for the black community and I'm proud to be seen as that. But sometimes I wish the black community would have a bit of pride in itself and see that there are greater things it can achieve. Slavery may have been abolished but a lot of black people are still living in mental slavery. It doesn't matter how high a black lawyer, doctor or even sportsman has gone in his profession, if he's the only black face in a room, he still feels like the little jumped-on nigger. You can't blame white people for that all the time because there are just as many bad black people as there are white; it's a case of self-pride and self-worth. We have to break free of those bonds. As Bob Marley put it, we have to emancipate ourselves.

(1997, p. 108)

Wright thus manages to misread the critique expressed by black intellectuals from Fanon to Marley about the effects on black subject formation of white racism as a personal and psychological fault of black people themselves, for whom racism is largely a mental construction of *perceived*, not real, racial discrimination. Wright, also rails against the Commission for Racial Equalities' long-standing, if overdue, campaign to "Kick Racism Out of Football". Wright dismisses the efforts of the CRE and others, and defends his limited support, on the basis that the campaign did not end racism. "How on earth is a trendy campaign going to stop such ingrained hatred? I don't pretend to know the answer, but putting posters up and waving banners around isn't going to do the trick" (1997, p. 110). This rather reactionary, unfair and caricatured dismissal of the CRE's campaign misses the point. There are, indeed, problems with liberal campaigns that *only* define racism in narrow ways, and no doubt many clubs did "support" the campaign if only to be seen to be doing something. One of the key concerns of many commentators was the way the CRE, at least earlier in the campaign, focused exclusively on understanding racism as overt racial abuse from "hooligans", thus leaving elements of more banal forms of racism in "normal" fan culture unexamined and totally failing to address issues of institutional racism found in the manager's offices, the boardrooms and press boxes. But Wright's response, which paradoxically mirrored those conservative elements within the game who questioned the need for *any* anti-racist campaign as football, according to them, did not have a problem with racism, only serves to undermine anti-racist politics. Wright's response would appear to be to do nothing as he has no alternatives. While requiring clubs to take moral, if not legal, responsibility for the actions of their staff and supporters, to ensure they have racial equality policies that are put into place, and to make clubs aware of the effects of their presence on local communities is not in and of itself sufficient to eradicate certain forms of racism, it is none the less a necessary first step.

Thus the rhetorical positioning of Wright *vis à vis* racism often lacks substance and understanding when he moves beyond the rhetoric of radicalism.[9] It is "the apparently limitless post-modern plasticity of Malcolm" (Gilroy, 1993, p. 13) that allows Wright to appropriate Malcolm X's legacy. It is a decontextualized and depoliticized Malcolm that Wright invokes, meaning that Malcolm X comes to stand for no more than a signifier of progressive black politics giving the user the appearance of being "radical" even if no oppositional politics is actually articulated.

Commodity blackness

In the late 1990s the Mercury mobile phone company used a series of high profile British stars to promote their new "one to one" mobile phone service. The adverts digitally remastered film clips of previous historic figures so that the contemporary stars could have a "one to one" phone conversation with their chosen hero. Given his popular positioning, Wright seemed the perfect choice (other stars such as model Kate Moss and comedian Vic Reeves were also used) – Wright being able to appeal across boundaries of "race" and class to give marketers access to the prized high spending youth market. His choice of hero was revealing. Wright was transposed to 1960s' America so as to talk to Martin Luther King and asks, "If I could have a one to one with him I would ask how he maintained his principle of peaceful protest in the face of such provocation." The ad then skilfully weaved parts of King's "I Have a Dream" speech, with images of white racists attacking black civil rights protesters, and black and white shots of Ian Wright looking determinedly off camera.

In many ways this illustrates well the notion of postmodern blackness that Wright signifies. At one level Wright is clearly attempting to link black politics from the past to the present. We might ask, however, why it was that Wright chose Martin Luther King, and not Malcolm X, with whom he wanted to have his "one to one" – even this advertising slogan perhaps inadvertently shows the shrinking of the space for *collective* political *action* to the *individual* who merely *talks*. It was claimed that Wright had asked for Malcolm X but the advertising agency could not find enough montage news reel clips of Malcolm X, and suggested King instead to which Wright agreed. A more likely scenario given that there are clearly many such clips of Malcolm X available, was the nervousness on the part of a corporate company who only wanted the *appearance* of the cool black radical and not the real thing. Thus Wright's acquiescence to the demands of the advertising and corporate world to "tone down" his beliefs, so as to choose the more acceptable King over Malcolm, demonstrates the actual politics Wright is willing to adopt.

As Marqusee points out, the "inflation of wages, prize-money and endorsements may have liberated sports stars from their serf-like status of the past, but it has also made them more dependent on and integrated with corporate power, and intensified the pressures for conformity" (1999, p. 298; see also Marqusee, 2000). The effect is that the demands of the Civil Rights movement of the 1960s – which both Malcolm X and Martin Luther King, in their final days, linked to wider Pan-African struggles against forms of *economic* and well as racial injustice – get emptied out of their serious socio-economic critique of global capitalism and colonial racism and effectively repackaged in order to help sell mobile phones to the affluent of the overdeveloped West, King's politics being reduced to no more than a set of historical stylized images lacking any serious political content or contemporary relevance. Wright, in effect, has sought to commodify his blackness, and elements of black radicalism with it, which can now be bought and sold within the media culture whenever elements of urban, streetwise "cool" need to be invoked, while disavowing any genuine political resistance, let alone praxis. Such postmodern politics is a form of "manufactured discontent" that offers the *appearance* of opposition, but in a commodified, and therefore easily assimilated, and controllable form. As Angela Y. Davis has warned, the symbiotic embrace of corporate culture and black popular signifiers risks negating the potentially revolutionary aspects of black vernacular cultures: "Where cultural representations do not reach out beyond themselves, there is the danger that they will function as surrogates for activism, that they will constitute both the beginning and end of political practice" (1992, p. 324).

Some may argue that it is unfair to judge Wright by the standards of black radical leaders from a different epoch who were clearly prepared to sacrifice personal gain for the benefit of their communities in the pursuit of social change and justice. Yet it is Wright *himself* who has asked to be considered in the same light through his public declarations of black politics. The oft-heard refrain that politics and sport should remain separate, thereby excusing the apolitical stances of many contemporary sports stars, black and white, misunderstands the inherently politicized nature of sports as a cultural arena whereby dominant ideologies of "race", gender, class and nation are displayed, and therefore reinforced – or challenged. The examples of Tommie Smith and John Carlos, and the earlier Muhammad Ali, through to Viv Richards testify to a mode of engagement that *is* possible, should individuals be willing to do so.[10] As Hartmann has observed, "Popular cultural institutions such as sport are not only sites in and through which racial formations are constructed and reproduced but also sites where racialized structures can be acted on, utilized, or even struggled against" (2000, p. 246). At a time when black Britons are still having to make the argument for an unequivocal right to be part of a nation which we ourselves have helped to build and fashion, the failure of black athletes – who have come whether they like it or not, to represent the imagined community of millions – to speak out is itself a political decision *not to do so*. In this context Wright can be seen as exemplifying wider socio-historical changes within black politics in Britain, highlighting the increasing individualization of collectivist politics; that is the shift of collectivist politics of the 1960s and 1970s to an articulation of more individualized forms of politics centred around the self and personal mobility.

Conclusion

If (post)modernist subjectivity can be defined as a reflexive and continuous process of "becoming", and the self-accumulation of wealth, knowledge and experience, then Wright's ability to continually re-invent his identity by transforming himself into a commodity spectacle would appear to be a perfect example of such a capacity for personal development. Yet he has done so across and between the different cultural spheres of the sports and media/celebrity worlds, and, in a somewhat paradoxical twist, achieved his greatest fame as his actual sporting ability has decreased. His subsequent movement "downwards" in footballing terms from Arsenal to West Ham, Nottingham Forest and Celtic, before playing Second Division football with Burnley, coincided with his meteoric climb *up* the celebrity ladder. Wright the cool black signifier has been more appealing to the media culture world despite the declining sporting referent of the actual Wright.

Indeed, in relation to the discourses of racial and national identity, we should not underestimate some of the shifts Wright can be seen as having expressed. His "heroic" performances for England and his particular style have enabled him to become a national hero in a way that few black athletes have been able to achieve, while retaining, however problematically, a sense of black identity.

Wright has come to personify a form of street-wise urban black cool – representative of a new black English sensibility that has offered a powerful counter to contemporary British mono-cultural racisms, in a political context where, increasingly, black sporting bodies have been the metonymic site through which the country's identity crises have been played out.

We might suggest, then, the mediated persona of Wright marks a shift from blackness being incorporated into a prescriptive version of *Britishness* that required a disavowal of our black identities and outer-national identifications (encapsulated by Frank Bruno), to the formation of a *black British* identity that more confidently expressed a sense of racial subjectivity *and* a sense of Britishness but on a conditional submission to an uncritical national allegiance (Linford Christie perhaps being the clearest example of this) to a newly emergent, though still tentative, sense of *black Englishness* at a time of imminent crisis for the very concept of Britishness (of which Wright would be a clear example). This is a form of blackness that is more secure in its performance and position, such that it no longer requires nor asks for "majority" affirmation for its legitimation. Such articulations are all the more urgent at a time when right-wing commentators such as Simon Heffer, Peter Hitchens and Roger Scruton still yearn for the magical return to the days of an old England, with its class-inflected, hierarchical and patriarchal sterile projections of the "sceptred isles", within which Britain's black population is still schematically viewed as an "alien" presence. Such imperialist fantasies of a return to colonial, and even *pre*-colonial, times can only function in our modern political landscape to legitimate the practices of the Far Right. It would be a mistake then to underplay the significance – whether conscious or otherwise – that black athletes have played, and continue to play, in undercutting the effectivity of such nationalist imaginings.

Nevertheless, the costs for this inclusion may be too high if it means that we are unable to engage with (re)defining what constitutes the borders of such an identity beyond its more populist nationalist appeals. An expansive and inherently protean sense of black Englishness that could include the positionings adopted by Wright *and* Barnes, and even Bruno, is one to be preferred to a situation where only those willing to cry for their country can be accepted. However, it is questionable whether the twenty-first century will produce sports stars capable of articulating what such a model will look like in the context of the logic of capitalism emptying out both the possibilities of sport as a transformative sphere, and of black culture as a site of resistance. Indeed, it may even be that sport's potential radical role in cultural politics will simply serve to distort and disguise wider social inequalities. As Marqusee has observed on the American condition:

> the high-profile affluence of a small number of black sports stars has now turned sports into a distorting mirror and in some ways an outright lie about a society in which, for example, white Americans enjoy a six-year advantage in life expectancy over blacks. Sports, which

did so much to force whites to acknowledge the black presence in America, now contribute to the invisibility of both the real hardships suffered in black communities and the persistence of racism.

(1999, pp. 295–6)

Unless black, and indeed white, athletes attempt to redefine the future possibilities of sports culture in the twenty-first century, Britain will follow a similar path. The possibilities of rejoining a radical and empowering form of contestation, with a critical reconceptualization of the public sphere, are opened up with the pivotal role of black cultural producers including black athletes. Whether black athletes will have the courage to carry out this role given the intensification of commodity saturation of black popular culture remains to be seen.

Notes

1 Glanvill's biography provides a detailed excavation of the charged atmosphere of racial attacks and police harassment that black communities faced in London during the 1970s and early 1980s where Wright grew up, though at times Glanvill's narrative slides into a questionable anthropological determinism in understanding Wright:

> Those who didn't live through the seventies might find it hard to appreciate what things were like at the time Ian was growing up. Racially-motivated attacks were common in Lewisham; it was not unusual for whites to scream "Immigrant!" at black passers-by; graffiti everywhere related the ritual battle: "Black power!", "NF", "Repatriate now". In a society where possibilities were already restricted in the fields of employment and housing, black people's lives were qualitatively worsened by the indifference and active antipathy of the indigenous people. Those who look for a clue to Ian's fiery temper as a player could do worse than examine the background to his developing years, his first years outside the protection of school, for clues.
>
> (1996, p. 70)

2 This fact has subsequently been used to frame Wright within a racialized discourse of the volatile and temperamental "rough diamond"; that is a (black) player with "natural" talent, but who lacks the discipline, "control" and cognitive skills of his professionally trained (white) peers. George Graham, one of Wright's former managers, remarked "I don't think Ian can play in control. He's intuitive and instinctive. If you make him think, the intuition is lost" (quoted in Glanvill, 1996, p. 127). Wright's dangerous "unpredictability" is summarized by Glanvill (ibid., p. 3) when he notes that Wright has

> suffered the worst slings and arrows of outrageous press coverage. He is a "Wright Nutter" and "Public Enemy Number One". And despite nurturing influence through his friends in the press, Ian doesn't seem able to shake off that image. The player most likely to score a dazzling hat-trick is also the man most liable to aim a punch at your centre back.

The "instinctive" propensity to irrational violence has been a feature of most profiles of Wright throughout his professional career, see, for example, Mott (1993); Powell (1997); Rampton (1999).

3 For most of his international career Barnes was constantly booed by large sections of the England supporters who believed that he did not try as hard for England as he did for his club side – Orakwue has termed the constant abuse he received, the level and duration of which is unprecedented, a form of "verbal lynching" (1998, p. 60). When Terry Venables recalled Barnes to the England squad during his tenure as England manager it attracted back and front page news coverage in the tabloids. As the *Daily Star* put it, "Terry Venables brought John Barnes back from England obscurity yesterday and told a stunned nation: 'Nobody likes him – I don't care!' " (*Daily Star*, 31 August 1994, p. 48). The same article referred to Barnes as "Jamaican Barnes", reinforcing the view that "he's not *really* one of us". The back cover to Barnes' paperback edition of his autobiography figuratively encapsulates this double presence of Barnes within the nationalist imagination that shifts between celebration of the athletic black hero to abject abuse. One photo, in grainy black and white, shows Barnes nonchalantly backheeling a banana thrown at him during a game off the pitch, while below a colour photograph shows Barnes in celebration after his amazing goal against Brazil in 1984 which is supposed to show Barnes' unfulfilled (international) promise. For an analysis of the racism that Barnes endured during his Liverpool career see Hill (1989).

4 That said, Barnes re-affirms the worst of sporting racial stereotypes (which are deeply embedded within British football culture) in discussing his own "natural ability" which he actually describes at one point as an "animal instinct" (1999, p. 146). Barnes informs us:

> Coming from Jamaica, I am blessed with rhythm. My innate balance and agility meant I could jump over all tackles flying my way at Watford and Liverpool. Footballers from the Caribbean and other warm climates are far suppler than the English, who are notoriously stiff ... It's too cold in northern Europe to possess the sort of physical flexibility ... I once had. In my younger days, when my sinews were more elastic, I glided through tackles. The only British player who matches the agility of the Caribbeans and Latin Americans is Ryan Giggs. His suppleness stems from the fact that he is half-black.
>
> (1999, p. 145)

Such nonsense – think of how many counter-examples refute the theory – is hardly worth a response, but those interested should see Fleming's (2001) critique of the pseudo-science that underpins such views which, disappointingly, is still propagated by some sport scientists.

5 Earlier in Wright's career Barnes gave him the following conservative and paternalistic advice on how to deal with racist abuse:

> Ian has not directly brought any problems on to himself. But the way he reacts to the taunts may determine whether the abuse will continue. I haven't had any problems myself since the days when they threw bananas on to the pitch – because I did not react. As Ian is Black it means he has to put up with it.
>
> (Hutchinson, 1992, p. 48)

6 In classic right-wing style Powell goes on to describe Wright as having "not just a chip on each shoulder but two Harry Ramsden bagfulls, drenched in sour vinegar" (1997, p. 77). Black public figures who speak out against racism are often dismissed by the mainstream white media as being paranoid and ungrateful, thus the implication that such people harbour unjustified resentments that they carry around with them. In this instance the comparison between Wright and Barnes is a similar one

often made by the very same journalists as that between "the uppity" Linford Christie and "the loveable" Frank Bruno (see Carrington, 2000).

7 Barnes' autobiography opens and ends with a discussion of racism in Britain, and throughout makes clear that his "acceptance" has always been conditional on his position as a famous footballer, and that his class position does not negate racism:

> Racism is a way of life for black people. The majority of motorists stopped by Merseyside Police are black. When I played for Liverpool, my car was often flagged down. Once they saw it was John Barnes inside, they would say, "Sorry, John, we've only stopped you because we've had a report that a car like yours has been stolen. It's an easy mistake to make, Sir." Mistake? They were simply targeting black people ... Although it is so obvious I have been stopped because of the colour of my skin, I always remain polite. I am lucky I am a footballer. Friends of mine who own nice cars but are not footballers are forever having their cars searched. But then that's the racist society we live in.
>
> (Barnes, 1999, p. 5)

8 I am mindful of the fact that most sports biographies are "ghost-written" by a professional journalist so it is often difficult to ascertain the degree to which such *auto*biographies are genuinely so. Nevertheless, I would argue that such expressions are still more easily associated with the vernacular adopted by Barnes.

9 Ian Wright's "radicalism" is exposed when you compare his pseudo-revolutionary stances to, for example, the actual activism of Harry Edwards and the athletes – black and white – involved in the Olympic Committee for Human Rights, in attempting to challenge white supremacy within America during the 1960s (see Edwards, 1969).

10 For example, what was most noticeable during the Stephen Lawrence murder trial, and subsequent enquiry by Sir William Macpherson, was the relative public silence and reluctance of black athletes, including Wright, and many other high profile black public figures to articulate the issues raised concerning continuing patterns of racial discrimination and violence. As Richie Moran argued:

> And what of Stephen Lawrence, whose tragic death has done more to make people examine their racism than most events? You would have to be made of stone to fail to be moved by the courage, dignity and persistence shown by his parents, Neville and Doreen ... But I do not recall one significant statement on the Stephen Lawrence case from a leading black player. Surely the black community would give massive respect to any of the leading black players who would actually speak openly about this anger and pain.
>
> (1999, p. 164)

For a detailed account of the Stephen Lawrence murder, the botched police investigation, the failed private prosecution and the subsequent Inquiry, see Cathcart (2000).

Bibliography

Back, L., Crabbe, T. and Solomos, J. (2001) "Lions and black skins: Race, nation and local patriotism in football". In B. Carrington and I. McDonald (eds) *"Race", Sport and British Society*. London: Routledge.

Barnes, J. (1999) *John Barnes: The Autobiography*. London: Headline (updated paperback edition, published 2000).

Carrington, B. (2000) "Double consciousness and the Black British Athlete". In K. Owusu (ed.) *Black British Culture and Society*. London: Routledge.

Cathcart, B. (2000) *The Case of Stephen Lawrence*. London: Penguin Books.

Edwards, H. (1969) *The Revolt of the Black Athlete*. New York: The Free Press.

Emmanus, B. (1996) "The interview". In *New Nation*, November 18.

Davis, A. (1992) "Black nationalism: the sixties and the nineties". In G. Dent (ed.) *Black Popular Culture*. Seattle: Bay Press.

Fleming, S. (2001) "Racial science and South Asian and black physicality". In B. Carrington and I. McDonald (eds), *"Race", Sport and British Society*. London: Routledge.

Flett, K. (2000) "Doing the Wright thing: men wept, women wrote about it in their diaries. Did you see Ian Wright on This Is Your Life?" In *The Observer Review*, January 30.

Gilroy, P. (1993) *Small Acts: Thoughts on the Politics of Black Cultures*. London: Serpent's Tail.

Glanvill, R. (1996) *The Wright Stuff: An Unauthorised Biography of Ian Wright*. London: Virgin Books.

Hall, S. (1998) "Aspiration and attitude ... reflections on black Britain in the nineties". *New Formations*, 33, Spring, 38–46.

Hartmann, D. (2000) "Rethinking the relationships between sport and race in American culture: golden ghettos and contested terrain". *Sociology of Sport Journal*, 17 (3), 229–53.

Hesse, B. (1997) "White governmentality: urbanism, nationalism, racism". In S. Westwood and J. Williams (eds) *Imagining Cities: Scripts, Signs, Memory*. London: Routledge.

Hill, D. (1989) *"Out of His Skin": The John Barnes Phenomenon*. London: Faber and Faber.

Huntington-Whiteley, J. (1998) *The Book of British Sporting Heroes*. London: National Portrait Gallery Publications.

Hutchinson, D. (1992) "It's not Wright: Barnes sympathises with Gunner taunted by racist fans". *The Voice*, November 17.

Lindsey, E. (1999) "Big mouth strikes again: Ian Wright is one of the greatest footballers this country has produced. Now he's a TV star to boot. And he's done it all by being full of himself". *The Sunday Express Magazine*, May 9.

Marqusee, M. (1999) *Redemption Song: Muhammad Ali and the Spirit of the Sixties*. London: Verso.

—— (2000) "This sporting lie". *Index on Censorship*, July/August, Issue 195.

Moran, R. (1999) "You send me bananas". In M. Perryman (ed.) *The Ingerland Factor: Home Truths from Football*. Edinburgh: Mainstream Publishing.

Mott, S. (1993) "Can he kick it?" *The Sunday Times*, Profile, 4 April.

Orakwue, S. (1998) *Pitch Invaders: The Modern Black Football Revolution*. London: Victor Gollancz.

Powell, J. (1997) "All the alleged wrongs cannot make a Wright". *Daily Mail*, 22 February.

Rampton, J. (1999) "Wright fights for his right to speak out: West Ham's voluble and sometimes volatile striker fervently believes in freedom on and off the pitch". *The Independent*, 7 May.

Sivanandan, A. (1982) "The passing of the king". In *A Different Hunger: Writings on Black Resistance*. London: Pluto Press.

Walters, M. (1997) "England striker revels in the greatest night of his soccer life: exclusive by Ian Wright". *The Mirror*, 13 October.

Wright, I. (1997) *Mr. Wright: The Explosive Autobiography of Ian Wright*. London: HarperCollins.

7

EVIL GENIE OR PURE GENIUS?

The (im)moral football and public career of Paul "Gazza" Gascoigne

Richard Giulianotti and Michael Gerrard

> How do you describe something that does not represent anything?
>
> (Barthes, 1977, p. 61)

> In a team full of hard men, Gascoigne was the lad, the Beniamino as Italians say. He may be an idiot, and a dire disappointment to all the women rash enough to imagine that they can domesticate him, but he is an idiot savant. His genius is for football, and football is an art more central to our culture than anything the Arts Council deigns to recognize.
>
> (Germaine Greer, *The Independent*, 28 June 1996)

As UK football (soccer) enters the new millennium, Paul "Gazza" Gascoigne is not its most important player. He has hardly featured at international level since 1998, and his better playing days at club level are certainly behind him. Gascoigne's media and merchandising profiles have been supplanted by a bland new generation of celebrity players, notably the young England stars David Beckham and Michael Owen. However, while the on-field achievements of these young talents will overshadow him, Gascoigne's social and historical significance, not to mention his public profile, may be a good deal more colourful and important. Unlike Gascoigne, the meaning of these players, particularly their off-field behaviour, is rarely the subject of such contested and often polarized debate.

In this chapter, we seek to provide a contemporary, cultural sociological assessment of Paul Gascoigne's public meaning. Drawing on Roland Barthes's semiological theory of myths, and Jean Baudrillard's reading of "the masses", we argue that Gascoigne cannot only be explained either by reference to the financial and cultural transformation of UK football or, less satisfactorily, as a simple representation of the negative side of xenophobic, patriarchal Englishness. Before commencing this analysis, however, we need to trace in some detail the turbulent history of Gascoigne's extraordinary career.

Newcastle to Everton the long way: Gascoigne's (im)moral career

Gascoigne's roots belong firmly in a most traditional football mythology of "rags to riches" success for a "street kid genius" (see Giulianotti, 1999, p. 140). Born in 1967, the second of four children, Gascoigne grew up in the working class housing estates of Gateshead, in north-east England. His father suffered a brain haemorrhage in 1974 and was unable to work again; the illness was later linked to head injuries sustained while playing football (Stein, 1994, p. 4). Gascoigne's mother became the family breadwinner, working a six-day week and shifts in a nearby glass factory. In this general climate of hardship Gascoigne was only able to take games at school by borrowing a PE kit (Hotten, 1997).

According to Mel Stein (1994, p. 2), Gascoigne's lawyer, the player showed potential at his junior school, proving himself "very bright particularly at maths", and winning a prize for best attendance. However, football became Gascoigne's preoccupation, and he became the youngest child to gain a place in his school team, aged 8. Ironically, given his tabloid image of "yob terrace culture", Gascoigne rarely attended Newcastle United matches. Local accounts of the juvenile Gascoigne have him playing long into the night under street-lights, "creating a floodlit pitch in his mind" (ibid., p. 5). Gascoigne suffered a second major trauma when he witnessed the death of his best friend's brother in a road accident. Gascoigne later commented: "I was shattered, I was 12 years old … I couldn't understand why God would want to take a harmless kid like that. It started me asking questions that have never been answered to this day." Stein (1994, p. 7) concludes: "There was always football to take his mind off everything." The incident – along with his father's disability – has frequently been linked to his "chaotic" personality and obsessive behavioural traits. At secondary school Gascoigne was in his own words "unteachable", seeing education as a distraction from football. He gained two CSE passes – grade four English and Environmental Studies – while his failure in maths is attributed to a collapsed desk, "after I fiddled with the nuts" (ibid., p. 16).

Gascoigne's early football career was remarkably consistent with the later one. Moments of individual brilliance were combined with often infuriating off-field actions. Weight problems, "self-destructive behaviour", "tantrums and tears" were attributed to a personal bewilderment and sense of persecution. In 1982 a "puppy-fat padded" Gascoigne was turned down by Bobby Robson's Ipswich; a trial at Middlesbrough ended when he injured his feet while watching an under-12 team play.

In May 1983, Gascoigne began an apprenticeship at Newcastle that was punctuated, according to Stein (1994, p. 18), by a series of paint fights, destruction of huts by lawn mowers, punishment training and fines. Youth coach Colin Suggett, though impressed by Gascoigne's immense natural talent, saw him as a disruptive influence, a "hyperactive, impossibly cheeky, overweight teenager, who compulsively guzzled Mars Bars and McDonald's" (Taylor, 1994, p. 16). In what again was to become a familiar theme, disciplinarian

Newcastle coaches like Arthur Cox and Jack Charlton decided, upon considering his sacking, that Gascoigne's football skills justified overlooking exuberant behaviour (Stubbs, 1997). He made his debut in April 1985 and quickly built an outstanding reputation, though his popularity among Newcastle fans seemed to remain uncertain.[1] Meanwhile, his reckless driving was legendary among team-mates who unanimously refused lifts. During Christmas 1986, he was fined £210 for failing to stop after hitting a pedestrian. On other occasions, the local police "tended to put away their notebooks, disarmed by his grin and an effusive apology" (ibid., p. 38). By 1988 Gascoigne had made 104 appearances for Newcastle, scored 25 goals, won a youth cup medal and earned an under-21 England cap (where his eccentric behaviour was first experienced by the English management team: Gascoigne's insomnia saw him wander into anybody's room at all times of day). His contract with Newcastle was due for renegotiation in 1989, attracting the attention of Liverpool, Manchester United and Tottenham Hotspur.

Gascoigne signed for Spurs in the summer of 1988 for £2 million. A league debut at Newcastle saw him pelted with sweets and frozen Mars Bars from a section of fans embittered by his departure. In the same month Gascoigne made his full English debut as a substitute against Denmark. By the end of his first season Gascoigne's club and international form – despite injury – had made him a popular candidate for England's future World Cup squad for Italia '90. Meanwhile, Gascoigne and his "minder", Jimmy "Five Bellies" Gardner (an unemployed ex-tarmac layer and father of two), were increasingly puzzled by the media attention attracted by their antics in London hotels and nightclubs. "He'd behaved no differently from a hundred such nights at the Dunston Excelsior [in north east England] and nobody had even complained about him up there" (ibid., p. 70).

Spurs had a poor season in 1989–90, and Gascoigne was only a late selection for the 1990 World Cup finals by England manager, Bobby Robson, on the grounds of his suspect temperament. In the early part of the season, Gascoigne had been consistently booked by referees (Nottage, 1995, p. 45). In November 1989, Gascoigne had been involved in an absurd warm-up incident with the Ipswich Town mascots. His playful wrestling of "Yogi Bear" and kicking of "Jess the Cat" had led to complaints that the latter had been hurt. But he gave a scintillating performance for England against Czechoslovakia, moving Rob Hughes to write, "what joy in performance. We have too few artists in our game to deny ourselves the wonder of this one" (*Sunday Times*, 21 April 1990). Nevertheless, days before he left for Italy, Gascoigne was caught up in a pub car park brawl that was publicized in the tabloids.

By the end of the 1990 World Cup finals, Gascoigne was established as one of the tournament's great stars. He was the creative spark in England's midfield, dictating the team's play. To an armchair audience at home and overseas, he was now firmly known by his tabloid sobriquet, Gazza. Off the field, he was embroiled in more controversy: having his value openly questioned by

England's manager, and throwing water at a journalist in Bologna. England survived a difficult group draw and dispatched Belgium and Cameroon in the later rounds before their epic semi-final against West Germany. Gascoigne played excellently, but was booked towards the end for a reckless tackle on Berthold, meaning that he would have missed the final should England have qualified. Before a worldwide television audience, Gascoigne struggled to maintain his composure, bursting into tears as the game entered a penalty competition that England lost. The abiding image of the match (and subsequently, of the tournament) for a record 25 million UK viewers remained a grief-stricken "Gazza", sucking child-like on a water bottle, as team-mates struggled to console him.

After the tournament, the national media embarked on a year of "Gazzamania". Within three months, he had split up with Gail Pringle, his girl-friend since the age of 15. He recorded a pop single with Lindisfarne, and a smorgasbord of Gazza merchandise was marketed. He was voted the Panasonic London Sports Personality, the Best Dressed Man of the Year and the BBC Sports Personality of the Year for 1990. He switched on the Christmas lights in London's Regent Street. A public engagement at Downing Street saw him cuddle the "Iron Lady", Margaret Thatcher, and talk to her about fishing; Buckingham Palace insisted on physical restraint when he later met Diana, Princess of Wales.

Gascoigne's football performances were "up and down". He was dropped from the England team in November 1990; "after a few months of Gazzamania ... he was in no state to go out on the pitch and play" (Nottage, 1995, p. 49). He was soon suffering from a groin/double hernia injury, but still inspired Spurs, a club in financial crisis, through the FA Cup, culminating in a spectacular free-kick goal against major rivals Arsenal in the semi-final at Wembley. His departure to the Italian club Lazio (of Rome) had been agreed, when he took the field against Nottingham Forest in the FA Cup final. Early in the first half, a wild tackle by Gascoigne shattered his knee's cruciate ligament, putting him out for over a year. Lazio persisted with the transfer, revising the fee down from a world-record £8 million to £5.5 million, even after another nightclub incident necessitated further surgery. The deal was remarkably complex, the final fee being divided between a number of parties, including a football agent and a London restaurateur (Fynn and Guest, 1994, pp. 218, 350).

At Lazio, Gascoigne played only forty-one games in four years, but was established as UK football's highest earner, accruing £3 million in the 1993–94 season. Early on, the Italian sports daily *Corriere dello Sport* calculated that enforced idleness was costing Lazio £400 per minute (Murray, 1996, pp. 161–2). Yet, an immediate hit with the fans, Gascoigne was welcomed with banners such as "Gazza's Men Are Here To Stay, Shag Women, Drink Beer". The UK Channel 4 network started televising live Italian league fixtures, and were preoccupied with Gascoigne's injuries and form for Lazio, at the expense of other, more significant football matters (Blain *et al.*, 1993, p. 31). In the highly charged derby match against Roma in November 1992, Gascoigne scored the equalizing goal in the last three minutes, and again was overcome with emotion. Off the field, three main controversies emerged. Prior to an international against Norway in October 1992, Gascoigne implored "Fuck off, Norway", when asked for a comment by Norwegian television. In January 1993, Gascoigne belched into a microphone when asked for a comment by Italian reporters, leading to an Italian MP raising the incident in Parliament. A month later, an Italian journalist accused Gascoigne of breaking wind at him in a hotel, though the player and his advisors disputed the exact source of the emission. Subsequently, he was at the centre of an entertaining spat involving English football's most venerable journalist (Brian Glanville) and a leading poet and essayist (Iain Hamilton). More seriously, Gascoigne's international career was blighted by the alien, "long-ball" tactics of new England manager Graham Taylor. An injury-hit team struggled at the 1992 European Championships in Sweden, then failed to qualify for the 1994 World Cup finals. After losing to Norway early in 1994, Taylor broke the cover surrounding Gascoigne's drinking habits, referring darkly to a "refuelling" problem (Glanville, 1997, p. 333). In April 1994, Gascoigne broke a leg in two places in training, signalling the end of his Italian sojourn. In the summer of 1995, he signed for Glasgow Rangers in a club-record £4.3 million deal.

Gascoigne had an excellent 1995–96 season, earning Scottish "Player of the Year" awards from both sportswriters and players, helping Rangers to win the domestic League and Cup "double". His old friend and new England manager Terry Venables made Gascoigne the fulcrum of the national team. Prior to the 1996 European Championships in England, Gascoigne and several other England players became involved in a highly publicized drunken party in a Hong Kong nightclub, featuring ripped tee-shirts and jets of alcohol being fired down the throats of those strapped into the bar's "dentist's chair". Venables resisted calls for Gascoigne's omission from the England squad, and the player responded with an outstanding goal against Scotland and a valiant, widely praised performance as England lost to Germany in the semi-finals.

A few days later, Gascoigne married his long-time partner, Sheryl, in a "private" wedding attended by the England football team and numerous showbiz celebrities; *Hello!* magazine paid a reported £150,000 for exclusive photographs and interviews. The union was in tatters after three months when Sheryl was photographed battered and bruised following a drunken assault on her by Gascoigne. The relationship immediately became a central metaphor in the public and media debate on domestic violence. A subsequent MORI Opinion Poll found that a small majority of women supported Gascoigne's selection to play for the England football team, rather than be omitted for "disciplinary" reasons (*Independent on Sunday*, 10 November 1996).

At Glasgow Rangers, Gascoigne consistently ran into disciplinary problems. He was booked regularly by Scottish referees, and sent off in key matches against Celtic and Ajax Amsterdam for violent play. In January 1998, he was fined £20,000 by the Scottish FA and strongly censured after he had responded to taunts from Celtic fans by mimicking an Orange Order flute-player.[2] The injury-prone Gascoigne left Glasgow in March 1998, signing for Middlesborough in a £3.45 million deal.

With a peculiar circularity, Gascoigne's World Cup affair ended in June 1998 as it had begun in 1990, in tears and frustration. The England manager Glenn Hoddle shocked the nation by omitting Gascoigne from his squad for the 1998 finals in France. Lack of match fitness was Hoddle's major premise, but earlier publicity about partying with notorious London celebrities, and late-night drinking, smoking and consumption of chicken kebabs had also weakened Gascoigne's cause. After the tournament, Gascoigne played an inadvertent but central part in Hoddle's downfall. The manager's sensationalized "diary" of the tournament had included allegations about Gascoigne's drunkenness and violence, contradicting Hoddle's earlier claims regarding the player. Many sportswriters and some England players criticized the book for its breach of trust, fatally undermining public confidence in Hoddle, who was sacked a few months later. In November 1998, Gascoigne spent sixteen days in a specialist clinic undergoing treatment for alcohol and stress-related problems. He also suffered the trauma of a close friend dying during a weekend drinking session. He performed creditably for Middlesborough that season, but faded out of the international team while continuing to make the news, with further tabloid stories about sex romps, aggressive behaviour, and the jailing of his minder, "Five Bellies". In November 1999, the full scale of Gascoigne's domestic violence was exposed when his former wife, Sheryl, conducted several television and press interviews on the subject. Gascoigne emerged as a pathological figure, given to irrational jealousies, persistent and prolonged outbursts of serious violence, and an obsession with controlling his spouse's every movement (*The Guardian*, 28 November 1999). A broader criticism centred on the complicity of Gascoigne's family and football acquaintances in shielding his systematic abuse from public view. On the field of play, Gascoigne's injury problems continued at Middlesborough, and he played in only forty league games over three seasons. In February 2000, one match against Coventry City ended, according to the UK media, in typical self-destruction: Gascoigne suffered a broken arm while attempting to elbow an opponent away from the ball. Middlesborough were keen to cut their wage bill and so allowed Gascoigne to move on a free transfer to Everton, where the player was reunited with his former manager at Rangers, Walter Smith. Some promising early performances for the club even led to nostalgic football figures arguing for the 33-year-old's return to the England national team.

Beyond representation: attempting a sociology of Gascoigne

Our argument is not that every moment, incident or action in Gascoigne's extraordinary biography betrays some kind of structural truth on class, masculinity or the footballing prowess of Mars bars consumers. Even the proto-structuralist Durkheim professed that "perfect" socialization was impossible, due to the diverse and deviant experiences between individuals who were ostensibly hewn from identical social strata. Gascoigne's difficult family life and detached experience of education may help to explain his genuine behavioural problems that are reported by those who know him well: the appalling domestic violence, the obsessive arranging of domestic objects, dysfunctional sleeping practices, a fear of crowds, weight problems, and binge eating and drinking. His self-destructive features surpass those of his peers: his tally of injuries is markedly higher than among most other professionals; the violence visited upon his spouse and his dietary well-being are also exceptional. Additionally, the publicity surrounding the Gazza myth is out of all proportion to that experienced by other UK sport stars, including the mercurial George Best.

Gascoigne's social deviance emerges within the football culture itself, and is principally a manifestation of excess: he takes the popular footballer habitus to absurd conclusions. In a sport renowned for low educational achievers, he has been described by fellow professionals as "daft as a brush" (Glanville, 1997, p. 307). Gascoigne has played at clubs (Newcastle, Rangers, Middlesbrough, Everton) and for managers (Terry Venables, Walter Smith, Bryan Robson) known for their relaxation with a drinking culture. Unlike many team-mates, he has had particular and consistent trouble in developing a reasonable toleration of alcohol and a capacity to stay fit. His relative lack of physical and emotional control is striking, and moves journalists and fellow players to describe him as "child-like" and "vulnerable". As one commentator has argued, "the whole British football club structure has perhaps been too efficient in cocooning him, keeping him in a state of arrested development" (Stubbs, 1997, p. 86). Off the field, Gascoigne's charitable instincts go far beyond the usual, professional calculation of positive public relations and tax-deductible benefaction. His loyalty to mates and family is of a different order to that usually found in football's occupational subculture.

This exceptional persona is fully congruent with the peerless talent that Gascoigne brought to bear within English football during the 1990s. For over a decade, public debate on the future of English football and the national team centred upon the fitness and form of Gascoigne. Brian Glanville (1997, p. 307) identified in Gascoigne "a flair, a superlative technique, a tactical sophistication, seldom matched by an England player since the war". We may forward two highly symbolic illustrations to sustain this point. First, during a World Cup match against Holland in 1990, Gascoigne pirouetted between two defenders to set up a chance; in doing so, he executed a Cruyff-like turn, *against Cruyff's team*, effortlessly (Kuper, 1994). Second, in the summer of 1999, after a decade of trophy-winning for Manchester United had been topped by an unprecedented "treble", the club's manager, Sir Alex Ferguson, admitted that he still rued his failure to purchase Gascoigne in 1988.

Making the Gazza myth: heroism, celebrity and the reinvention of English football

To develop a deeper reading on Gascoigne, it is useful to provide a historical perspective on the broader social meaning of professional players. Drawing upon Critcher (1979) and Featherstone (1995), Giulianotti has outlined a socio-historical taxonomy to explain elite footballers. "Traditional" players like Matthews and Lofthouse were local, working-class "heroes", while modern, international professionals such as Best, Law and Keegan became "stars" or "celebrities", well known for their off-the-field "personality" or "lifestyle". Giulianotti introduces a third category, the "postmodern" star, whose public meaning is much more reversible (e.g. Cantona) or popularly founded upon notoriety (e.g. Jones). There are certainly elements of the traditional and the modern in Gascoigne's career, given his close loyalties to old friends and family, and his peripatetic media career, respectively. But he does show a clearest approximation to the postmodern category, notably through the constant rein-vention of his public identity: alcoholic, philanthropist, jet-setter, local boy, wife-beater, sex object, athlete, slob, offender, victim, and so on. As we shall see, this postmodern form of celebrity has a rather striking congruence with the meaning of Gascoigne's audience, the football "masses".

Williams and Taylor (1994) have contrasted the public identity of Gascoigne with that of the ex-England captain, the late Bobby Moore. Hinting at a Barthesian approach, they take an established position in puncturing the popular deification of Moore, citing counter-evidence of his drinking and later work for a soft porn tabloid. Disappointingly, their inchoate homage to Barthes is then abandoned. No similar complexity is found in the case of Gascoigne who becomes merely emblematic of English football hooliganism, lager louts in Spanish resorts, political xenophobia and, quoting Ian Taylor, "the troubled and pressing condition of traditional British masculinity" (ibid., p. 232). This perspective is sustained elsewhere, notably by the feminist columnist, Suzanne Moore, who described Gascoigne as a "bleached, blubbering icon" and "carica-ture of addled masculinity" (*Independent*, 30 October 1996). Yet, as we have seen, Gascoigne's public identity may be a good deal more complex than such a portrait suggests.[3]

To counterpoise the more sweeping accounts, it is worth re-examining Barthes's conception of myth in greater detail. For Barthes (1972, p. 124), "myth is a type of speech defined by its intention much more than by its literal sense". Yet these intentions are hidden within the myth. Typically, they shelter inside a bourgeois conjuring trick, in which the myth "has turned reality inside out, it has emptied it of history and has filled it with nature" (ibid., p. 142). Otherwise stated, the myth portrays a "natural" relationship between concepts, people and objects; not one that is historically shaped and contested. There is certainly no incongruity in employing the Barthesian approach to sport. Barthes's semiology has an all-encompassing sweep, converting all social phenomena into a cavalcade of signs (Ritzer, 1997, p. 30). For example, sporting practices are surrounded by words and phrases like "sportsmanship", "gentlemanly conduct" and "play the game", but the "natural" connection between "fair play" and sport remains a mythological one. It masks the social struggles and negotiations of power that underlie the development of sports, and ignores the centrality of "gamesmanship" or outright cheating to sporting cultures.

Perhaps most importantly, Barthes recognizes that in visual texts such as films we are given an "obvious meaning" to follow by the author/director. He argues that we should look beyond this to find a third, "obtuse" meaning, which radically recasts or restructures the film. The third meaning may carry a certain emotion, and provide its art form (in this case film) with a crucial supplement, a subliminality, that cannot be described or articulated. It does not subvert the story, but remains oblivious to it (Barthes, 1982, p. 329). More substantively, Barthes (1977, p. 55) argues, the obtuse "belongs to the family of pun, buffoonery, useless expenditure. Indifferent to moral or aesthetic categories, it is on the side of carnival."

Working backwards into the Barthesian position, the relevance of a footballer renowned for his financial and behavioural excesses, for clowning around in public and private, for his apparent moral imperviousness, is immediately striking. It is here that we follow an established position in football culture, regarding the underlying symbiosis of Gascoigne's on- and off-field persona: curtailing his eccentricities or excesses would inevitably impact upon his extraordinary football prowess. Certainly, in transferring Barthes's filmic method into the world of football, the adjectives that follow Gascoigne's play slot also into the realms of the obtuse: intuitive, exquisite, superlative, "a natural" who has "everything". Moreover, we would argue that the affective, emotional meaning of Gascoigne operates at this level, most notably in his significance of pre-professional values, especially his antediluvian, self-absorbed and somewhat adolescent love of the game. Archetti (1997) discusses the special status within football culture of *pibes* ("boys"), players whose enthusiasm and style rekindle memories of childhood football matches, in the streets or wastelands in working-class locales. Susan Sontag (1982, p. xxi) notes that Roland Barthes divided writers into those who write something and those who write. While the former practice the routine, instrumental profession of writing, the latter writers champion an intransitive, personal and autotelic engagement that is "excessive, playful, intricate, subtle, sensuous". Similarly, most contemporary football players perform with a clear set of goals and tactical systems in mind, following the unadventurous or unimaginative "obvious" meanings of games, playing *for* something. Conversely, Gascoigne stands in the company of *pibes*, especially among South Americans like Maradona, Ortega, Valderrama and Denilson, whose subtlety, grace and style strike an emotional chord within the depths of football's folk culture, through the pure artifice of play.

The affective appeal of Gascoigne *qua* artistic player contrasts rather sharply with the cruder, melodramatic appropriation of the player's emotions (the tears at Italia '90) which lay behind the mythology of Gazza *qua* public celebrity. He was not the first athlete, nor will he be the last, to break down on the field of play. Yet, within a wider context, the images of Gascoigne's emotional disassembling were an open goal for those powerful forces within the UK game who were seeking to repackage and reinvent English football. The defeat to Germany, England's old foe, would have been enough alone to bind together the disparate, worldwide collection of English football fans into a pained, imagined community. However, the match was watched by the UK's largest-ever television audience at a time when both free-to-air and the emerging subscription stations were seeking to nurture the interest of transient sport viewers. Similarly, the UK football authorities were increasingly committed to marketing the game to new consumers, notably the typified "ABC1s" and women.[4] Hence, to sustain their high-brow packaging of Italia '90, the BBC's television coverage played upon the sophistication of Italian culture, employing Pavarotti's rendition of Puccini's *Nessun Dorma* as its signature anthem, and showing the Three Tenors (Pavarotti, Carreras and Domingo) in concert. Meanwhile, according to programming logic, Gascoigne's tears provided an uncomplicated, "human interest" side for female viewers or those with relatively limited grasp of the football aesthetic.[5] In short, a clear cultural distinction, in Bourdieu's sense, was referenced in the mythological construction of football's blighted, recent past and brave new future. Signifiers of the former were traditionally masculine fans and players, colourless playing styles, a pervasive distrust of foreigners, financial problems among clubs, dilapidated stadia, and a generalized atmosphere of cultural entropy. Conversely, Italia '90 came to sustain a fresh assembly of possibilities for the national game: a wider range of viewers and supporters, more inventive players, a more European or global sensibility, profits for investors and entrepreneurs, the construction or reinvention of UK stadia according to Italian design, and the association of the new game with *sophistication*, both internally and in new relationships to other cultural practices (such as fashion, advertising, music, literature and the performing arts). Invariably, the meaning of England's star player was enlisted in this fresh mythological construction of the national game. His technical skills and expressiveness (not only in the tears incident) suggested a schism from the regimented, opaque masculinity of English professionals and their formulaic strategy of play, or the joyless violence of xenophobic England fans at venues across Italy. Gascoigne, in short, was at the centre of this repackaging myth in English football, with its "natural" binary opposition of the bad old and the good new. Yet, as even a brief look at Gascoigne's biography demonstrates, the player's "obtuse" behaviour has not lent itself so readily to such a utopian vision.

Out of the mass: the seductive absurdity of the Gazza epic

To summarize, our argument is that the construction of the Gazza myth has certainly been conjunctural to the reinvention of English football's political economy and cultural standing. However, it would do some violence to the player to reduce his biography and diverse behaviours into a concise representation of contemporary masculinity, the occupational subculture of players, or xenophobic Englishness.

If there is a sense in which Gascoigne "represents" a social entity or cleavage, then we would suggest that this must be the "masses" of whom Jean Baudrillard speaks. For Baudrillard, the masses are a veritable black hole of meaning, where notions of the social or subjectivity meet their end (1983, p. 9). The masses have no interest in liberation or self-improvement, but prefer to delegate the burden of choice to others. More subtly, the masses "enjoy a long lead" over those that would seek to harness them (Baudrillard, 1993, p. 169). The masses toy with publicity machines, opinion polls, the media and intellectuals. The "experts" and "opinion-makers" are seduced into debating or locating the masses' wishes or desires, to "crack their code", when in truth there is no deeper pattern to be found, save for a delusive, playful and ironic strategy. Thus, the masses "exercise a passive and opaque sovereignty; they say nothing, but subtly, perhaps like animals in their brute indifference ... they neutralize the whole political scene and discourse" (Baudrillard, 1990a, p. 94). Their predominant strategy – one of disappearance and silence – must be seen as a "fatal strategy" in the context of an information-saturated world. Baudrillard thus conceives of the mass as an "object", an "evil genie", whose ruses and deceptions constantly evade and outfox the "subject". Baudrillard (1990b) counterpoises the seductive power of sign games and enchanting illusions with the overbearing rationality of the modern world that we seek to escape. He points to some specific "fatal strategies" that may be adopted to offset the threat of a disenchanted world. The masses may pursue a fatalistic hyperconformity in gleefully heeding advertising campaigns, absorbing their simulation by opinion polls, and forcing their media construction to its ecstatic, final form. We may note the generalized fatigue with which workers and consumers go about their daily business, which for Baudrillard (1998, p. 183) reflects a "latent, endemic revolt, unconscious of itself". Or we may consider the most romanticized strategy, involving the potlatch-style giving of absurd gifts (including one's life); such gifts become "accursed shares" that cannot be properly reciprocated without their recipients themselves dying (Baudrillard, 1993, pp. 36–7).[6]

Gascoigne's exceptional talent within the world's leading sport leaves him little scope for disappearance, save for a dreaded retirement from his beloved game. Nevertheless, while his actions and utterances are the subject of intensive scrutiny and evaluation, Gascoigne is relatively silent in the way of rendering them coherent, of imposing upon them some kind of evolutionary pattern or dominant meaning. Unlike his contemporary Eric Cantona, whose very "Frenchness" attracted a stream of banal deconstructions from football arrivistes in the media and academe, Gascoigne's carnival of colourful signifiers has no such existential depth. There is no code to crack for a man who stands grinning on open-topped buses, adorned in false breasts; or who answers tabloid charges of group sex with the correction that more people were involved (*Independent*, 30 May 1996). Instead, there is a curious hyperconformity, a fatiguing zealousness, with which Gascoigne stretches his public typification to its limits: the "bad boy" label is reified through more belches, farts, swearing and drinking; the "clown" image is extended by circus costumes, hair extensions, nudity and dramatic changes in body shape; the "violent male" is caricatured through pub fights, hitting his partner, and reckless tackles on opponents; the "inner child" is unleashed through public tears, on-field tantrums, the engagement of professional therapists. Gascoigne takes the public stereotypes about under-socialized football players to an exaggerated and hyperreal level that even his fellow professionals find somewhat grotesque. Yet even the worst excesses – most obviously the domestic violence – cannot end an underlying national empathy for him, for the myth that began in tears. Indeed, since the outset of Gazza's "image-making", there has been an appeal to a market hyperconformity, to join him in the absurd consumption of useless paraphernalia: the transparently dreadful record, the throwaway tee-shirts, his Italian football television programme (on which the stricken player cannot play), or the men's toiletries that he endorses (but cannot use personally for medical reasons). Through Baudrillard, we can also begin to see how Gascoigne may stand out as a conjunctural player, joining Matthews and Best in symbolizing the epistemic shifts in English football and in the wider social structure. The "heroic" Matthews validated working-class respectability, sociability and industry; he knew his place and literally refused to forsake it. Best's celebrity celebrated the new working-class dream of individualism, easy consumption and spectacular mobility. Subsequently, Best was buried in an avalanche of critical media signs, retiring at the age of 26 to reorder his life upon a reality principle. Conversely, Gascoigne's postmodern stardom embraces all ungrounded signifiers, and assembles a stream of reversible images and contradictory events that brook no meta-narrative. Perhaps most crucially, the Gazza saga does signify, in Baudrillard's terms here, the end of "class identity", the entropy of the social, the victory of the mass. His appeal is rooted in a fatigued acknowledgement of the artificiality of consumer society, of which football is a part, though he is better placed than the masses to push it all beyond reason.

On the field of play, Gascoigne has exercised a pragmatic "fatal strategy" *par excellence*; the "evil genie" characterized by deceptive dribbling and intuitive reading of play. Occasionally, there are indications that the prospect of complete "disappearance" is seductive, that he wishes to end the Gazza saga, only to return again with more public excesses or epic football moments. Yet, there is no question that, in terms of Baudrillard's symbolic exchange, Gascoigne has given too much: first, through the undisguised, anguished tears of self-pity before a global audience; second, through the series of injuries that were born of his reckless and epic commitment to football, and which have blighted the demonstration of his talents. In this sense at least, as he nears retirement, Gascoigne continues to exercise the minds of all English football people. In disappearing from the England team, he threw down an accursed challenge, to match his talent, to which no other player may adequately respond. And to the football world, he bequeaths the more seductive and unanswerable question, as to how truly great a player he might have been.

Notes

1　Nottage (1995. p. 45) suggests Gascoigne was a crowd darling, though Hamilton (1993) argues otherwise.
2　The Orange Order is a strictly Loyalist organization that celebrates the securing of Northern Ireland for British rule over the forces of Catholic nationalism. Historically, the Celtic football club originated among the Irish-Catholic community in Glasgow, and continues to carry a fan culture that relates to the nationalist side in Ireland.
3　Whannel (1994, p. 148) forwards a brief, more pleasing assessment of the Gascoigne myth. Perceptively, he argues that if England had won the semi-final against West Germany in 1990, Gascoigne's tears would have been overtaken by other images, thus reducing the scope for his mythical invention.
4　Reflecting the new commercial potential of the UK game, soon after the 1990 World Cup, the English FA joined with the top twenty English clubs to split with the old Football League. The new "Premier League" began in 1991, armed with an astronomical £304 million television deal, when less than fifteen years earlier the major television deal in English football had netted only £9.8 million (Giulianotti, 1999, p. 91).
5　A similar rationale was employed by American television stations in covering the 1996 Olympic Games. A large female audience was retained through the dramatizing of competition between athletes, and the use of short biopics on competitors that played upon emotional themes (for example, family tragedies, childhood traumas, medical problems).
6　There are some striking parallels between this form of self-destructive symbolic exchange and the romantic "hero" role, as outlined by Featherstone (1995). Heroes rise above the social context, are often driven by a "demonic force", are willing to risk all in the name of a greater cause, and thus, in a Wagnerian sense, flirt with personal disaster.

Bibliography

Archetti, E. (1997) "And Give Joy to my Heart". Ideology and emotions in the Argentinian cult of Maradona". In G. Armstrong and R. Giulianotti (eds) *Entering the Field: New Perspectives on World Football*. Oxford: Berg.
Armstrong, G. and Giulianotti, R. (eds) (1998) "From another angle: surveillance and football hooligans". In C. Norris, J. Moran and G. Armstrong (eds) *Surveillance, CCTV and Social Control*. Aldershot: Gower.
Barthes, R. (1972) *Mythologies*. London: Paladin.
—— (1977) *Image-Music-Text*. London: Collins.
—— (1982) *Barthes: Selected Writings*. London: Collins.
Baudrillard, J. (1983) *In the Shadow of the Silent Majorities*. New York: Semiotext(e).
—— (1990a) *Seduction*. London: Macmillan.
—— (1990b) *Fatal Strategies*. London: Pluto.
—— (1993) *The Transparency of Evil: Essays on Extreme Phenomena*. Trans. J. Benedict. London: Verso.

—— (1998) *The Consumer Society*. London: Sage.

Blain, N., Boyle, R. and O'Donnell, H. (1993) *Sport and National Identity in the European Media*. Leicester: Leicester University Press.

Critcher, C. (1979) "Football since the war". In J. Clarke, C. Critcher and R. Johnson (eds) *Working Class Culture: Studies in History and Theory*. London: Hutchinson.

Featherstone, M. (1995) *Undoing Culture*. London: Sage.

Fynn, A. and Guest, L. (1994) *Out of Time: Why Football Isn't Working*. London: Pocket Books.

Giulianotti, R. (1999) *Football: A Sociology of the Global Game*. Cambridge: Polity.

Glanville, B. (1997) *The Story of the World Cup*. London: Faber and Faber.

Hamilton, I. (1993) *Gazza Agonistes*. (*Granta*: 45). London: Penguin.

Hotten, J. (1997) "The greatest player of his generation: Gascoigne". *Four-Four-Two*, September.

Kuper, S. (1994) *Football Against the Enemy*. London: Orion.

Murray, W. (1996) *The World's Game: A History of Soccer*, Urbana, IL: University of Illinois Press.

Nottage, J. (1995) *Paul Gascoigne: The Inside Story*. London: Victor Gollancz.

Pickering, D. (1997) *The Cassell Soccer Companion*. London: Cassell.

Polley, M. (1998) *Moving the Goalposts: A History of Sport and Society since 1945*. London: Routledge.

Poster, M. (1988) *Jean Baudrillard: Selected Writings*. Stanford: Stanford University Press.

Ritzer, G. (1997) *Postmodern Social Theory*. New York: McGraw-Hill.

Sontag, S. (1982) "Writing itself: on Roland Barthes". In *Barthes: Selected Writings*. London: Collins.

Stein, M. (1994) *Ha'way the Lad: The Authorized Biography of Paul Gascoigne*. London: Transworld.

Stubbs, D. (1997) "Fool, genius, hero, clown, victim, brute, saviour". *Goal*, March, p. 86.

Taylor, L. (1994) "Paul Gascoigne: the naughty boy who has never grown up". In *The Sunday Times Illustrated History of Football*. London: Hamlyn.

Whannel, G. (1994) *Fields in Vision: Television Sport and Cultural Transformation*. London: Routledge.

Williams, J. and Taylor, R. (1994) "Boys keep swinging". In E. Stanko (ed.) *Just Boys Doing Business*. London: Routledge.

8

PUNISHMENT, REDEMPTION AND CELEBRATION IN THE POPULAR PRESS

The case of David Beckham

Garry Whannel

Today's heroes should be giving their young fans more to live up to.

(Letter of the week in *Woman's Realm*, 6 February 1997)

It is frequently suggested, by newspapers and by figures in public life, that sport stars should be moral exemplars – role models for the young. When, as is often the case, their behaviour hits the headlines for "negative" reasons, they are castigated for their failure to set a "good example". The concept of sport star as "role model", however, postulates a crude and over-simplified model of the relation between young people, the media and sport stars (Whannel, 1995). Rather, sport star images involve complex condensations of discourses of masculinity, and morality, shaped by the self-referential and intertextual constructions of celebrityhood.

David Beckham has all the attributes of a "golden boy" – football talent, good looks, highly publicized romance with another media star, Victoria Adams (Posh Spice in the pop group, The Spice Girls). He plays for a team, Manchester United, that attracts both massive support and considerable loathing, because they have become a symbol of the dominance of football by the richest clubs. In summer 1998, a widely publicized photograph of him, on holiday with Victoria, wearing a garment described as "a sarong", was presented in the tabloid press in terms of deviance from the conventions of masculinity, with hints of his supposed "emasculation". Shortly after this episode, Beckham's sending-off in England's key match in the World Cup provided a point of condensation for discourses of morality and fair play in sport, in which national pride became national shame. Yet after a season spent shrugging off the abuse, winning Premiership, FA Cup and European Champions League medals, fathering a child, and marrying Victoria, the story in the popular press became a narrative of redemption and triumph.

Tabloid news values: the personal is sensational

Media news is highly personalized. Sports is given its own distinctive part of the paper and its own set of alternative news values (Hall, in Ingham, 1978), and consequently sport stories that break out of the sports page ghetto and hit the front page have an added resonance. Sensationalism in the press is nothing new, but a series of recent developments has shifted the relation of public and private spheres dramatically. The British tabloid revolution of the 1980s, in which full computerization and colour printing accelerated the drift away from traditional page layout, has fostered a collage style of layout in which headlines and photo displays dominate the page. This in turn heightened the force and impact of stories about easily recognized star figures. Any clear division between public and private spheres has been blurred, and areas of life once resolutely private are now in the public domain.

As with any new sport star, the initial tone of representation is celebratory. The back cover of an early biography by Bobby Blake (1997) proclaims, "In just two incredible seasons, David Beckham has become Manchester United's greatest young star." Beckham's goal from the half way line against Wimbledon (17 August 1996) is described in a chapter entitled Goal of the Century. Beckham's rise to fame is "phenomenal", he is "a heart throb to millions of teenage girls, a hero to as many football-mad boys" (Blake, 1997, p. 10). He is represented as fun loving but disciplined, constructed in terms of "responsibility": "He likes a few beers with the lads occasionally, or a glass of wine with a meal. But never more than once a week. 'You have to take care of yourself at this level,' he says" (ibid., p. 44).

He is ordinary but glamorous too, being pictured on celebrity pages and associated with models (ibid., p. 47). However, hubris awaited. Good-looking, successful without apparent effort or sacrifice, and a player for England's top club side, he was already the target of abuse from fans. In 1998, England's defeat by Argentina in a key World Cup game was blamed on Beckham, who was sent off halfway through the match. Throughout history, societies have generally evolved means of publicly castigating infringements of the conventions of correct behaviour: "Throughout the pre-modern period the courts had a variety of shaming punishments at their disposal. One of the most characteristic was the pillory ... pillorying usually took place at midday and usually on market day" (Briggs *et al.* 1996, p. 79). Just as pillorying took place in the most public place available – town squares at midday on market day; so contemporary pillorying happens in that most public of places – the tabloid press. The tabloids offer us judgements that can have the stark simplicity of a medieval morality play, yet these messages about morality take place in the context of the moral ambiguities and uncertainties of late modernity.

Tabloid castigation and fan anger combined to create a hostile climate for Beckham – "the pretty boy scapegoat was lynched in effigy ... when the 1998–99 season began, any football fan who'd ever loathed Manchester United pilloried their preening, blond-streaked right winger with chants inventive and profane" (*Vanity Fair*, September 99). Subsequent accounts of his career make much of this hostility and of the way in which Beckham coped with it: "When George Best played he was offered booze after every game; Beckham gets boos before, during and after every game whether he wants it or not. He even gets abused in the street" (*GQ*, May 1999).

However, given the furore over the sarong picture just before the World Cup, he was not only being punished for being sent off, and infringing the conventions of fair play, but for being rich and successful, and for not conforming to the conventions of masculinity. He was more adventurous with style than the cautious and defensive conservatism of the working class football subculture, with its fears of any hint of "effeminacy", would accept.

Envy, humour, abuse and emasculation

The subsequent abuse of Beckham is rooted in three main factors – the hatred of Manchester United prevalent among football fans, the tall poppy factor, and Beckham's sending off in the 1998 World Cup. The dominance of the English game in the 1990s by Manchester United, the perception of them as domi- nating the game through their wealth, and the perception that many of their fans are "glory hunters" with no organic links to Manchester, have combined to make the chant of "stand up if you hate Man U" commonly heard at English League grounds. Beckham's display of wealth and fashion becomes a metonym for the wealth of his club.

Undeniably a highly gifted footballer, good-looking, stylish, and married to the best-looking Spice Girl, he appears as someone who has it all. The elegance of his football masks effort: he appears to have acquired "it all" without conspicuous striving. He is a tall poppy, there to be cut down, as *Time Out* sardonically noted:

> After all, he's better looking than most footballers, he once wore a sarong, he plays for the super-successful Manchester United (who he has treacherously supported all his life, despite being born in Leytonstone) and he's going out with a pop singer – oh yeah, hanging offences, every one of them.
>
> (31 March–7 April 1999)

In the World Cup game against Argentina, the result was crucial to England, the game was in the balance when he was sent off, and the kicking offence seemed unnecessary. Retaliating to a challenge in the heat of the moment is undisciplined, but, in the macho codes of football, forgivable. However, Beckham had a moment to reflect, and still, rather lazily, kicked out at his opponent, Simeone, in full view of the referee. Indeed, the languid nature of the kick fitted the construction of Beckham as slightly foppish. Clearly he was provoked, and it may well be that Simeone exaggerated the effect of the rather half-hearted kick, but the moment allowed Beckham to be constructed as a sacrificial victim and as scapegoat for England's defeat.

The episode was the subject of hostile press comment; it unleashed a torrent of abuse from the terraces, and Beckham became the butt of jokes, many of which featured his supposed dull-wittedness. One BBC comedy programme[1] featured a running gag about Beckham and Posh, in which they sat at a baronial length table, eating dinner. One joke was that they have nothing in common and nothing to talk about until the subject of unit trusts arose, at which point they were suddenly both animated and well informed. A running gag throughout the programme, concerned Beckham's supposed gauche unfamiliarity with fancy food:

Beckham: This bacon's cold.
Posh: It's Parma ham, David.
Beckham: These cucumbers are hot.
Posh: They're courgettes, David.
Beckham: These peas are still in the pod.
Posh: They're mange-tout, David.

Among jokes circulating on the Internet is "The Beckham Diary", which features suggestions that he is thick (it reports on wise-cracks of his team-mates that he doesn't get); and "a whingeing egotistical bastard". Another elaborate Internet joke contrasts intelligent foreigners Arsene Wenger, Dennis Bergkamp, and Jaap Stam with dull-witted Brits Alex Ferguson and David Beckham.

Part of the terrace hostility to Beckham can be related to the fear of emasculation engendered by a public figure who strays beyond the rigid versions of masculinity favoured in English football culture. The suggestion is that Victoria dominates him; that his clothes are chosen by her; that this is un-masculine; that he looks like a prat, a wally, and that he is not too bright.

The extensive press attention given to a picture of Beckham (on a beach holiday) in a sarong has become one of the featured elements in most narrativizations of his story. The sarong, one magazine commented "made him look a right twerp" (*GQ*, May 1999), and the picture is captioned "Becks and Posh with their hers and hers wardrobe" (ibid.). Beckham does "un-masculine" things; attending fashion events like London Fashion Week fashion show (*Evening Standard*, 15 January 1999). His sartorial adventurousness transgresses the laddish code in which sharp and stylish means Hugo Boss – a little flash but in the solidly "masculine" tradition of the sharp suit. A cartoon in *The Sun* (26 April 1999) showed Beckham dressed in a Spice Girl Union Jack mini dress and platform shoes, with a musical agent saying, "So, David ... what other tips on being a pop star did Posh give you?". The popular press was constructing Beckham as feminized and emasculated.

Much working-class male terrace humour centres on sexual infidelity and sexual humiliation of the players. Songs and chants about players' wives having affairs are not uncommon. One chant aimed at the visiting goalkeeper is "dodgy keeper, dodgy keeper, takes it up the arse", and the chant most commonly aimed at Beckham, or more precisely at Posh, is "does she take it up the arse?" Newspapers refer to this obliquely, without a direct quote. Freud has discussed the function of aggressiveness in humour and also the presence of feelings of shame in sexual references: "By the utterance of the obscene words it compels the person who is assailed to imagine the part of the body or the procedure in question and shows her that the assailant is himself imagining it" (Freud, 1960, p. 98). So footballers are humiliated by a process in which the private domain of sexuality is rendered public. Humour here functions as a weapon. Writing on humour, Henri Bergson argues that: "laughter is incompatible with emotion or with sympathy with its object ... it always implies a certain callousness, even a touch of malice" (Mathewson, 1920, p. 6).

Such humour is in certain circumstances, a distinctive feature of masculine cameraderie. Laughter, Bergson suggests, belongs to men in groups (ibid., p. 6) and "Being intended to humiliate, it must make a painful impression on the person against whom it is directed. By laughter, society avenges itself for liberties taken with it. It would fail in its object if it bore the stamp of sympathy or kindness" (quoted in ibid., pp. 6–7).

Both jokes and abuse are typically dealing with the repressed; with awkward and disturbing psychological fears. The obsession with anal sex, which can signify both submission and humiliation, is suggestive of a working-class masculine culture disturbed by fears both of the feminine and of the homo-erotic. In this context, the supposedly emasculated Beckham offered a convenient symbol onto which such fears could be condensed.

Beckham played well throughout the season, betraying few signs that he was distracted by the abusive chants. During the 1998–99 season, the Beckham narrative was that in his handling of the abuse from the terraces, and in his key role in Manchester United's route to the treble (they won the English Premier League, the FA Cup, and the European Champions League, the three major trophies for which they competed) he had demonstrated his "maturity" and was thus to be forgiven and "rehabilitated": "Beckham took strength from his adversity, demonstrated impressive resilience" (*Evening Standard*, 26 May 1999). This resilient maturation is attributed to his becoming, unlike George Best, a family man: "fatherhood and his pending marriage to Spice Girl Victoria Adams, suggest that at 24 he is already capable of controlling his own destiny" (ibid.).

The theme of redemption through love was developed in dramatic fashion in Easter week by *Time Out* (31 March–7 April 1999) which featured David Beckham on the front cover in white trousers and a white see through shirt in a pose evocative of Christ and the crucifixion, with the caption "Easter Exclusive: The Resurrection of David Beckham" making the religious reference explicit. Inside, the accompanying article was titled "The Gospel according to David" and a subtitle referred to him as "back from the reputation wilderness". *TV*

142

Times (22–28 May 99) later used a similar picture from the same photo-shoot, and ran a shortened version of the same article. Their caption read "David Beckham from sinner to saint: Red Hot and Spicy". Here then, was a perfect Christ for the 1990s – good-looking, stylish, talented, and engaged to a successful female pop singer.

Vortextuality: the wedding and the vortex effect

The growth in the range of media outlets, and the vastly increased speed of circulation of information have combined to create the phenomenon of a "vortex" effect, which I term here "vortextuality". The various media constantly feed off each other and, in an era of electronic and digital information exchange, the speed at which this happens has become very rapid. Certain super-major events come to dominate the headlines to such an extent that it becomes temporarily difficult for columnists and commentators to discuss anything else. They are drawn in, as if by a vortex. The death of Princess Diana was a case in point, dominating the media for days, almost to the extent of removing most other issues from the agenda. During a World Cup or an Olympic Games, even writers with no declared interest in sport feel impelled to comment on events, as Germaine Greer and A.S. Byatt, among others, did during Euro 96, the European Nations football championships.

If not on the same scale, the wedding of Beckham and Posh was also an example of the vortex effect at work. Television presenters alluded to it, politicians made asides about it, radio phone-ins discussed it, and comedians made jokes about it. In 1999, Beckham, sometimes alone, but more usually with, Posh, featured on the front covers, among others, of the *Radio Times* (13–19 March), *Time Out* (31 March–7 April), *Midweek* (19 April 1999), *GQ* (May), *Now* (May 19), *TV Times* (22–28 May), *OK* (July 16 and 23), *Vanity Fair* (September 99), and *Marie Claire* (October 99). The *Vanity Fair* (September 99) cover proclaimed the story as "The matching outfits! The salacious rumors! The secret tattoo!". The self-referential and intertextual intensity of focus on the couple became self-generating, producing a pressure impelling even broadsheet newspapers and political journals to comment. The couple sold rights to the wedding itself to *OK* magazine. The Wedding Special Part one (16 July 1999) ran thirty-six pages on the wedding, while Part two (23 July 1999) focusing on "Baby Brooklyn at the wedding" ran to another twenty-nine pages.

The first *OK* (16 July 1999) issue was flagged on the front as "The Wedding of the Decade", the "Biggest Ever Issue" and "World Exclusive". The event was proclaimed as "the wedding the whole world had been waiting to see" *OK* (16 July 1999), and the hyperbole was justified by the intense attention paid to the event in the rest of the media. A cartoon in the *Evening Standard* (5 July 1999) showed God in an armchair saying "I've postponed the end of the world until I've seen the Beckham wedding pictures."

The people's royalty?

The event was represented as a Royal wedding. It occupied the same space, attracted the same form of coverage in the tabloid press. The apparent mobilization of public attention through the media, resembled the media mobilization of an audience for royal weddings (see Philips and Whannel, 1998). The staging of the event, and its media representation, focused on regal splendour, royal connections, and comparisons with royalty. Explicit comparisons were made with the Marriage of Prince Edward and Sophie Rhys-Jones, with more than one paper suggesting that David and Victoria were far more glamorous:

> After Edward and Sophie's low key affair, the Spice Girl and the soccer star show them how to stage a proper Royal Wedding.
>
> (*Daily Mail*, 5 July 1999)

> The supreme glitziness of their marriage makes Prince Edward's marriage to Sophie Rhys-Jones look a comparatively frumpy occasion.
>
> (*The Guardian*, 3 July 1999)

Posh was described as the "queen of the castle" *The Guardian* (3 July 1999), while the *Daily Mail* (5 July 1999) ran the headline I, QUEEN POSH TAKE THEE, KING BECKS. It was reported that Posh had a 20-ft train and a retinue of 125 security guards (ibid.) and that the splendour of the event was more regal than the recent royal wedding:

> From the regal "thrones" at the reception to the imperial purple carpets and rows of liveried attendants, the sheer spectacle of yesterday's event could not have been more of a contrast to the real Royal Wedding last month.
>
> (*Daily Mail*, 5 July 1999)

> Prince Edward and his bride Sophie Rhys-Jones wanted their wedding to be a relatively low key family day with as little fuss as possible. David and Victoria didn't. They wanted pomp and splendour and they made sure they got it.
>
> (ibid.)

In an anthropological discussion of British Royalty, Hayden has commented that "The Queen's majesty needs other individuals to radiate and enhance it" (1987, p. 35). In the case of Posh and Beckham's wedding, the couple, their designers, the celebrity guests, the security guards, and the media all contributed to the production, radiation and enhancement of "majesty". *The Sun* (6 July 1999) remade its front page layout to report the wedding, moving its mast-head into the middle, and running the headline MR AND MRS BECKS. Below a rather blurred and clearly covertly taken picture of the couple on their wedding thrones, the caption reads "Soccer's David Beckham and pop queen Posh Spice sit on regal thrones at their fairy-tale wedding banquet". Inside, a headline reads "Victoria looked like a queen", while the text relates that "ecstatic bride Posh Spice sits like a queen on a throne at her lavish wedding – with love for her 'king' David Beckham glowing in her eyes" (ibid.).

The following day, The Sun extended the royal metaphor into the political domain with the headline:

THE SUN ASKS THE BIG QUESTION

WHO RULES ?

WHICH COUPLE IS MORE POPULAR IN BRITAIN TODAY ?
CALL AND VOTE NOW

(*The Sun*, 7 July 1999)

The layout featured two pictures of the weddings of Posh and Becks and Sophie and Edward with phone numbers for readers to vote on the issue.

Media representations highlighted links with royalty. According to *Now* (19 May 1999), "The hottest ticket of the year was sent out on parchment paper emblazoned with gold leaf to the elite circle invited." The wedding was organized by a company, owned by Lord Snowdon's half-brother, that was also responsible for Princess Anne's 40th birthday and for the 21st birthday celebrations for her son. Flowers were provided by "two of the most respected florists in the business"; one did the flowers for the film *Four Weddings and a Funeral* and the other did the floral arrangements for the party to celebrate the Queen's ruby wedding. Victoria wore a beautiful diamond and gold coronet by Slim Barrett, a jeweller who made pieces for the late Princess of Wales (*GQ*, 16 July 1999). The general air of royal patronage evoked in such journalism almost leads one to expect the appearance of crested plaques announcing "by appointment to Posh and Becks". Even the intensity of the press attention was evoked as proof that the couple were even more fascinating than the Royals:

> the near-suicidal actions of the press desperadoes say a lot about the unique position Beckham and Adams currently occupy in British life. After all there are no paparazzi risking their lives for pictures of Edward Windsor and Sophie Rhys-Jones.
>
> (*Vanity Fair*, Sep. 99)

Conspicuous consumption and display

The *Radio Times* (13–19 March 1999) featured Beckham and ex-Liverpool and Scotland football star turned television pundit, Alan Hansen on the cover for a story captioned "the money and the madness of soccer superstardom – what a difference a decade makes". The article highlights footballers' dramatic increase in earnings since Hansen's days just a decade earlier. The lavishness of the wedding exemplified Veblen's (1970) concept of conspicuous consumption, in which wealthy elites advertise their riches through highly visible forms of display.

In much of the coverage, everything is related in terms of monetary value, with obsessive detail about designer labels. *OK* it was reported, "turfed out a cool million" for the wedding rights (*Vanity Fair*, Sep. 1999). The wedding required "an army of private security experts" *NOW* (19 May 1999). *The Mirror* (1 July 1999) referred to it as the showbiz wedding of the year. The couple booked "every available limousine in Ireland – and are getting more sent over from the UK – so that family, friends and celebrity guests can travel in style" *NOW* (19 May 1999). It was reported that the couple spent £120,000 on the rings alone (ibid.) and every aspect of the display of lavishness was lovingly detailed:

> 3 grain-set baguette diamonds and set in 18 carat yellow gold. Each side of the shank of the ring is set with six diamonds with the total diamond weight adding up to 5.82 carats. David's ring is a full eternity ring set with 4 baguette diamonds with 24 smaller diamonds set on one side of the shank, in 18 carat yellow gold adding up to a total diamond weight of 7.44 carats. As a wedding gift, David gave Victoria a pair of Asprey and Garrard emerald-cut diamond earrings set in 18 carat gold to match her wedding ring.
>
> (*OK*, 16 July 1999)

The bridesmaids were "dressed as woodland flower fairies" in outfits made by theatrical costumiers Angels and Bermans. The best man received a specially engraved Cartier watch; the usher received a gold and silver Rolex watch. The couple "personally conducted a taste test of dozens of different dishes to decide what they wanted to include on their wedding menu". Music was provided by an 18 piece string orchestra and the cake was a "lavish three tier creation by Rachel Mount" (*OK*, 16 July 1999). Over 400 people were involved in the wedding arrangements and there were three articulated lorries full of flowers (*OK*, 23 July 1999). After the wedding, Posh and Becks "retired to spend their first night of married life in the castle's $3,900 a night Royal Suite" (*Daily Mail*, 5 July 1999). The descriptive language in representations of the wedding evoked an exotic and decadent luxury:

> carpeted in sumptuous deep red, with the walls lined with a pleated ivory taffeta lining, the marquee was more than fitting for the most famous celebrity couple in the world. The spectacular flower arrangements were in three colours: burgundy, green and purple, which created a suitably regal effect.
>
> (*OK*, 16 July 1999)

The 236 marquee guests had sat in gold-coloured chairs at 12 round tables. They would have marvelled at the ornately designed 7ft naked gold figurines and the two huge Egyptian black cats with piercing green eyes'.

(*The Sun*, 6 July 1999)

At work here is an element of nostalgia for earlier periods of excess which the real Royal Family could no longer stage. It is as if the Beckham wedding had been staged by the Prince Regent in Brighton Pavilion. Press reactions to the spectacle differed between tabloid and broadsheet in a manner that revealed the links between "class" and "taste". *The Observer* describes them as pleasant looking, not particularly bright, and rounded up other press reaction:

The Sun called the wedding a fairy-tale, *The Mirror* a dream come true. The *Daily Express* declared that Mr and Mrs Beckham elevated vulgarity into an art form. *The Guardian* said that it was "confirmation of a country's coarsening, a dissonant hymn in praise of mammon".

(*The Observer*, 11 July 1999)

Sue Carroll in *The Mirror* acknowledged the "tackiness" of the wedding and defended it:

Well, I admit it was breathtakingly tacky. Barbiedom meets Brookside, Versace-cum-Spanish brothel … There was something splendid about their fascinating show business excess. Something so utterly over the top it made your heart soar to witness the noble tradition of the truly tacky wedding in all its flamboyant glory.

(*The Mirror*, 7 July 1999)

She went on to describe them as "a couple so totally besotted and wrapped up in one another even their most hardened footie mates respect their displays of soppy sentimentality" (ibid.). It was indeed striking how often their love for each other was evoked in articles to legitimate the excess. The presiding bishop at the ceremony said that "seeing Victoria and David on the day it was clear to all of the guests who were lucky enough to be there that the couple were totally in touch with their innermost feelings" (*OK*, 16 July 1999).

Several portrayals of the couple revolved around the theme of their modesty. One quoted Posh as saying, "If I'd had a more low-key wedding I would have been called a tight cow. As it is people say we were flash and over the top. Well, that's fine. But we had the most amazing day and that's all that counts" (*Marie Claire*, Oct. 99). A spokeswoman for Victoria Adams said, "They honestly regard it as a family event. They don't go to many celebrity parties" (*The Guardian*, 3 July 1999). Unusually among the papers, the *Daily Record* (3 June 1999) discussed their largely unpublicized lavish charity donations and work for

147

charities. When asked about football achievements, Beckham said, "They're all important but having a child means more than anything" (*GQ*, May 1999). Here, then, the lavish display is excused and legitimated as the ritualistic excess and abundance that precedes the responsibilities of family and parenthood.

Postmodernity: new lads and old lads

David Beckham is a postmodern celebrity, a point that can be illustrated by comparison with Liverpool's Robbie Fowler. Fowler may be a "new lad" but in many ways he is an old lad, a pre- "new-lad" lad. He is forged in the mould of northern working-class masculinity and has a workerist and socialist sensibility (lifting his football shirt to reveal a tee shirt with a slogan supporting the striking dockers, empathizing with homeless people). His homophobia was revealed in his baiting of Chelsea's Grahame Le Saux (actually heterosexual, but as a *Guardian*-reading art lover from the Channel Islands, clearly "suspect" from the perspective of the constricting limits of working-class terrace subculture masculinity.) From Liverpool, Fowler is a scouse scally – with a roguish desire to see what he can get away with. Despite his considerable wealth, he has not adopted some of the more overt trappings of flamboyant, up-to-the-minute style. In representation, he is the working-class boy made good, but still utterly grounded in a particular northern working-class masculinity and behaving in consistency with it (see Critcher's (1979) typology of football stardom).

David Beckham, by contrast, is a post-new-lad man. Growing up in an environment in which men's interest in fashion, style, narcissism and the possibility of being objectified have all been nurtured by a decade of the style press (*Arena, GQ, FHM*), in a period in which sport and fashion have become more closely linked, in which footballers and pop stars gravitate to one another's glamour, and in which fame has itself become commodified, he is subsumed by his own image. His star persona has become the substance, the marketable object – all, that is solid melts into air, or at least, into magazine pages. Where Fowler is grounded, Beckham appears rootless: he can be dressed in anything because surface appearance is all.

Victoria Adams' attitude to their conspicuous display includes a distinct postmodern ironic sensibility: "We've got matching dogs [rottweilers] matching watches (gold Rolexes], similar wardrobes, matching Jags. I like all that. I mean, I know its tacky, but it makes me laugh" (*The Guardian*, 3 July 1999).

And when an expert at the 500-year-old College of Arms slated the design of an invented coat of arms for the wedding as "tacky and amateurish" (*Now*, 19 May 1999) she responded:

> "... so what if the poxy swan is the wrong way?", snaps the woman who was once dubbed Relatively Posh Spice. "Does anybody really give a shit – d'you know what I mean? Having your own crest – it's one of them, innit?" Adams pokes her tongue into her cheek. "We're

just thinking, this is the biggest day of our lives – we're just going to go over the top and make it entertaining for everybody. Much as we want it, it's still one of those." Tongue meets cheek again.

(*Vanity Fair*, Sep. 1999)

Indeed, the whole event was distinctly hyper-real. It was itself constructed from media representations. Posh got the idea of staging the wedding ceremony in a semi-derelict folly from Ross's wedding in *Friends*. Before the event, the *News of the World* produced a spread simulating the wedding. *The Evening Standard* (5 July 1999), unable to get anything other than pictures of guests leaving the wedding, included a spread of celebrity look alikes acting out what the wedding might have looked like. Below a headline SEALED WITH A KITSCH, the *Evening Standard* (5 July 1999) described the wedding as "fairytale or kitsch depending on whether the news was relayed by broadsheet or tabloid". *The Guardian* (7 May 1999) pointed out that the pair were "the only couple in Britain to have figured individually on the covers of separate PlayStation games: Becks on FIFA 98; a pixellated Posh on SpiceWorld". Indeed, the lack of any serious fuss about the implicitly blasphemous *Time Out* cover seems to support the reading that Beckham, at least in representation, is a thoroughly post-modern figure. Dress him as Christ and it doesn't really matter, because he's not "real". In this vortextual media event, consumption is the new democracy; style the new cultural capital. The performative talent of David Beckham and Victoria Adams provided the potential for their commodification. Now they are so thoroughly "well known for being well known", their abilities as footballer and singer appear oddly and rather sadly, de-centred.

Acknowledgements

The author would like to thank Ian Wellard and Carlton Brick, and also Deborah Philips, whose sub-editing skills and keen eye for pertinent media material were invaluable.

Note

1   Alistair McGowan, BBC1 September 1999.

Bibliography

Blake, B. (1997) *New United Legend: A Tribute to David Beckham*. Edinburgh: Main-stream.
Briggs, J., Harrison, C., McInnes, A. and Vincent, D. (1996) *Crime and Punishment in England: An Introductory History*. London: UCL Press.
Critcher, C. (1979) Football since the war. In J. Clarke, C. Critcher and R. Johnson (eds) *Working Class Culture*. London: Hutchinson.
Freud, S. (1960) *Jokes and their Relation to the Unconscious*. London: RKP.

Hayden, I. (1987) *Symbol and Privilege: The Ritual Context of British Royalty.* Tucson, AZ: The University of Arizona Press.

Ingham, R. (ed.) (1978) *Football Hooliganism: The Wider Context.* London: Interaction Inprint.

Mathewson, L. (1920) Bergson's theory of the comic in the light of English comedy. *Studies in Language, Literature and Criticism* 5, Nebraska: University of Nebraska.

Philips, D. and Whannel G. (1998) The fierce light: the royal romance with television. In M. Wayne (ed.) *Dissident Voices.* London: Pluto.

Veblen, T. (1970) *The Theory of the Leisure Class.* London: Allen and Unwin.

Whannel, G. (1995) Sport stars, youth and morality in the print media. In G. McFee, W. Murphy and G. Whannel (eds) *Leisure Cultures: Values, Genders, Lifestyles* (pp. 21–136). Eastbourne: LSA.

9

THE SPECTACLE OF A HEROIC LIFE

The case of Diego Maradona

Eduardo P. Archetti

In a special issue of *El País*, a leading Spanish newspaper, devoted to the analysis of the universal craziness of soccer, we read:

> In Argentina, a country traditionally crazy about soccer, and to which this sport has provided the major expression of national pride, Diego Maradona is and will continue to be a hero as important as the legendary liberator from colonial rule, General San Martín.
>
> (Carlin, 1999: 29)

In fact, many years ago Juanse, an Argentinian rock star singer, declared that "Maradona is only comparable to General San Martín with a temperature of 40 degrees crossing the Andean mountains for the liberation of Chile" (*Página 12*, 1 December 1994, p. 2). Most Argentinians will agree with this characterization and will include him in a kind of heroic triangle in which Maradona is not only similar to San Martín but also very similar to another Argentinian hero and mythical figure, the tango singer Carlos Gardel who died young and tragically in 1933.

Since his discovery by the general public, soccer aficionados and journalists in 1971, at the age of 11, Maradona has been defined as an exceptionally talented player and, indeed for many, "a new genius". In the 1970s when the ideologies and methods of coaches, crystallized in the values of physical effort, tactics and discipline, dominated world football, and Pelé, the great Brazilian player, and Cruyff, the charismatic Dutch striker, abandoned soccer, the number of players able to win a decisive match on their own was dwindling. The spontaneous abilities of players were overruled by the belief in collectivism and the tyranny of a style of playing designed by managers and coaches. Systems were discussed, discovered and experimented with, and the crucial role of individual players was dismissed. Maradona was in this context, both locally and internationally, an unexpected appearance, a "divine gift" according to one of my informants. He perceived him in the following way:

Maradona united technique and imagination, and since he was a child he has amazed the entire world. He is a different player because he always makes beautiful moves, simple or complicated, and, most of all, because he cannot be predicted. Any part of the field is like a natural place for him; his left foot is able to change a movement in a fraction of a second creating a new situation, and when the adversary thinks that he stops, he will run, and when he thinks he will run, he will stop. He will always make unexpected moves. He has been playing in all the grounds you can imagine, defying the laws of gravity and equilibrium, and he has been, since childhood, offering happiness to millions and millions of football lovers and supporters of the teams he played with.

Maradona has been a "winner" since the start of his career. As a very young player with Argentinos Juniors, a club from Buenos Aires, he won everything in local competitions. He then began his journey to the first division with the same club, shortly before his sixteenth birthday. His precocity and talent made possible his debut in the senior national team before he was 17 years old. In 1979, in Tokyo, at the age of 18 he won, as a captain of the team and indisputable leader, the title of the World Junior Cup with the Argentinian national team. Later he went to Boca Juniors in Argentina, won the league in 1981, moved to Barcelona FC in 1982, where he won the Copa del Rey in 1983, and to Naples two years later. In Naples he became an idol, helping the hometown team to win the Italian league in 1987, the first time a southern team had done so. Naples repeated their League title triumph in 1990, won the Italian Cup in 1987 and the European Cup in 1989. At the peak of his career Maradona was the captain of the Argentinian team, winners of the 1986 World Cup in Mexico. The Argentinian national team "depended" on him, and he never refused to play, becoming the symbol of Argentinian football in the 1980s. Maradona was a global player, a nomad, living in a new age of football, like his predecessors as world's best football players: Pelé, Di Stéfano and Cruyff, and, like them, he was also a winner.

His life was also marked by scandal. It was well known in Naples in 1990 that Maradona had taken drugs and participated in dubious parties. On 17 March 1991 Maradona was randomly dope-tested after a home match against Bari. The tests proved positive. Maradona's urine was found to contain cocaine. There were only small traces of it, the remnants of the drugs he had snorted a couple of nights earlier. He was immediately suspended by the Italian football authorities. He left Naples, tired and tearful, on 1 April 1991. Four weeks later in Buenos Aires the Federal police raided an apartment where Maradona was in bed after a day of drinking and drug-taking with some women friends. His life since has been marked by drugs and cocaine. He left football temporarily and made a return in October 1993 with Newell's Old Boys, a first division team from Rosario in Argentina. Maradona played a few games. The Argentinian national team had unexpected problems in qualifying for the 1994 World Cup in the United States of America. Football experts and above all supporters clamoured for the return of Maradona. Maradona surrendered to this, in many ways, irrational demand and he committed himself to a physical effort that an addict could not normally afford. Maradona joined the national team and travelled to the United States of America. Maradona led Argentina to a convincing 4–0 win over Greece and a hard-earned 2–1 victory over Nigeria. After this second match he was chosen for the dope test. The test was positive, and he was suspended. It was reported that when Maradona was told he cried, "I killed myself training, I killed myself training, and now they do this to me" before breaking into sobs. Maradona summarized what he felt when, at a press conference, two days later, he said: "They have cut my legs off." The game against Nigeria was his last one: he left football for ever.

One of my informants summed up Maradona's career in the following way:

> Winning is not the only thing in soccer or sport; there is all that drama. The life of Maradona is a constant melodrama, full of scandals, emotional crisis, drug consumption when he was taken in 1991 in Italy and later on, in 1992, in Argentina. Always the psychodrama involving him and his group of permissive managers and opportunist friends. Maradona's life is full of the stuff of how we live: exceptional talent but fragile morality; endless tradeoffs between what we want and what we get, or what we pay for what we want. I cannot think of many films, plays or television shows that are honest about how a set of important stars are conditioned by the circumstances of their lives. Maradona's life was in this sense exceptional and open to constant scrutiny. He was not a prisoner of fame; he used fame in a self-destructive way. He knew all the risks he was taking while playing football and consuming drugs. His career was not only spectacular but a public spectacle.

Heroic sports figures must be seen in their cultural context in order to understand their social meaning and to observe their communal impact (see Holt and Mangan, 1996). In this chapter, my analysis of Maradona as an example of heroic masculinity will touch upon the logic of creating differences and how this impacts on discourses concerning agency, personhood, morality, and identity. A sports hero can be any person admired for given qualities or achievements and regarded as an ideal or model. A sports hero is an idol and an icon who belongs to a specific time: the time of heroes. The time of heroes, opposed to other times which encapsulate daily routines or scheduled rituals, represents in the mind of the adoring public a glorious dream-like time during which the daily mediocrity of normal life is suddenly transcended. The world of sports heroes is a world of creative enchantments because, in some moments, like flashes of intense light, athletes become mythical icons representing mastery over mortality (Novak, 1993, p. 163). The heroes stand *alone*, alone against a world of opponents and alone against an underworld full of dangers.

The solitude of heroes is of great value in their transformation into cultural icons (see Rank, 1990).

In many cases sporting heroes are a source of collective identity and pride in both national and supra-national settings and, paradoxically, very local settings – the cities of Naples or Barcelona, or a neighbourhood of Buenos Aires. The case of Maradona, as I observed above, is a clear illustration of "transnational" heroism. He was a God-like hero in Naples while he was playing for the Naples Football Club and in Argentina while playing on the national team. I have not carried out fieldwork in any other city apart from Buenos Aires. Thus, the analysis of Maradona's heroic status will be limited to Argentina.[1] This chapter reflects two periods of my research. In 1988 I was working on the meaning of football for Argentinian national identity and masculine constructions; the first part of the chapter is based on the way football heroes are represented as *pibes* (young boy players). In July 1994 I went back to Buenos Aires after Maradona's second drug scandal. The second part of the chapter will be devoted to the analysis of the impact of this dramatic turnover of his career. The two parts, I hope, will permit the reader to understand the mythical standing of Maradona. The examination of concrete performances makes it possible to see how every performance (and every man) has some significance for the audiences that adore him.

The *pibe* and the *potrero*: Maradona as a symbol of a national style

No identity can ever exist by itself and without an array of opposites, negatives and contradictions. The emergence of contrasting styles in sport, particularly in football, is intimately related to a search for national identity. Football was introduced to Argentina by British immigrants in the 1880s, and this initial period of amateur football in Buenos Aires was dominated by British clubs. The emergence of a truly *criollo* (creole) foundation began in 1913 when Racing Club, a football association started by Argentinian natives and Italian immigrants, without a single player of British origin, won the first division championship for the first time. Two styles were thus contrasted, the *british* and the *criollo*. "Britishness" was identified with being phlegmatic, disciplined, methodical, and concentrated on elements of the collective, of force and of physical power. These virtues help to create a repetitive style, similar to that of a "machine". The *criollo*, due to the Latin influence, was exactly the opposite: restless, individualistic, undisciplined, based on personal effort, agile and skilful (see Archetti, 1995, 1996).

The conceptual oppositions between British and *criollo* physical virtues have become enmeshed in common perceptions of football. The British (English) physical virtues are still associated with "force and physical power", while the virtues of the *criollos* are those of agility and virtuoso movement. The metaphor of the "machine", as opposed to individual creativity, is constant in contemporary Argentinian football imagery.[2] "Britishness" is still associated with the industrial, and the *criollo* with the pre-industrial social system. During a game, when faced with the British machine or repetitive play, the typical *criollo* response would be the "dribble" or the *gambeta* in Argentinian Spanish. This manifestation of style is eminently individual and cannot be programmed. It is the opposite of the industrial, collective game of the machine. A crucial event in the life of Maradona will clearly illustrate this reasoning.

For sheer drama Maradona's performance in Argentina's quarter-final clash with England was to hang in the memory of millions of Argentinian (and world) fans long after Mexico '86 was over. The press presented the match as a struggle not so much between two countries (or two teams), as between two outstanding players – Maradona and the English goalkeeper Peter Shilton. Five minutes into the second half of the match, and with no goals scored, Maradona scored one of the most controversial goals in the history of World Cups. He went to a ball together with Shilton, and the clash involved not only bodies but hands: Maradona scored with his hand (what he called later "the hand of God"). The linesman and the referee did not see the infringement of a basic rule in football; they agreed it was a goal. For Maradona that was all he needed. Four minutes later, Maradona scored again, this time with a goal that was to go down as one of the best in footballing history. Burns described it in the following way:

> In the words of Brian Glanville, it was a goal "so unusual, almost romantic, that it might have been scored by some schoolboy hero, or some remote Corinthian, from the days when dribbling was the vogue. It hardly belonged to so apparently rational and rationalized an era as ours, to a period in football when the dribbler seemed almost as extinct as the pterodactyl." Picking up the ball inside his own half and keeping it so close to his boots as to make it seemed glued to them, Maradona proceeded to carve his way through the English side, with the effortless movement of a racing skier in slalom … Having shrugged off Fenwick and without for a instant losing his control of the ball, Maradona found the time to assess Shilton's position. The English goalkeeper seemed desperate to second-guess the Argentine's next move, so Maradona kept going, leaving his strike to the last possible moment. The split-second delay prompted a final rearguard action by Butcher. He tried to break Maradona's momentum with an attempted tackle, again to no avail. The Argentine checked himself and effortlessly passed the ball from his right foot to his left before casually slipping it past Shilton.
>
> (1996, p. 160)

Brian Glanville, one of the best football journalists in any language, understood the "essences" reproduced in this second goal: Maradona was suddenly a dribbling schoolboy or a Corinthian hero (a devotee of amateur sports) and, in the second goal, he was *alone* dribbling past the entire English defence. What he did was done alone without any help from his team-mates. His raid into the English lines was a lonely performance. At that moment, moreover, Maradona was not only the creative *criollo* player defeating the English machine, but in doing this he was a young boy, a *pibe*. In the Argentinian mythical account of playing, the *pibe*, without any form of teaching, becomes the inventor of the *criollo* style in the *potrero* – a small patch of irregular ground in the city or in the countryside which has not been cemented over. The *pibe* is placed in a mythical territory that inherently empowers those who belong to it. This image, commonly accepted by Argentinians of all times and ages, partly emphasized the infantile beginning of Argentinian football (as is manifest perhaps in any game), but also points to the importance of freshness, spontaneity and freedom during play. These values are commonly associated with childhood and are usually lost with the advent of maturity and resulting adult responsibilities. The authentic Argentinian player will never stop being a child. Football allows a man to go on playing and remain a *pibe*. One could say that the imaginary world of football reflects the power of freedom and creativity in the face of discipline, order and hierarchy. The best Argentinian players do not come from the playgrounds of primary or secondary schools or from the clubs, the spaces controlled by teachers and trainers. The *potrero* is portrayed as exclusively open and free. Consequently, the great players are considered the pure products of this freedom, which allowed them to be creative and improvise without the constraint and rules imposed by experts or pedagogues. *Pibes* came to be seen as liminal figures in the construction of Argentinian masculinities, and *potreros* became territories associated with the experience of freedom and creativity. The foreign British and English styles offered an image very much opposed to that of the liminal figures of the *pibes*. Maradona is the best *pibe* Argentina ever produced, and he was called before his second goal against England and, of course, after: *el pibe de oro* (the golden young boy).

To be, and remain, a *pibe* is a powerful image because, in football, the most creative period for some players is associated with immaturity. My informants do not deny the role of experience and the passing of the years (*el paso de los años*), in the development of physical automatism and tactical sense. These qualities are also considered important for expected performances. But a *pibe* is, by definition, an unpredictable player finding unexpected solutions in the most difficult moments of a game. The magic of Maradona is always under-stood as a performing skill, for it produces inexplicable effects and illusions – paralysing opposing players and charming his audience. This is defined as a powerful, bewitching quality. This image of the childish, unruly *pibe* serves to portray football as a game to be fully enjoyed only when total freedom is granted, and achieved. Conversely, football is ideally perceived as a perfect game for children.

The imagery of Maradona is even more complete because he is the product of one of the poorest neighbourhoods of Buenos Aires, where *potreros* still exist. He was born in Villa Fiorito in 1960, and Casas and Chacón (1996, p. 5) write, "everything started in Villa Fiorito, a forever forgotten neighbourhood where prosperity never arrived, in a remote day ... in a humble house." It is easy to presume that in Villa Fiorito the streets were without asphalt and there was a plethora of *potreros*. The most original Argentinian player comes from the *potrero* of Fiorito which is now used as a mythical name, as the essence of *potrero* (see Fontanarrosa and Sanz, 1994, pp. 53–4). We are not told to which school Maradona went (this is not important), and we are told that when he joined his first serious club he was already a crack player (Gilbert, 1996, p. 17). What has not been learnt in the *potrero* cannot be taught elsewhere. Carlos, one of my informants in the first piece of fieldwork, reminded me in 1988 that "Maradona is pure *potrero* even when he is not playing football. Well, I can put it this way: he still lacks civilized manners, and he has obvious problems in accepting boundaries and control. In the *potrero*, you learn how to be free and to improvise." He commented that Maradona was born in a neighbourhood where fathers and mothers take buses to work when it still is night and and do not return home until it is dark once again. He added, "*Pibes* without shoes who play football in the *potreros* see in the ball a symbol of a future that can be different. It is not only the joy of playing; football is a way of changing their fate."[3]

Juanjo, one of my best informants during my fieldwork, summed up the meaning of the second goal of Maradona at Aztec Stadium in Mexico that historical day of June 1986:

> You can say that this day – and during twenty seconds – Maradona was able to produce the most important performance in the history of Argentinian football. It was done against the English machine, it was done against England, and it was done against the most rugged defenders of the world. It was the victory of the *criollo* style. It was not against Brazil or France or Italy; in such games his performance would never have had the same emotional impact. I can say that it was like pure magic because his moves were difficult to realize but also an illustration of Maradona's destiny that day. He also demonstrated that dribbling is the essence of our style of playing. He dribbled and dribbled, and in fact these few seconds are still in my memory like a prolonged time; it is still part of me, and as pure images they have persisted for years and years. I will never forget the second goal against England. It was an eternal performance. He demonstrated why we call him *el pibe de oro*. He is made of pure gold, and nobody will replace him in the pedestal of remembering and gratitude. I thought after this goal that to speak about Maradona will be not only difficult but

impossible, and I said to myself that this is understandable because he is like a feeling. Yes, Maradona is a feeling.[4]

It is important to remember that on the global scene the production of local territories and identities is difficult to sustain because of the dispersed nature of globalism and nationhood, and the life-worlds of local subjects tend to become deterritorialized, diasporic and transnational (in other words, the life of Maradona). Argentinian football supporters and sports writers tend in the opposite direction. The heroes ought to be local. The modes of belonging to the *potrero* and the *pibe* in no way contradict a simultaneous sense of belonging to the imaginary territory of a nation. The two become intrinsically connected on the playing fields of a nation. Maradona, thus, is transformed into a mythical Argentinian sport hero, and not only his football exploits, but also his entire life, concern the citizens of the country. This dependency and the tragic consequences of it will be explored in the next section.

The 1994 World Cup in the USA: the fall of Maradona

We can imagine that heroes are normal beings who just do the right things in precise moments. Maradona's second goal against England is a kind of performance that can be understood according to this logic. However, I have suggested that heroic sport figures must be seen in their cultural context. The cultural meanings of *pibes* and *potreros* make it possible to understand the national impact of Maradona. The drug scandal in the 1994 World Cup belongs to another human dimension of the heroes: their fall and decadence. Maradona was suspended for several years in September 1994. He commented that with this sanction his "legs were cut off but also his body was expropriated. I am empty ... I was killed as player and as a man" (*Clarin*, 3 September 1994, p. 47). Suddenly Maradona was left alone, and nobody could help him against "their enemies" and his own personal ghosts. He then saw himself as a kind of falling Che Guevara, his confessed idol, alone in the jungles of Bolivia fighting an impossible war against a powerful army. In his case the Bolivian army was replaced by the authorities of the Fédération Internationale de Football Association (FIFA) (ibid.). Let us go back to Buenos Aires in the first week of July 1994.

The front pages of two Buenos Aires newspapers on 1 July are a synthesis of national feelings and cultural emotional reactions. In *Clarin* it was a picture of Maradona with a single word: Pain. In *Página 12* Maradona was symbolically replaced by a *pibe*, a sad, crying *pibe*, who, with an Argentinian flag in his left hand, expressed the title indicated: Mourning. The sad *pibe* not only represented the world of suffering supporters but, as I pointed out before, the mythical foundation of the Argentinian style of playing. Maradona was "killed", as he himself said later, and the Argentinian nation was in sorrow, mourning its fallen idol. A journalist described how Buenos Aires reacted:

The real sadness and craziness was clearly perceived in the streets of Buenos Aires. In bars and restaurants, supermarkets, small neighbour-hood shops, in intense discussions in the busses and the underground. A general reaction was dominant among common people: we will forgive Diego; we will always forgive Diego Maradona. The arguments presented were diverse. Some saw the dope test as a plot against Maradona and Argentina; others identified the main author, Havelange, the Brazilian president of FIFA, who always defined Maradona as his adversary because he was critical of many of his deci-sions. But all of them, without a single distinct voice, asserted that Maradona was the essence of joy in the practice of football, and if he used Ephedrine he was not responsible; others were responsible.

(*Cronista Comercial*, 1 July 1994, p. 2)

Before coming back to the images of pain and mourning I would like to comment on the question of responsibility which appears clearly in the descrip-tion made by the journalist. We must capture the multifaceted meaning of the *pibe* and the different dimensions related to the social construction of the stereotype so well crystallized in the figure of Maradona. One important feature is the small body, particularly in terms of height. In addition to body shape, the content of bodily performances, as we have seen above, seems to be an another important feature. The image of a typical *pibe* player is based on an exuberance of skill, cunning, individual creativity, artistic feeling, vulnerability and improvi-sation. In this sense it is easy to understand that the image of a powerful, disciplined and perfect athletic body is absent. A third related feature is the kind of daily life *pibes* lead. In the case of a *pibe*, a considerable amount of disorder is expected, and tolerated. Chaotic behaviour can be the norm. They have a tendency to recompense, penalize or forgive others in an exaggerated way, to convey arbitrary judgements and choices, to display stupid and irrational heroism. They also have a capacity to "die", metaphorically (by being impris-oned or becoming a drug addict, as in the real life of Maradona), and be resurrected, and a special talent in critical games to make the unexpected move, ensuring victory to the team. Thus, a *pibe* is creative, free of strong feelings of guilt, self-destructive and, eventually, a bad moral example to other players. In the global moral evaluation of this kind of player the ultimate criterion is the creativity of their bodies. My informants, like the informants of the journalist writing about "responsibility", and I imagine supporters in general, tend to forgive the lack of moral and social responsibility of the *pibes*. In this sense, Maradona is not alone. The amount of joy provided by the *pibes* is more impor-tant to the public than any consistent moral statement they might make. Tomás, one of my informants, explained to me that:

to be a *pibe* is not only to be liberated from several responsibilities. To be a *pibe* means that one does not feel the pressures from the authority of family, parents, and school ... but also to be a *pibe* implies that it is easier for others to see only the positive aspects and forgive the imperfections. It is common to say here, "but he is a *pibe*, just a *pibe*; let him be a *pibe*". Maradona is a *pibe* and will remain a *pibe*. He represents this state of perfection and freedom, when we disregard the most negative traits of an individual. This spontaneity, to be fresh and to do things just right without thought of negative consequences, is a quality we appreciate. A great football player must have these qualities.

The imperfections of Maradona, in Tomás' interpretation, are contrasted to what is expected of a mature person. Yet for him, Maradona, a real *pibe*, is not perfect as a man, but he is perfect as a player. His perfection is attained, and maintained, because he is still a *pibe*. Many voices opposed to this representation were also heard during this critical month. A psychiatrist, Jorge Kury, critically analysed the Argentinian devotion for *pibes* and Maradona:

> this accepted ideal shows some features that express an infantile origin, shared by all men, but in the case of our modern idols (word derived from ideal) this characteristic is very exaggerated, provoking situations like the one experienced by Maradona. If the social models could be more measured and mature, our life could be better, without so many disappointments.
>
> (*La Nación*, 16 July 1994, p. 24)

Related to lack of responsibility and, in spite of this, the certainty that strong sanctions from FIFA were expected, supporters reacted with an incredible sense of guilt. The general idea was that Maradona was obliged to make his comeback in football in order to save Argentinian honour and to increase the chances of winning a third World Cup. It was thought that Maradona reacted to popular pressure with a tremendous physical self-sacrifice and in doing this, at the end, he was immolated. He sacrificed himself in order to provide joy and hope. Tomás explored this when he said to me:

> I assume my guilt and, if it could be possible, I would ask for mercy from Maradona. I feel that I demanded so much from him and that he gave me more than I gave him. Now, when I know that perhaps he will never return to a ground and even worse, that I will never cry his name in an important game – against Brazil or Italy, for instance – I feel, like him, that my heart has been destroyed.

Ideas of destruction and self-destruction were associated with tragedy and the definition of Maradona as "a tragic figure" or " a tragic hero". Tomás believed that Maradona was a sort of tragic hero because he surpassed limits and when this was no longer tolerated he was punished without mercy. He also said that

160

he was put in this situation, and, in the last instance, the people and the supporters of Argentina destroyed him. He insisted that Maradona was defying the limits of our ordered life, and the fact that most men are ordinary now implied that his behaviour was a provocation for many. I felt, discussing with Tomás, that he was trying to convey the idea that in almost every tragedy the atmosphere is one of doom from the beginning, and that what Argentinians experienced as a national tragedy needed a tragic hero: Maradona. At the same time, the belief that the tragic hero is "one of us" was present. He is not necessarily virtuous in everything; he is a man who reminds us of our own humanity, who can be accepted as standing for us. However, the ultimate effect of Maradona's tragedy is to sharpen the feeling of responsibility, to make supporters fully aware that they have erred as the tragic figures have erred. We can say that the notable thing with this tragic event is that people feel that they have something to do with the situation and they are still desperately concerned with it. The anguish and the sense of guilt were increased because Maradona shared with common people the human condition. They transformed Maradona into a historical figure of the past, not only recent but contemporary, because he could not be brought back to the stadiums: he was taken as an exemplary character in drama. The fall of an idol breaks the fiction of the life and transforms it into a public spectacle.

I think that the sadness observed during the month of July in Buenos Aires (and I imagine in the rest of Argentina) had this component: supporters knew that this was the last act by Maradona as an active player. What emerged forcefully was the significance of tragedy as performance, as public spectacle, and as rite. I felt that the narratives collected showed that tragedy is an account of the fortunes of heroic characters in adversity. Maradona's life began with joy and ended in grief. Moreover, Maradona was great in grief; even then he maintained his position as a hero, but Argentinians would have preferred him in happiness. We can conclude by saying that there is no real tragedy without the complex relations between being guilty and being innocent. Maradona was guilty, but he felt that he was innocent. His logic was shared by his audience. The audience missed a "son"; Argentinians were suddenly *huérfanos* (orphans) (see Osvaldo Soriano, 1994). Tomás expressed this imagining himself as a "father": "he is like our son and we as fathers place our dreams on them; we prefer of course that they achieve something in their lives; we are afraid of their failures".

I began this section pointing out that pain was a generalized emotional reaction. Disregarding age and gender, "*Siento dolor*" (I feel pain) was what many Argentinians said in public – in television programmes, radios, newspapers and magazines. It was a diffuse pain related to his act, to his past life and to his career as a player that ended this day. A strong discomfort was easily transmitted, and, of course, anguish, anxiety, disappointment, sadness and grief were intimately associated with "feeling pain". It was a generalized reflection on the importance of pain in modifying the perception of things and evaluation of human condition. Pain was related to compassion. Compassionate statements were heard, a shared compassion: compassion for Maradona but also compassion for oneself. A suffering community was visible showing in public loyalty and devotion to the fallen idol. My informants emphasized that "feeling compassion is much better than judging Maradona", and that "compassion is a noble feeling" (*la piedad es un sentimiento mucho mejor y más noble que el enjuiciamiento*, according to Manucho). Compassion was also connected with the idea of suffering and enduring. A typical football supporter knows that his team and his players are not all regular and stable. Argentinians have developed what they call *aguante*, a capacity to endure and overcome bad moments in their supporting lives. This virtue, however, was contested and many Argentinians reacted strongly against the connection between compassion and enduring. Many concluded, like Juanjo, that, "we must learn to live without Maradona and try to forget his loss".

Conclusion

I have tried to show that the idealized Maradona is not just a given man, independent of his outstanding qualities; he is a part of a cultural system for producing differences. Some players will be transformed into heroes and cultural icons, and others never will achieve this status. The qualities of Maradona transcended the limits of nationality and, in this sense, can direct attention to a variety of ideas concerning how one should, or could, be a sporting hero. Ideological similarities between Argentinians and Italians have been advanced. This, however, has not been discussed in this article. I emphasized the importance of dramatic events for grasping the meaning of Maradona's performances as a sport hero. I believe that it has been made clear that, in the dramatic spectacles I have described, we find ideas, opinions, and symbols that reflect upon themselves, the participants, and us, the observers. The display of the imagery and emotions associated with Maradona is central in such a perspective. Maradona himself expressed it thus:

> If I succeeded in being a living myth, I did not search for this. I am very grateful for having been transformed into a myth, but I am just a normal human being. I do not see myself as a myth because, after all, I was only successful in some football struggles.
>
> (Arcucci, 1999, p. 40)

Notes

1   I have previously published two articles on the meaning of Maradona in Argentina (1997 and 1998). The original contribution of this chapter lies in the way I concentrate my analysis on "dramatic events" and give voice to my informants in the city of Buenos Aires, men of different age and class. On my methodological approach to the study of football I have presented my framework elsewhere (see Archetti, 1999).

2   Kanikar (1994) argues that the imperial British created the image of the "sporting boy". The games recommended were team sports which required qualities of leader-

ship, working together and loyalty. To be part of a team was conceived as being part of a perfect machine.

3 Maradona has refused several times to be identified with a national tradition. His talent, according to him, is an individual and "divine gift" (*Corriere della Sera*, 11 November 1985, p. 1). However, he usually accepts that he learned everything as a *pibe* in the Argentinian *potreros*.

4 Juanjo confines Argentinian victory to a match of football. However, it occurred after the Argentinian defeat in the Falklands War in 1982. Players denied before the match that politics or revenge were at stake during this crucial game. Maradona has, however, reinterpreted the feelings of the players before the match. He said that, "to win over England in 1986 was more than to win over another national team: the victory was against a country" (Arcucci, 1999, p. 38).

Bibliography

Archetti, E.P. (1995) "Estilos y virtudes masculinas en *El Gráfico*: la creación del imaginario del fútbol argentino". *Desarrollo Económico*, 35: 419–42.

—— (1996) "Playing styles and masculine virtues in Argentine football". In M. Melhuus and K.A. Stølen (eds), *Machos, Madonnas, Mistresses: Contesting the Power of Gender Imagery in Latin America*. London: Verso.

—— (1997) "And Give Joy to my Heart". Ideology and emotions in the Argentinian cult of Maradona". In G. Armstrong and R. Giulianotti (eds), *Entering the Field: New Perspectives on World Football*, Oxford: Berg.

—— (1998) "The *potrero* and the *pibe*: territory and belonging in the mythical account of Argentinean football". In N. Lovell (ed.), *Territory and Belonging*. London: Routledge.

—— (1999) *Masculinities. Football, Polo and the Tango in Argentina*. Oxford: Berg.

Arcucci, D. (1999) "Diego Maradona. honestidad brutal", *Rolling Stone*, 14: 32–40.

Burns, J. (1996) *Hand of God: The Life of Maradona*. London: Bloomsbury.

Carlin, J. (1999) "Locos por el fútbol". *El País Semanal*, 1195: 20–9.

Casas, F. and Chacón, P. (1996) "San Dieguito. La novela de Maradona. La Película de Maradona", *Página 30*, 5 (69): 6–11.

Fontanarrosa, A. and Sanz, A. (1994) *El Pequeño Diccionario Ilustrado: el Fútbol Argentino*. Buenos Aires: Clarin-Aguilar.

Gilbert, A. (1996) "Cebolla de Fiorito. Maradona Jurásico", *Página 30*, 5 (69): 16–21.

Holt, R. and Mangan, J.A. (1996) "Prologue: heroes of a European past". *The International Journal of the History of Sport*, 13 (1): 1–13.

Kanikar, H. (1994) " 'Real true boys'; moulding the cadets of imperialism". In A. Cornwall and N. Lindisfarne (eds), *Dislocating Masculinities: Comparative Ethnographies*. London: Routledge.

Novak, M. (1993) "The joy of sports". In C.S. Prebish (ed.), *Religion and Sport: The Meeting of the Sacred and the Profane*. Westport, CT: Greenwood Press.

Rank, O. (1990) *In Quest of the Hero*. Princeton, NJ: Princeton University Press.

Soriano, O. (1994) "Huérfanos", *Página 12*, 1 July 1994: 1, 32.

10

GRETZKY NATION

Canada, crisis and Americanization

Steven J. Jackson

Be happy for Gretzky. He's finally free. He's been a celebrity since
he was six. He's been in national magazines since he was 11. Been
a pro since high school. After 32 years, the pressure is finally off.
Starting this week, Gretzky never has to be Great again.

(Rick Reilly, *Sports Illustrated*)

The fact that he is simply known as "The Great One" reveals something unique
about ice hockey star Wayne Gretzky. Indeed, trying to write about Gretzky
without falling into the trappings of either a celebrity profile or a eulogy is
nearly impossible. On Sunday, April 18, 1999 Wayne Gretzky played the final
game of his twenty-year professional ice hockey career. Although his New York
Rangers lost in overtime to the Pittsburgh Penguins Gretzky received what
might have been the longest standing ovation in sport history and was called
upon to return to the ice several times to the chants of "encore". In some
respects the fanfare was simply a demonstration of appreciation for the star who
had dominated his sport for so many years. Even a cursory look at his list of
exploits and achievements are testimony to this extraordinary individual:

- Gretzky holds 61 NHL records including most goals (940) and assists
  (2,223) for a total of 3,163 points.
- Gretzky scored more than 200 points per year six times (no other player
  even reached 200 in a season) and scored over 100 points 15 times over 20
  NHL seasons.
- He won 4 Stanley Cups, played in 19 All Star games, won 10 Art Ross
  trophies (leading scorer), 9 Hart trophies (Most Valuable Player), 2 Conn
  Smyth trophies (MVP in the Playoffs) and 4 Lady Byng awards (Most
  Gentlemanly Player).
- Such was his dominance that by comparison Michael Jordan would have
  had to score 50 points every game of his career to equal Gretzky.

However, while these statistics provide a rather crude measure of his quantitative output, it is Gretzky's status as ice hockey's only transcendent sporting icon
(Swift, 1999) that enables us to gain some understanding of his wider cultural

and symbolic meaning. In 1984 he was appointed an officer of the Order of Canada; in November, 1999 he was inducted into the Hockey Hall of Fame; and, on June 5, 2000 he received an Honorary Doctor of Laws degree from the University of Alberta. Nevertheless, even these awards pale in comparison to the emotional display witnessed during his final game in April, 1999. Gretzky had hinted at his possible retirement during the 1999 season but it was only made official a few days before the Rangers last game of the year. It was a farewell sporting spectacle like no other. Above and beyond Gretzky's extended standing ovation, the career highlights displayed on Madison Square Garden's big screens and the long list of speeches and gifts, consider the following symbolic events that marked the special day:

• Gretzky's number "99" was painted behind both goals. His jersey number would later be retired, not from the team, *but from the league*.
• Former team-mates of Gretzky's (e.g., Paul Coffey) were given the day off by their owners so that they could watch the Great One in his final performance.
• Both the American and Canadian national anthems were adapted to make reference to Wayne Gretzky. The Star Spangled Banner included the phrase: "For the land of the *Wayne* and the home of the brave". In turn, during the singing of Canada's national anthem pop star Bryan Adams changed the last line which normally reads "O Canada we stand on guard for thee" substituting the lyrics "We're gonna miss you W-A-Y-N-E ... G-R-E-T-Z-K-Y".

The latter example is particularly striking. While many sport celebrities, including Gretzky, have had songs written about and/or dedicated to them, it is difficult to imagine any other athlete having something as sacred as a national anthem transformed on their behalf. In Gretzky's case the anthems of two different nations were changed revealing his status on both sides of the 49th parallel. These brief examples may seem trivial yet they demonstrate Gretzky's unparalleled status not only as a sporting celebrity but as a national icon. Gretzky's retirement in 1999 left the hockey world wondering if there would ever be another one like him. Moreover, his departure left Canadians wondering if they would ever have another global sporting star that could serve as their ambassador. Even the Prime Minister, Jean Chretien, begged him to play "one more year".

The purpose of the preceding prologue is to update the life and cultural significance of "All Canadian" sport star Wayne Gretzky. Arguably, the end of his career and the beginning of a new millennium provide an opportune point at which to reflect upon the sport celebrity who became the focal point of a crisis of national identity just over a decade ago (Jackson, 1994). The alleged crisis emerged as a consequence of the articulation of particular political, economic and cultural events in Canada during 1988. Among these events were the Canada–United States Free Trade Agreement (FTA), the ensuing federal election and, curiously, the marriage and subsequent trade of Wayne Gretzky from the Edmonton Oilers to the Los Angeles Kings. What was most striking about these seemingly unrelated events was the fact that all were linked, by particular interest groups, to a debate about the future of Canadian culture, identity and sovereignty. More specifically, Wayne Gretzky came to symbolize the fate of Canada, a seemingly victimized nation, trying to withstand the threat of "Americanization". Notably, the same debate, albeit within a different context, continues today. For example, reporting on a recent meeting of 200 of Canada's most influential citizens, *Washington Post* writer Steven Pearlstein asserted that: "With reluctance and resignation, Canadians are concluding that what they once celebrated as the world's longest undefended border is quickly vanishing. Economically, culturally, socially, demographically, even politically, Canada ... is becoming indistinguishable from the United States" (2000, p. 11). Arguably, concerns about Canada's relationship with the United States and the implications for Canadian culture and identity are seemingly just as, if not more, important as we begin the twenty-first century.

In this chapter I reflect upon the 1988 crisis of Canadian identity by tracing the discourses that linked the fate of one particular sport star, Wayne Gretzky, to the fate of the nation within the context of an impending threat of "Americanization". I begin by providing a brief socio-historical context within which to understand the issue of Americanization in relation to Canadian culture and identity. In turn, I revisit the media coverage of the 1988 marriage and trade of hockey star Wayne Gretzky to illustrate how they were articulated within a discourse of crisis (Jackson, 1994). Finally, I discuss the politics and contradictions associated with the notion of a national crisis of identity with respect to the threat of Americanization.

Globalization, Americanization and Canadian identity

Globalization has emerged as the most important theoretical, political, economic and cultural issue of our times (cf. Appadurai, 1990; 1996; Albrow and King, 1990; Featherstone, 1990; Ferguson, 1992; Hall, 1991; Hirst and Thompson, 1996; King, 1990; Robertson, 1992a; 1992b; Sklar, 1992). While it no doubt oversimplifies the matter the two main groups of proponents within the debate can be categorized as either the homogenizers or the heterogenizers. According to Andrews *et al.* (1996) those who might be described as the *homogenizers* pessimistically anticipate the emergence of a globally shared, universalized culture. Conversely, the *heterogenizers* refute such a determinist view of globalization, arguing instead for a recognition and celebration of every particular localized culture. With respect to the former theoretical strand, the homogenization of culture, there are critics who have identified the United States and the process of Americanization as potential threats. Whether the notion of Americanization has any real theoretical or concrete validity is open to debate. However, there is no denying the concept exists within both popular and academic discourse (cf. Allison, 1991; Lealand, 1994; Klein, 1991; McKay and Miller, 1991).

In sport the issue has been examined employing a variety of conceptualizations including: globalization, modernization, homogenization and even mundialization (Andrews, 1997; Guttmann, 1991; Jackson and Andrews, 1999; Maguire, 1990, 1993, 1999; McKay *et al.*, 1993; Sabo, 1993; Wagner, 1990). In several cases the more specific conceptual category of "Americanization" has been employed (Kidd, 1970; 1991; Klein, 1991, McKay and Miller, 1991).

The use of the term Americanization, however, has also been subject to criticism (Heron, 1977; Kidd, 1991; Maguire, 1990). Kidd (1991), while acknowledging the relative usefulness of the term Americanization in the Canadian case, is quick to point out that perhaps "American capitalist hegemony" is an even more appropriate term, in light of the explicit influence that the United States has had on the organization of sport in Canada. According to Kidd the term Americanization "tends to reify the abstraction of Canadian sport and to oversimplify the complexity of its social determinations" (ibid., p. 180).

Perhaps more than any other nation, Canada has directly been confronted with the issue of Americanization (Jackson, 1992; Jackson, 1994; Kilbourn, 1988; Smith, 1980). Guttmann (1991) acknowledges that the Canadian case is particularly striking in light of the coexisting nature of its political sovereignty and its simultaneous economic and cultural dependence on the United States. Canada's cultural dependency has largely been attributed to its wary, yet largely unrestricted, attitude towards American media products. As McPhail (1992) notes, Canada is about twenty years ahead of the European Community in terms of its experience in confronting the media and the Americanization phenomenon. Thus, Canada may provide some unique opportunities for investigations of the process of Americanization beyond that of simple geographic proximity. This analysis is a case study that focuses on Canada and illustrates some of the problematics associated with the current debate. To be clear from the outset, however, the focus is less upon the issue of whether Americanization is but one, or the dominant, manifestation of a more general economic and technological process and more upon how the concept itself was represented by the media. Specifically, this analysis traces the discourses of crisis surrounding Canada's most prominent sporting hero, Wayne Gretzky, as they were articulated to the notion of Americanization by both Canadian and American media in 1988.

Americanization and Canadian identity in socio-historical perspective

The problem of Americanization as it impacts on Canadian identity is not new. Indeed, it is impossible to overlook the unending influence of the country with which Canada shares the longest undefended border in the world. As Graubard remarks: "No Canadian is ever able to ignore or forget the United States, though the reciprocal sentiment is decidedly uncommon" (1988, p. ix).

Evidence of this enduring influence abounds in the number of scholarly works which address the issue, giving some indication of its captivating significance to Canadians who have been described by Gwyn as: "the world champions at collective self-analysis" (1985, p. 188). Early works such as Goldwin Smith's (1891) *Canada and the Canadian Question* to later titles including: *The Canadian Quandary* (Johnson, 1963); *Neighbors Taken For Granted* (Merchant, 1966); *Life With Uncle* (Holmes, 1981); *On Guard for Thee* (Bowker, 1988); *From Nation to Colony* (Scott, 1988); and, *In the Eye of the Eagle* (Lisee, 1990) are testimony to a pervasive concern with Canada's relationship to the United States. Moreover, numerous works specifically employ the term Americanization in their titles, including Gullett (1911), Lumsden (1970), and Moffett's (1972) *The Americanization of Canada*. Each of these works focuses on various aspects of culture and identity with respect to Canada's confrontation with Americanization.

In the 1980s one feature of this relationship was highlighted in Richard Gwyn's (1985) book, *The 49th Paradox*. Gwyn's title is an insightful turn of phrase in reference to the fact that the 49th parallel, which acts as the border between Canada and the United States, is considered to serve as much more than a symbolic geographical marker. Canadian Peter Newman notes: "that boundary is the most important fact about this country. It defines not only our citizenship but how we behave collectively and what we think individually. It determines who we are" (1989, p. 24). Such statements highlight an important feature of the socially constructed and hegemonic basis of national identities.

The dialectical nature of a national identity is expressed with respect to how it is defined out of both similarity and difference. A nation tends to be defined "out of difference" to other nations through the use of stereotypes, symbols, and practices (including sport) which supposedly embody a sense of cultural uniqueness. However, the process of defining a nation out of difference is intimately interrelated to its hegemonic capacity. In effect, discourses that employ terms such as "we", "us", and "our" in order to signify "the nation" have become naturalized and taken for granted. Consequently, a nation becomes an all-inclusive concept that ignores and marginalizes other existing cultural identities. Crucially, it is the criticism of external "Others", including the United States, that serves to both bolster national identity and mask its hegemonic relations. Strikingly, more than ten years later his comments about the importance of the 49th parallel to national identity, Newman remains rather pessimistic about Canada's future:

> Without Canadians being aware of it, the Americanisation of the economy has entered a disturbing new reality ... We find ourselves on the cusp of the millennium well on the way to becoming an economic

colony of the Americans – self governing still, but indentured to the Yankee dollah, just the same.

(Pearlstein, 2000, p. 11)

Arguably, any understanding of the basis and meaning of Canadian identity must examine its network of interrelationships, including those with the USA.

Americanization and Canadian identity in 1988

Conceptualized as a "conjunctural moment", the intersection of a specific set of political, economic, and cultural events led some people to label 1988 a "year of crisis" in Canadian identity. The ascription of "crisis" arose in part from the campaign for the 1988 Canadian federal election and, more specifically, the central debate within it, the Canada–United States Free Trade Agreement (FTA). The significance of the FTA was captured by McDonald who noted that: "[it] had loomed as the most fundamental decision on national identity that the country would likely make for the remainder of the century" (1989, p. 28). Likewise, Davies noted the importance of the issue when he suggested that the government was "signing away Canada's soul" (1989, p. 28).

In brief, the goal of the Free Trade Agreement (FTA), which took effect January 1, 1989, was to reduce and eventually remove any remaining tariffs and trade barriers between the two countries over the ensuing ten-year period. Arguing in 1988, Canadian opponents of the Agreement asserted that free trade with the U.S. would lead to American economic domination of the Canadian economy (Bowker, 1988; Lapierre, 1987; Scott, 1988). As one newspaper headline of the time put it: "Canadian Identity is embedded in Free Trade Pact". Notably, since 1989 these same arguments have continued to be voiced (Andley, 1998; Winter, 2000). The current fragile state of the Canadian economy undermined by recent trade agreements between the United States and Mexico (in which Canada was also a partner) has only amplified resentment (Hurtig, 1992). Consequently, Canadian sovereignty, Canadian culture, a Canadian way of life, in essence, "a Canadian identity" continues to be represented as being under threat of extinction at the hands of Americanization.

Notwithstanding the defensive nationalist stance, the attitude expressed by some of the more conservative ranks of the "American" press and academia suggested that the perceived threat on the part of many Canadians is perhaps not unfounded. Consider, for example, the following comments from an article entitled: "Come to Uncle" that was published in *The New Republic*:

Canada needs us. Indeed, it's hard not to suspect that in briefly threatening to reject this obviously sensible treaty, Canada – as is so often the case with stagy suicide attempts – was simply trying to draw attention to itself. The entire election was a cry for help … it doesn't take a Ph.D. in psychology to realize that Canadians' mock horror at the thought of

169

becoming part of the United States actually masks a deep desire to do precisely that. They protest too much. Their lips say "no, no", but their eyes say "yes, yes" … There is only one cure for this complex neurosis. We must purge it once and for all by giving Canadians what they secretly want. We must embrace them, adopt them, love them, annex them. In short, we must make Canada the 51st state.

(1988, p. 4)

While undoubtedly satirical, this is significant because it captures one of the prevailing moods in Canada represented by the media during the FTA debates; a mood based on an assumption of the US desire to assimilate, merge or otherwise incorporate Canada. Despite these indictments, it must be recognized that Canada and the United States have long engaged in the most unrestricted trade of any two countries in the world, with an estimated annual exchange of goods and services worth over $US 1 billion per day (Pearlstein, 2000). In fact, 80 percent of trade between Canada and the USA was already "free" prior to the signing of the FTA. Such a contradiction prompted critics such as Peter Brimelow to charge that the current popularization of Canadian nationalism and identification "is a fraud, designed primarily to benefit particular interest groups in Canada" (1986, p. 1).

There is little doubt that the FTA was being translated as the "Americanization" of Canada. It is also clear that resistance to the Agreement became a rallying point for Canadian nationalists and a political platform for the two major opposition parties, the Liberals and the New Democratic Party. The Liberals said they would renegotiate the deal; the NDP wanted it thrown out. The political and cultural ramifications stemming from the label of a "crisis" of national identity was noted by Desaulniers (1987). He suggests that in an age of political anomie statespersons often attempt to reintroduce those time-honoured symbols that have consistently served to capture and mobilize the national collective. He also argues that a national identity becomes an all-embracing cultural concept representing collective attitudes, styles and emotions and that a crisis can be utilized politically by linking patriot and partisan interests. The following declaration by then Liberal party leader John Turner illustrates this point quite well by linking the FTA with Canadian sovereignty: "I'm not going to allow Mr. Mulroney to destroy a great 120-year-old dream called Canada … This is more than an election. It is your future" (Burns, 1988, p. A-2).

Yet, despite considerable nationalist opposition, the voting Canadian populace re-elected Prime Minister Brian Mulroney and his Progressive Conservative party on November 21, 1988. Such a result might be interpreted as indicating Canadians' confidence in and support of the government, and a denial of any suggested fear of Americanization. Alternatively, the re-election of Brian Mulroney could indicate a simple lack of candidate choice or reflect the inherent limitations of the parliamentary system of government. As Clarke *et al.* (1991) note, there was no "national" mandate in the 1988 election. Despite the fact that Brian Mulroney's Conservatives held office, they were supported by only 43 percent of the popular vote, down from 50 percent in 1984. More voters actually deserted the Conservatives in 1988 than were moving towards them. The previous section has highlighted the economic and political context of Canada in 1988. Clearly, there were tensions amidst the pending Free Trade Agreement and the FTA was certainly being used by particular interest groups to further their political ends. How, then, did an ice hockey star like Wayne Gretzky become so entangled in such a complex and politically charged debate? To even begin to understand the issue demands some understanding of the cultural significance of sport in Canada, and in particular ice hockey in Canada.

Sport, popular culture, and Canadian identity

Sport has long played a major role in the social construction of national identity in Canada. However, since the 1960s the specific use of government policy to exploit sport's role in defining Canadian culture and identity out of difference to the United States has gathered momentum. For example, during the 1968 federal election the issue of national unity became a central platform for eventual Prime Minister Pierre Trudeau. It was Trudeau who saw culture as central to unity, and who saw sport as an important part of culture. In 1969, the year following his election, Trudeau commissioned a report titled the *Task Force on Sport*, as part of his "Unity through Sport" campaign. In part, the report argued that sport was "an effective antidote to economic and cultural domination by the United States" (Macintosh *et al.*, 1987, p. 74). Here was one of the first direct articulations of the role of sport, as a cultural buffer, in defining Canadian identity with respect to the United States.

Throughout the next twenty years sport remained at the forefront of state initiatives in order to construct a national identity in relation to the United States. As Macintosh *et al.* note: "[sport] has an important role to play in any government attempt to promote unity and a unique Canadian identity" (1987, p. 186); and, "in countering the threat to Canadian identity of the pervasive mass culture of the United States" (ibid., p. 174). This brief overview helps illustrate the role of sport in state policy for the ongoing signification of the vulnerability of Canadian identity in relation to Americanization.

Unfortunately, despite its apparent significance within the Canadian social formation, sport, as a form of popular culture, has too often been neglected as a site for serious scholarly analysis. Gruneau has acknowledged this problem by charging that there has been a "marginalization of research on popular cultural forms and practices", including sport, and a "failure to pay sufficient attention to the politics of the popular" (1988, pp. 16–17). In light of this inattention to popular cultural forms, it is duly noted that two events in the life of hockey star Wayne Gretzky in 1988 could be interpreted within a discourse of crisis; specifically, his marriage to American actress Janet Jones and his trade from the Edmonton Oilers to the Los Angeles Kings. The meaning of these events can only be understood by grasping the significance, however mythical, of ice hockey in Canada.

Strikingly, in 1987, Doug Beardsley, while writing a book about the meaning of ice hockey in Canada was unable to refrain from a social commentary on the current and future status of Canadian identity and its relationship to the United States. He insisted that:

> Canadians do not wish to have a distinctive national identity. This indifferent country, that worships mostly money and mediocrity, sees the quest for a national identity as a passing phase, a gently warming wave that comes once a generation, then subsides on the same rocky shore. With the possibility of free trade, we open ourselves even more – if that's possible – to American influence and domination.
>
> (1987, p. 183)

The "loss" of Wayne Gretzky came to embody many Canadians' worst fear regarding this American influence and domination. According to the media his personal fate signified the inevitable impact that Americanization would have on Canada. But, who is Wayne Gretzky and why did his story carry such significance in 1988?

Canadian identity, Wayne Gretzky (the man who would be (a) king)

A few excerpts from Beardsley's (1987) book *Country on Ice* help put hockey, and its 1988 Canadian personification, Wayne Gretzky, into perspective. According to Beardsley:

> because hockey so clearly defines the Canadian experience, Wayne Gretzky is the latest in a long line of hockey heroes who personify the hopes, wishes, and dreams of the Canadian people ... by finding greatness in him, we find it in ourselves.
>
> (1987, p. 109).

Gretzky himself acknowledges the distinct nature of his rise to national hero symbol, admitting that:

> my childhood was a little different from most. I could skate at two. I was nationally known at six. I was signing autographs at ten. I had a national magazine article written about me at eleven and a thirty-minute national television show done on me at fifteen. I turned pro and kept going to high school.
>
> (1990, p. 7)

As strange as it sounds it seems to be a bit of an understatement to call Wayne Gretzky a "good" or even "great" hockey player. Reflecting on the most famous trade in sports one soon realizes that Wayne Gretzky was already a King before he left for Los Angeles back in 1988.

Indeed, it could be argued that the vast majority of Wayne Gretzky's NHL career has been couched in terms of a royal, if not immortal existence. The year 1988 proved the zenith of this adulation, with interestingly but not surprisingly, an event not directly connected to hockey – his marriage to American actress, Janet Jones. The Canadian "Royal Wedding", while re-affirming Gretzky's noble status, also evoked a fear that was to become a reality later in the year – perhaps this "Hollywood Princess" would lure the King from his Canadian castle, which would result in his eventual abdication.

The royal wedding

The anxiety of the Canadian press was obvious. Even from the announcement of the engagement on January 12, 1988 concern was being directed not only at the player's short-term playing prospects, but also at the couple's longer-term, life prospects. In this respect, the future "Mrs. Wayne Gretzky" was viewed as a double threat to Canada's most prized possession. Janet Jones was described as a Jezebel, Dragon Lady and another Yoko Ono, in reference to Ono's purported role in stealing John Lennon and breaking up the Beatles (Friedman *et al.*, 1988). As Gretzky (1990, p. 143) described the reaction of the Canadian people:

> Some were offended that I'd fallen in love with an American and not a Canadian. Others were upset that I was going out with a *Playboy* magazine centerfold ... . I thought it was stupid that so many Canadians saw a relationship between the Playboy pictures and Janet being an American.

In defense, Gretzky takes the liberty of naming some of the "Canadian" *Playboy* centerfolds including Kimberly Conrad, Shannon Tweed and Dorothy Stratten. In essence, Gretzky tries to highlight the irony of the attacks on his wife in light of the fact that the Canadian public had taken great pride in claiming the success of its own Playboy centerfolds. Further attempts were made to down-play the "national" significance of the relationship. Gretzky, for example, stated that: "We're just two normal people, a Canadian and an American, getting married" (Strachan, 1988a, p. A24). Such an assertion displayed a complete disregard for not only his elevated position within the Canadian socio-cultural structure at the time, but also the press's role in creating the Gretzky "dynasty". Interestingly though, he felt it necessary to refute the concerns of the press, regarding his forthcoming marriage: "There's no question she has rejuvenated my life," he said, "she has been a big influence on my career" (ibid., p. A24). In this way Gretzky himself is contributing to the discourse, created by the press, in which his actions have been interpreted within the context of a crisis in Canadian identity.

Despite pleas for anonymity, the coverage and hype of the wedding continued. According to one member of the Canadian media: "This will probably be the highest-profile wedding in Canadian history and there have been comments that it's almost a Canadian version of a royal wedding" (ibid., p. A24). Even the wedding reception emcee, actor Alan Thicke added to the hype, comparing the wedding to that of Lady Diana and Prince Charles, ... telling guests that Gretzky had gotten his hair cut "so his ears would look bigger, like those of the Prince of Wales" (Wulf, 1988, p. 12).

In actual fact "The Wedding" did not reflect its media billing. As Al Strachan described it in his editorial, it was "a pleasant, low-keyed affair" (Strachan, 1988b, p. D5). This was not the wedding the Canadian press wanted, and it certainly wasn't the "Royal Wedding" it created elsewhere.

While the discourse emanating from media coverage of the wedding indicated a concern for Gretzky's tenure in Canada, direct links were being made between the wedding and the Free Trade Agreement. One observer wrote:

> the marriage of the hockey hero and the Hollywood starlet projected an apt symbolism at a time of often-bitter political debate over the proposed Canada–U.S. free trade agreement, which some critics say will tie Canada too closely to the United States.
>
> (*Maclean's*, July 25, 1988, p. 31)

The implication is that Gretzky's decision to "tie the knot" was symbolic of the feared excessively close political, economic, and cultural ties Canada will have with the USA. Furthermore, it is implied that Gretzky is not being true to his roots; that he is selling out to the USA. As editor John Robert Colombo of *New Canadian Quotations* put it: "It is, shall we say, free trade in action" (*Maclean's*, July 25, 1988, p. 31). In a further example Ross (1988, p. 4) commented that: "The 'royal' wedding reads partly like the Canada–U.S. free trade deal. Wayne Gretzky's (Canada) gifts to Janet Jones: a very expensive engagement ring (one estimate put the price at $125,000 although Gretzky denies this), a $250,000 car, plus other gifts. Jones's (United States) gift to Gretzky: a kiss."

This reference suggests what many critics of the Free Trade Agreement have noted elsewhere, namely that Canada will get short-changed by the USA. The assumption is that the USA will enjoy an expansion of an already large consumer market and reap the benefits of access to an oasis of natural resources. Conversely, Canada is portrayed as having its generous nature being taken advantage of.

The "wedding" may have provided one concrete example of Gretzky's importance to Canada created by the indigenous press. However, the events of August 9 and beyond, not only reinforced the fears expressed earlier in the year, but also provided the press with another example of linking the cultural hysteria created by the Free Trade debate, with a prominent cultural form, namely hockey, in the persona of Wayne Gretzky.

It was on August 9 (often referred to as Black Tuesday) that Gretzky was traded from the Edmonton Oilers, to the Los Angeles Kings. Undoubtedly this turn of events shocked the hockey world, and certainly we are left in no doubt that it had equally as profound an effect upon Canada itself. It was noted that the trade was the biggest headline for the *Edmonton Journal* newspaper since the end of World War II (Gretzky, 1990). The following newspaper headlines are reflective of the media reaction:

Defection of "national treasure" stuns fans, players, executives
> (*Globe and Mail*, August 10, 1988, pp. 1–2)

Grieving for the Great One
> (*Vancouver Sun*, August 13, 1988, p. B1)

A nation in mourning
> (*Sports Illustrated*, August 22, 1988, p. 94)

In addition Houston wrote of the event:

As you will know by now, history was made yesterday. We're aware of this because the reports tell us it was the world's biggest trade, ever. You could pick your sport, never mind that hockey is up there with snowshoeing and darts in laidback L.A. Still, in Canada the Great One was abdicating his throne to be with the woman he loved, and he shed a tear.

> (1988, p. A14)

The discourse of crisis and its articulation to the threat of Americanization continued. Quickfall (1988, p. 22) suggested that: "Canadians are being forced into Americans' way of thinking. This is an example of it." What is being implied is that the Gretzky trade symbolized an ideological shift in Canadian values perhaps underscored by what Kidd (1991) refers to as American cultural hegemony. One aspect of an American cultural hegemony emerged in the search for a US perspective on the controversial event. For example, Mark Mulvoy, the managing editor of *Sports Illustrated*, remarked that: "This is a terrible blow to Canadian pride. Canada, as a nation, always had an inferiority complex. Now it must feel like a long lost stepchild" (Fischler, 1988, p. 12).

These remarks emphasize two important conceptual points regarding Americanization and Canadian national identity. First, the American media also contributed to the discourse of crisis. They did so by perpetuating the myth of the centrality of ice hockey in Canada and by reproducing a discourse which focused on Canada's supposed inferiority complex. And, second, there is a need to recognize that the American media were able to contribute to the discourse of crisis both within and outside of the USA, through such publications as *Sports Illustrated* and *The Hockey News* might be fairly limited both in Canada and elsewhere. Consequently, while the discourse of crisis evident in the American press cannot be assumed to have any guaranteed effects, the fact remains that these media products and their meanings were in circulation and hence available.

While it can be argued that the discourses located in all of the previous articles could be indirectly positioned within the Free Trade debate and the threat of Americanization, the next set of examples are far more blatant in their connections. The first set focuses on the impending economic threat of the USA via Free Trade signified by Gretzky's move to Los Angeles. Said one unhappy fan who called *The Globe and Mail* newspaper in Toronto: "This is what happens with free trade. We export a national hero to the United States. We lose a national treasure to the Los Angeles Kings" (Strachan, 1988, p. A2). Another fan said: "If this is an indication of the free trade between Canada and the U.S., then Canada is in trouble" (Hansen, 1988, p. 21). And third, a Canadian sports journalist stated: "Who cares why Gretzky is gone? He's gone. He's not our star any more, he's theirs. If this be free trade, stuff it" (Taylor, 1988, p. 94). Thus, Gretzky's personal fate is articulated to the fate of Canada as a nation with the media linking the Free Trade Agreement and the threat of Americanization.

A striking connection was further drawn between the economy, culture and the environment. According to Fotheringham: "This is what happens with Free Trade, they get Gretzky, we get acid rain" (1989, p. 84). In this case Americanization is represented in terms of a pervasive Canadian view of the US uncaring and irresponsible attitude towards pollution and its environmental consequences.

In addition to the previous examples of a perceived "threat of Americanization", Gretzky's own father, Walter, contributed to the despair on the part of Canadians stating that: "He's a Canadian institution and what's Canadian should remain Canadian. It's a son-of-a-gun when Americans can take away something like that"; he further states: "You Americans think you can buy anything we have, that's not the way I feel, that's reality" (Barol *et al.* 1988, p. 61). Such a statement indicates how a central character amid a story can contribute to the construction of a crisis through media discourse. Walter Gretzky claims that his perspective is not personal opinion but reflects "reality".

Even scholars contributed to the discourse of crisis. A *USA Today* article entitled: "Gretzky trade triggers U.S.–Canada *War*" featured insights provided by sociologist Neil Snarr. The article begins by referring to the political climate between the two nations in 1988:

President Bush/Dukakis said he received a final message from the prime minister Thursday demanding the immediate return of Wayne Gretzky. The U.S. has refused. The Pentagon said all available troops have been rushed to the border in anticipation of an all-out attack by millions of crazed Canadians pushing toward Los Angeles and yelling "Remember the Wayne".

(Snarr, August 12, 1988, p. 2C)

Furthermore, Snarr injects that: "The Gretzky deal could hurt the pending U.S.–Canada trade agreement .... I'm not saying the Gretzky trade to Los Angeles will kill (the agreement) ... But I wouldn't be surprised to see it happen ... They [Canadians] view it as another example of the U.S. flexing its big-money muscle to get something from Canada" (*USA Today*, August 12, 1988, p. 2C). Each of the aforementioned cases indicates how the media articulated the Wayne Gretzky trade to the notion of an impending American economic threat. The next set of examples indicate how a discourse of crisis is further reproduced through the media's incorporation of key political figures into the story.

Consider the response of then New Democratic Party House Leader Nelson Riis, who issued a tongue-in-cheek press release suggesting that the federal government intervene to stop the hockey star's trade. Referring to Gretzky as an irreplaceable Canadian commodity Riis stated:

Wayne Gretzky is a national symbol like the beaver, Pierre Berton and Harold Ballard .... It's like the *Wheel of Fortune* without Vanna White .... They may as well have sent Wayne to the moon as send him to L.A. Everybody knows that Los Angeles isn't a hockey town – they wouldn't know a hockey puck from a beach ball.

(Strachan, 1988, p. A2)

Ironically, Riis happens to draw upon an American comparison of the Wheel of Fortune in order to express the significance of the event. He further called upon Sports Minister Jean Charest to buy Gretzky's contract and at least confine the trade to a Canadian team. The previous extract is a clear, if trite, example of a prominent politician entering the debate regarding the distinctive cultural identity of Canada, which would "inevitably" be eroded by an increase in the American influence in Canada, thus bringing in the spectre of the Free Trade Agreement.

Politicians were also indirectly positioned with respect to the crisis by the media. One reporter stated that: "Considering what Gretzky did to Canada, Prime Minister Mulroney may need a legion of shrinks to shape up the national psyche" (Fischler, 1988, p. 12). Here the media contribute to a discourse of crisis by articulating Gretzky's departure as an assumed national problem facing the Prime Minister as Canada's political leader.

Finally, when asked if Prime Minister Mulroney couldn't summon the powers of his office in a case of such national emergency, PM spokesman Bruce Phillips laughed, stating that Gretzky will continue to be a great representative of hockey and Canada. The last example, although highlighting a lighter side of the event, nevertheless reveals how the media contributed to a discourse of crisis.

This section has attempted to show how the media, for whatever reason and intent (if any), articulated the Wayne Gretzky scenario within the discourse of a culturally based Canadian identity, which they suggest, is constantly and increasingly under threat from its overbearing southern neighbour. Gretzky is characterized as portraying the supposed plight of Canada, with Janet Jones representing the American threat even though her influence on his move was really never substantiated.

Although the Gretzky saga was overwhelmingly articulated within the framework of a discourse of crisis, it would be foolish and inaccurate to presume that this representation guaranteed any influence upon the Canadian populace. Moreover, there was some evidence of alternative and/or counterhegemonic responses to the trade within the media. Acknowledging the interpretive limitations of poll findings it is noted that one carried out shortly after the trade found: "Few crying over Gretzky" (*Vancouver Sun*, August 27, 1988, p. A2); and that "Gretzky means little to most Canadians" (*Montreal Gazette*, August 27, 1988, p. D17).

In addition, Molinari (1988, p. 14) noted that:

> we have survived Armageddon. Two months after "The Day the Earth Stood Still", the planet hadn't altered its rotation, you can still see sunrises, and Edmonton is still on the map .... for all Wayne Gretzky is, he never was and never will be – despite those howls from so many – a Canadian treasure. A Canadian citizen, sure. A modest and wondrously skilled athlete, certainly. An exemplary role model for youngsters, absolutely. But sorry, folks, Gretzky wasn't one of his country's greatest natural resources.

According to these indicators not only were Canadians rejecting the overstated importance of Gretzky, and hence hockey, to the construction of a national identity, but also it suggests that the Canadian cultural plight (whether real or imagined) of which this case is presumably a symptom, is treated with indifference. Yet, it must be remembered that even these alternative representations emerged from the media. And, as previously noted there can be no assumption of any guaranteed media effects on Canadians, either individually or collectively.

The federal election results of November 21, 1988 that re-elected Brian Mulroney and his Progressive Conservative Party were widely interpreted as a vote in support of Free Trade. However, as previously noted, post-election surveys would suggest that this was not necessarily the case. In the end one is left with a very confusing picture. On the one hand, it could be argued that both sets of public indicators (the reaction to the Gretzky deal and the federal election result) refuted any "apparent" crisis of national identity, perhaps signalling the underlying strength and substance of a distinct Canadian autonomy. On the other hand, there were individuals who interpreted Gretzky's fate as symbolic of their nation's future subordination chiefly characterized in terms of Americanization. In either case, however, there was considerable evidence to suggest that there were attempts by the media and specific political factions, the Liberals and New Democrats in particular, to forge a crisis through the signification of Americanization. Indeed, in at least one case politicians made a direct link between Gretzky's and Canada's ultimate fate.

The pros and cons of the Canada–US Free Trade Agreement as well as other global free trade pacts continue to be debated. There seems to be a never-ending stream of discourses fixated on the economic colonization of Canada, the demise of social programs and the kinder, gentler society and the dreaded "brain drain". Moreover, a cursory view of the more recent socio-political climate would certainly lead one to assume that the Canadian social formation is in an ongoing state of crisis. From immigration to Aboriginal rights to continued separatist threats in Quebec, various segments of the media and the particular interest groups which influence them continue to represent Canada as unstable and unsure of its identity. Yet, regardless of the specific crisis emerging, there is a pervasive discourse that continues to construct the nation through reference to a threat of Americanization. The politics and contradictions associated with such discourses are highlighted by Mackey (1999, p. 145):

> The constant attempt to construct an authentic, differentiated, and bounded identity has been central to the project of Canadian nation-building, and is often shaped through comparison with, and demonisation of, the United States ... The USA has been used as an important external "other" many times in Canadian history ... Ironically, while one of Canada's defining and supposedly essential characteristics is tolerance to difference, one of the major socially acceptable forms of overt *in*tolerance has been that directed at the United States.

The serious nature of Canada's resentment towards the United States and the threat of Americanization is revealed in some recent Molson Canadian beer advertisements. The first one, "The Rant", which Garfield (2000) describes as a "manifesto of national identity", features a rather unassuming Canadian named Joe. Commencing rather reservedly the speech assumes increasing volume and passion as the Canadian reveals that he is *"not a lumberjack nor a fur trader, doesn't live in an igloo, eat blubber or own a dogsled and that he has a prime minister, not a president, speaks English and French, not American ... believes in peacekeeping, not policing, diversity, not assimilation, that Canada is the first nation of ice hockey and the best part of North America"*. The second Molson ad, "No doot aboot it" uses a Canadian presumably starting a new job at an American company (perhaps a subtle reference to the brain drain?) as its theme. The ad uses an obnoxious American co-worker who relentlessly taunts the new Canadian arrival with a selection of stereotypes ranging from toques and curling to lumberjacks and Canada's infamous employment of the word "eh". Reaching his breaking point the Canadian pulls the American's suit jacket over his head, as experienced ice hockey fighters do, in order to silence him. In combination, the two Molson advertisements appeal to a sense of anti-Americanism while at the same time expressing a revitalized sense of what it means to be a Canadian. Indeed, there does seem to be a trend that suggests there is a new attitude emerging, a sort of "Canada kicks ass" spirit although not all Canadians like it. A case in point was the backlash against Olympic 100 metre gold medallist Donovan Bailey after he defeated American Michael Johnson in the million-dollar race at the Toronto Skydome in 1997 (Jackson and Meier, 1999). Many Canadians felt that Bailey's ungracious post-victory behavior was unsportsman-like and in at least one case it was actually described as "un-Canadian" (Brunt, 1997, p. D12).

The extent to which Canadian culture and identity express a new form of confidence and nationalism is questionable. Returning to the story of Wayne Gretzky's retirement there were certainly many demonstrations of nationalism towards the man who had quietly assumed the role of representing the nation for so many years. For the most part his role in defining Canadian identity was unspoken except for the rare Canada Cup and Olympic moments where he donned the maple leaf jersey. Perhaps it was because Gretzky played in a North American professional sporting cartel where corporations are of primary importance. People tend to forget that Gretzky played the majority of his professional career in the United States not Canada. Following his move to Los Angeles in 1988, Gretzky moved twice, first to St. Louis in 1996 and then the following year to New York where he played his last three seasons. He may have been Canada's ambassador but he was also hockey's and the NHL's ambassador. Everywhere he went he attracted attention and fans. Most experts agree that Gretzky, almost single-handedly, made ice hockey popular in the United States. Evaluating Gretzky's impact Deacon's (1999, p. 20) notes that:

> The NHL that he joined in 1979 was poorly managed, had no U.S. network TV contract and had few prospects for growth. Since then, the league has expanded from 21 to 27 teams, and league officials attribute much of that to Gretzky's impact – to the success of the Los Angeles Kings and the subsequent profile it gave the game. Entertainment giants like Disney and Blockbuster suddenly wanted to play, so teams in Anaheim, Calif. and Miami, respectively, were born.

> Thanks in no small part to Gretzky, the NHL … could bill itself "The
> coolest game on earth" without blushing.

However, Gretzky's success in making the Canadian game popular in the
United States may reflect the very fears that nationalists expressed and fore-
warned during debates about free trade during the crisis of 1988. Wayne
Gretzky's personal career has certainly flourished since 1988, gaining fame and
fortune while remaining Canada's most cherished athlete. Likewise, the NHL,
as a professional sport entertainment corporation, has enjoyed increasing
success and seems to be making some inroads into the highly competitive US
market. Moreover, two Canadian cities have been successful in obtaining NBA
franchises: the Toronto Raptors and the Vancouver Grizzlies. However, one
only needs to think of former Canadian NHL franchises such as the Quebec
Nordiques and the Winnipeg Jets or even current vulnerable franchises such as
Ottawa, Calgary and Edmonton, to realize that "free trade" with the United
States, whether within or outside of sport has a downside. The reality is that the
NHL is more American-dominated than ever before with new teams emerging
in unlikely locations including: Nashville, Miami, Tampa Bay, Anaheim, Dallas
and Phoenix. However, it isn't so much the location of the new franchises it is
the political economy that underlies them that may be the real concern. In
simple terms, although "free trade" may work in theory there is no level playing
field between the Canadian and American economies. NHL franchises based in
the United States are subsidized by a range of municipal, state and federal tax
incentives that, combined with a stronger currency and larger fan base, make
American cities more attractive to players, owners and administrators.

The link between Wayne Gretzky, Canada and national identity provides one
site at which to specify the complexities inherent within the "Americanization of
culture" debate. And, while the concept of Americanization seems to be losing
favour with most theorists interested in the nature and consequences of globalization, its use within discourses associated with nationalist backlashes in
Canada and in other parts of the world prevails. I would like to suggest that if
the term is going to be used then a number of factors need to be taken into
consideration. First, and foremost, there is a need for a clearer understanding of
the concept of "Americanization" with respect to both its implicit and explicit
meanings, politics, and effects. Second, there is a need to differentiate between
ascriptive or "other imposed" notions of Americanization which simply serve as
a metaphor for social change and the actual effects the phenomenon may have
on the lived experiences of individuals and groups. Third, it is important to
identify and explore the role of human agency by recognizing how local
cultures challenge, resist and/or rearticulate American cultural products and
ideas (see Forgacs, 1992). Fourth, and finally, it is important to identify the
nature and extent to which "Americanization" is employed politically to
attribute indigenous social problems to an external source (Jackson, 1994). For

example, with respect to the notion of crisis and cultural politics in Canada Mackey (1999, p. 13) argues that:

> contrary to the common sense that circulates about national identity and cultural pluralism in Canada, national identity is not so much in a constant state of crisis, but that the reproduction of "crisis" allows the nation state to be a site of a constantly regulated politics of identity.

Those interested in exploring this issue specifically in relation to sport in Canada may wish to examine the research done on Ben Johnson (Jackson, 1998a, 1998b; Jackson *et al.*, 1998) and Donovan Bailey (Jackson and Meier, 1999).

Number 99 has retired but his influence as a popular cultural figure continues. Before he had even officially retired, Gretzky was questioned about his interest in becoming an NHL franchise owner. Indeed, he is now a part owner of the Phoenix Coyotes. At the same time there are voices crying out from the great white north pleading with Gretzky to save Canada's national game by buying one of the existing troubled franchises. Only time will tell whether Gretzky's sense of nationalism and his instincts for success in business can be married. For better or worse chances are that Gretzky, despite his retirement, will still be expected to be "The Great One" on or off the ice.

Bibliography

Albrow, M. and King, E. (1990) *Globalization, Knowledge and Society*. London: Sage.

Allison, P. (1991) Big Macs and baseball caps: the Americanisation of Auckland. *Metro*, *124*, 124–30.

Andley, P. (1998) *Culture or Commerce? Canadian Culture after Free Trade*. Toronto: Stoddart Publishing.

Andrews, D. (1997) The (Trans)National Basketball Association: American commodity-sign culture and global-local conjuncturalism. In A. Cvetovitch and D. Kellner (eds), *Politics and Cultural Studies Between the Global and the Local* (pp. 72–101). Boulder, CO: Westview Press.

Andrews, D., Carrington, B., Mazur, Z. and Jackson, S. (1996) Jordanscapes: a preliminary analysis of the global popular. *Sociology of Sport Journal*, 13, 428–57.

Appadurai, A. (1990) Disjuncture and difference in the global cultural economy. *Theory, Culture and Society*, 7, 295–310.

—— (1996) *Modernity at Large: Cultural Dimensions of Globalization*. Minneapolis: University of Minnesota Press.

Barol, B., Wright, L. and Lazarovici, L. (1988) Gretzky puts Edmonton on ice. *Newsweek*, August 22, pp. 60–1.

Beardsley, D. (1987) *Country on Ice*. Markham: Paperjacks Ltd.

Bowker, M.M. (1988) *On Guard for Thee: An Independent Review of the Free Trade Agreement*. Hull: Voyageur Publishing.

Brimelow, P. (1986) *The Patriot Game*. Toronto: Key Porter.

Brunt, S. (1997) Bailey fits modern hero model. *Globe and Mail*, June 2, p. D12.

Burns, J.F. (1988) Canada elections called for Nov. 21. *The New York Times*, October 2, p. A-2.

Canada prepares for royal wedding. (1988) *The Montreal Gazette*, June 19, p. D3.

Christie, J. and Hynes, M. (1988) Defection of national treasure stuns fans, players, executives. *Globe and Mail*, August 10, pp. A-1, A-2.

Clarke, H.D., Jenson, J., Le Duc, L. and Pammett, J.H. (1991) *Absent Mandate: Interpreting Change in Canadian Elections* (2nd edn). Toronto: Gage Educational Publishing Company.

Come to Uncle. (1988) *The New Republic*, December 12, p. 4.

Davies, R. (1989) Signing away Canada's soul: culture, identity, and the free trade agreement. *Harper's*, 278, 43–7.

Deacon, J. (1999) The great one. *Maclean's*, 112 (17), April 26, 16–21.

Desaulniers, J.P. (1987) What does Canada want? *Media, Culture and Society*, 9, 149–57.

Featherstone, M. (1990) Global culture: an introduction. *Theory, Culture and Society*, 7, 1–14.

Ferguson, M. (1992) The myth about globalization. *European Journal of Communication*, 7, 69–93.

Few crying over Gretzky. (1988) *The Vancouver Sun*, August 27, p. A2.

Fischler, S. (1988) Jones, Pocklington are big winners in trade. *The Hockey News*, 41, September 9, p. 12.

Forgacs, D. (1992) Americanisation: the Italian case, 1938–1954. Paper presented at the Americanization of Culture conference, University of Wales, Swansea, September 16–18.

Fotheringham, A. (1989) Different – in a manner of speaking. *Maclean's*, July, p. 84.

Friedman, J., Sheff, V. and Balfour, V. (1988) Trading places. *People Weekly*, August 29, pp. 38–41.

Garfield, B. (2000) Blame Canada and Molson for brilliant "Rant" at States. http://www.adage.com/news_and_features/ad_review/archives/ar20000508.html

Graubard, S.R. (1988) Preface: In search of Canada. *Daedalus*, 117, ix.

Gretzky, W. (with Rick Reilly) (1990) *Gretzky: An Autobiography*. New York: Harper-Collins Publishers.

Grieving for the Great One. (1988) *The Vancouver Sun*, August 13, p. B-1.

Gruneau, R. (1988) Notes on popular cultures and political practices. In R. Gruneau (ed.). *Popular Cultures and Political Practices* (pp. 11–32). Toronto: Garamond Press.

Gullett, H.S. (1911) The Americanization of Canada: an Australian's impressions. *United Empire*, 2, (6), June, p. 418.

Guttmann, A. (1991) Sports diffusion: a response to Maguire and the Americanization commentaries. *Sociology of Sport Journal*, 8, 185–90.

Gwyn, R. (1985) *The 49th Paradox: Canada in North America*. Toronto: Totem Books.

Hall, S. (1991) The local and the global: globalization and ethnicity. In A.D. King (ed.) *Culture, Globalization and the World-System*. London: Macmillan.

Hansen, G. (1988) Response to Gretzky trade [special phone-in response to The Great Trade in Armchair Critic]. *The Edmonton Sun*, August 11, p. 21.

Heron, C. (1977) *Imperialism, Nationalism and Canada*. Toronto: New Hogtown.

Hirst, P. and Thompson, G. (1996) *Globalization in Question*. Cambridge: Polity.

Hobsbawm, E. and Ranger, T. (1983) *The Invention of Tradition*. Cambridge: Cambridge University Press.

Holmes, J.W. (1981) *Life with Uncle*. Toronto: University of Toronto Press.

Houlihan, B. (1994) Homogenization, Americanization and creolization of sport: varieties of globalization. *Sociology of Sport Journal*, 11, 356–75.

Houston, W. (1988) Pocklington not the villain, after all. *The Globe and Mail*, August 10, p. A14.

Hurtig, M. (1992) *The Betrayal of Canada* (2nd edn). Toronto: Stoddart.

Jackson, S.J. (1992) Sport, crisis and Canadian identity in 1988: a cultural analysis. Unpublished doctoral dissertation, University of Illinois, Urbana.

—— (1994) Gretzky, crisis, and Canadian identity in 1988: rearticulating the Americanization of culture debate. *Sociology of Sport Journal*, 11 (4), 428–46.

—— (1998a) A twist of race: Ben Johnson and the Canadian crisis of racial and national identity. *Sociology of Sport Journal*, 15, 21–40.

—— (1998b) Life in the (mediated) Faust lane: Ben Johnson, national affect and the 1988 crisis of Canadian identity. *International Review for the Sociology of Sport*. 33 (3), 227–38.

Jackson, S.J. and Andrews, D.L. (1999) Between and beyond the global and the local: American popular sporting culture in New Zealand. *International Review for the Sociology of Sport*, 34 (1), 31–42.

Jackson, S.J., Andrews, D.L. and Cole, C.L. (1998) Race, nation, and authenticity of identity: interrogating the "Everywhere" man (Michael Jordan) and the nowhere man (Ben Johnson). *Journal of Immigrants and Minorities*, 17 (1), 82–102.

Jackson, S.J. and Meier, K.V. (1999) Hijacking the hegemonic hyphen: Donovan Bailey and the politics of racial and national identity in Canada. In R. Sands (ed.) *Global Jocks: Anthropology, Sport and Culture* (pp. 173–88). Westport, CT: Greenwood Press.

Johnson, H. (1963) *The Canadian Quandary*. New York: McGraw-Hill.

Kidd, B. (1970) Canada's "national" sport. In I. Lumsden (ed.) *Close the 49th Parallel etc.: The Americanization of Canada* (pp. 257–74). Toronto: University of Toronto Press.

—— (1991) How do we find our own voices in the "New World Order"? A commentary on Americanization. *Sociology of Sport Journal*, 8, 178–84.

Kilbourn, W. (1988) The peaceable kingdom still. *Daedalus*, 117, 1–29.

King, A. (1990) *Culture, Globalization and the World System*. Basingstoke: Macmillan.

Klein, A. (1991) Sport and culture as contested terrain: Americanization in the Caribbean. *Sociology of Sport Journal*, 8, 79–85.

Lapierre, L. (1987) *If You Love This Country: Facts and Feelings on Free Trade*. Toronto: McClelland and Stewart Ltd.

Lealand, G. (1994) American popular culture and emerging nationalism in New Zealand. *National forum: The Phi Kappa Phi Journal*, 74 (4), 34–37.

Lisee, J.-F. (1990) *In the Eye of the Eagle*. Toronto: HarperCollins Publishers.

Lumsden, I. (1970) *Close the 49th Parallel etc: The Americanization of Canada*. Toronto: University of Toronto Press.

McArthur, C. (1986) The dialectic of national identity: the Glasgow Empire Exhibition of 1938. In T. Bennett, C. Mercer, and J. Woollacott (eds) *Popular Culture and Social Relations* (pp. 117–34). Milton Keynes: Open University Press.

McDonald, M. (1989) Fields of force. *Maclean's Magazine*, 102, July 3, pp. 26–30.

Macintosh, D., Bedecki, T. and C.E.S. Franks (1987) *Sport and Politics in Canada*. Kingston: McGill-Queens University Press.

McKay, J., Lawrence, G., Miller, T. and Rowe, D. (1993) Globalization and Australian sport. *Sport Science Review*, 2, 10–28.

McKay, J. and Miller, T. (1991) From old boys to men of the corporation: the Americanization and commodification of Australian sport. *Sociology of Sport Journal*, 8, 86–94.

McPhail, T. (1992) Canada as a laboratory of media regulation to counter the Americanization phenomenon. Paper presented at the Americanisation of Culture conference, University of Wales, Swansea, September 16–18.

Mackey, E. (1999) *The House of Difference: Cultural Politics and National Identity in Canada*. London: Routledge.

Maguire, J. (1990) More than a sporting touchdown: the making of American football in England 1982–1990. *Sociology of Sport Journal*, 7, 213–238.

—— (1993) Globalization, sport development, and the media/sport production complex. *Sport Science Review*, 2, 29–47.

—— (1999) *Global Sport: Identities, Societies, Civilizations*. Cambridge: Polity Press.

Merchant, L. (ed.). (1966) *Neighbors Taken for Granted*. New York: Praeger.

Metcalfe, A. (1987) *Canada Learns to Play*. Toronto: McClelland and Stewart.

Moffett, S.E. (1972) *The Americanization of Canada*. Toronto: University of Toronto Press.

Molinari, D. (1988) Can't call deal an outrage until fans boycott. *The Hockey News*, 42 (2), 14.

Newman, P.C. (1989) Bold and cautious. *Maclean's*, July 3, pp. 24–5.

Pearlstein, S. (2000) Canadians contemplate future across a vanishing border. *Otago Daily Times*, September 20, p. 11.

Quickfall, J. (1988) Canadians are being forced into Americans' way of thinking. [special phone-in response to The Great Trade in Armchair Critic]. *The Edmonton Sun*, August 11, p. 22.

Reilly, R. (1999) No fuss necessary in Wayne's world. April 20. http://sportsillustrated.cnn.com/inside_game/magazine/life_of_reilly/news/life-ofreilly

Resnick, P. (1977) *The Land of Cain: Class and Nationalism in English Canada, 1945–1975*. Vancouver: New Star Books.

Robertson, R. (1990) Mapping the global condition: globalization as the central concept. *Theory, Culture and Society*, 7, 15–30.

—— (1992a) *Globalization, Social Theory and Global Culture*. New York: Russell Sage.

—— (1992b) *Globalization*. London: Sage.

Ross, V. (1988) Cross-border trade. [Letter to the editor]. *Maclean's*, August 15, p. 4.

Sabo, D. (1993) Sociology of Sport and the New World Order. *Sport Science Review*, 2, 1–9.

Scott, M. (1988) *From Nation to Colony*. Lindsay, Ont.: Tri-M Publishing.

Sklar, H. (1992) Brave new world order. In C. Peters (ed.), *Collateral Damage: The New World Order at Home and Abroad* (pp. 3–46). Boston: South End Press.

Smith, A. (1980) *The Geopolitics of Information: How Western Culture Dominates the World*. New York: Oxford University Press.

Smith, G. (1891) *Canada and the Canadian Question*. Toronto: Macmillan.

Snarr, N. (1988) Gretzky trade triggers U.S.–Canada War. *USA Today*, August 12, p. 2C.

Strachan, A. (1988) Criticism stings Gretzky. *Globe and Mail*, May 5, p. A-24.

Strachan, A. (1988) Media clangers amid wedding's bells. Editorial in the *Globe and Mail*, July 18, p. D-5.

Strachan, A. (1988) Gretzky goes to L.A., *Globe and Mail*, August 10, p. A-1, A-2.

Swift, E.M. (1999) One of a kind. *Sports Illustrated*, 90 (17), April 26, pp. 32–41.

Taylor, J. (1988) A nation in mourning. *Sports Illustrated*, August 22, p. 94.

Wagner, E. (1990) Sport in Asia and Africa: Americanization or mundalization? *Sociology of Sport Journal*, 7, 399–402.

Wayne Gretzky: a Hamlet, a prodigal son for our times. (1988) *The Montreal Gazette*, August 21, p. B-3.

Winter, J.P. (2000) *The Silent Revolution: Media, Democracy, and the Free Trade Debate.* Ottawa: University of Ottawa Press.

Wulf, S. (1988) The great wedding. *Sports Illustrated*, July 25, pp. 9, 12.

11

HIDEO NOMO

Pioneer or defector?

Hajime Hirai

Nomo mania

On July 11, 1995, the Prime Minister of Japan, Tomiichi Murayama, sent a letter by facsimile to Hideo Nomo, then with the Los Angeles Dodgers, who was scheduled to be a starting pitcher in the annual Major League All-Star game on the same day:

> Congratulations. The Japanese people are proud of you as the first Japanese selected to play at the All-Star Game. Your performance has brought tremendous excitement here. We are looking forward to the game with great expectation. Do your best, Mr. Nomo.
>
> (*Asahi Shinbun*, 1995c, p. 9)

NHK, the Japanese Broadcasting Corporation, televised the game live from Arlington, Texas. The game started at 9.30 Japanese time on Monday morning, July 12. In spite of it being a weekday morning, more than thirty million Japanese watched Nomo playing with the Major League all-stars. At a public square in front of the Shinjuku Station, one of the busiest railroad terminals in Tokyo, about a thousand people stopped to watch the game on a giant television screen. They gave huge cheers whenever Nomo struck batters out. One man told a reporter that he stopped over at the Shinjuku Station on the way to his office to watch the "pitch of the century". Another middle-aged man expressed his excitement by saying, "I took a day off today to come here and watch him play. Nomo realized his American dream. I am thrilled as if I were there" (*Asahi Shinbun*, 1995d, p. 12).

NHK, by cancelling regular programs on its satellite channel, had broadcast live almost every game that Nomo had pitched since making his debut in Major League Baseball on May 2 that year. Nomo's sensational achievements in the United States were "Kamikaze", God's Wind, for NHK, who had been struggling to promote their satellite broadcasting system. For, thanks to Nomo's appearances, the sale of satellite dishes significantly increased.

Subsequently, package tours from Japan were planned to watch Nomo pitch. The most popular tour was a five-day trip including visits to Disneyland,

Universal Studios and Dodger Stadium, which cost approximately $1000 to $2400 (these and subsequent figures in US dollars). Various kinds of merchandise related to Nomo appeared on the market, and many of them were in heavy demand (Sato, 1995). At a Major League Baseball official souvenir shop in Tokyo, a warm-up jacket with Nomo's autograph was selling for about $500. A baseball and a card with his autograph sold for about $130 and a T-shirt with Nomo's name and his number, 16, for about $40. Numerous books and magazines on Nomo, the Dodgers and Major League Baseball (MLB) were also published. Nomo was the Japanese sport celebrity of the moment.

However, Nomo's profile within North America was also on the rise. Attendance at Los Angeles' Dodger Stadium had grown, especially when Nomo pitched. Newspapers and magazines such as *The New York Times* and *The Wall Street Journal* published articles on Nomo. His photos graced the front pages of weekly magazines such as *Newsweek* (July 10, 1995), *Sports Illustrated* (July 10, 1995) and *Time* (July 24, 1995). These articles covered everything from his unique pitching form (nicknamed "Tornado") and powerful forkball, to how he had contributed to the recovery of baseball's popularity after the players' strike, and a better mutual understanding between Japan and the United States.

In this chapter, issues relating to the globalization of sports, especially the international migration of athletes, will be discussed focusing on Nomo, Japanese baseball's most prominent export to the United States and the prototypical transpacific sport star.[1] First, the history of baseball in Japan will be briefly reviewed, and historical factors which have made Japanese baseball what it is today will be examined.[2] Then, details of Nomo's challenge to the major league and his subsequent career will be introduced. Finally, after analysing the impact of Nomo on Japanese baseball and society, the context and motives behind his decision to relocate to the US will be examined.

Yakyu in Japan[3]

It is necessary to understand the history of baseball in Japan before we discuss whether Hideo Nomo is a pioneer or defector in Japanese baseball. Americans teaching English and western culture at colleges in Japan first introduced baseball to the Japanese in the early 1870s. The game, which is called "Yakyu" literally meaning "field ball" in Japanese, instantly became a popular extracurricular activity among college students. For example, students at prestigious colleges founded baseball clubs. Ichiko, which later became a part of the University of Tokyo, dominated baseball from the late 1880s until the early 1900s. They not only were undefeated by any other college team, but they also beat US teams in Japan. When the club beat a team of expatriate Americans from the Yokohama Country Athletic Club in 1896, their victory made newspaper headlines across the nation. For a country that had opened its doors to western civilization only a few decades earlier, this triumph represented more than a small victory (Roden, 1980).

By the early twentieth century, intercollegiate games had become a major spectator phenomenon. Thousands of spectators packed stadiums and millions of people all over Japan listened to games on the radio. College and semi-professional teams from the United States visited Japan. Major League All-Stars and All-American teams, including such legendary players as Babe Ruth, Jimmy Foxx, and Lou Gehrig, played exhibition games in Japan. In his autobiography, Ruth recalled how the Japanese people enthusiastically welcomed them on and off the baseball grounds (cited in Whiting, 1989).

The social environment did not always favour the development of baseball, however, as the exceedingly frenzied supporters started causing social problems. This climate was intensified as the militarism and nationalism of the period gradually took control of Japanese society. The Ministry of Education issued the Baseball Control Act, whose aim was to promote the "healthy development" of baseball among college and high school students.

The Baseball Control Act resulted, ironically, in facilitating the birth of the first professional team in Japan. Since the act prohibited amateurs from playing with professionals, the *Yomiuri Shinbun*, a major national newspaper which was planning to invite the Major League All-Stars in 1934, had to organize the All-Japan team, whose players were naturally regarded as professionals. The first professional team, established in 1934, was named the Tokyo Giants who became the Yomiuri Giants the next year. Even though the Japanese Professional Baseball Association was formed by seven clubs in 1936, professional baseball gained support slowly in its early days. Major newspapers, except the *Yomiuri*, tended to ignore it. Moreover, many Japanese regarded earning money by playing sports as somewhat vulgar (Whiting, 1989).

By 1945, World War II interrupted the fortunes of baseball. Nationalists and militarists insisted that baseball should be banned because it came from the enemy, the United States. In 1943, baseball terminology in English was prohibited and replaced by Japanese terms. Eventually baseball, whether amateur or professional, was suspended altogether as the war intensified. Nonetheless, the Japanese returned to baseball quite quickly after World War II. Professional baseball resumed in 1946, and was split into the Pacific and Central leagues in 1949. Although the franchises and sponsoring companies have changed many times since then, the number of clubs in each league has remained at six since 1958.

In the 1950s professional baseball firmly established its status as the most popular spectator sport in Japan. For example, the total annual attendance of both leagues jumped from 2.5 million in 1950 to 9 million in 1959. Nationwide radio networks started broadcasting live games every night, and tabloid newspapers featuring professional baseball radically increased their circulation. Television, however, had the most decisive impact on professional baseball.

The 1960s and 1970s were the era of the Yomiuri Giants. They won nine Japanese Championships in a row from 1965 to 1973. The club drew the largest crowds in both leagues, and its annual home game attendance consistently exceeded three million. Yomiuri's television station broadcast all their home games, and other stations aired the away games. Although the Giants remain the most popular team, they are no longer as dominant as they used to be in the 1960s and early 1970s. Over time circumstances surrounding professional baseball have changed the sport. The amateur players' draft, started in 1965, gradually helped to disperse promising young talent to teams other than the Giants.

Japanese baseball is now entering a new era. In the past, the relationship between Japanese and American baseball was essentially one-way, that is, from the United States to Japan. In the early days Japanese baseball imported most of its knowledge and technology from the United States. International games, frequently held in the early twentieth century, dwindled after World War II. In professional baseball, exchange activities with US major leagues were limited to only importing players and hosting exhibition games.

Japanese baseball, at least at the professional level, never seriously looked overseas. It virtually isolated itself and was resting in peace for quite a long period. Under the isolation policy, baseball in Japan has developed to a level that is very different from baseball across the Pacific Ocean. Even though baseball in Japan is an imported culture, it has been naturalized as a Japanese culture of "Yakyu" (Whiting, 1989; Fagen, 1995).

The main reason that Japanese baseball has kept itself isolated so successfully for such a long period is, ironically, the popularity of "Yakyu" in Japan (Katayama and Seki, 1995). Because "Yakyu" has been so dominant as a form of popular culture, none of the baseball organizations, players, or fans has sought opportunities to turn their eyes to baseball overseas (Ninomiya, 1995). Those engaged in the management of professional teams did not have to worry financially. Most of the players were satisfied with the fame and financial rewards that they received. Fans, having their own favourite clubs and players, scarcely paid any attention to the major leagues in the United States. To sum up, neither management, players nor fans felt the necessity to turn their eyes overseas.

Another reason why Japanese baseball has been so successful in its isolation is because historically personnel exchanges between major league and Japanese professional baseball have been limited to only a handful of American and Hispanic players recruited to play for Japanese teams. However, most of them have been players who were either too old to play in the major leagues, or who could not make it to the major league in the first place. In Japan these players are called "Gaijin Suketto", meaning foreign aid or helper, the term is a derogatory one and suggests that such players are hired because Japanese baseball needs them. But, they are a "necessary evil".

However, many aspects of these characteristics of Japanese baseball have changed since the mid-1980s. At the amateur level, international exchanges have been as active as ever, particularly since baseball was admitted to the Olympic Games in 1984. All-Japan national teams, at the amateur level, have participated in many international tournaments. At the professional level, satellite television channels, which started service in the mid-1980s, have been broadcasting American sports such as the Major League Baseball (MLB), the National Football League (NFL), the National Basketball Association (NBA) and National Hockey League (NHL). There has been a clear increase in global television programming as evidenced by the presence of cable television stations carrying channels such as ESPN and CNN-News. These changes in the mass media have made many Japanese feel closer than ever to major league baseball in the United States. However, perhaps the most significant event in further intensifying the attention was when Hideo, ace pitcher of the Kintetsu Buffaloes, began playing with the Los Angeles Dodgers in 1995.

From a Buffalo to a Dodger

In January 1995, Hideo Nomo made a public announcement at a press conference to announce that the Kintetsu Buffaloes had accepted his request for voluntary retirement from the club. He declared that he would challenge for his right to play major league baseball in North America (*Asahi Shinbun*, 1995a).

Nomo, who had won more games and had struck out more batters than any other pitcher in the Pacific League for the fourth consecutive year beginning with his rookie season, had not pitched well in the previous year, due to pain in his right shoulder. The pitcher, distrusting the club's potentially unfaithful treatment of him, and feeling insecure about his future career, requested a multi-year contract to be negotiated by his agent (*Asahi Shinbun*, 1995a). Up to this point, professional baseball organizations in Japan had never officially accepted this kind of request from any Japanese player. Nomo would be no exception as Kintetsu, a member of the organization, refused to accept his request (Tabuchi, 1995).

After a series of heated bargaining sessions, Kintetsu, realizing that it was no longer possible to hold Nomo on the roster, could not help but accept his request to be released from his contract with the club. So he was freed to negotiate with American clubs (*Asahi Shinbun*, 1995a). Notably, in *The Collective Agreement of Japanese Professional Baseball*, there were no regulations or rules that even considered the possibility of a Japanese player wishing to play in MLB. Because this was the first such case in the history of Japanese professional baseball, things had to be dealt with as a special procedure beyond the existing rules and regulations.

Public opinion regarding this incident was completely divided (Tabuchi, 1995). Some people praised Nomo as a pioneer, while others regarded him as a rebel (Okada, 1995; Fagen, 1995). Those who supported him were impressed with his strong will to make his dream come true, even risking losing fame, status, and financial security. Conversely, those who did not support him regarded his actions as selfish. Many of them, including the commissioner, worried that other star players might follow him to North America (Rodman, 1996).

Most of the mass media appeared unwilling to express a clear view on this matter with the exception of several newspapers, magazines and TV stations, belonging to the Yomiuri Group which owned the Yomiuri Giants. They were critical or at least skeptical of his action, fearing that the orderly situation of Japanese baseball might be jeopardized. The tone of most of the daily newspapers, sports tabloid papers and weekly magazines was: "We can understand and are sympathetic with him. But the actions he took were not appropriate. He should take more time and try (or at least pretend to try) to obtain everybody's consent." Nomo stood at the centre of this controversy.

Shortly thereafter, Nomo flew to the United States, with his outspoken and controversial agent, for contract negotiations with major league clubs that had shown interest in him. Ultimately, he chose the Los Angeles Dodgers. He later wrote in his autobiography that the most important factor in making his decision was the presence of Peter O'Malley, the owner of the Dodgers (Nomo, 1995). O'Malley strongly believed that baseball should be more international, and he was active in international activities with Asian nations, Japan in particular. "O'Malley helped to foster the internationalisation of baseball. This had always been dear to his heart" (Fagen, 1995, p. 65). For a man like O'Malley, and a baseball club proud of its history as a pioneer of ethnic and racial integration in the sport, Nomo was definitely an attractive player. Although no one in O'Malley's organization had seen him pitch in the previous year except in a 2-minute long "highlight video" (Verducci, 1995, p. 45), the Dodgers offered Nomo a contract with a signing bonus of $2 million. However, the contract was not for a major league player, but for a minor leaguer, because it was during the MLB's players' strike. Since technically Nomo was a minor league player, the Japanese mass media adopted a "wait and see" stance.

When spring training started in 1995, the atmosphere seemed to change gradually. Expectations were rising steadily in Japan, as Nomo cleared barriers to pitch in the major league. Reporters and cameramen rushed to the Dodgers' camp in Florida. They followed Nomo so as not to miss any action that he made, or any comment made about him by the Dodgers coaching staff. Now, Nomo was becoming a "hot topic" in Japan. Televisions, newspapers and magazines began to cover him through talk shows and special articles in regular news section.

Nomo made his major league debut as a starting pitcher for the Los Angeles club in a game against San Francisco on May 2. Unfortunately he did not win a game for a month despite some brilliant pitching performances. However, once he recorded his first win, in June, he proved that he had the potential to be a dominant pitcher at the major league level, too. This fact was confirmed when he was nominated as a member of the National League All Stars. The Tornado Boy, nicknamed after his unique pitching form, had attracted enormous attention from both American and Japanese media. The American media invented a word, "Nomo Mania" while the Japanese used "Nomo Fever" to describe the hyped attention to him and the social and economic ripple effect aroused by him. He was no longer just a rebel. He was a celebrity. The Japanese cheered him as a pioneer, and called him "the man who chased his dream" (*Asahi Shinbun*, 1995d). His status rose as he kept pitching well in the second half of the season, and contributed to the Dodgers' division title. He finished the season with a record of thirteen wins and six defeats, led the league with the most strikeouts, and won the league's Rookie of the Year Award.

Nomo played for the Dodgers for two and a half more years. It was evident, however, that his performance was on the wane and he was not as happy at the club under the new owner and the new manager (Nishiyama, 1998). When he asked to be traded in 1998, the Dodgers sent him to the New York Mets. However, he was released from the Mets early in the 1999 season. After his first career experience in the minor league, he agreed to a one-year contract with the Milwaukee Brewers. In the 2000 season, he reached an agreement to play for the Detroit Tigers. He was the opening pitcher of the season, and remained as one of the club's starters, winning eight games. In 2001, Nomo moved to Boston as a free agent, beginning the season with the Red Sox with the second no-hit game of his career against the Baltimore Orioles on April 4.

As seen above, the image of Nomo within Japan changed from anti-establishment rebel to a pioneer chasing his dream. Nomo Fever had reached its peak twice when he appeared at the All-Star Game in July, and when the Dodgers clinched the division title via his pitching in October. The attention given to Nomo gradually diminished in the next few years, however, partly because he was unable to maintain his performance, slowly things began to change along with Nomo's celebrity status. The Dodgers did not win the championship, and other Japanese players such as Hideki Irabu joined Nomo in the major leagues. When he was traded and released in 1998 and 1999, many Japanese as well as American fans felt that Nomo might have been "finished" (Yamamoto, 1999; Cannella, 1999).

On the contrary, however, Nomo recovered again in 1999, and made yet another strong impact on many Japanese. The fan's new image is one of a strong-minded and disciplined Japanese player who overcame hardship in a foreign land (Asari, 1999). His revival has been compared to the middle-aged workers worrying about the chance of layoff and unemployment under the difficult economic conditions of Japan. Shibazaki (1999, p. 3), for instance, suggested that people's new perception of the revival of the Tornado Boy represented aspects of a distressed Japanese society, which had been disconcerted by employment anxiety and a distorted attitude towards America. Such observations highlight the importance of context in explaining the significance of particular individuals and events in shaping history of sports, baseball in Japan in particular.

After Nomo

The case of Nomo provides a good example of how baseball and its players have been perceived in Japan. It also provides an important point of discussion for the "globalization of sports". Many scholars have addressed globalization, from a variety of topics, geographical areas and nations, and events, and from a number of interpretive perspectives (Donnelly, 1996). But, generally speaking, contemporary discussion about globalization may be summarized as a concern with the basis and consequences of post-industrial capitalism, economic flows, new media technologies, and the influence of largely, but not exclusively, American popular culture on contemporary social life throughout the world (Jackson and Andrews, 1999, p. 31).

Among the factors mentioned above, the impact of globalization and the reactions of recipient local culture to exposure to global culture are one of the key aspects of the globalization of sports (Houlihan, 1994). Some scholars, including Wagner (1990) and Guttman (1994), have been investigating the process and results of the diffusion and naturalization of western sports into Asia. As well as these factors, however, the issue of talented athletes crossing national borders, whether amateurs or professionals, is certainly one of the important aspects of the globalization of sports (Bale and Maguire, 1994).

Maguire (1996), for instance, developed a typology of sport labour to describe sport players crossing national boundaries. Migrating athletes are thus categorized as pioneers, settlers, returnees, mercenaries, and nomadic cosmopolitans. Even though I have frequently called Nomo a pioneer, it is evident that my use of the term is different from that used by Maguire in his typology. According to his definition, a pioneer is a person possessing an almost evangelical zeal in extolling the virtues of his/her respective sport. He cited nineteenth-century missionaries of the empire, the nineteenth-century Sokol/Turner movements and the twentieth-century YMCA movement as examples (Maguire, 1996). In Nomo's case, it is safe to say that he did not leave Japan for the United States in order to convert Americans to Japanese baseball habitus and culture.

Judging from his statements, it seems there are two important reasons why Nomo said Sayonara to Japanese baseball, and it seems that their roots are the same. We may call them the pursuit of the pure joy of playing baseball, and the hatred for the established order preserved by conservative authorities. Curiously, no sports sociologists have ever paid attention to these factors when discussing issues of sport labour immigrants. For instance, Nomo recalled his reason for challenging the major league in his autobiography:

I like a "power to power confrontation". Deliberately waiting for a walk, choosing a bunt, stealing each other's signs, all these cheap tricks don't fit into my baseball style. To say it extremely, [it must be either] a strikeout or homerun. Throw balls as hard as you can, and hit balls as hard as you can. I like such a kind of baseball.

(Nomo, 1995, p. 26)

When Nomo was invited to a special press conference before the All-Star Game and asked for his comments on the match, he flatly replied in his well-known blunt style: "I am very honoured [to be selected]. I feel sorry for fans, but it is me who wants to enjoy the game most. I don't feel any pressure at all. I don't care about strikeouts. I want fans watch me enjoying on the field" (*Asahi Shinbun*, 1995b).

For Nomo, who had played against teams from North America and Cuba, and who had watched many games from the United States on satellite channels, the conservative and authoritarian style of Japanese baseball, from organizational management to daily pre-game practice, was a matter of disappointment and indignation. Multi-year contracts and agents were not (and still are not) approved of by owners in Japan. Even though free agency was finally introduced in 1993, conditions for acquiring this right are much stricter in Japan than in the United States. Nomo complained that his field manager and coaching staff at Kintetsu had never listened to players, only sticking to conventional training methods and playing strategies (Nomo, 1995). Under these conditions, having felt impatience and despair, he chose to pursue his dream. This might have been an inevitable decision for a person like Nomo. In this sense, he may be labeled a defector, not a pioneer at all. But, in another sense, he is a pioneer who let Japanese players and fans showed that there is a totally different type of baseball from Yakyu.

Some talented pitchers, such as Hideki Irabu of the New York Yankees/Montreal Expos, Shigeru Hasegawa of the California Angeles, Masato Yoshii of the New York Mets/Colorado Rockies, and Kazuhiro Sasaki of the Seattle Mariners, followed the path that Nomo paved. Significantly the motives that drove them to make it to major league baseball seem similar to those of Nomo. It is the pursuit of the pure joy of playing baseball. For example, a combative Irabu threatened his Japanese club, by declaring he would retire from Japanese baseball, unless the club let him negotiate with the Yankees (*Asahi Shinbun*, 1997, p. 12). Likewise Yoshii chose the Mets over Japanese clubs, even though the latter offered better financial conditions (*Asahi Shinbun*, 1998). It is evident that money and fame are not the only factors influencing Japanese players' decisions to move to MLB. When discussing sport labour immigration across borders, we have neglected to consider one important factor, that is, the "pure joy of playing". I doubt if this factor is applicable only to the case of Japanese baseball players who crossed the Pacific Ocean.

Under the influence of the globalization of sports, it is natural to anticipate that the values, norms and standards among players and fans would change. One of the most distinctive changes in Japanese sports in the second half of the 1990s, with regard to the globalization of sports, is the fact that more athletes than ever prefer to play overseas. In baseball, the number of players trying to make their fortunes in the major leagues is increasing. Some of them are established players in professional baseball here, but the rest are those who are not good enough to play in the first team of professional ball clubs. Because Japanese baseball organizations are imposing tough requirements on players to obtain the right of free agency, and because an agreement regulating players' trade between Japanese and American clubs was concluded in December 1998, the number of top class Japanese players moving to the United States at the peak of their careers will not increase in the near future. Rather, some young talented prospects, bypassing semi-professional or collegiate careers, and avoiding apprenticeship in the minor leagues, are now considering playing in the United States as an alternative (Miyata, 1998). It is expected that this trend will accelerate, since many major league clubs have been intensifying their recruiting activities in Japan (Harashima and Higuchi, 1995).

Outflows of talented athletes are happening in other sports, too. In soccer, two promising players, who were members of Japan's national team which played at the 1998 World Cup in France, transferred to clubs in Italy. The number of young soccer players playing in Brazil and Europe is also increasing. In volleyball, Rugby Union, and table tennis, which do not have professional organizations in Japan, some players have left to play overseas. It is interesting that most of these athletes had already reached their peaks when they sought these new challenges. A volleyball player, who used to be the captain of the national team, left for an Italian club when he was 35 years old, saying that he didn't want to hesitate to take his first and last chance (Shiga, 1999). In Japan, even elite athletes in most sports are either amateurs or semi-professionals employed by big companies. Even in professional sports such as baseball and soccer, most players usually stay in one club for their entire playing careers. Apart from several world class athletes in individual sports such as golf and tennis, playing overseas looked unrealistic in most cases until Nomo emerged.

Nomo's challenge and his presence in MLB have had a tremendous impact on the Japanese view of baseball. According to a survey of Japanese viewing habits of professional baseball by satellite television, the number of respondents who thought that American Major League Baseball was more interesting to watch is almost the same as the number of respondents who thought Japanese baseball was more interesting to watch (Hirai, 1995). But what they see or expect to see in Japanese and American baseball are not the same. The primary point of interest for Japanese baseball comes from familiarity with the clubs and players, while for American baseball it is the nature of the sport, such as powerful and fast plays and sophisticated playing techniques. They are expecting to see what they cannot see in Japanese baseball when they watch American games.

Asked about Nomo's move to the major league, 75 percent of respondents answered that their interest in the American game had increased since his debut. The majority of respondents said that they would anticipate more Japanese players moving to the United States to play, and that they wouldn't mind this. One surprise was that over 80 percent of respondents regarded it as good for Japanese baseball organizations, even though it means that local leagues might be downgraded to a second-class level. If a similar survey is repeated in the future, we may be able to anticipate a more open-minded view of players going overseas.

As we have seen, Nomo has been recognized as an international celebrity among the Japanese. What we have to keep it in mind here, however, is the fact that Japan has always had a sense of awe of and respect for Western civilization since the Meiji Era, and this mentality among Japanese has a great influence on how Nomo has been regarded.[4]

In popular cultures including sports, the impact of the United States has been enormous, particularly since the end of World War II, and has been expanded and intensified recently because of the increasing influence of mass media. It is interesting to observe that so-called Americanization, or cultural imperialism, has caused many Japanese to cling to their own cultural heritages. Yakyu (along with some other popular cultural forms such as "Enka": traditional popular music) for instance, is the symbol of the tendency for many Japanese to be inward-looking. Those people have made their own "small world", living comfortably and never wanting to look outside. For them, Nomo's behaviour, which overstepped existing standards, looked more puzzling and reckless at first. Then, when they witnessed that he had achieved more than expected, their awe turned to joy. They eventually started to see Nomo as if he was representing Japan, and a saviour fighting against the conqueror.

Of course, there are many other Japanese who have become global celebrities in arts and sports. For instance, Akira Kurosawa, the Oscar-winning movie director, Seiji Ozawa, conductor of the Boston Symphonic Orchestra, Ayako Okamoto, golfer, and Kimiko Date, tennis player are regarded by many Japanese as being global celebrities. But the impact Nomo has made on Japanese society seems greater than that of any other Japanese celebrity, mainly because he plays the most popular sport in Japan. Furthermore, his performance was very visible thanks to intense coverage by the mass media, particularly television. At the end of the 1995 season, some people claimed that the Japanese government should give Nomo the National Honour Award, which only twelve Japanese, including five sports figures, have ever received. Even though he actually did not receive it, this may indicate that he was regarded as the visible symbol of Japan's growing number of global individual success stories in a diverse set of fields.

As Simple As Can Be

Nomo has had a tremendous impact on not only the world of baseball but also societies in general in both Japan and the United States, as revealed in the notion of "Nomo Mania". But if we focus upon his statements and actions, we will notice that these were made and/or taken based upon one simple philosophy. It is the pursuit of pure joy in playing baseball. It doesn't seem to be a big deal for him, no matter where he plays, no matter which team he plays for, or no matter whom his teammates are, as long as he is sticking with his philosophy. On the contrary, if there is something that may interfere with his approach, he will do his best to either put it out of his way or avoid confrontation, no matter whether it is the sturdy authority of the Japanese baseball organization or the noisy and curious mass media.

It is a well-known fact that Nomo does not always enjoy a good relationship with the mass media, especially Japanese reporters and cameramen. He bluntly, and sometimes angrily, refuses to be interviewed and have his picture taken, by saying, for instance, that he would like to concentrate on pre-game practice, or that they will be a nuisance to his team-mates. But I suspect that what he really means is his feeling of dislike and disdain toward some journalists who flatter authorities and who do their jobs not because they love them, but because they are ordered to do so.

It is unlikely that Nomo views himself as either pioneer or defector. Rather, he seems intent on pursuing his dream in the sport he loves. Nomo once said that he hoped that American fans would see him as just one of the players, not as a rare Japanese playing in the majors (Nightingale, 1995, p. 36). With his constant efforts and strong beliefs, he is pursuing his dream in Major League Baseball, where players are enjoying themselves and yet engaging in the battle of survival regardless of races and nationalities. Nationalities and national borders may not be a factor for him any more, at least in the ballpark. Arguably, he is the first Japanese athlete to refuse to be the subject of a debate on sport and national identity. For him, receiving a letter of encouragement from the Prime Minister Murayama might just be a matter of " Thank you. But no thanks."

Notes

1   Nomo is not the first Japanese player to play in the major league. Masanori "Massy" Murakami played with the San Francisco Giants in 1964 and 1965. His records in major league were five wins, one loss and nine saves. Young Murakami, originally a player of the Nankai Hawks in Japan, was sent to the Giants organization to "study baseball". He pitched far better than he was expected. After a short stint in the Giants' minor league team, he was promoted to the Giants. This move caused a problem between the Hawks and the Giants after the 1964 season. The Hawks maintained that he was on loan, and the Giants claimed he was their property (Wulf, 1995, pp. 25–6). Even though he continued playing well with the Giants in 1965, he decided to come back to the Hawks, citing "fundamental precepts of obligation and humanity" (ibid., p. 25). This bitter experience occasioned a so-called "gentleman's agreement", which asked American clubs to refrain from the recruitment of active players in the Japanese professional baseball organization.
2   Historical reviews on Japanese baseball are based on the discussion in the *Encyclopedia of World Sports* (Hirai, 1996).
3   For more information on the history of Japanese baseball, see Whiting (1989).
4   For those interested in the mentalities of Japanese toward the cultural and economic invasion by the United States, I recommend the book, *The Japan that Can Say No* by Shintaro Ishihara, a well-known novelist and the Governor of Tokyo.

Bibliography

Asahi Shinbun (1995a) Nomo, dai leaguehe. Morning edition, January 10, p. 21.

Asahi Shinbun (1995b) Bei kyuen asu senpatsu, tanoshimitai. Evening Edition, July 11, p. 15.

Asahi Shinbun (1995c) Nomo kun ganbare. Morning Edition, July 12, p. 9.

Asahi Shinbun (1995d) Seikino 25 kyu, tanoshinda. Evening Edition, July 12, p. 15.

Asahi Shinbun (1997) Irabuyo dokohe yuku. Morning Edition, April 12, p. 12.

Asahi Shinbun (1998) Mets Yoshii debyuwo kazaru. Evening Edition, April 6, p. 5.

Asari, K. (1999) Nomono kakugo. *Nihon Keizai Shinbun*, Evening Edition, May 11, p. 1.

Bale, J. and Maguire, J. (eds) (1994) *The Global Sports Arena: Athletic Talent Migration in an Interdependent World*. London: Cass.

Cannella, S. (1999) No more heat, no more Nomo? *Sports Illustrated*, April 26, pp. 84 and 86.

Donnelly, P. (1996) The local and the global: globalisation in the sociology of sports. *Journal of Sport and Social Issues*, 23, 239–257.

Fagen, H. (1996) *Nomo: The Inside Story on Baseball's Hottest Sensation*. New York: Penguin Books.

Guttman, A. (1994) *Games and Empires*. New York: Columbia University Press.

Harashima, Y. and Higuchi, F. (1995) Dainino Nomowo hakkenseyo. *Asahi Shinbun*, Evening Edition. August 22, p. 1.

Hirai, H. (1995) Can Nomo change "Yakyu" to baseball? Impact of major league baseball on Japanese baseball fans. Paper presented at North American Society for the Sociology of Sport, Sacramento, CA. November 5, 1995.

—— (1996) Japanese baseball. In D. Levinson and K. Christensen (eds), *Encyclopedia of World Sports*, Santa Barbara, CA: ABC Clio. vol. 1, pp. 80–4.

Houlihan, B. (1994) Homogenisation, Americanization, and creolization of sport: Varieties of globalization. *Sociology of Sport Journal*, 11, 356–75.

Ishihara, S. (1991) *The Japan that Can Say No*. Trans. F. Baldwin. New York: Simon & Schuster.

Jackson, S. and Andrews, D. (1999) Between and beyond the global and the local: American popular sporting culture in New Zealand. *International Review for the Sociology of Sport*, 34, 31–42.

Katayama, K. and Seki, H. (1995) Nomono katsuyakude miete kita shinno World Seriesno yume. *Shukan Yomiuri*, October 22, 38–43.

Maguire, J. (1996) Blade runners: Canadian migrants, ice hockey, and the global sports process. *Journal of Sport and Social Issues*, 23, 335–60.

Miyata, K. (1998) *Asahi Shinbun* Morning Edition, November 10, p. 31.

Nightingale, B. (1995) LA Times kishano me. (Translated into Japanese by N. Sakano). *Sports Graphic Number*. November, 34–7.

Ninomiya, S. (1995) Commentary on Nomo. In H. Nomo, *Bokuno Torunedo Senki* (pp. 39–41), Tokyo: Shueisha.

Nishiyama, R. (1998) Nomo houshutsuronga kasoku. *Asahi Shinbun*, Morning Edition, May 23, p. 23.

Nomoga nini intai. (1995) *Shukan Yomiuri*, January 29, 144–5.

Nomo, H. (1995) *Bokuno Torunedo Senki*. Tokyo: Shueisha.

Okada, T. (1995) Chosenka, kyudan karano touhika. *Asahi Shinbun*, Morning Edition, January 10, p. 21.

Roden, D. (1980) Baseball and the quest for national dignity in Meiji Japan. *American Historical Review*, 85, 511–34.

Rodman, E.J. (1996) *Nomo: The Tornado who Took America by Storm*. Los Angeles: Lowell House Juvenile.

Sato, H. (1995) Shokon, Nomoni nore. *Shukan Yomiuri*, August 6, 166–9.

Shibazaki, S. (1999) Nomo shinwato koyo fuan. *Nihon Keizai Shinbun*, Evening Edition, May 21, p. 1.

Shiga, H. (1999) Hito: Manabe Masayoshi san. *Asahi Shinbun*, Morning Edition, July 9, p. 3.

Tabuchi, E. (1995) Aa, Kintetsuno hitowo miru me. *Shukan Yomiuri*, July 23, 159–61.

Verducci, T. (1995) He's over here. *Sports Illustrated*, May 15, 44–6.

Wagner, E.A. (1990) Sport in Asia and Africa: Americanization or mundialization? *Sociology of Sport Journal*, 7, 399–402.

Whiting, R. (1989) *You Gotta Have Wa*. New York: Macmillan.

Wulf, S. (1995) The starting pitcher. *Time*, July 24, 24–5.

Yamamoto, H. (1999) Nomo kounenpoga neck. *Asahi Shinbun*, Morning Edition, March 28, p. 27.

12

GLOBAL HINGIS

Flexible citizenship and the transnational celebrity[1]

Michael D. Giardina

Hingis combines calculating maturity with the undaunted spirit of
youth. She grins in the face of fear … With her uncanny timing
and devilish drop shots, Hingis' arsenal is completed by the shield
of self-confidence.

(Robbins, 1997, p. 1C)

Proem

In 1994, a 14-year-old Swiss female named Martina Hingis made her professional debut on the Women's Tennis Association tour.[2] Almost immediately, her
impact was felt throughout the tennis world as she became the youngest player
ever to hold the Number One ranking (16 years, 6 months and one day). A
scant three years after her debut, Hingis posted a 75–5 record, won three of the
four Grand Slam singles championships and twelve tournaments overall; she was
subsequently selected the "Player of the Year" by the WTA Tour, the
International Tennis Federation and *Tennis Magazine*, and was named "Female
Athlete of the Year" by the Associated Press. This marked her transition into the
media spotlight and, with it, her own transformation into a transnational
celebrity. Amidst this rise to glory, Hingis would become known around the
world as one of the most quotable and fascinating players. As the highest paid
female athlete in the world,[3] Hingis has come to be represented within the
media in a multiplicity of character incarnations ranging from "cultured
European" to "postfeminist woman."

This chapter focuses on the flexibility of Martina Hingis in relation to the
construction of her transnational celebrity status. I begin by offering a touristic
journey[4] through what I term "Travels in Hingis-reality"[5] – a postmodern
voyage that uncovers the polymorphous media representations of Hingis
throughout the world. From there, I delve into the flexibility of Hingis' citizenship that enables her to negotiate various borders of the global market. In the
process, I put forth a reading of the "Global Hingis" paradigm – Hingis as an
exemplar of transnational celebrity. I conclude by excavating the three distinct
phases of her rise to celebrity standing which, when layered together, reveal a

flexibly global celebrity capable of adapting her identity to meet the ever-changing climate of global capitalism.

Travels in Hingis-reality

San Diego, California, 1998. The Toshiba Tennis Classic. Here I am, huddled in a corner of a bustling pressroom with a few sports journalists, all eagerly awaiting the up-coming post-match press conference. The topic of conversation on everyone's lips this evening is teenage phenomenon Martina Hingis, the undisputed World Number One in women's tennis. We had just watched Hingis strategically dismantle Joennette Kruger (a top-30 player from the Republic of South Africa) in just under fifty minutes, her game plan executed with such surgical precision and Gary Kasparov-like cunning that one veteran tennis columnist remarked: "She has the most intricate shot making ability I've ever seen; no one is as smart as she is on the court." However, not all the talk in the pressroom is on her tennis game. One reporter, commenting on the new "look" Hingis sported during the tournament – a short hair cut, dyed black – says, "She looks grown up now, more mature, cultured ... she's trying to move away from being so unfiltered and outspoken." Additionally, others speak of the stinging comments Hingis made about Venus and Serena Williams at a previous tournament, about how her brashness (or enigmatic charm, depending on whom I speak with) is actually positive in terms of generating interest in a women's game that is trying to reinvent itself since the retirements of Chris Evert and Martina Navratilova, the demise of Jennifer Capriati, and the stabbing of Monica Seles. Still others gossip over whom she may or may not be dating at the time, one going so far as to remark, "Even if Hingis and [Spanish tennis professional Julian] Alonso aren't serious, it does wonders for her image and the image of tennis."

The press liaison signals to us that Hingis will be entering the interview room in a few minutes. I take my seat, not sure what to expect. The representations of her in both print and electronic media portray her not only as a stellar player, but also as a celebrity wise beyond her years; she is the sophisticated, cultured European changing the face of women's tennis and generating media interest in the women's tour. Clearly, the player I had just seen from my seat in the press row demonstrated immense athletic and artistic talent, but what about the off-court aspect of her celebrity persona? A few minutes later, Hingis enters the room dressed plainly in multi-colored spandex shorts and a Sergio Tacchini T-shirt. Her hair is awry, her face bare of make-up and all the trappings of celebrity. From just a few feet away, she looks like a very plain teenager, not the glamour girl the Women's Tennis Association (WTA) takes pleasure in parading around at every opportunity. However, it soon becomes apparent that, both on and off the court, she exudes the confidence of being the Number One ranked player in the world.

As the press conference evolves, Hingis answers most of her questions diplomatically (in both English and, for the sake of one reporter, German), but throws in a few verbal jabs at the Williams sisters and their unending comments about how they are going to be ranked Numbers One and Two in the world before long. In one instance she reminds me of a young Monica Seles, who used to laugh and giggle her way through her press conferences; in the next, when speaking on the issue of equal prize money in Grand Slam tournaments, she appears as articulate and intense as Billie Jean King has been on the same subject. To the majority of us in the pressroom, there exists more depth and substance to Hingis than any other player on the tour.

Fast forward two years, where my travels bring me to Birmingham, England – the veritable birthplace of cultural studies – for a conference at which I am to present a paper on the media representation of Hingis. On my first night there, I venture off the campus of the University of Birmingham and, few hundred yards from the main gate, I notice a striking black and white billboard advertising – as part of her new product endorsement for Berlei – the image of a sports bra-wearing Anna Kournikova accompanied by the tag line "Only the ball should bounce". Inside a nearby gas station/food mart, I leaf through several tabloid dailies, all of which are gearing up for Wimbledon by featuring the "Spice Girls of Tennis" in columns having nothing to do with tennis at all. I pick up a British copy of *Esquire Magazine* (the "sharper read for men"), which features a close-up shot of Kournikova on the cover and an article including pictures suitable for *Sports Illustrated's Swimsuit Issue*. In the article, Kournikova asserts that the number one priority on her list of career goals is to win Grand Slam championships, as well as describing how comfortable she has become with being a celebrity. For a player with yearly endorsements hovering near the $10 million mark while never having won a WTA singles title (0-for-74), I wonder how true this statement can possibly be. At least with Hingis, owner of thirty-four WTA singles titles and five Grand Slam tournament victories (not to mention the rare Doubles Grand Slam in 1998), a similar comment would carry with it a greater degree of legitimacy. Back at the conference the following day I speak with a professor from Australia who tells me she has been working on a piece involving Hingis as Australia's adoptive daughter. She also tells me that a colleague of hers in New Zealand has also identified similar trends while working on a paper regarding Hingis as representative of Kiwi identity. It occurs to me just how far the reach of Hingis' celebrity appeal stretches. Thinking back, I can recall having seen her in advertisements and articles in English, French, Japanese, and Romanian media; her appeal is definitely not limited to one culture or age group.

Following the conference, I travel south to Florence, Italy. Strolling through the Piazza dell Duomo, I come across a portrait artist named Fumanti who displays a glamorous sketch of Hingis to serve as an example of his work (by contrast, other artists in the piazza display sketches of such celebrity icons as Tom Cruise and Julia Roberts). When I inquire about the portrait, the man shows me a copy of *La Gazzetta dello Sport* that features Hingis on the cover. In broken English he explains, "She is beautiful ... I could not think to sketch anyone as more beautiful than she ... she has *sprezzatura*."[6] This (re)presentation of Hingis the Glamour Girl reveals itself once again later in the week. While in Paris, the style capital of the world, Hingis is featured in several magazines that present her as glamorous and alluring. Playing on her media-constructed European refinement, Hingis is (re)presented as a model of glamour and sophistication. Furthermore, the accompanying articles on this theme, presenting her as more cultured than the other players on the tour and including pictures of her dressed in fashionable clothing to support this claim.

A week later finds me at Wimbledon on the hallowed grounds of the All England Lawn Tennis and Croquet Club – the virtual Mecca of the tennis world – where Hingis and Venus Williams hook up in one of the quarterfinal matches. For Hingis, the 1997 Wimbledon champion, this year's tournament has been kinder to her than 1999, when she was unceremoniously dispatched in the first round by then-unknown Australian teenager Jelena Dokic in an embarrassing first-round loss. At the time, Hingis had been mired in a post-French Open slump, attributed to her crushing defeat in the Finals by Steffi Graf. Her image tarnished by what some saw as petulance taken to the extreme, Hingis made a conscious effort to keep her emotions in check on the court, refine her comments off it and, as one reporter put it, "grow up".

A few months later, back in my central Illinois apartment, I tune in to the 2000 US Open, where talk of a "Survivor"-like atmosphere hovers over Hingis, the Williams Sisters, and the oft-overlooked Lindsay Davenport. Throughout the entire two-week event Hingis, though swept aside by the mainstream media in favor of Venus and Serena Williams, still maintained her unique position in the WTA by speaking out against performance-enhancing supplements, promoting her involvement with the World Health Organization's "Match Point Against Polio" campaign,[7] and headlining the Arthur Ashe Kids' Day festivities.

During my "travels in Hingis-reality," I was truly amazed at how Martina's celebrity had extended throughout the world. In terms of transnational celebrities in general and Hingis in particular, she comes to inhabit the local by playing off both her known celebrity qualities as well as, and at the same time, appearing as a *tabula rasa* on which local meanings and desires are inscribed. For this reason, she seems perfectly at ease appearing as a European sophisticate in Paris, a symbol of women's empowerment within the United States, or a model of Western freedom and individuality in Asia. By unraveling the power of her celebrity identity across (trans)national boundaries, we can gain keen insights into the rapidly changing landscape of global capitalism, as well as how flexible citizens such as Hingis contribute to our understanding of the postmodern moment.

Flexibly global

So, how do we begin to understand that which Martina Hingis has come to represent across (trans)national boundaries? Building on my travels through Hingis-reality, the following sections focus specifically on the construction of Martina Hingis as a transnational celebrity. Informed throughout by Norman Denzin's understanding of postmodernity (1986, 1989, 1991, and 1997), I seek to deconstruct Hingis within an interpretive space that frames her as a free-floating celebrity commodity-sign. Employing Aihwa Ong's (1998, 1999) concept of "flexible citizenship," I trace the vectors of Hingis' celebrity identity within the landscape of global capitalism. This entails examining the nature of global sport celebrities within the growing transnational economy, the role of media in the construction/production of such celebrity, and the materiality of the celebrity performer. Approaching her in this manner allows us to view the "postmodern scene as a series of cultural formations which impinge upon, shape, and define contemporary human group life" (Denzin, 1991, p. viii). By excavating her positioning within these (con)texts, I unveil what I call the "Global Hingis" paradigm – Hingis as an exemplar of flexible citizenship and transnational celebrity.

The heart of this project is centered on concepts of celebrity as it relates to the globalizing effects of sport and culture. For purposes of this discussion, I broadly define globalization as the breaking down of old structures and boundaries of nation-states and communities by what Anthony Giddens (1986) would call "features of time-space compression" (quoted in Maguire, 1999, p. 129). This involves the rapid intensity, extensity, and velocity of cultural flows – the "movement of capital, technologies, people, and mediated images" – that guide and shape the logics of global capitalism (ibid.). Further, I see globalization as the "increasing transnationalization of economic and cultural life, frequently imagined in terms of the creation of a global space and community" (Robins, 1997, p. 12). It is this idea of transnationality – the condition of cultural interconnectedness and mobility across space – that entails "the intensification of world-wide social relations which link distinct localities in such a way that local happenings are shaped by events occurring miles and miles away and vice versa" (Giddens, 1990, p. 64). In effect, as technologies of communication expand at an exponential rate, as transnational corporations operate in a multiplicity of countries worldwide, and as local identities become increasingly open to new cultural ideas and practices, a new type of figure emerges – the flexible citizen.

According to cultural anthropologist Aihwa Ong, the era of globalization has led both individuals and governments to develop a "flexible notion of citizenship and sovereignty as strategies to accumulate capital and power" (1999, p. 6). This idea of flexible citizenship "refers to the cultural logics of capitalist accumulation, travel, and displacement that induce subjects to respond fluidly and opportunistically to changing political-economic conditions" (ibid., p. 6). As such, movement and celebrity status across national boundaries are grounded within particular structures of meaning about family, gender, nationality, class mobility, and social power which vary from place to place (ibid.).

It is within this overarching idea of cosmopolitanism that several new communities emerge. The new "traveler" group is one such community – the new elite of the globalization era. It is here that these new flexible citizens – athletes, movie stars, media moguls, international business players – have the agency to manipulate traditional forms of citizenship to their own advantage and utilize technological innovations in mass media, wireless communication and transportation to harness the flexibility necessary for success in a global-izing world. With regard to Hingis, she is aided in her "quest to accumulate capital and social prestige in the global arena" (Ong, 1999, p. 6) by her management team at Octagon Marketing (a global sport marketing firm), which acts as a cultural intermediary that carefully guards her aura as a star performer. This ranges from pursuing only those endorsement deals that perpetuate her global appeal (such as with Adidas) to promoting her charity work with the World Health Organization; as guardian of her official biog-raphy, Octagon Marketing is able to influence and create a constructed narrative of authenticity specific to any given locale. This is key because transna-tional figures both emphasize and are regulated by practices favoring "flexibility, mobility, and repositioning in relation to markets, governments, and cultural regimes" (ibid.).

Concurrent with this repositioning, flexible citizens are more concerned with global market conditions than traditional meanings of citizenship in a particular nation. That is to say, traditional notions of citizenship no longer carry the sort of passionate attachment one expects to be associated with the idea of national citizenship. Instead, transnational celebrities have become flexible with respect to the formalities of their citizenship: they have separated their citizenship from their culture, where the former is flexible and amorphous and the latter is stable and tied to one's country of origin. For example, while Hingis has a "home" in Switzerland and travels to the Czech Republic several times per year, she main-tains a "home base" in Florida during the US swing of the WTA Tour to cut down on extreme travel schedules and to take advantage of Florida's perfect tennis weather. However, this attachment to Florida and the USA remains one of economic and professional convenience; she manages to negotiate various forms of belonging as a cosmopolitan citizen and transnational celebrity without accepting (or requiring) ties to a single nation, imagined community, or identity.

In the age of global sport, there is an increasing trend among (trans)national sporting leagues and organizations that engenders an environment conducive to the emergence of flexible citizens. This is seen in both team and individual sports. For example, the National Hockey League and Major League Baseball are both heavily populated with individuals from around the world who migrate to the United States and Canada to increase their material wealth. While not as dramatically populated, the National Basketball Association is beginning to see a significant rise in the number of European players entering the league as products of US collegiate programs or European professional leagues. Individual sports – golf, tennis, or track and field – are slightly different. The WTA, for example, is not tied to the United States or England the way the National Basketball Association or Premier League football are; rather, it is a global regulatory body that facilitates tournaments and establishes a uniform set of rules. While there has been a rise in the popularity of golf in the United States – a rise primarily attributed to the emergence of Tiger Woods – its worldwide media appeal is harder to gauge. With regard to the WTA, I see it as the leader among women's professional sports considering that its growing appeal is not confined strictly to the United States; over seventy-five countries are represented by players on the tour, and there are over sixty events per year spanning six continents. Currently, six different countries ranging from the United States and Spain to France and Germany are represented in the top ten rankings for the WTA (that number rises to eleven different countries if you include the top twenty players). Furthermore, the WTA Tour promotional video bills itself as a global sport offering "11 billion yearly impressions" worldwide that advertisers and sponsors can buy into.

Although a case can be made for either Anna Kournikova or the Williams sisters as representative flexible citizens, I believe that the most flexible of the WTA's transnational celebrities is Martina Hingis. While Venus and Serena Williams are recognized throughout the world as star performers, they are understood primarily through American narratives and a celebrity identity that marks them as Americans. Furthermore, where Anna Kournikova is globally recognized and celebrated, I would argue that her celebrity status is fixed around her image as a glamour girl (or "Spice Girl"). In essence, she's always the same person wherever she goes (i.e., she's sexy in London, sexy in Paris, sexy in New York). Whereas Hingis is able to maneuver in and out of whichever narrative(s) best fits the moment, advertisements featuring Kournikova that try to break away from overcoded notions of her sexuality and glamour become viewed as inauthentic. It is here that I wish to introduce Hingis as what C.L. Cole and Samantha King might call a "representative figure implicated in [trans]national fantasies of origin, organization, and character" (1998, p. 56). In response to the growing discourse of globalization, I have come to characterize Hingis' transnational appeal and positioning within this arena as the "Global Hingis" paradigm. By this, I mean the concept that a "representative figure" like Hingis is the prototypical "flexible citizen" – one who becomes tied to the foundational characteristics of a given locality *while at the same time* operating amidst a multi-faceted global plane which transcends (inter)national boundaries. As this phenomenon unfolds, Hingis' (celebrity) subjectivity is remade time and again to appeal to ever-changing and contrasting local consumer markets.

MICHAEL D. GIARDINA

Swiss Miss celebrity

> Coziness under strict control, anachronism versus state-of-the-art technology: strange bedfellows in a storybook land. Nowhere else in Europe can you find a combination as welcoming and as alien, as comfortable and as remote, as engaging and as disengaged as a glass cable car to the clouds. This is the paradox of the Swiss, whose primary national aesthetic pitches rustic Alpine homeyness against high-tech urban efficiency.
>
> (Fodor's Switzerland, 2000)

Although Martina Hingis is a Swiss citizen, she was born in what was then Czechoslovakia (now Slovakia) and spent several of her early years in what is now the Czech Republic. After moving to Switzerland when she was 7 years old, she assumed the cultural identity of Switzerland insofar as she calls herself "Swiss," plays on the Swiss Olympic and Federation Cup (international tennis tournament equivalent to the Davis Cup) teams and speaks Swiss-German, the favored language of the area to which she moved. At first, Hingis had a hard time learning Swiss-German, which is an unwritten everyday language that varies greatly from region to region (Roberts, 1998, p. 25). The grammar and vowels of these dialects, known by the collective term "Schweizerdeutsch," can be traced back to Middle High German. In school, children here are taught this cultivated official language, High German, which native speakers call "written German." Within three months, Hingis had mastered the language, and says "half a year later, nobody could tell that I wasn't Swiss" (quoted in Roberts, 1998, p. 25). She also learned English from a private tutor and from playing in various tournaments, where English is the official language of tennis. She now speaks four languages fluently (English, German, Swiss-German, and Czech, as well as some French).

It was these formative years in Switzerland – a country whose citizens are known for having won more Nobel Prizes and having registered more patents per capita than any other nation – which gave rise to a personality that would first catapult her to the international stage, that of the "Swiss Miss". Maturing rapidly as a tennis prodigy, Hingis dominated the Junior tennis ranks: at age 8, she won the Swiss sub-12 outdoor championship; at 9, the Swiss sub-14 outdoor championship; at 10, the Swiss sub-16 outdoor championship and the European sub-14 Championship. At the age of 11, when most kids are in grade school, Martina won the Swiss sub-18 outdoor championship, as well as the European junior (sub-14) championship in Athens, Greece. By the age of 12, she had become the youngest-ever Grand Slam junior titlist (1993 at Roland Garros), replacing the former record-holder Jennifer Capriati. Just prior to her 1993 appearance in the Junior Wimbledon tournament, the *Daily Telegraph* in London printed its first feature article on the 12-year-old Hingis, describing her as "porcelain pretty, pony-tailed – and powerful when she has to be," as well as portraying one opponent as looking "wretchedly gauche against her beautifully composed opponent [Hingis]" (Mair, 1993, p. 37). Furthermore, her on-court intelligence was discussed in terms of its (near) superiority to those already on the WTA tour. The article concluded by posing the question: "Is the child really that good or is she merely at an age where she has her older opponents freezing?" (ibid.).

When she first burst onto the professional tennis scene, Hingis was primarily understood through what Richard DeCordova (1990) has deemed "physical performance" – the physical characteristics that make her unique in the field of tennis players or athletes. This discourse emphasizes beauty or lack thereof, body type, tangible skills, and other visually stimulating characteristics (Marshall, 1997, p. 95). At the age of 14, Hingis was necessarily identified as displaying a childlike demeanor and being a welcomed personality on the tour. Invariably, the "Heidi" references soon followed her into the press. Although she displayed a petulant, sometimes overly cocky attitude on the court, it was often dismissed as being a part of her youth or justified as being a part of her appeal.

While her tennis game has been crafted to perfection by her Czechoslovakian-trained mother/coach Melanie Molitor, it is represented in terms of its "Swissness." Aside from the obvious qualities of efficiency and technical perfection, her game draws on the inherent ability of the Swiss to incorporate differing aspects of culture and make them their own. A breakdown of her tennis game (and her personality) would show just how amorphous it really is: from Maureen Connolly, an endless love for horses and a desire for living outside the norm; from Chris Evert, a strong baseline game and two-handed backhand, as well as her appeal as "Mme. Americana"; from Martina Navratilova, her name and her Czechoslovak roots; from Billie Jean King, a dedication to social justice; from Steffi Graf, power and precision; and from Seles, an unbridled passion for the game.

Positioned in terms of "Swissness," she is described in the media as being an intellectual player, someone who sets up highly intricate points, and plays almost-perfect technical tennis. Broadcasters and journalists speak of her game as being like that of chess master Gary Kasparov, as she almost toys with opponents seemingly because she is so much more mentally gifted in terms of tennis knowledge. Furthermore, US Davis Cup captain and Hall-of-Famer John McEnroe once said of Hingis' game that "She's a step or two ahead of all human beings out there on the court ... mentally, she sees things virtually no one else sees" (McEnroe, 1999, US Open Broadcast).

It is also interesting to note that, as Hingis has gone about asserting a distinct Swissness of character, her flexibility has also allowed her to circumvent her distinctly *un*-Swiss roots to the point that she is no longer looked upon as having a connection to Czechoslovakia at all.

MICHAEL D. GIARDINA

Pan-European flair

> There is a common high culture in Europe, and a common
> popular culture. However, the high culture tends to be a culture
> of elites.
>
> (Field, 1996, p. 1)

With the evolution of Hingis' media personality, she has come to represent not
only "Swissness," but also an over-arching pan-European appeal. Through carefully crafted management of her image, Hingis projects an aura of
"Europeanness" – a cross between old-world, nineteenth-century charm and its
twenty-first-century counterpoint: the high-tech, jet-set glamour that exemplifies London, Paris, and Milan. As Kum-Kum Bhavnani argues, the unification of
Europe in 1993 led to the encouragement of a collective European identity
whereby those "who live in these countries are being urged to be Europeans,
and not lay claim to national identities such as being French, or Dutch, or
German" (1993, p. 33).[8] Thus Hingis, by moving onto the public stage via the
media, projects images of Otherness – other people and other places – which
contributes to her being seen as a differentiated and cosmopolitan figure within
commodified sports. This theme is then repeated in her various sponsorship
agreements.

Specific to her endorsements, transnational corporations have gravitated
toward Hingis in droves. As of this writing (late 2000), Hingis is one of the
main celebrity endorsers of global products such as Clairol beauty products,
American Express credit cards ("Femme Fatale since '99"), Bolle sunglasses,
Opel cars, Omega watches and Adidas sportswear. I see these last two products
as especially indicative of Hingis' global appeal in each market (Omega as high-
class or elite audience and Adidas as mass-audience global product). Of all of
her endorsement deals, the one Hingis has with Omega is most representative
of her ascribed high-class/elite lifestyle. A subsidiary of the Swatch Group,
Omega bills itself as symbolizing "accomplishment and perfection – qualities
that have been inherent in every Omega watch since the company's foundation
in La Chaux-de-Fonds, Switzerland, in 1848" (Omega Website). Other
celebrity endorsers of Omega include actor Pierce Brosnan, who plays the latest
incarnation of international special agent 007 James Bond; supermodel Cindy
Crawford; Formula-1 racing car driver Michael Schumacher; and two-time
America's Cup winner Sir Peter Blake. At first glance, Hingis seems almost out
of place among such world-renowned, sophisticated figures. However, I would
argue that the notion of her "Europeanness" of character (i.e., her "worldly"
image, cultured tastes, and fashionable image) is a powerful signifier of sophistication, which is exactly the image Omega portrays. This notion repeats itself in
the following example.

With regard to her Adidas endorsement, she is presented as a part of what
Adidas likes to call its "Tennis Club." This "club" of product endorsers includes

Hingis, Kournikova, Austria's Barbara Schett, US Open champion Marat Safin of Russia and Swedish star Magnus Norman. Presenting the "club" as a melting pot of identities united in the name of sport embraces Adidas' goal of being the sports apparel leader in the global market. In particular, Hingis and Kournikova appeared in a televisual advertisement for the Tennis Club that aired during the 2000 Australian Open which can best be characterized as a disjointed pastiche of postmodern filmmaking, reconciled only when viewed as an image as a whole, not of its parts. The ad, set in a smoky rave-scene warehouse which could exist in practically any locale, stresses lifestyle – particularly *Hingis'* perceived European lifestyle. It is the role of "lifestyle" politics in late-capitalist consumption that Donald M. Lowe has argued "become signifier for product characteristics, which in turn are the signifier for exchange value ... [D]econtextualized, the image of social, cultural values can then be juxtaposed with the image and sign of product characteristics to connote a particular lifestyle" (1995, p. 67). Thus, David Andrews, incorporating Frank (1991) states that "[the] postmodern body is essentially an outgrowth of the absorption of this commodity-sign culture, for 'As the body sees the object it immediately aligns itself in some fit with that object; its desire is to make the object part of its image of itself' " (Frank, 1991, p. 62, quoted in Andrews, 1993, p. 52).

This "media personality" – Martina Hingis the commodity-sign – is a hyper-real product of the conjuncturally-specific technologies of advertising/media which drive postmodern consumptive practices. Marked as a (European) body of fitness, beauty, fashion, and success through various advertising campaigns, the consumption of Hingis' sign-value (through licensed apparel, racquets, endorsed products, etc.) serves as a means for the acquisition of her sign-value. By moving into the arena of (North) American media, this notion is taken to an even higher level, and Hingis becomes at once both European and American.

Mme. Americana

> The public self and its masks are increasingly defined by a media-oriented mass culture in which youth, health, and sexuality have taken on premium values.
>
> (Denzin, 1991, p. 5)

Specific to Hingis and her arrival in the United States are two separate but mutually contingent occurrences: the "mapping" of Hingis onto Chris Evert and the rise of "Girl Power!" discourse in the mainstream media. As Hingis' image is introduced through such narratives, she becomes ensnared into an already existing pattern of cultural representation; as a new potential star, Hingis is "mapped" onto a type of female tennis player that predates her appearance on the tour (Marshall, 1997, p. 97). Most notably, she becomes mapped onto the legacy and media representations of Chris Evert.

Perpetuating this comparison is Evert herself, who says of Hingis:

> She is the closest one, I feel, that plays the way I used to play. I think when Martina [Hingis] came along, I saw a player who doesn't necessarily blow people off the court and doesn't have that one big weapon necessarily. She uses her head at a young age, is very composed and anticipates well.
>
> (Harwitt, 1997)

Furthermore, as part of the Partners for Success program (the mentor division of the Tour's Player Development Program), Evert was selected to team up with Hingis and offer advice on life on the tour.

That she becomes mapped onto Evert is a curious development in that there are obvious correlates to her namesake, Martina Navratilova; namely, a non-American heritage (read: Czechoslovakian) and the fact that she was specifically named after her. Being mapped onto Evert, however, opens the door for Hingis to begin to be established in the mainstream of contemporary (American) sporting subculture. With Evert operating as an archetype that works to define the organization of Hingis as an emergent celebrity, Hingis becomes linked to ideas of femininity, grace, and success. Most importantly, though, is that she becomes linked to Evert in terms of an affective representation of traditional American values (read: heteronormative).

With her image (loosely) tied to Evert, she is then appropriated and understood through the rise of "Girl Power!" discourse. In this context, Hingis is presented as containing American qualities of individualism and freedom; she is a success story, someone who "escaped" the perils of Communist Czechoslovakia for a better life. Furthermore, by containing such American qualities (not to mention an attractive physical appearance), Hingis is appropriated into the discourse of women's empowerment through sport and becomes incorporated into "Girl Power!" campaigns. That she isn't American is not important; with her flexible citizenship and heteronormative exterior as currency – but also a subjectivity grounded in a decidedly (imagined) European national identity – Hingis is able to manipulate images of both the European sophisticate and the empowered postfeminist woman. This (re)presentation enables her to position herself on the margins of the nation as an outsider, but also, and at the same time, at the center of its cultural capital(ist) industry.

However, before we can look at Hingis as an embodiment of "Girl Power!," it is important to take a step back and try to understand just what is meant by this 1990s' buzzword for commodified feminism. The term, often linked to the British pop group the Spice Girls, has been popularly defined as "the empowerment and freedom of young females from gender stereotyping" (Mesbah, 1998, p. 26). On a more politically-motivated and sport-oriented level, the aim of the "Girl Power!" campaign – under the direction of the Department of Health and Human Services (DHHS) in the United States – is to "encourage and empower

9–14-year-old girls to make the most of their lives" (DHHS/Girl Power! Official Website). Donna Shalala, Secretary of the DHHS, said of this campaign:

> With "Girl Power!" we see physical activity as a cornerstone of our strategy to give 9–14 year old girls the confidence and resilience they need to stay away from the dangers like tobacco, drugs, and teen pregnancy and make the most of their lives ... Getting involved in sports such as basketball, tennis, and soccer builds self-confidence and self-esteem while also keeping young girls physically active. These are vital skills and attitudes that will help girls throughout their adult lives.
>
> (DHHS/Girl Power! Official Website)

These notions have been quickly adopted by girls, and even more swiftly by marketers who want to get the attention of these young consumers. In the case of athletics in general, and women's tennis in particular, I would prefer to characterize "Girl Power!" as a subversion of stereotypical notions of female body culture whereby binaries of weak/strong, feminine/masculine, and soft/hard are imploded and reconstructed with both empowering and productive results. By productive I mean the way in which unequal power relations, while appearing to celebrate and promote women's achievement in sport, actually perpetuate the subjugation of female athletes. This is because "Girl Power!," for all its positive (re)configurations within the media, still remains framed within dominant structures of male hegemony. What results is that hetero-social normativity among participants is promoted, athletes are routinely and overtly sexualized within the media, and non-normative groups such as lesbians and racial minorities are marginalized.

Coinciding with the launch of the "Girl Power!" campaign and its attendant appropriations within the media have been the remarkable strides made by women's athletics on a general level. On the heels of the 1996 Olympic Games, the 1999 Women's World Cup of Soccer, and the launching of the Women's National Basketball Association, women's soccer and basketball have achieved both unprecedented success and a new level of media attention, especially within the United States. Instead of being relegated to the back pages of *Sports Illustrated* or the last five minutes of ESPN's "SportsCenter," a whole new culture of women's sports magazines (i.e., *Sports Illustrated for Women*, *Women's Sports and Fitness*, and *Real Sport*) has emerged, and television ratings for women's sporting events have shown a steady increase. However, this popularity is largely a matter of advertising, public relations, and the workings of the media. The breakthrough moments of women's sports of the last decade have been decidedly media events; that is, they have been staged by and interpreted by the various media outlets that cover them. Of course, as Norman Denzin (1996) points out, events such as these contain a "kernel of utopian fantasy", each being (re)presented in terms of the prevailing political, economic, social, and cultural formations. Thus Hingis, in relation to the United States, is (re)presented as a (trans)nationally embodied (and appropriated) stereotype of an empowered postfeminist vision of the future that serves to bind those who consume her image to a discourse of normalization. In particular, I draw my understanding of postfeminism from the work of C.L. Cole and Amy Hribar (1995), who explain:

> Postfeminism can be characterized as the process through which movement feminism was reterritorialized through the normalizing logic ... governing 1980s America. While movement feminism generated spaces and identities that interrogated distribution and relational inequalities, meanings, differences, and identities, the postfeminist movement includes spaces that work to homogenize, generate conformity, and mark Others, while discouraging questioning ... In other words, a normalizing discourse.
>
> (1995, p. 356)

Thus, by effectively normalizing "Girl Power!" discourse, everyone from the WTA to her American sponsors is able to capitalize on the "Girl Power!" phenomenon in such a way that a discursive space is created that spawns the production of (something like) Hingis' sign-value. This newly created space, however, is not one of resistance, but rather one of conformity; *by normalizing "Girl Power!" the media removes from it connotations of it as a political movement and renders it acceptable in mainstream America.*

Conclusion: The intricacy of (being) a postmodern celebrity

Throughout our journey in Hingis-reality, we have traversed a multiplicity of boundaries and experienced first-hand the interconnected nature of Martina Hingis' flexible citizenship and transnational celebrity appeal. As she becomes recognized more fully in the scope of global sports, her image comes to represent Jean Baudrillard's notion of "simulacra," a copy for which there is no original. Appropriated in the mainstream media of various cultures for her global/local appeal, Hingis' flexible citizenship can become tied to virtually any locale. Where she is praised in the USA media for her outspokenness, the Swiss press vilify her; where she is accepted as Australia's adoptive daughter, she is loathed by the French; where she is considered a representation of Swiss intellectual thinking (her adoptive home), she is also represented as Martina II, the second-coming of Martina Navratilova (who shares with her a Czechoslovakian heritage); and where she is the model of European culture and sophistication, she is also appropriated in the USA for what places her celebrity in the most normalized narrative, that of an affective representation of "Girl Power!" discourse.

Through overcoded exposure in the media, mass-produced images replace (or, at least, invade and influence) personal lived experience with events where free-floating signifiers such as Hingis come to represent and stand in for an unquestioned social reality. It is here that, as a simulacrum of her images is reproduced and reified over and against the prevailing cultural climate, the media "become the locus of the *illusion* of reality" (Denzin, 1986, p. 196). Thus, the body comes to serve as a site for the "construction of norms and normative positions about what the body should represent and what the ideal body should be" (Marshall, 1997, p. 144).

As the vectors of her celebrity collide within the USA, Hingis (likewise Kournikova, the Williams sisters, etc.) becomes ensnared in a discourse which promotes a necessary heteronormativity and locates her in an unquestioned and depoliticized narrative of women's empowerment.[9] However, unlike her contemporaries who are seemingly bound to such a discourse, Hingis' flexibility enables her to transgress such boundaries while at the same time employing/utilizing them for personal gain. In selecting different sites for work, investment, and family, Hingis both circumvents and benefits from different nation-state regimes (Ong, 1999). To echo the words of Leo Braudy, it is as if Hingis "has become a free agent – mobile, self-possessed, the image of the ideal individual" (Braudy, 1986, p. 569).

In the last three weeks of writing this chapter, Hingis has gone on to add three more WTA singles titles to her impressive resume – including her first-ever tournament victory on Swiss soil – and has strengthened her grip on the Number One ranking. She has also consolidated her doubles partnership with Anna Kournikova, rekindling interest in and projecting them once again as the "Spice Girls of Tennis." This version of Hingis the Spice Girl, however, portrays an image of the upwardly-mobile, professional woman; with a more mature outlook on life and a flourishing career, Hingis is transformed into the imagined outcome of female athletic participation. With the "material and symbolic resources to manipulate the global schemes of cultural difference, racial hierarchy, and citizenship" (Ong, 1998, p. 135), Hingis has once again remade and repositioned herself and her image in the most lucrative narrative.

Notes

1 The author wishes to thank Synthia Sydnor and Jennifer L. Metz for their keen insights and comments that helped to organize my thoughts, as well as Laura Hess for thought-provoking conversation. Special thanks to David L. Andrews for his suggestions regarding the terms "amorphous subjectivity" and "polymorphous subjectivity" as they relate to Hingis, and for invaluable discussions that arose during the formulation of this chapter.

2 Some 240 journalists from around the world descended on Zurich, Switzerland, to see Hingis' professional debut at the Swisscom Challenge. The 4,500 spectators in the sold out Saalsporthalle witnessed Hingis defeat Patty Fendick 6–4 6–3. Following the match, many believed they had witnessed the future Number One player in the world.

3 In 2001, Hingis was one of five female tennis players named in *Forbes Magazine's* "Power 100 in Fame and Fortune List." The highest ranked female athlete on the list at number 22, Hingis moved up 29 places from the previous year's list.

4   This follows in the tradition of Robert E. Rinehart's (1998) *Players all: Performances in Contemporary Sport*, and is informed by Norman K. Denzin's (1997) *Interpretive Ethnography: Ethnographic Practices for the 21st Century*.

5   This is a play on the title of Umberto Eco's (1973) *Travels in Hyperreality*.

6   *Sprezzatura* loosely means "the ability to make something difficult look easy and offhand, flowing naturally from the personality and nature of the doer, instead of being laborious." This definition is taken from Castiglione's *The Courtier*, alluded to in Leo Braudy's (1986) *The Frenzy of Renown: Fame and its History*.

7   The "Match Point Against Polio" campaign, spearheaded by the World Health Organization, is committed to raising awareness and funds for worldwide polio eradication. Major partners involved in the polio eradication initiative include Nelson Mandela, the United Nations Foundation, the Bill and Melinda Gates Foundation, and the U.S. Centers for Disease Control.

8   Although encouraged, a collective European identity has not garnered widespread support.

9   It is important to note that these norms and normative positions are necessarily tied to a specific locale; Hingis, ever the transnational celebrity, is able to maneuver in and around these norms whenever she deems it necessary.

Bibliography

Andrews, D.L. (1993) Deconstructing Michael Jordan: popular culture, politics, and postmodern America. Unpublished doctoral dissertation, Urbana: University of Illinois, Urbana-Champaign.

Bhavnani, K. (1993) Towards a multicultural Europe? "Race", nation, and identity, 1992 and beyond. *Feminist Review*, 45, 30–45.

Braudy, L. ([1986] 1997) *The Frenzy of Renown: Fame and its History*. New York: Vintage Books.

Cole, C.L. and Hribar, A. (1995) Celebrity feminism: Nike-style post-Fordism, transcendence, and consumer power. *Sociology of Sport Journal*, 12 (4), 347–69.

Cole, C.L. and King, S.J. (1998) Representing black masculinity and urban possibilities: Racism, realism, and *Hoop Dreams*. In G. Rail (ed.), *Sport and Postmodern Times*. Albany, NY: State University of New York Press.

DeCordova, R. (1990) *Picture Personalities: The Emergence of the Star System in America*. Urbana: University of Illinois Press.

Denzin, N.K. (1986) Postmodern social theory. *Sociological Theory*, 4, 194–204.

—— (1989) *Interpretive Interactionism*. Newbury Park: Sage Publications.

—— (1991) *Images of Postmodern Society: Social Theory and Contemporary Cinema*. Newbury Park: Sage Publications.

—— (1996) More rare air: Michael Jordan on Michael Jordan. *Sociology of Sport Journal*, 13, 319–24.

—— (1997) *Interpretive Ethnography: Ethnographic Practices for the 21st Century*. Newbury Park: Sage Publications.

Eco, U. (1973) *Travels in Hyperreality*. San Diego: Harcourt Brace Jovanovich.

Field, H. (1996) Creating a European identity. Paper presented at the Inaugural conference of the Australian Key Center for Cultural and Media Policy, Brisbane, Australia.

Fodor's Switzerland. (2000) The good, the bad, and the tidy. [Online]. Available: http://www.fodors.com/miniguides/mgfeatures.cfm?section_list=ove,sig,din,lod,nig,sho,tra,web,fea&destination=geneva

Frank, A.W. (1991) For a sociology of the body: an analytical review. In M. Featherstone, M. Hepworth, and B.S. Turner (eds), *The Body: Social Process and Cultural History* (pp. 36–102). London: Sage Publications.

Giardina, M.D. (2000) Dueling cyborgs: Martina Hingis and Venus Williams as marked bodies of consumption. Paper presented at the Third Annual Crossroads in Cultural Studies Conference, Birmingham, United Kingdom.

Giddens, A. (1986) *The Constitution of Society*. Cambridge: Polity Press.

—— (1990) *The Consequences of Modernity*. Cambridge: Polity Press.

Grossberg, L. (1992) *We Gotta Get out of this Place: Popular Conservatism and Post-modern Culture*. New York: Routledge.

Harwitt, S. (1997) Martina II. [Online] Available: http://www.sportsforwomen.com/features/year/1997/feat_hingis.html

Lowe, D.M. (1995) *The Body in Late-capitalist USA*. Durham: Duke University Press.

McEnroe, J. (1999) Quoted during the United States Open Finals telecast of Martina Hingis versus Serena Williams on CBS.

Maguire, J. (1999) *Global Sport: Identities, Societies, and Civilizations*. Cambridge: Polity Press.

Mair, L. (1993) New Martina prepares for the bigtime. *The Daily Telegraph*, June 30, p. 37.

Marshall, P.D. (1997) *Celebrity and Power: Fame in Contemporary Culture*. Minneapolis, MN: University of Minnesota Press.

Mesbah, M. (1998) "Spice Girl" power: marketers really, really like it. *Kidscreen*, September 1, p. 26.

Omega Watch Official Website. [Online] Available: http://www.omega.ch

Ong, A. (1998) Flexible citizenship among Chinese cosmopolitans. In P. Cheah and B. Robbins (eds), *Cosmopolitics: Thinking and Feeling Beyond the Nation* (pp. 134–162). Minneapolis: University of Minnesota Press.

Ong, A. (1999) *Flexible Citizenship: The Cultural Politics of Transnationality*. Durham: Duke University Press.

Rinehart, R.E. (1998) *Players All: Performances in Contemporary Sport*. Bloomington: Indiana University Press.

Robbins, L. (1997) Fearless Hingis: Teen tennis star has the swagger of a champion, and the talent and Grand Slam titles to back it up. *The Plain Dealer* (Cleveland), August 24, p. 1C.

Roberts, J. (1998) Hingis and mother: perfect partners. *The Independent* (London), June 9, p. 25.

Robins, K. (1997) What in the world's going on? In P.D. Gray (ed.), *Production of Culture/Cultures of Production* (pp. 11–66). London: The Open University.

United States Department of Health and Human Services. Girl Power! press release. [Online]. Available: http://www.hhs.gov

13

NYANDIKA MAIYORO AND KIPCHOGE KEINO

Transgression, colonial rhetoric and the postcolonial athlete

John Bale

Introduction

In what ways can elite African athletes be read as postcolonial? To what extent can postcolonial status contribute to an athlete being regarded as a hero? Is the postcolonial athlete an agent of resistance, a quality that further contributes to heroic rank? This chapter seeks to answer these questions in the context of two former Kenyan sports stars, Nyandika Maiyoro and Kipchoge Keino. While embracing a conventional approach to the description of their heroic deeds, I also interrogate their representation in (post)colonial texts. In doing so I draw on what David Spurr (1994, p. 1) refers to as "rhetorical analysis rather than historical narrative" and reveal that colonial writing about these athletes was far from monolithic. Put differently, I seek to show that the heroic status of "the colonized athlete", as represented by "the colonizer", is unstable and riven with contradiction.

The European gaze has long viewed "the African body" as a raw material, available for conversion by the Euro-American global sports complex. The physical transformation of African corporeality was part of the colonial project and occurred in mission stations, colonial schools and later, on the campuses of American universities. But the African body was also transformed into familiar cultural forms on the printed pages of a variety of colonial and neo-colonial texts. The "colonial machine" and the "processing" of the natives – a "conversionist fantasy" – were persuasive metaphors in colonial rhetoric (Brantlinger 1988, p. 18; Bale and Sang, 1996, p. 97). In 1923 the French sports magazine, *L'Auto*, carried a cartoon of a semi-naked African native who, in 1922, was shown carrying a shield and spear, surrounded by a landscape of palm trees. An adjoining sketch, representing the situation by 1925, depicted the native transformed into a uniformed and sports-shod athlete, carrying a trophy and bedecked with a victor's garland. He was shown standing in what was the unmistakable sportscape of the athletic arena (Deville-Danthu, 1997, p. 25). Having witnessed the successes of African-Americans at the 1936 Olympics,

French journalists, anticipating the French team for the (aborted) 1940 Games, remarked that research should be undertaken in "the bush" which would hopefully result in the "French race" being represented by the "outstanding contribution" of Africans from the colonies (quoted in ibid., p. 68). In such visual and written representations the African was textually appropriated for the west. However, as late as the early 1950s it was still possible to deny that "the African" would ever seriously contest the athletic records set by athletes from "the west" (Richards, 1953). Hence, rather than an unambiguous colonial gaze that constructed a monolithic colonial "other" as a variation of the "noble savage", a variety of rhetorics were employed. The appropriation of the black body, valorized for the world of the colonizer, was only one form of colonial textual representation. This chapter seeks to employ four rhetorical modes to explore a selection of western representations of two African sports heroes, the Kenyan middle-distance runners Maiyoro and Keino.

Today, Kenyan runners are highly visible and disproportionately successful in world spectacles such as the World Championships and Olympic Games (Bale and Sang, 1996). It was Maiyoro who was the first Kenyan runner to achieve any kind of publicity in the western sports media and Keino was Kenya's first truly world class athlete, world record holder and Olympic champion. It was these achievements that, in essence, made these athletes heroes and, at least at the district or provincial level, celebrities.[1] However, I suggest that for "the African", heroic status may be given only grudgingly by western writers, with reservation and equivocation. Although Richard Holt (1998) has elegantly demonstrated the different categories of sports hero, little has been done to reveal the plurality and contradiction among the western voices seeking to represent sports heroes from Africa. Indeed, there appears to be relatively little ambiguity in popular representation of the sporting hero *per se* and it is only in recent years that a re-writing of such figures has been attempted (see, for example, Baker, 1988). In the case of African sports heroes, the western representation of their heroism has consistently juxtaposed the tropes of idealization and naturalization with that of negation.

This introductory section is followed by three further sections. The first presents Maiyoro and Keino as postcolonial and transgressive athletes and briefly examines their careers as middle-distance runners. I suggest, however, that their heroic rank is, partly at least, related to their status as postcolonial athletes. Next, I excavate a variety of texts to reveal the ambivalent occidental representation of these heroes. Finally, I offer a brief conclusion in which I try to integrate the broad themes of this chapter.

Maiyoro and Keino: postcolonial athletes

Whether Maiyoro and Keino were celebrities – that they were created by "the media" – is debatable. That they were heroes is more convincing. But what made them heroic figures? To be sure, their athletic performances were major factors but they were also, in some senses, among the first "postcolonial athletes". They were "Third World" athletes who arrived in a "First World" sport. And this is not unrelated, I think, to their status as heroes. But did they also symbolize postcolonial resistance? I will return to this question later but at this stage simply aver that resistance (of, say, a political nature) is less readily achieved through the highly repressive character of competitive sports than in, for example, writing, dance or art. In these latter forms of representation, the "rules" are less rigidly enforced and individual "expression" and improvisation are more encouraged.

Maiyoro burst on to the world sport stage in the mid-1950s as his country gained political independence, reminiscent of the Finnish runners of the 1920s. The athleticism of Maiyoro and Keino boosted not only the newly independent Kenya, but also the emerging world of post-independence Africa. But these runners may be also read as postcolonial athletes because they overturned the colonial way of seeing the black African athlete. They transgressed the norms of sports-space and in doing so unsettled the occidental sports establishment. Maiyoro was a role model for other Kenyans. Among them was Keino who became an iconic figure and a role model for black athletes everywhere.

In the early 1950s the prevailing western view was that African track athletes, like African Americans, possessed "great speed but little stamina" (Wiggins, 1989). Middle-distance running (that is, track racing beyond 800 metres) was read as being the preserve of the "white" athlete, epitomised mainly by Nordic runners such as Paavo Nurmi in the 1920s, Taisto Mäki in the 1930s, and Gunder Hägg in the 1940s. During the 1950s it was the Czech, Emil Zatopek, who was the nonpareil of distance running. To be sure, in the 1948 Olympics Alain Mimoun from Algeria, who ran in the colours of France, gained second place in the 10,000 metres. He went on to win two silver medals, in the 5,000 and 10,000 metres at the 1952 Games and capped his career by winning the 1956 Olympic Marathon. In 1952 he was the only African in the top 60 5,000 metre runners in the world (Quercetani and Regli, 1953, pp. 30–1). But by representing France Mimoun could immediately be read as an ambiguous African hero. Indeed, he could be argued to have represented France in more ways than one. He assumed "French-ness" by dropping the Algerian element in his surname (O'katcha) and supported France in the war against Algeria.[2] He was the colonized athlete and did not represent "blackness" in the way that athletes from central and southern Africa might. It was the "Arab north" rather than "Black Africa" that Mimoun represented – if he represented Africa at all.[3] Not until the Rome Olympics in 1960 was the black athlete with stamina made visible to a global audience when the Ethiopian athlete, Abebe Bikila, claimed victory in the Marathon.

Maiyoro, and subsequently Keino, can be read as transgressors who crossed the boundary between the perceived preserve of the "white" and that of the "black". And in these cases there was no ambiguity about who they represented. In short, Maiyoro and Keino confounded the prevailing stereotype of the black athlete but this "out-of-placeness", I stress, presented difficulties for those who sought to represent it; hence the contradictions within the neo-colonial discourse discussed later.

Nyandika Maiyoro

Born in 1930 in the Kisii district of Nyanza province in the Rift Valley of western Kenya, Maiyoro was an heroic figure for Kenyan runners in the 1950s and early '60s. Outside Kenya, however, he was known only to track and field *aficionados*. As a young man he took part in district and provincial meetings before becoming a national champion and record holder. Maiyoro seems to have made his first international appearance, at least outside of British East Africa, in a meet in Madagascar in 1953. He was entered for the 3,000 metres race and emerged a local hero. Apparently he failed to arrive at the start in time and only started when the rest of the field was 100 metres down the track. He closed the gap after 4 laps and proceeded to win the race by 50 metres. The following year a team of Kenyan athletes took part in the Empire Games in Vancouver. En route they broke their journey in London and took part in the Amateur Athletic Association championships held in the (appropri- ately named, from an ethnic perspective) White City Stadium, London. Maiyoro was one of two distance runners included in the party. He competed in the 3 mile event and surprised many of the 30,000 British spectators by leading for much of the distance. During the course of the race he periodically opened up a considerable lead on the pack of English runners behind him, only to let them catch him and then sprint off again. Eventually, they overtook him and the British runners, Fred Green and Chris Chataway each broke the world's record. Maiyoro finished in fourth place, breaking his Kenyan record in the process.

The British press far from predicted Maiyoro's performance but it was a defining moment in the history of athletics. Following the race the editor of the British track magazine, *Athletics Weekly*, noted that "never again shall we nurse the idea that the coloured races (sic) are no good at anything beyond a mile" (quoted in Bale and Sang, 1996, p. 6). The world of British track and field, if not the world beyond, had been alerted to the fact that Maiyoro was an excep- tion to the notion that black athletes lacked stamina. Maiyoro also achieved fourth place in the 3 miles championship at Vancouver and again improved on his Kenyan record. The next major international event in which he competed was the 1956 Olympic Games at Melbourne. This was the first time a Kenyan team had competed at the Olympics and Maiyoro was entered for the 1,500 metres and the 5,000 metres. He met with little success in the former but finished seventh in the latter, in a race that included global luminaries such as world record holders Vladimir Kuts and Gordon Pirie. Maiyoro did not run particularly well in the 1958 Empire Games in Cardiff but in 1960 he brought his career to a climax by achieving sixth place in the Olympic 5,000 metres in

Rome. He did not achieve the global visibility of Bikila but his time of 13 minutes 52.8 seconds was an "African record".

Maiyoro's heroic status is justified by the fact that he was the first black athlete from Africa south of the Sahara to achieve world-class status as a middle-distance runner. His achievement in the 1960 Rome Olympics ranked him the world's twelfth fastest 5,000 metres runner that year, the only black athlete among the 70 fastest runners over the distance in the world (Quercetani, 1961, pp. 55–7). He ventured where black athletes had been traditionally absent, transgressing the "purified" space of the 5,000 metres track race. He broke with tradition and drew attention to what had previously been considered "natural" and "taken for granted". Tim Cresswell (1996, p. 26) would argue that in doing so he revealed the "historical and mutable nature of that which is usually considered 'the way things are'". Given that football (soccer) is the most popular sport in most African countries, including Kenya, his fame may not have even been national. But within the southern Rift Valley and Nyanza he was celebrated as a popular local figure and an inspiration to younger runners. Among them was Kipchoge Keino.

Kipchoge Keino

Keino was born in Kipsano in 1940, in the Nandi district in the southern part of Rift Valley province. His father had worked on a tea plantation and was, himself, a runner of a good enough standard to win prizes in plantation-sponsored races (Noronha, 1970, 21). As a youngster in the 1950s, Kipchoge was inspired by the exploits of Kenyan runners such as Maiyoro and Kiptalem Keter. By the 1960s he had become a global track icon. Keino was a role model for black athletes in Kenya but his fame was much greater than that of his own hero, Maiyoro. What is more, his name was known beyond the world of track and field. Celebrity, heroism and stardom are, however, multi-scaled and relative. While his athletic achievements may have served to advertise Kenya to the broader global scene, he was also celebrated by the ethnic group of which he was a member, the Nandi. They recorded his heroism in one of their songs:

Laleyo laleyo laleyo laleyo
See Kipchoge the man
Who runs for his country Kenya.
Kipchoge, the man Kipchoge,
Who runs for Kenya ...
(repeated continuously)

(quoted in Langley, 1979)

Keino made his first major international appearance in the Commonwealth Games of 1962 in Kingston, Jamaica, finishing eleventh in the three miles. His name lies buried in the results but it was an initiation to international running. He developed his speed and stamina, basing his training on the scientific methodology of interval running and maintained meticulous records of his performances (Noronha, 1970). By the mid-1960s he was achieving world class times and was fifth in the 5,000 metres at the Tokyo Olympics. A year later he broke the world records in this event and the 3,000 metres. While modest about his performances he displayed a degree of flamboyance by sometimes wearing a baseball cap during his races. He was described by Britain's foremost athletics writer as the "world's most exciting athlete" (Watman, 1965) and was Kenya's first world-famous sporting hero. He was a role model for schoolboys in not only Kenya but also the USA.[4] It is arguable that Keino's performances at the Mexico Olympics of 1968 were the most incredible in the annals of middle-distance running history. The British track magazine, *Athletics Weekly*, dubbed him the track runner of the year, ahead of the likes of Tommie Smith and Ron Clarke (Watman, 1969, p. 4). This plaudit was only partly based on Keino's 1,500 metres Olympic victory over the world's record holder, Jim Ryun, in an Olympic record time. This was the second fastest time for the 1,500 metres in the event's history, which in 1968 was thought impossible at altitude. Keino had previously raced five times (heats, semi-finals and finals) in the previous week and suffered stomach trouble. In addition to this victory, he finished second in the 5,000 metres and made the final of the 10,000 metres, dropping out with three laps to go with stomach pains which turned out be a gall bladder infection. Mexico City was not the only site of Keino's Olympic successes. As his career neared its end he decided his best chance of a gold medal in the 1972 Olympics at Munich was to enter the steeplechase. A novice in this event, he won it with relative ease and, in addition, earned a silver medal in the 1,500 metres.[5]

Back in Kenya he was awarded the Order of the Burning Spear by the president and, upon his retirement assumed a coaching role and bought a farm. In 1998 he was the leader of the Kenyan Olympic team. Keino also bought a sports shop and from income generated by it and the farm he established accommodation for orphans in Eldoret in north-west Kenya. Soon the number of orphans outnumbered the available space and in 1989 a larger plot was purchased for the Kip Keino Childrens' Home where seventy orphan children were accommodated. It was not simply through his sporting associations that Keino is seen as a hero.

Rhetorics of empire

There are doubts about whether the notion of the "postcolonial" is anything other than an illusion. We are, it is suggested, in a neo-colonial world in which colonialism still exists in everything but name. But postcolonialism can be seen as more than simply an epoch. "Postcolonial" can apply to method as well as to period and content and I believe that there is some value in applying postcolonial methodology to modern sports. Broadly speaking, post-colonial theory (method) includes the excavating of colonial and neo-colonial

223

texts for "meanings" hitherto obscured by status quo readings. New readings of such texts reveal fresh insights.

The "straightforward" – the taken for granted – reporting of the feats of Maiyoro and Keino, as outlined in the previous section, is typical of the coverage afforded many sports heroes. At worst, they are gazetteers of sporting facts and figures, which are taken at face value and are uncontested. What I have represented so far is only a partial record. I will now attempt to demonstrate that the western representations of these Africans' performances were far from monolithic. Spurr argues that colonial discourse is made up of a "profusion of different voices", assuming "a number of widely divergent rhetorical forms". These often clash with one another and yet "all enter equally into the matrix of relations of power that characterizes the colonial situation" (Spurr, 1994, p. 7). Spurr recognizes twelve rhetorical modes or ways of writing about non-western people. They represent a "repertoire for colonial discourse, a range of tropes, conceptual categories, and logical operations available for purposes of representation" (ibid, 3). Four of these modes – surveillance, appropriation, idealization and negation – are used here to reveal the instability and slippage in the discourse surrounding Maiyoro and Keino. In this section I want to excavate the discourses surrounding Maiyoro and Keino by using the modes noted above. Although these overlap with each other, they are presented sequentially for purposes of organization. The texts used to explore the representation of these athletes are mainly reports and articles in British and North American track magazines and newspapers.

Surveillance

Kenyan running has long been subjected to the colonial gaze of surveillance (Bale and Sang, 1996) and it remains one of the major forms of writing about African athletes. For sports agents and college recruiters, knowledge is power when it comes to successful conscription. Part of the colonial project was to quantitatively record Africa and the African. Africa was mapped by the geographical agencies of Empire while "the African" body was mapped by the methods of anthropometry and, concurrently, by the stopwatch and measuring tape. Indeed, the stopwatch had been used to time races in Kenya from the turn of the century (ibid., p. 75). The discourse of Kenyan track and field is one that provided the west with information about the black athlete. Track and field is a world of record(ing)s and statistics – a world of surveillance. It was the times that Maiyoro and Keino took to cover a particular distance, rather than their performance in a race, that would enable them to be compared with, and rhetorically appropriated by, the sports system of the colonial power. The times and distances achieved by athletes in the track and field meets of colonial Kenya were, from the 1930s, entered as local records and used for comparison with western equivalents. To take part in sport, African athletes, of necessity, have to be judged by the (western) standards of the stopwatch and tape measure. As

Walter Benjamin noted in one of his fleeting allusions to sports, there was nothing more typical of "the test" in its modern form "as measuring the human being against an apparatus" (Buck-Morss, 1989, p. 326).

A globally organized ledger which claimed to rank all track and field performances above a certain standard was established in 1950, following the formation of the Association of Track and Field Statisticians. Monitored and maintained by an international group of respondents (initially almost entirely European and north American) who were intent on surveilling and recording the performances of athletes throughout the world, "world class athletes" could now be defined by quantitative data. In this way, the Kenyan performances of Maiyoro and Keino could be judged against the norms of the west. The categorization of records by continent (Maiyoro's so-called "African record") supplied evidence of racial difference. Until the 1970s and 1980s, these data, when compared to the records of Europe, simply confirmed the African's perceived inferiority. But through their record(ing)s the Kenyans were not only negated but also valorized, their bodies being seen as a potential resource for the future global supply of sports labour.

The rank-ordering of athletes in the style outlined above is based purely on a timed record, irrespective of any other variables. During the 1930s Benjamin had compared such records to the industrial science of Taylorism that employed the stopwatch to analyse minutely the bodily actions of factory workers (Buck-Morss, 1989, p. 326). The cold statistic, authoritative and privileged, yet distanced, bares itself devoid of any context (i.e. weather, track conditions, opposition, tactics). In this way, for example, Maiyoro's best mile time in 1958 of "precisely" 4 minutes 9.6 seconds could be identified as occupying the modest position of 86th in the world's best performers' list, with no indication at all of the context in which it was achieved. The track statistics of modernity, like the anthropometrists' data of yesteryear, reflected scientism – but also spuriousness.

Appropriation

When Henry Morton Stanley looked over the nineteenth-century landscape of the shores of Lake Tanganyika he extrapolated the African environment by describing what it would be like when colonized – a landscape of English meadows, churches and pretty villages (Spurr 1994, p. 30). European writing about Maiyoro and Keino appropriated them for the world of Olympism, international championships and world records. Witnessing Maiyoro finishing in fourth place in the AAA championships, the British track and field magazine *Athletics World* (1954) read his performance as a revelation of "a physical ability in the greatest 'Caucasian' traditions" – an aberration of "the African". Even so, under such a gaze, the athletes' bodies are prepared for union with western sport; "everything is in order; it is a question of simple substitution and supplement rather than true transformation"; the "African body" waits for western sport to bring it into being (Spurr, 1994, p. 30).

The western view of progress, carrying with it a hint of negation with respect to the African, was reflected in the view that Maiyoro would, "with the *right* training and competition, be a match for any runner in the world" (quoted in Bale and Sang, 1996, p. 6, italics added). Like African "art", Maiyoro's running reflected simply a "stage" in the "development" towards a "civilized" culture of racing. Drawing on the observations of Christopher Miller (1985) on African art, such writing as that noted above "*rewards* Africa for conforming to a European image of [athletics], for acting as a mirror in which the European can contemplate a European idea of [sport]". But what would happen to the world records and Olympic championships if such Africans were to emerge in significant numbers? This was a sentiment that was to haunt the European world of track and field into the twenty-first century (Hoberman 1997, p. 100).

Appropriation – the "conversionist fantasy" – was symbolically inscribed in the physical landscape as well as on the written page. The running track, often built by schoolteachers or missionaries, on which Maiyoro sometimes raced, and the home made track on which Keino recorded his progress, were uniform sites reflecting the mastery of space. The 100 yards stretch was a sporting analogue of the railway line from Mombasa to Nairobi. Each was a colonial "reaction to the winding, African footpath"; each was "a straight line, a man-made construct … indicative of order and control" (Cairns, 1965, p. 78).

Idealization

The idealization and naturalization of the Kenyan runner have a long pedigree. The idealized African athlete is the sporting analogue of Rousseau's "noble savage". The French geographer, Elisée Réclus had, in the 1870s, eulogized the Masai in the last quarter of the nineteenth century, observing that they have "slim, wiry figures, admirable for running" (quoted in Bale and Sang, 1996, p. 51). Here the trope of idealization merges almost seamlessly with that of naturalization. The British track coach and journalist, P.W. Green commented on Maiyoro's style of running by noting that it was "as near the perfect action as I have seen" (ibid., p. 6). He had "exploded the age-old 'no stamina' myth about negroes" applauded the *Athletics World* (1954) reporter.

Maiyoro and Keino are, of course, embedded in a deeper rhetoric about the "natural athlete". In attempts to "explain" Kenyan success in long distance running allusions are often made to the naturalness of the Kenyan "way of life". Such "explanations" of Kenyan running success are those of environmental determinism. Consider for example, the view of the American journalist, Kenny Moore (1990):

> Africa can be seen to be a sieve of afflictions through which only the hardy may pass. The largest, fastest, wildest, strangest beasts are here.

Every poisonous bug, screaming bird and thorned shrub has arrived at this moment through the most severe environments ... Sport is a pale shadow of the competitive life that has gone on for ever across this high, fierce, first continent. Is it any wonder that frail European visitors feel threatened?

Such a landscape "produces" the noble savage, the natural athlete. Culture and history are denied any place in such accounts.

The mode of idealization can easily overlap with those of negation and denial. The "natural athlete" is not only the Corinthian ideal; he is also seen to be in possession of an unfair advantage over those who have to train hard to achieve results. The juxtaposition of the modes of appropriation and idealization to those of negation and denial is common in colonial and neo-colonial discourse. The mode of idealization may also find its way into the rhetoric of the African athlete himself. Kenyan athletes have been thought to possess a distinctive "style". Keino can be seen as representing what might be termed "ethno-Africanism" when he claimed that:

Our style of running was not like theirs. When I ran, I liked to "front run". European athletes, on the other hand, used to pace themselves with the aim of saving themselves for the final lap sprint finish. On the contrary, I started slowly and would up the pace ... as far as I was concerned, it was only the athletes who could muster the stamina and strength to stay with my pace who could pose a challenge to my abiilty to win. They were amazed to see us run the way we did.

(quoted in Bale and Sang, 1996, p. 81)

Here Keino himself speaks the words of the European, essentializing both Kenyan and European runners.

Negation

It has been suggested that the most popular form of representing "the African" is one of negation (e.g. Pieterse, 1995). This chapter has, of course, shown that this is far from being the case but, even in the case of the heroic runners of Kenya, negation can be seen to lie next to idealization as a mode of representation. The British reaction to Maiyoro's performance at London's White City in 1954 is illustrative. The three-mile race, observed the liberal *Manchester Guardian*, was "made confusing" by Maiyoro's "ludicrously fast pace", while *The Times* (London) stated that it was "inevitable" that he would be overtaken by the British runners (quoted in Bale and Sang, 1996, p. 6). During the Empire Games in the same year he was patronizingly referred to as "the popular Black Jack from Kenya" by one of Britain's most respected athletics writers (ibid., p. 7). And the fact that Maiyoro ran without shoes was regularly alluded to. It was a sign of difference, signifying "the Other". When he burst into the lead and interspersed his running with faster efforts he was thought naïve. When the Russian, Vladimir Kuts, employed a similar strategy against Chris Chataway in an epic duel in the autumn of 1954, he was being tactical.

Denigration of Keino's great performances in Mexico City was widespread. During the 1950s the possible influence of altitude on the Kenyans' performances was hardly part of the discourse surrounding the Kenyan athletes. But by 1968 the Kenyans had begun to make their mark and occidental observers referred to their Olympic victories as "unfair" (Bank, 1969, p. 21). The Mexico City Olympics were labelled "the unfair games" because it was widely assumed that the Kenyans, having lived at high altitude, had a crucial advantage over other runners. This ignored the fact that success in sport is the result of a variety of factors and that no athletes from a number of other high altitude nations, including Kenya's neighbours in East Africa, won any medals at all. Traditional economic and cultural advantages accruing to athletes from north America and Europe have rarely, if ever, been invoked to "explain" their sports success over athletes from the global "periphery". It was also suggested that Keino's colleague, Ben Jipcho, had unfairly undertaken the pace-making in the 1,500 metres in order to draw the sting out of the American world record holder, Jim Ryun, whose defeat allowed the American journalist, Dick Bank (1969, 21), to engage in a vitriolic attack on Keino. He repeated the kinds of comments levelled at Maiyoro in 1954, suggesting that Keino "must be the most stupid tactician of all time" and that he had "such an exaggerated opinion of himself that he [thought] he [could] outsprint everyone". Additionally, Keino was labelled as being "greedy" having (been) entered (for) three middle-distance events (ibid., p. 20). To my knowledge, this insult was never directed at the Finnish running hero, Paavo Nurmi, nor to the Czech legend, Emil Zatopek, each of whom embarked on equally – if not more – arduous Olympic schedules. Of course, they had white skin.

Conclusion

The world of sport is criss-crossed by a huge number of postcolonial athletes. They are postcolonial in a literal sense – legacies of colonial powers. An essential element of postcolonial studies is the re-writing of colonial texts and the search for resistance within such texts and within postcolonial corporeal activities. Could the black sports heroes described above also be re-written as agents of a postcolonial resistance? Sports seem less appropriate than literature or dance as sources of resistance because while providing the oppressed with the opportunity of defeating the (neo)colonial master, they do so on his terms. Sports like track and field are highly conservative activities – indeed, reactionary, according to Benjamin (Buck-Morss, 1989, p. 326). To display resistance to something an athlete dislikes (colonialism, neo-colonialism, bureaucracy, discrimination) is not readily undertaken during the course of a sports event. Unlike the fictional

Colin Smith, in Alan Sillitoe's *Loneliness of the Long Distance Runner* (1961), few world class athletes are likely to draw attention to their cause by withdrawing from a race just before the finishing line when clearly within reach of victory (Bale, 1999).

Arguably the most well-known "resistant act" in track and field, the black power salute at Mexico City, was undertaken *after* the athletes had won their medals. To resist in sport is seen to be un-sporting or taking oneself out of sport. Failure to adopt western sports involves opting out of the global sports system. The hybrid body culture of Trobriand Cricket represents a graphic example of postcolonial body culture as resistance. The Caribbean "style" of cricket, and "Kenyan running", by contrast, are simply cosmetics, a thin veneer on standardized world sport. Resistance implies intentionality (Cresswell, 1996). Transgression, on the other hand, can be said to be seen as being "out of place". It is, I suggest, acts of transgression that best describe, and help to explain, the heroic status of the two Kenyans who have formed the focus for this chapter. They were heroes but not rebels. Perhaps Keino could be termed a "proto-celebrity" but neither he nor Maiyoro could be said to have degenerated into "mere celebrities" (Vande Berg, 1998, p. 137). Having said this, the heroism of these two athletes needs to be read within a variety of rhetorical modes; there was no single neo-colonial gaze. The sports star – in this case the postcolonial athlete – can therefore be read as a textual construct, but one that is equivocal, ambivalent and contested.

Notes

1   On the distinction between heroes and celebrities see, for example, Vande Berg (1998).
2   I am grateful to Pierre Lanfranchi for this information.
3   The distinction – if such a distinction exists – between the "Arab north" and "Black Africa" is strongly drawn by Wole Soyinka (quoted in Howe, 1998, p. 243).
4   This assertion is based on an email communication from Dave Sobal, 12 August 1999. He refers to a successful US high school runner who, in the 1970s, wore an old orange baseball cap, Keino-style, and threw it on to the infield when he began his sprint finish. "Keino was a hero to be emulated by an inner city kid in a dying steel town in northwest Indiana."
5   Keino's ability to achieve Olympian performances in events from 1,500 to 10,000 metres, including the steeplechase, reflects a range rarely, if ever, found in modern track and field. In an interview in 1999 Keino claimed that he had also run 21 seconds for 200 metres and in the "low 46s" for 400 (email communication from Larry Rawson, 6 October 1999). If so, his track ability was superlative.

Bibliography

Baker, W. (1988) *Jesse Owens: An American Life*. New York, The Free Press.
Bale, J. (1999) "Sport as power: Running as resistance?". In J. Sharp, P. Routledge, C. Philo and R. Pattison (eds), *Entanglements of Power: Geographies of Domination/Resistance*. London, Routledge, 148–63.

Bale, J. and Sang, J. (1996) *Kenyan Running: Movement Culture, Geography and Global Change*. London: Cass.

Bank, D. (1969) "Dick Bank's Mexico Reflections". *Athletics Weekly*, 23 (1), 18–23.

Brantlinger, P. (1988) *Rules of Darkness: British Literature and Imperialism, 1830–1914*. Ithaca, NY: Cornell University Press.

Buck-Morss, S. (1989) *The Dialectics of Seeing*. Boston: The MIT Press.

Cairns, A. (1965) *Prelude to Imperialism*. London: Routledge.

Cresswell, T. (1996) *In Place/Out of Place: Geography, Ideology, and Transgression*. Minneapolis: University of Minnesota Press.

Deville-Danthu, B. (1997) *Sport en Noir et Blanc*. Paris: L'Harmattan.

Hoberman, J. (1997) *Darwin's Athletes: How Sport has Damaged Black America and Preserved the Myth of Race*. Boston: Houghton Mifflin.

Holt, R. (1998) "Champions, heroes and celebrities: sporting greatness and the British public". In J. Huntington-Whiteley (ed.), *The Book of British Sporting Heroes*. London: The National Portrait Gallery.

Howe, S. (1998) *Afrocentism: Mythical Pasts and Imagined Homes*. London: Verso.

Langley, M. (1979) *The Nandi of Kenya: Life Crisis in a Period of Change*. London: Hurst.

Miller, C. (1985) "Theories of Africans: the question of literacy and anthropology". In H.L. Gates (ed.), *"Race", Writing and Difference*. Chicago: Chicago University Press, 281–300.

Moore, K. (1990) "Sons of the wind". *Sports Illustrated*, 78, 8, 72–84.

Noronha, F. (1970) *Kipchoge of Kenya*. Nakuru: Elimu Publishers.

Pieterse, J. (1995) *White on Black: Images of Africa and Blacks in Western Popular Culture*. New Haven, CT: Yale University Press.

Quercetani, R. (ed.) (1961) *International Athletics Annual*. London: World Sports.

Quercetani, R. and Fulvio R. (eds) (1953) *International Athletics Annual*. London: World Sports.

Richards, D.J.P. (1953) "Athletic records and achievements in relation to climatic, social and environmental factors". Unpublished master's thesis, University of Wales.

Sillitoe, A. (1961) *The Loneliness of the Long Distance Runner*. London: Pan.

Spurr, D. (1994) *The Rhetoric of Empire*. Durham, NC: Duke University Press.

Vande Berg, L. (1998) "The sports hero meets mediated celebrityhood". In L. Wenner (ed.), *Media Sport*. London: Routledge, 170–85.

Watman, M. (1965) "Keino: the world's most exciting athlete". *Athletics Weekly*, 19, 51, 16.

—— (1969) "They were the 'mostest' in 1968 – 1". *Athletics Weekly*, 23, 1, 4–5.

Wiggins, D. (1989) " 'Great speed but little stamina': the historical debate over black athletic supremacy" *Journal of Sport History*, 16, 2, 158–85.

14

IMRAN KHAN

The road from cricket to politics

Peter Corrigan

Like many social phenomena, sport is both suffused with concepts greater than itself (aesthetics, ethics, economics, class, senses of the local, the national and the global, community, ethnicity, race, leadership, colonialism, gender, politics – to mention only the most obvious) and deploys these concepts in particular ways, reshaping in its turn what we might understand by them. Indeed, sport is one way through which we learn what such notions actually mean in specific contexts. This conceptual apprenticeship offers both follower and participant the possibility of making the imaginative leap to further involvement with these ideas in a non-sport setting, and in this chapter we explore how the Pakistani cricketer Imran Khan has done this. First, however, let us consider the game of cricket more generally.

Cricket, colonialism, nationalism, class and race

One way in which sports may be differentiated from each other is through the different concepts associated with each and the varying weights and impor-tances of these concepts with respect to each other. Even where concepts are shared across sports, they will not operate in the same way in each case. Synchronized swimming and rugby league may have many concepts in common, but the relative importance to each of, say, the aesthetic dimension may be rather different. Followers, participants, commentators and writers on sport may, of course, each provide different accounts of the conceptual compo-sition of a given game, and thus the "same" sport exists in different ways for different actors within and across specific occasions (and for the "same" actor in different roles). In this section, the focus is on writers on cricket and on those concepts they deploy in their accounts that resonate with the sociological imagi-nation of the present writer. This, then, is a sociologist's analysis of a selection of writings on cricket.

Given the above, what appear to be cricket's leading concepts and how do those concepts operate? At the most abstract level, cricket has to do with large questions of social solidarity and social differentiation, particularly senses of colonialism, the national, class and race.

International sport of all kinds, particularly team games, allows for both solidarity and differentiation. The European Football Championships, for example, both create a sense of togetherness (the Championships permit the participants access to the identity "European", confirming their right to it through the playing of the game) and differentiation (Europeanness of a defined sort, such as "Italian" as opposed to "Czech" or "Norwegian" or any other European nationality, the differences being mobilized most intensely during matches). The togetherness and difference of cricket, however, are very much a formerly imperial one, as this A-to-Z listing of the main cricket-playing countries strikingly indicates: Australia, Bangladesh, England, India, New Zealand, Pakistan, South Africa, Sri Lanka, West Indies and Zimbabwe. Cricket was one way through which imperial links were forged, maintained and preserved between England and the rather extensive patches of the world it colonized, Sandiford (1994, p. 42) going so far as to describe it as "an integral feature of the process of imperial assimilation". Playing the game marked one as a participant in the Empire, but was also an opportunity to show that one existed differently as, say, "Australian". Beating the imperial metropole at the game it had invented could always be understood as demonstrating that one's own (colonial) identity more than measured up – at least in the context of sport. At the same time, it was likely to confirm the cultural dependence of the colonies by admitting that they could not compete on that level: the English may have had Milton, but the Australians had Bradman to compensate (Keneally, 1987 [1981], p. 275). James (1993 [1963], p. 233) makes a similar point with respect to the relationship between England, with its deep historical well of national traditions of all kinds, and the West Indies, where this space was occupied by the wrecking of English batting.

Cricket has created and reflected senses of national identity within societies as well as between them. It has been an important component in the construction of Englishness (the late nineteenth-century masculine version of it, at least), first, by marking England off from the countries of continental Europe, where the game even now has almost no existence, and, second, by supposedly encapsulating qualities considered to be peculiarly English. For W.G. Grace (1997 [1892], pp. 86–7), the practice of cricket brought into being "the modest, manly and self-reliant cheerful type of boy we like to associate with English boyhood", Lang (1987 [1893], p. 6) praises the fairness and generosity of the English cricketing crowd ("It is not so in all countries ..."), while the novelist George Orwell (1987 [1944], p. 131) sees the game as expressing an English tendency to esteem form or style more than success. In Sir Henry Newbolt's (1910) poem *Vitaï Lampada*, the lessons learned in schoolboy cricket rally the ranks of a regiment under attack, despite the remoteness of England from the blood-sodden desert of the battle. It is easy to see, then, that an important function of cricket in the imperial era was the transmission of certain English cultural values to the colonies, both to remind the colonizers of who they were (or, rather, who they were supposed to be) and to display to the colonized what they were. Assimilation of these values was to a degree a way in which certain sections of the colonized could access some of the spoils of the imperial adventure for themselves (Sandiford, 1994, p. 158).

Cricket has also been part of the nation-building process in Pakistan, a country of many ethnicities, languages and often antagonistic caste groups that has been in existence only since the partition of the Indian subcontinent in 1947. There have been perhaps three major ways in which such a divided social space has been united: Islam, war and cricket. The Muslim community crosses many nations, and so although Islam may unite people, it does not unite them as members of a particular nation: the members of the *umma* are linked by religion, not nationality. Furthermore, the Sunni/Shia division in Pakistan does little for a sense of unity. War with another country is a traditional way of uniting a fractured nation, and several have been fought between Pakistan and India. War, however, is hardly conducive to long-term stable unity. Cricket, on the other hand, seems to be. Noman (1998, p. 35) goes so far as to say that the two "most widely celebrated post-independence events both relate to cricket: the winning of the World Cup in Australia in 1992, and the last-ball six by Javed Miandad which won the Sharjah trophy against the great rival [India]". It may seem odd that a game introduced by colonizers should play such an important role in producing a sense of national togetherness, but Noman (ibid., p. 50) suggests that it was precisely because it was the game of the elite that it was actively propagated and consequently served as a means of social mobility to those who would otherwise not have a way of accessing the upper echelons of society. Cricket promised a path to social success in a way that the other great sport of Pakistan, hockey, did not, and has become more a mass than an elite sport. Test cricket was deliberately brought to places other than the twin centres of the game in Karachi and Lahore as part of a nation-building exercise in the 1950s (ibid., p. 91), and the sport was one of the few ways in which Pakistan existed as a nation on the world stage at this period (or at least on the world stage as composed of the after-effects of the Empire). Later, television brought the exploits of the national team right into the rural villages. By the austere 1980s of General Zia, cricket "was the only source of popular joy" (ibid., p. 248) and so we find a remarkably strong correspondence between the nation as existing through cricket and the experiencing of popular pleasures. This was also the era of Imran Khan's captaincy, and we can see in the hindsight vouchsafed to the historical sociologist that the bringing together of a sense of the nation, popular joy and leadership in the body of one Oxford-educated person made Imran's later move to national politics almost inevitable. Indeed, it is a combination of qualities most political leaders could only dream of, and most sports captains could never approach with the peculiar intensity possible in the circumstances of 1980s' Pakistan.

Like nationality, class and race are concepts that create both togetherness and apartness through the same gesture – the togetherness of those who claim membership of class X or race Y (or have such memberships forced upon them), and their apartness from other classes and races. In both cases, cricket provides a space where these apartnesses themselves are brought together in what we might call a unity under dominance. That is, the structures of inequality with which difference is often intertwined are not necessarily touched by shared participation in a game, and may even be reinforced and legitimized. Social superiority was maintained in the English game for the ninety years up to 1962 by the division of players into (gentlemen) amateurs and (working class) professionals and a consequent division of labour and conditions that reflected this: the gentlemen batted and the professionals bowled, they occupied separate dressing rooms and entered the field through different gates, their initials came before or after their names depending upon whether they were amateurs or professionals respectively (Brookes, 1997 [1978], p. 66, Frith, 1997 [1978], p. 112, Sandiford, 1994, p. 80). In the earlier days of West Indian cricket, the traditional order saw "a line of white batsmen and a line of black bowlers" (James, 1993 [1963], p. 94), and just as the traditional captain of England was a gentleman amateur (until 1952) so the traditional captain of the West Indies until 1960 was white. Among the spectators, class and race, and sometimes both, were displayed and realized through their location at different physical spots in the grounds (Sandiford, 1994, p. 81, Thompson, 1995, p. 176). Class and racial inequalities, then, were maintained by similar mechanisms. In Pakistan, cricket was an elite game in the early years, and indeed broadcast commentary was exclusively in English (which would not have been understood by most of the population) until the 1970s, when Urdu commentary finally began to gain airtime (Noman, 1998, p. 50, 173). But the use of the game in the nation-building exercises already mentioned, and the path to social mobility later reinforced through sponsorships by the likes of banks, railways, airlines and other corporate bodies (ibid., p. 48) led to the shift from an elite game to one a much broader section of the population could use as a way towards a better life.

So much for the central concepts of cricket in the broader sense. What of Imran Khan?

Imran Khan: representing the self, representing the country

This chapter is concerned not with media or other representations of Imran, but rather with Imran's own representations of himself and his ideas. The texts analysed include the autobiographies of 1983 and 1988, the travel books *Indus Journey* of 1990 and *Warrior Race* of 1993, and a selection of interviews and texts on political and religious matters from *The Electronic Telegraph* (29 April 1996), *Resurgence* (1997) and *Chowk* (16 January 1998) – not quite the *œuvre* of the average sports star, but not out of line with a tradition that expected Pakistan cricket captains to be able to hold forth on matters wider than their sport (Noman, 1998, pp. 75–6). Such an expectation is hardly surprising given that many of the earlier captains were members of a highly educated elite, and Imran certainly fitted that traditional mould.

The three different sets of texts as classified above are marked by somewhat different sets of concepts. Colonialism and race, leadership in the context of cricket captaincy and to some degree politics are to be found in the autobiographies, the travel books are of course marked by geography and history generally, but also by questions of conservation and politics as well as by Imran's attempts at locating his family in the history of Pakistan, while the late texts pay much attention to politics and government, Pakistan and its people, religion, Islam and the West. Political ideas are present throughout, but develop from being relatively insignificant in the early books to being absolutely central to the later texts. The concern with colonialism and race seems to have been transformed into a broader concern with the characteristics of Western societies in general and the place of Islam in the contemporary world. Imran does different sorts of (re)presentational work on Pakistan across the three groups of texts: he (re)presents Pakistan as a cricketer, (re)presents the country in geographical, historical and conservational terms, and (re)presents the way the country ought to be in political and religious terms. There thus appears to be a progressive broadening-out from cricketing specificity to history and geography to higher-level notions of social organization more generally. Those who have been leaders on the field rarely get much beyond the first of these stages, and it is perhaps an indication of the depth of Imran's "star quality" that he has gone considerably further.

My reading of Imran's writings is obviously through the twin prisms of my particular sociological concerns and the present knowledge of his activities. It is now difficult to read the autobiographies without having one's antennae already finely tuned to pick up any political concepts that may be found therein, and the latter will appear to be of much more significance than they did in 1983 or 1988. Similarly, the more purely cricketing aspects of the texts (such as discussions of leadership and captaincy) will appear rather less important from the perspective of the early twenty-first century than they would have at the time of publication. Such caveats entered, let us now consider the principal Imranian concepts.

The autobiographies

We have already seen that cricket was part of the cultural arm of colonial domination. Imran picks up on this theme several times, as well as commenting on the double standards of colonialist practices and the question of race. Cultural dominance was manifest both in the effects it had on the behaviours of certain Pakistanis and in the ways in which cricketing matters were treated by certain elements in England. Some of the effects of colonialism in Pakistan are discussed on the very first page of *All Round View*, which in itself would seem to indicate something of the foundational quality of the concept for Imran.

Having established his parents as anti-colonial, he recalls his father commenting upon the *Kala sahibs* who acted out and even adopted the ways of the English, speaking English to their children and Urdu, if at all, with an English accent (Khan, 1988, p. 1). For this section of the Pakistani elite, particularly the polo players, to live was to exist through colonially-given categories. Such cultural dominance even accompanied the travelling Pakistan cricket team at times, the manager of the 1971 tour to England embarrassing the players at an MCC dinner by claiming that they had learned proper behaviour thanks to English cricket – including how to hold a knife and fork (Khan, 1983, p. 18). Imran's belief in the value of one's cultural location, which will later come out in his discussion of Islam and the West, is clear in his praise of Viv Richards. Proud to be who he is, the West Indian captain is unlike those of his compatriots who mimic English ways (Khan, 1988, p. 117). He despairs of those Pakistanis who could only see some derogatory English press criticism of the manager of the 1987 tour to England through the eyes of their former colonial masters (ibid., p. 87). It is possible to interpret the later travel books as an attempt to overcome this colonized perspective on the world by presenting Pakistan and its culture in a positive way both to Pakistanis and others.

Colonial double standards in cricket are evoked in the context of umpires and the relationship to apartheid-era South Africa. On the one hand, it was considered appropriate for the head of the [English] Test and County Cricket Board to criticize Australian umpires, but on the other it was not considered sporting for the Pakistan captain to criticize English umpires (Khan, 1983, pp. 121–2). Imran further complains of the "colonial arrogance" of English opinion in its opposition to an international panel of umpires on the grounds of the allegedly superior experience, competence and fairness of English umpires (Khan, 1988, p. 174) – which would seem to imply that non-English umpires by comparison were inexperienced, incompetent and unfair. In the case of South Africa, colonialism, race and double standards came together directly. When the West Indies, India and Pakistan did not want to play England teams containing players who had unofficially toured apartheid South Africa, it was argued that this would be a limitation on individual rights, yet all the players who took part in the Packer-organized World Series Cricket in the late 1970s were simply forbidden to play Test cricket – the question of individual rights was not raised at all (Khan, 1988, p. 175). Cricket was still dealing with its colonial legacy.

Government involvement in Pakistani cricket and the political situation in Pakistan generally are both discussed in the autobiographies. We have already seen how important cricket was to the nation-building process in Pakistan, and so it is not really surprising to find the figure of General Zia ul-Haq, President for the ten years until his death in 1988, occasionally stalking the Imranian stage. As a successful and personable representative of the country in sport at a time when military presidents lacked a wholly appealing image in the West (Zia had, among other things, overthrown elected Prime Minister Zulfikar Ali

Bhutto in 1977 and had him hanged in 1979), Imran must have appeared to be a very valuable commodity to the general. Hence the expensive treatment of Imran's leg injury was partly funded by the government on the president's advice (Khan, 1988, p. 65), and Zia persuaded him to come back from retirement with the argument that he had to transcend his own inclinations because his country needed him (ibid., p. xiv). The game itself was an important piece on the general's diplomatic chess board: he instructed the Board of Control for Cricket in Pakistan to reinstate the banned Packer players for a tour of India (against whom a loss could have unpredictably dangerous consequences for life, limb and social and political stability), and twice ensured that the team continued to play when they did not want to (because of violence at Colombo and a sub-standard pitch at Jaipur) (Khan, 1983, p. 45; 1988, pp. 74, 80–1). Continuing to play kept available a means of continuing to maintain relations with Sri Lanka and India, while refusing to play could have endangered them. Cricket, then, was an instrument of foreign policy as well as a way of building domestic solidarity.

In the case of politics more generally, Imran was already making his intent clear in the first autobiography (Khan, 1983, p. 154), an interest that had expanded to a discussion over several pages in his 1988 book. Although he briefly talks about race in pre-Mandela South Africa and the economic consequences of the arms race between what have since become the openly nuclear powers of the subcontinent, his main interests are in the internal problems of Pakistan: population growth, soil erosion, poor health care, corruption and the tendencies leading towards the fragmentation of the country (Khan, 1983, p. 154; 1988, pp. 182–3). Even if not yet a political manifesto, Imran's future direction seems clear in his observation that revolutionary change would be required in order to overcome the problem of corruption (ibid., p. 184). The magnitude of this problem may be grasped through the fact that Pakistan was named as the second most corrupt country in the world (53 out of 54) in 1996 by Transparency International, the Bhutto government being dismissed by the president that year precisely on corruption charges (Rashid, 1996b). Little changed in the following years, with Pakistan ranked 48 of 52, 71 of 85 and 87 of 99 in 1997, 1998 and 1999 respectively (Transparency International, 1996, 1997, 1998, 1999).

The travel books

The travel books, unsurprisingly, pay much attention to geographical description and historical narrative, but they also touch on some political themes. Imran discusses the shift away from his socialist leanings of the early 1970s that was brought about by his assessment of the failure of nationalization policies in Pakistan, which he considers to have resulted in corruption, high inflation, lower land productivity and negative effects on the environment. It is the latter that causes him to praise the feudal landlords for keeping up their game reserves and thus retaining forest cover and animal life – and, incidentally, the partridge he is so fond of shooting (Khan, 1990, pp. 17–19, 23). *Indus Journey* is peppered with concern for the conservation of buildings as well as of forests and animals, often with calls for the government to help (ibid., pp. 64, 72, 78, 86). In *Warrior Race*, he extols the democratic nature of Pathan traditions, where poverty does not prevent an individual from the dignity of feeling the equal of any other (Khan 1993: 5). A first sign of the broadening of the earlier anti-colonial interests of the autobiographies comes with his discussion of Western (as opposed to simply British) media dominance of Pakistan and its deleterious impact on Pakistani elite views of their own society and culture. Imran deplores what we might call the Ataturk effect, where that leader's Westernization of Turkey in the 1920s led, in Imran's eyes, to the devaluation of the local culture but only to a sort of second-class European identity (ibid., p. 152).

Possibly more important for Imran's later political career, though, is the persistent location of himself across both travel books as a member of a family that transcends its present setting in contemporary Pakistan and stretches backwards in time to find a heritage of ruling. He establishes his father's Pathan tribe, the Niazi, as moving from Afghanistan to India in the thirteenth or fourteenth century, and spends much time discussing the exploits of his ancestor Haibat Khan Niazi, a general of the sixteenth-century Emperor of North India Sher Shah Suri and a governor of Punjab (Khan, 1990, pp. 24, 85–90; 1993, pp. 117, 139, 142–3). He also discusses the history of his mother's tribe, another Pathan group called the Burkis. (Khan, 1993, p. 20). All told, Imran's locations of his family in history crop up on eleven pages out of the seventy-five containing text in *Indus Journey* and on sixteen of the 104 text-bearing pages in *Warrior Race*.

Through the travel books, then, Imran establishes a ground of historical legitimation for himself that makes his move to politics seem a natural step. He is no longer Imran Khan, international cricketer from 1971 to 1992, but Imran Khan of the Niazi tribe, millennial descendant of the King of Ghor in Afghanistan (Khan, 1993, p. 17), inheritor of the Pathan traditions of soldiering, democracy and equality, and with the blood of a governor of the Punjab running through his veins.

The political texts

We have seen that there are a number of factors that can be understood as coming together to shape Imran as a political character, and his strongly expressed views on what makes a good cricket captain (Khan, 1983, pp. 25, 101, 105, 107–8; 1988, pp. 50, 61, 102, 126, 129–46), although not discussed here due to lack of space, meant that he was always likely to be interested in a leadership position. There is a still quite a leap, however, to the position of political actor leading a new party. The death of his mother from cancer was the catalyst that shifted Imran from political potential to political action, along with a little help from the government of the day. Her illness led him to discover the seriously deprived state of the health service in Pakistan and in particular the lack of access of the poor to adequate health care (Khan, 1988, pp. 183–4). He consequently set about raising funds to build what became the Shaukat Khanum Memorial Cancer Hospital and Research Centre in Lahore, which opened in 1994. According to its Objectives and Mission Statement (nd), "The objectives of the SKM Hospital and Research Centre are to provide the highest quality diagnostic and therapeutic care to patients with cancer, irrespective of ability to pay". The phrase "irrespective of ability to pay" is easy to interpret as a political statement in favour of the poorer classes and a criticism of the government for not providing proper health care. Indeed, this is how the government led by Benazir Bhutto chose to interpret matters. It then went on the offensive, claiming that money was being embezzled, the poor were not being treated for free, and ensuring an advertising shutout from national radio and television (Khan, 1996). By thus picking up and amplifying the political dimensions of the hospital, the government itself helped create Imran as a national political actor, despite the latter's protestations that his only interest was social work. In April 1996, eighteen months after its opening, Imran announced he was founding the Tehrik-e-Insaaf (Movement for Justice), an event marked by the bombing of the hospital (Rashid, 1996a). The bombing would seem simply to confirm the institution's political importance, as originally recognized by Benazir's government.

Although Imran lists a series of political issues with which he is concerned, such as the economy, health, literacy, corruption and law and order (Khan, 1996), the principal concepts underlying his political texts (Khan, 1996, 1997, 1998) relate to the associations between colonialism and the West on the one hand and Pakistan and Islam on the other. A series of oppositions that structure Imran's views on the matter across the three texts is shown in Table 14.1.

Table 14.1 The oppositional structure of Imranian political discourse

Colonialism and the West	Pakistan and Islam
Slaves of western culture	Extreme radicals
Colonial system	Home-grown roots
Westernized elite	Mass of people
Centralization and globalization	Decentralization and localization
Bureaucracy	Community and family
Colonial education	Learning local crafts
Separation of religion and politics	No separation of religion and politics
Immorality	Morality
Arrogance of West	Tolerance of Islam
Materialism	Spirituality
Individualism	Family and community
Strong institutions	Weak institutions
Weak family ties	Strong family ties

For Imran, the colonial system left a legacy of nefarious consequences which are only being reinforced by Westernization and globalization today, and he finds a set of answers to these consequences in a return to local cultural and religious roots. In particular, the people of Pakistan themselves ended up divided into two main groups: a Westernized elite that inherited the ways of the colonizers and benefit from the global economy, and a mass of people that suffer political and economic exploitation (Khan, 1997). In more general terms, the nature of family and community life in Pakistan is contrasted favourably with Western tendencies to individualism and immorality, and even to the centralized institution of the bureaucracy (Khan, 1997, 1998): decisions made at the local level appear to be an important way of reclaiming cultural and political autonomy. The arrogance and intolerance of the West have to do with the power of the Westernized elite to impose a definition of the situation that Imran sees as rebarbative to the people of Pakistan. Imran points out that Islam is based on tolerance because it does not teach compulsion, thus reversing the usual Western cultural stereotypes of the liberal, tolerant Westerner and the intolerant Muslim (Khan, 1997). Intolerant, however, remain the extreme radicals who are the furthest product of a reaction against the Westernized elite (Khan, 1996). Imran does not see them as an appropriate solution precisely because of their intolerance, and proposes that the Westernized elite begin to study Islam so that they could fight sectarianism and extremism (Khan, 1998).

For Imran, then, the answers to Pakistan's problems are already present in Pakistani culture and religion. He does not completely dismiss the West, however, recognizing the strength of its institutions and pointing out that the systems of justice and the protection offered to citizens' rights in some Western countries give them more Islamic characteristics than Pakistan. But in an echo of an earlier point made above about colonial double standards, he remarks that such countries do not treat the citizens of other countries in the same manner, exporting to the developing world toxic waste and drugs illegal in the West. He also sees the Environmental and Green movements as anti-materialist and pro-spirituality, which would put them on the "good" side of his oppositions (Khan, 1998).

The Tehrik-e-Insaaf did not win a single seat at the General Election of 1997, but the movement continues with Imran as leader. The government, this time led by Nawaz Sharif of the Muslim League rather than Benazir of the Pakistan People's Party, continued to construct him as a genuine political rival by giving Imran the opportunity to claim that the prosecution of his wife, Jemima Khan, for allegedly illegally shipping tiles out of the country was a "smear campaign" (Barwick, 1998) and a case of "political victimisation" (Siddiqui, 1999). She was cleared in April 2000 (Paterson 2000) when Pakistan was ruled by the government of General Pervez Musharraf, who had ousted Sharif in a coup in October 1999. Imran greeted the coup with approval on the grounds that the army was trying to save democracy (Rashid, 1999) and saw in the new regime the hope of putting an end to the political corruption personified by Sharif and Benazir (Anonymous, 1999). The story will hardly end there, however, and it seems more than likely that further political activities and texts are still to come from Imran Khan.

Conclusion

This article began with a discussion of the ideas of differentiation and solidarity and with the notions of colonialism, nationalism, class and race in the context of cricket. An examination of Imran's writings has shown that these concepts have been picked up and transformed into the more specific contexts of the West, Islam and Pakistan, as well as an explicit commitment to the poorer classes of Pakistani society. Imran seems to have made the most of any conceptual apprenticeship that his experiences as cricketer provided. The analysis presented here also suggests that his road from cricket to politics was a very hard one to avoid.

Bibliography

Anonymous (1999) "Imran fears civil war if system not changed". *Dawn*, 16 November. Available http://www.insaaf.com/pressreleases/CivilWar.htm (accessed 3 October 2000).

Barwick, S. (1998) "Imran accuses Pakistan of smear campaign". *The Electronic Telegraph*, 15 December. Online. Available http://www.telegraph.co.uk (accessed 24 August 1999).

Brookes, C. (1997 [1978]) "Amateurs and professionals 1873–1962". In C. Lee (ed.), *Through the Covers. An Anthology of Cricket Writing*. Oxford: Oxford University Press.

Frith, D. (1997 [1978]) "Edwardian Cricket". In C. Lee (ed.), *Through the Covers. An Anthology of Cricket Writing* (pp. 111–24). Oxford: Oxford University Press.

Grace, W.G. (1997 [1892]) "Cricket as a sport". In C. Lee (ed.), *Through the Covers. An Anthology of Cricket Writing* (pp. 85–90). Oxford: Oxford University Press.

James, C.L.R. (1993 [1963]) *Beyond a Boundary*, Durham, North Carolina: Duke University Press.

Keneally, T. (1987 [1981]) "A bloody Drongo". In M. Davie and S. Davie (eds) *The Faber Book of Cricket* (pp. 274–8). London: Faber and Faber.

Khan, I. (1983) *The Autobiography of Imran Khan*. London: Pelham Books.

—— (1988) *All Round View*. London: Chatto & Windus.

—— (1990) *Indus Journey: A Personal View of Pakistan*. London: Chatto & Windus.

—— (1993) *Warrior Race. A Journey Through the Land of the Tribal Pathans*. London: Chatto & Windus.

—— (1996) "My dream for Pakistan". *The Electronic Telegraph*, 29 April. Online. Available http://www.telegraph.co.uk (accessed 24 August 1999).

—— (1997) "Politics In Pakistan". *Resurgence*. Online. Available http://www.gn.apc.org/resurgence/articles/khan.htm (accessed 24 August 1999).

—— (1998) "'Selective Islam' in Pakistan". *Chowk*. 16 January. Online. Available http://www.chowk.com/Gulberg/Madrasa/imran_jan1698.html (accessed 24 August 1999).

Lang, A. (1987 [1893]) "A liberal education". In M. Davie and S. Davie (eds) *The Faber Book of Cricket* (pp. 4–11). London: Faber and Faber.

Newbolt, H. (1910) "Vitaï Lampada", in *Collected Poems 1897–1907* (pp. 131–3). London: Thomas Nelson.

Noman, O. (1998) *Pride and Passion. An Exhilarating Half Century of Cricket in Pakistan*. Karachi: Oxford University Press.

Objectives and Mission Statement (nd) Shaukat Khanum Memorial Cancer Hospital and Research Centre. Online. Available http://www.shaukatkhanum.org.pk/index.html (accessed 23 September 1999).

Orwell, G. (1987 [1944]) "Raffles and morality". In M. Davie and S. Davie (eds) *The Faber Book of Cricket* (pp. 131–2). London: Faber and Faber.

Paterson, M. (2000) "Jemima Khan cleared of smuggling antique tiles". *The Electronic Telegraph*, 6 April. Online. Available http://www.telegraph.co.uk (accessed 3 October 2000).

Rashid, A. (1996a) "Imran makes stand for justice". *The Electronic Telegraph*, 26 April. Online. Available http://www.telegraph.co.uk (accessed 24 August 1999).

—— (1996b) "Imran Khan urges death penalty for corruption". *The Electronic Telegraph*, 21 December. Online. Available http://www.telegraph.co.uk (accessed 24 August 1999).

—— (1999) "The army was right, says Imran Khan". *The Electronic Telegraph*, 15 October. Online. Available http://www.telegraph.co.uk (accessed 3 October 2000).

Sandiford, K. (1994) *Cricket and the Victorians*. Aldershot: Scolar Press.

Siddiqui, K. (1999) "Imran alleges Sharif ploy in tiles case". *The Indian Express*, 13 January. Online. Available http://www.expressindia.com/ie/daily/19990113/01350795.html (accessed 19 August 1999).

Thompson, L. O'B. (1995) "How cricket is West Indian cricket? Class, racial, and color conflict". In H. McD. Beckles and B. Stoddart (eds), *Liberation Cricket: West Indies Cricket Culture*. Manchester: Manchester University Press.

Transparency International (1996) *1996 Corruption Perceptions Index*. Online. Available http://www.gwdg.de/~uwvw/ (accessed 3 October 2000).

—— (1997) *1997 Corruption Perceptions Index*. Online. Available http://www.gwdg.de/~uwvw/ (accessed 3 October 2000).

—— (1998) *1998 Corruption Perceptions Index*. Online. Available http://www.gwdg.de/~uwvw/ (accessed 3 October 2000).

—— (1999) *1999 Corruption Perceptions Index*. Online. Available http://www.transparency.de/documents/cpi/index.html (3 October 2000).

15

BRIAN LARA

(Con)testing the Caribbean imagination

Hilary Beckles

Cricket in the anglophone Caribbean is no sporting matter. Though the quintessentially English imperial sport, it was embraced by the disenfranchised African and Asian communities during the nineteenth century. Despite attempts by white colonial elites to monopolize and racially segregate the game, the popular demand for open access provided it with a radical, democratizing mandate. Such contests became closely interwoven with the wider agendas of anti-colonial political movement that gave rise to mid-twentieth-century national society.[1]

Historians of the game have painted a picture of postcolonial cultural identity and nationalism that frames the painful but rewarding subaltern struggle to tear cricket away from its oppressive, imperial scaffold and make of it an instrument of political liberation within civil society. Furthermore, they have conceptualized this narrative in a nuanced way that typifies much of the West Indian experience of anti-colonialism. While the game came to constitute an arena within which the civil rights movement fashioned a culture of political and social transformation it continued to serve as an ideological space in which there was celebration of the traditional morality and values of the targeted colonial elite.

In this dialectical way, then, cricket was firmly wedded to both the radical process of nation-building and the reactionary interests of politically retreating white elites. While the defeat of colonialism was won in part on the battlefield of the game, attempts at the preservation of Victorian social outlooks with respect to the role of the individual in society remained an enduring effect. The black cricket hero especially became the representative of progressive political nationalism as well as the champion of social traditionalism.[2]

The movement for political change featured the rise of black consciousness that conceived whiteness, particularly Englishness, as an oppressive ideology from which the individual and the "nation" should be liberated. It took a regional mass movement during the 1950s which was led by radical intellectuals, labour leaders, and anti-colonial liberal politicians to wrest the captaincy of West Indies cricket from the clutches of white elites that had assumed a right to lead as a metaphor of their dominance of civic society and the colonial State.[3]

243

The appointment of Frank Worrell as tour captain in 1960, the first black to occupy this position, was understood in the West Indies as a victory for blacks and the wider democratic and anti-colonial movements. He was idolized as a symbol of a successful strike against colonial supremacy at home and abroad. The young nations that emerged shortly thereafter represented Worrell's character as an expression of all the things they wished to be; he was considered graceful, sincere, smart, mature, sound, and visionary. Worrell served his wider West Indian "nation" as a statesman and ambassador. In this way the cricket hero was enshrined within the dominant political project, and his private and public conduct judged and approved accordingly.

The cricket hero, then, in the age of nationalism, became a super icon, stretching and shaping the national imagination to encompass a new, dignified and respected location within the postcolonial world. These mostly black and Indian "stars", beginning with Learie Constantine in the 1920s, George Headley in the 1930s, Frank Worrell in the 1950s and 1960s, Gary Sobers and Rohan Kanhai in the 1960s, and Viv Richards and Clive Lloyd in the 1970/80s have all been declared "national heroes". Constantine was given an English peerage and served in the House of Lords; some of the others have been knighted by the Queen of England on the recommendation of their national governments.[4]

Between the period represented by the career of George Headley and Viv Richards, the West Indies Test team rose from the status of comical entertainers to world champions. They established after 1978 an enviable domination of the international game, crushing all competitors. It was an awesome, unprecedented record of achievement. Not surprisingly, cricket in these newly independent jurisdictions became "King", and all other sports were its subjects. West Indians raised the game's performance standards, redefined its methods of play, and created a system of scientific approaches that enabled them to brush away other teams with childlike ease.

This magnificent edifice came crashing down in the mid-1990s. Today, the West Indian Test team is ranked among the weakest in the international arena. It is ridiculed by opponents, its members heckled around the world as pathetic amateurs not worthy of attracting a gate. Their descent from awesomeness to awfulness is considered one of the most extraordinary dislocations in the modern history of sports. In the midst of this collapse and fall to ruin, Brian Lara emerged as the latest superstar of the West Indian and international game. A highly artistic and courageous player he is rated the best batsman in the world on the basis of his spectacular and extraordinary accomplishments, all of which have been achieved as a relatively young and inexperienced international player.[5]

On April 18, 1994, at the age of 25, Lara broke the World Test record of 365 runs set by the incomparable Gary Sobers in 1958, when he scored 375 runs against England in Antigua. On June 3, while playing as an "overseas" professional for Warwickshire County in the English domestic competition, he became the first player to score seven centuries in eight first class innings. Lara did not stop there. He proceeded three days later to record the highest first class score, still playing for Warwickshire, against Durham; a massive 501 runs not out breaking the previous best of 424 runs made by Archie MacLaren of Lancashire county 99 years earlier in 1895.

These record-breaking performances were preceded by a majestic innings of 277 runs against Australia at Sydney in 1993. The locals, longing for this rare quality in batsmanship, dubbed him the "Prince of Cricket". This performance was described by many critics as the greatest ever played on Australian soil, a fittingly wonderful prelude to the smashing of three world records the following season. West Indians too embraced him with regal language but preferred the designation "Crown Prince" – recognizing that Gary Sobers remained the "King". With these extraordinary feats, Lara became the latest political icon in the region and his achievements were celebrated in 1994 with the award of the highest national honour of his native Trinidad and Tobago – The Trinity Cross. Finally, to crown it all he was appointed captain of the West Indies Test team in 1996, though the announcement was greeted by a whirl-wind of public controversy.[6]

The end of this golden stretch in Lara's career also signalled the beginning of rough patches that further highlighted the systematic decline of the West Indies team. His record-breaking journeys had taken place at the beginning of the crisis of collective performance. The team in which he stood tall in 1994/95 is easily dwarfed by Viv Richards' "dream team" in which he made his test debut in 1990. Critics and supporters alike have drawn the inescapable conclusion that his rise to stardom has not impacted positively upon the fortunes of West Indies cricket. But this is not how the cricket hero is framed within nationalist ideology. His genius is expected to lift the team to a height of accomplishment that in turn enables the nation, the extended spectatorship, to celebrate and marvel at its capability.

The simultaneous fall of West Indies cricket and rise of Brian Lara, both against a backdrop of the collapse of West Indian economies and the decay of civil society movements, have contributed to a situation within which postcolo-nial tensions serve to divide deeply public opinion on Lara's status and role within cricket culture. No cricket icon has ever had such a divisive impact upon the public perception and imagination within development discourse. The failure of the cricket team to compensate for the spreading sense of socio-economic decline has led to an interpretation of Lara's success as anti-social, individualistic, and egocentric, constituting a rupture of the traditional under-standing that the super-hero is driven to performance excellence in order to satisfy the public imagination rather than to promote his own status.[7]

The public feels, furthermore, that it has made an enormous social and psychological investment in this game which is now hijacked by mercenary professionals, players and administrators, who have stripped it of its high cultural meaning – the ideological representation of the "nation". While perceiving on a daily basis the meaning of moral, political and economic crisis

245

within the postcolonial state, particularly the growing hollowness of nationalist symbols, West Indian citizens are not prepared to renegotiate cricket's role within the turbulent but ongoing nation-building exercise. Lara, moreover, is believed to be the leader of this unwelcome rethinking process. The general fear is that at the end of the discussion cricket will have unhinged itself from nationalist sentiments, be alienated from community ownership, and be throwing itself headlong into globalized market driven sports commodification.[8]

Lara, in his own way, is aware that the conceptual integration of the nationalist project and social constructions of the cricket hero, as well as the assumption of their joint mission, continue to be riddled with paradoxes and supportive of a fair measure of personal exploitation. The vast majority of cricket heroes who preceded him, some of them his role models and career guides, were never financially compensated at a level commensurate with the degree of hero-worship they attracted. Financially distressed and embarrassed stars were casually cast aside as new ones emerged, and Lara has encountered a trail of bitterness along the path of his achievement of wealth and fame.[9]

Also, cricket stars as social icons were expected to subordinate their social and political opinions and actions to the State that offered in return pitiful levels of token financial support. Relationships between "star" and State were often sour, unhealthy, and not mutually supportive. This history and images of dejected has-beens have shaped the social field within which Lara came to define his identity as a postcolonial sport icon.

What has happened during Lara's meteoric rise is that the nationalist dream of building a West Indian State as a real home for the West Indies team has become a nightmare, collapsed under the weight of a cocktail of political opportunism and mismanagement, and corporate incompetence and corruption. The reality of a string of impoverished Antillean micro-states that after thirty years cannot legitimize their existence in serious fora in a sound and rational way, and are insecure or pessimistic about the future, cannot be separated from the circumstances surrounding the Lara litany. West Indianness, as a "lived" and imagined social experience, now seems buried under the rubble of inter-nation acrimony within the region, and is struggling to emerge as a construction of technocrats tinkering with financial instruments and institutions of trade.

Lara has admitted on more than one occasion, with a greater telling force after the dismal performance against South Africa in 1998, that a major part of his difficulty in leading the West Indies team was that the players are drawn from different societies in a region where the people are segregated in nation-states built by their grandparents as instruments of liberation and development. But the team in which he made his debut, and those he hero-worshipped as a youth, were also constituted in this way and were winning enterprises. Something new therefore may have surfaced under Lara's regime which is subverting the regional cohesion that was expected to grow in intensity.

The evidence of developments outside of the cricket world is supportive of Lara's suspicion and the direction of his explanation. Many other public institutions in the region are reeling under the impact of such intraWest Indian tension and conflict. The "spirit and soul" of integrative West Indianness which found solitary refuge within the bowels of the populist cricket culture, and remained marooned there for three decades, is broken and is on the retreat. To proclaim one's West Indian identity in some public places today is to invite indiscreet humorous responses. Furthermore, it is now commonplace for West Indians to assert boldly that outside of cricket they are not "West Indian", and that their interest in the regional integration movement goes no further.[10]

Writing in the Barbados *Daily Nation* during a heated public ventilation over one of Lara's many controversial actions, Angus Wilkie argued that the "lack of national unity" is the "cause of present fragmentation" in West Indies cricket. Despite the lack of political unity and functional nationalism in the 1960s and 1970s, he said, West Indians were "driven by hope and a vision of West Indian political unity within a reasonably short time. But the reality today is of doubt and pessimism. Unconsciously, I believe, the gloom has affected our cricket performance." Wilkie's argument is a compelling one that connects Lara's stated opinion to the wider reality of political governance within the region. For him, West Indies cricket under Lara's leadership was asked to do the impossible – perform at a level of excellence in a "political void without any unifying force".[11]

Within a short time a regional call was on for Lara's neck as captain. His detractors were clear in their view that he was not an effective leader because he did not understand or respect the traditional role of the captain within West Indian society. They did not question his ability as a player, but asserted that the magnitude of the office was rather too great for his kind of mentality. Senior and junior team-mates deeply admire him as a player but were divided in their respect for him as a captain and person. What they all feared, however, was that if officials stripped him of the captaincy, as they publicly threatened to do, he would retire from the international Test game and throw West Indies cricket even deeper into the doldrums.

Lara's supporters have responded by stating that removing him as captain was not likely to promote higher levels of performance from him or the team so long as the deepening crisis of West Indian nationalism continues to divide and disable them. Only the construction of a real rather than an imaginary West Indian State, that is, an integrated socio-economic and political system of collective responsibility and duties, they said, could create the conditions for West Indies cricket resurgence in the age of globalization. The nationalisms of other major competing countries are said to be undergoing substantial strengthening as a result of their strategic responses to the global challenge. In the West Indies, it is said, societies are weakening on account of the parade of parochialism which is exposing their collective vulnerability to the manipulative strategies of larger, more organized nationalistic competitors.[12]

The uniqueness of Lara's social and political context helps to illuminate the extent to which the popular democratic movement has shuffled to a halt, and is considered defeated in some quarters. The leadership of many regional principal public institutions, including those charged with the administration of cricket, is now dictated by a professionally conservative corporate elite who see the abandonment of significant aspects of political sovereignty and national pride as a necessary prerequisite or unavoidable condition of global integration and success. The subjugation of the nation-state and cricket administration to the rule of traditional big business interests has combined to create a devastating moral and spiritual assault upon the democratic movements and expectations of mass society. Today, the kinds of working-class communities that have produced Lara are more likely to be seen by the property-owning elites as places that produce incurable criminals rather than cricketing geniuses.

It follows, then, that the renegotiation of cricket culture within the nationalist discourse in an age of globalization is a part of changing class relations in the wider society and the scramble of cricketers as citizens to participate autonomously in the wealth being generated by the refashioned international situation. The division of public opinion on Lara's suitability to represent West Indian aspiration tells us a great deal about the nature of these contests. Citizens are getting around and going beyond the State and traditional arrangements in seeking assistance in order to engage national and international processes. They are attempting to break free of marginalizing constraints. Many state leaders can no longer speak with conviction to them on issues such as national identity, patriotic pride, and social freedom because they are seen as financial beneficiaries from the national prostration to North Atlantic financial agencies.

Lara's image and reputation as a cricket icon have suffered immeasurably on account of the fact that there is no organized counter-movement that roots postcolonial cricket contests within the ongoing historic struggle for social equality and material justice for the masses. In fact, these objectives are considered politically infeasible by ruling political parties on account of their ability to implement the structural adjustment programmes of the neoliberal right that is waving in triumph the flag of the global dawn. One very noticeable and telling consequence of the defeat of the democratic mass movement is that disenchanted citizens are running for shelter and iconic leadership within the walls of revivalist evangelical churches that now attracts the kinds of large crowds that were once associated only with cricket matches.

The relegation to memory of the earlier cricket triumphalism and the communal explosion of born-again religious escapism signal the victimization of Lara's generation by regressive economic forces and social discourses. It highlights the retreat of the populist movements to which cricket has been hinged since the 1920s. Cricket cannot carry, and certainly not alone, the cross of these crippled political agendas whose leaders, like Lara, are unable to attract and mobilize significant emotional support. What in fact the region is trying to understand and cope with is the growing realization that the political process is in crisis, and that cricket culture is in the middle of a paradigmatic shift.

The turbulence resulting from the nature of Lara's postures and decision-making, therefore, belongs properly to the realm of social effects associated with an ineffective, discredited political process. The politics of social decline is, in the final instance, the central cause of the discord that surrounds the inner relations of West Indies cricket. It has less to do with Lara's alleged lack of discipline and commitment, though objectively the moral imperatives of the traditional paradigm of national society have been questioned and are being rejected. The new paradigm has its own distinctive moral features, even though Lara at times appears to be seeking a reconciliation in order to rescue and harness aspects of tradition for the future. This, of course, is possible as the best features of colonial cricket were embraced and retrieved by champions of the nationalist phase.

An important feature of Lara's verbal expressions is an indication that while he wishes to be admired and respected, he has no warmth for the traditional perception of the cricket hero as national ambassador. Nor is he impressed with the social role model construction which he sees as politically manipulative and personally oppressive. To some extent he is reacting to the long line of abandoned former heroes who fill his space with hard luck stories about selector and management victimization. In general, he has no time for the probing press, critical spectators, and does not trust cricket administrators, most of whom he sees as his opponents. These attitudes when perceived have had disturbing effects on the West Indian psyche.

There have been many instances supportive of this view, though but a few have produced an avalanche of publicly expressed West Indian hostility to Lara. In all instances the emotions ventilated are the result of an interpretation that Lara is not cut from the same gentleman player cloth as the "greats" who went before. When he walked out of the West Indies tour to England in 1995 after a dressing room conflict with Captain Richie Richardson, and other senior player, it was reported that conduct with respect to the manager, the legendary Wes Hall, was "abominable". There was no precedent of this kind of development in the prior sixty to seventy years of West Indies test cricket. This case, furthermore, should be put within the context of a threat to do the same thing on his inaugural tour, the 1991 tour to England under Viv Richards, after an adversarial encounter with manager Lance Gibbs, also a legendary West Indian player. Lara discusses both incidents in his book, and casts Richardson and Gibbs in the role of villain.[13]

When Lara pulled out of the winter tour to Australia as a result of the fine imposed for his actions in England during the summer, and threatened to sue the President and the Board, the West Indian public was dismayed but not to the same extent as it was when he withdrew from the training camp to prepare the team for the Pakistan tour in February 2000 because of his carnival engagements. In his own words, the responsibility of being the latest icon of West Indies cricket culture became "too much of a burden" and cricket had "ruined" his life. At the same time, however, according to Tony Cozier, Lara's refusal to tour Australia was a "political statement that he wished to see the leadership of the West Indies Cricket Board changed". In this he succeeded as the debates which followed resulted in the toppling of Peter Short's presidency.[14]

The events surrounding Lara's conduct and performances during the 1995 West Indies tour to England illustrate clearly why the West Indian public is so deeply divided on his status and importance within the cricket culture. The English tour took place immediately after the defeat at home by the Australians in May during the final match in Jamaica. The tourists won the series 2–1 and in the process put an end to the phenomenal twenty-year rule of the West Indies. It was a shattering moment for West Indians who felt that the team lacked motivation, a fighting spirit, and the desire to win. Lara's performance was outstandingly weak. The press reported that mutual dissatisfaction had developed in the relationship between Lara and captain – Richie Richardson – and indicated that it played a significant part in the team's lacklustre performance.

The tour to England began in June under a cloud of despair and internal bickering. Lara did little to set aside public reports that he was critical of Richardson's leadership. Nor did he deny convincingly reports that he had expressed a desire to lead. Those who backed the alleged claim argued that Lara was tactically superior and had demonstrated this during his service as captain of the Trinidad and Tobago national team and the West Indies youth team. At the mid-point of the tour open verbal conflict between Lara and his captain threatened its continuation.

The moment of reckoning was a team meeting at which Manager Wes Hall asked players to freely ventilate their opinions. It is reported that Lara made criticisms of the captain's method and style which constituted a call for his stepping down from the leadership. Richardson, it is stated in the Manager's Report, took Lara's assertions personally and responded that he was not going to resign the leadership on account of the egomania and selfishness of any one player but would readily do so if the team felt that it was in its collective interest. The team stood behind the captain. Lara, feeling betrayed, stormed out of the meeting and stated that he no longer wished to play with the team and announced his resignation from international cricket.

Lara's disappearance from the tour party struck a devastating blow to team morale. Manager Hall did all he could to secure his return. It was a difficult moment for management and players. The international press had detected that a major crisis was in the touring camp but could not get the details. Lara finally returned to the team and met with the President of the West Indies Cricket Board, Peter Short, who he said, had agreed to reinstate him without penalty. Back on board Lara proceeded to give a series of superlative performances. He scored three centuries in consecutive matches, brought the team back from the brink of defeat, and secured an honourable 2–2 tie in the series. The English were confident they could win the series. Their manager, Ray Illingsworth, a former England captain, stated that Lara was all that stood between his team and success. Lara won the man of the series prize and returned home to both cheers and condemnation.

Richardson's tenure as captain soon collapsed after a series of embarrassing defeats including one by Kenya, a country without Test ranking. His fall, however, was surrounded by rumours of Lara's perceived lack of support that amounted to sabotage. Short's leadership of the board also collapsed on account of the way in which he handled the impasse in England. He was accused by his board of pandering to Lara's ego and condoning his flagrant misconduct. The board did not accept that Short was in a position to make a deal with Lara, and the disciplinary committee proceeded to impose penalties. Lara claimed that he had made a deal with the President by which he was assured that the matter was over and put to rest.

When the selectors met a few weeks later to identify the West Indies team to tour Australia Lara announced his unavailability claiming the need for rest and relaxation. The public was appalled by the development. The Australians were the principal opposition and Lara was the leading batsman. Predictably, the team was well beaten and Lara was vilified in sections of the home media for his lack of commitment to the national cause. Within a year, however, he was appointed captain. But within three years his regime had collapsed under the weight of 5–0 and 2–0 "whitewashes" at the hands of South Africa and New Zealand respectively. The dominant view in the society is that he reaped as captain some of what he sowed as a player.[15]

The horror expressed by Test players of earlier generations at Lara's temporary withdrawal from the touring party in England, and subsequent refusal to tour Australia for the World Series Cup, confirms the view that something altogether unfamiliar and non-traditional had surfaced in West Indies cricket. Clarvis Joseph, at the time president of the Leeward Islands Cricket Board, now vice-president of the West Indies Cricket Board, described Lara's conduct as the "height of indiscipline". Viv Richards expressed the view that these developments would undoubtedly affect the team's future performance. He told the English press: "I carry no weight with the Board, but I am so dismayed by the affair that, here and now, I volunteer to mediate in an attempt to get a batsman [Lara] better than I ever was, back on track."[16]

Bob Woolmer, Lara's coach at Warwickshire County, described him as an egocentric person who places neither team nor nation before self. Ian Botham, former English superstar, said that Lara "needs his bum kicked and quickly". Reflecting on his own career, Botham noted, "I was no angel but I never let England down." Colin Croft, former West Indies star, was perhaps most incensed. "If I had anything to do with the Board meeting," he said, "[Lara] would not play for the West Indies for a long time." Michael Holding, Croft's contemporary, added that Lara needed to see a psychiatrist.[17]

What these altogether predictable comments reflect are the ideological perspectives of a new paradigm coming into conflict with the sentiments of tradition. The division of popular opinion with respect to Brian Lara is an early indication of the beginning of this process. The evidence of this phenomenon is clearer in many other areas of civil society. The point should be made, then, that Brian Lara is enormously misunderstood, ill conceived, and therefore unimaginatively judged. Since this is so, it is likely that the generation which comes immediately after him will also be incorrectly understood.

The débâcle of the West Indies inaugural Test tour to South Africa in December 1998–January 1999 best illustrates the depth of rejection of nationalist sentiment and the fullness of the embrace of market economy principles by West Indies players led from the front by Lara. The whole world understood that it was a seminal moment of enormous magnitude. They were going to be the first black test cricket team to compete in post-apartheid South Africa. This society had not witnessed the glory days of West Indies cricket and a substantial amount of nostalgia and romanticism surrounded the event. Nelson Mandela was as eager to see the West Indians as the children of Soweto. The West Indian cricket establishment had done a great deal to isolate the racist regime, and the team, Lara especially, were hailed as heroes and world achievers by black communities desperate to identify with role models drawn from civil society.

Before the tour got on the road news of a pay dispute between the players and the Board, and a strike, had flared. This kind of thing had not occurred before in West Indies cricket. The relationship between players and the Board had long been turbulent, but no captain had ever organized a team strike. The bomb was dropped, however, when it was announced the Lara had flown to London instead of Johannesburg and with his vice-captain, Carl Hooper, were demanding at the eleventh hour additional fees for the tour.

The West Indies Cricket Board refused to negotiate. The President issued a statement that Lara was fired as captain, and that with Hooper, was no longer a member of the touring party. The team stood firmly behind the captain and forced the Board to reinstate both players without penalty. The President summoned Lara to a meeting at headquarters in Antigua. Lara refused and told the President to find his way to London. The President ate humble pie, backed down, and boarded a plane to London. Meanwhile, President Mandela and South African cricket officials were doing all they could to salvage the tour. South Africans, black, white and coloured, were appalled by Lara's leadership, and the West Indian public was shamed by it all. The tour did finally get on the way and the West Indies team went down 5–0, its worst ever Test defeat.[18]

Lara had a dismal tour. He seemed incapable of rising to the special challenges of the encounter. Both the on and off field circumstances overwhelmed him. At home he was branded a money-chasing loser who felt no shame in the disgrace that engulfed his team and nation. The press reported endless stories of his alienation from players and highlighted his on-tour preference for golf and girls. No captain of West Indies cricket has ever been so persistently criticized by the entire cricket world. The global feeling seems to be that Lara represents most perfectly the fall from grace of West Indies cricket as a culture of social elegance and nationalist commitment. The condemnation has been as extraordinary as the praise on earlier occasions.[19]

Much of this criticism carries a greater load of perception than fact, but this distinction is hardly made on the streets by the disenchanted. A destructive tendency in young nations, particularly those emerging from a colonial experience, is to personalize social contests that result from underlying structural change and transformation. But West Indian cricketers and communities need not be acrimoniously divided on the matter. It is the absence of an effective conceptual grasp and understanding of the process that has enabled the media and society to construct a scenario in which nationalism and "Laraism" are juxtaposed as the team collapses further into ruin. The unhealthy focus on Lara's persona rather than the process of change has blurred the critical issues involved. The new paradigm – cricket in the age of globalization – in which cricketers see themselves more as entrepreneurs than professionals should not be moralized in terms established during the age of nationalism. It has to be negotiated on its own terms and judged for the contribution it makes to revised notions of development.

Brian Lara wanted to lead and to do well for his team and country, but on new terms and conditions. Tim Hector, critic and commentator, expressed views on Lara's desire to lead that speak to the circumstances that confront West Indian cricket and society in the age of globalization. "For too long", he said, "the West Indies have been playing the aristocratic game. We are resentful of anybody who shows an anxiety to lead and does so openly. We prefer them to behave like British aristocrats, concealing the desire to lead." Focusing on Lara's bid for the captaincy, Hector noted that "we have picked up a disproportionate hostility to Lara because of this. It is precisely that desire and hunger to lead which the West Indies need now to lift it out of the doldrums." Richardson was clearly the last heroic captain of the age when national pride more than anything else seemed the motivation for performance on the field. Lara is the first hero of a new paradigm that is characterized by individual performance, privatization through sponsorship, and event and action commodification by global television that has become the principal money earner for the game.[20]

There is no turning back. Lara, the first multimillionaire cricket entrepreneur from the West Indies, has opened doors for the next generation. It will see his corporate style and global connections as the norm, and will articulate its entrepreneurial interests in ways that transcend cricket officials' traditional notions of what is good for cricket. The West Indies Cricket Board, which also lost much of its public credibility in the early 1990s, will not be allowed to define exclusively what is in the interest of players. Indeed, the thinking across the region is that these officials are not in the game's interest by virtue of many of its decisions being clearly hostile to players and spectators alike.

If Lara is now cast as an anti-hero of the mature adult generations he remains undoubtedly an esteemed hero, even if a reluctant role model for teenage West Indians. There are many reasons why, for them, he is an iconic leader, all of which relate to the social and ideological circumstances faced by West Indian citizens. For some, his unprecedented financial success represents proof of the arrival of their generation at the gates of the global corporate economy. At a time when the region's economy is characterized by structural decline and a general inability to guarantee that living conditions for the majority will improve, Lara's success brings a gloss to an otherwise dull and dreary economic landscape.

Some adults, it should be noted, also admire his courage and tenacity in telling cricket officials that they cannot rule or ruin his life or determine the contents of his decision-making. In addition, his declaration of a right to be his own man, based on his personal success, represents for the youth a triumphalist mentality that is not intimidated by traditional convention rooted in the authority of conservative elders. For all these reasons, the youth are in support of his style and strategic reactions while turning their backs on what officials represent and the anti-player positions they adopt and defend.

There is, furthermore, a recognition among the youth that Lara's success will pave the way for their own ascendency. Public resistance to his agenda and methods, then, is considered anti-youth in some quarters, and hostile to the principle of openness with regard to the empowerment discourse. If Lara is fettered, they believe, then West Indies cricket has turned its back on them at the beginning of the twenty-first century. The symbolic implication of the discussion is not lost on them, and they are watching in eager anticipation. The significance of Lara's economic accumulation and his reputation as a sports entrepreneur possess a certain magic for these mostly working-class youth whose attraction to sport in general is largely motivated by the search for socio-economic betterment.

The question of cricket's divorce from nationalism, and the abandonment of nationalist sentiment under Lara's influence, has more to do with how this generation is preparing for the challenges ahead. The only rational form of nationalism which they will recognize and respond to is one that offers open access to the wider Caribbean and beyond. Only seamless entry into the wider Caribbean world, an effective engagement of the global economy, will hold their imagination in ways that insular nationhood cannot. From this expanded base they will be positioned to articulate the national and the global, and to do so aggressively.

The self-confidence of Lara's generation, bolstered by a pertinent educational exposure, and rooted within a postmodern sense of national identity, is slowly providing an important and decisive site for the promotion of a more relevant nationalism. Citizens have shown no intention of delinking identity discourse from popular culture – in which cricket remains King. It follows, then, that the protection and promotion of the game will be an essential part of new strategies of self-empowerment and self-definition. It is here, then, that the text of Lara's personal journey should be read and understood.

Notes

1 This thesis is best represented in the classic work of C.L.R James, *Beyond a Boundary*. London; Hutchinson, 1963; also, *Cricket*. London; Allison and Busby, 1989.

2 See Brian Stoddart, "Cricket and colonialism in the English-speaking Caribbean to 1914: towards a cultural analysis". In Hilary Beckles and Brian Stoddart (eds), *Liberation Cricket: West Indies Cricket Culture*. London: Manchester University Press, 1995.

3 See Hilary Beckles, *The Development of West Indies Cricket: Vol. 1, The Age of Nationalism*. London: Pluto, 1999.

4 This discussion is set out in Michael Manley, *A History of West Indies Cricket*. London: André Deutsch, 1988.

5 See Hilary Beckles, *The Development of West Indies Cricket: Vol. 2, The Age of Globalisation*. London: Pluto, 1999.

6 Ibid.

7 Colin Croft, "Brian Lara: prince or king?" *CricInfo Interactive Magazine*, April 2, 1999; Peter Roebuck, "How our man in Washington made Lara a winner again". *Electronic Telegraph*, April 4, 1999.

8 See Beckles, *The Development of West Indies Cricket, Vol. 2*; Vijay Lokapally, "Brian Lara out on a mission". *The Hindu*, May 19, 1996.

9 No player in the history of West Indies cricket has ever received the high level of income from sponsorship and other commercial sources as Lara, not even his mentor and friend, the incomparable Sir Garfield Sobers. This had given him a unique sense of his autonomy with respect to his employers, the West Indies Cricket Board, with whom he has had numerous contests, most, if not all, of which he has won.

10 See June Soomer, "Cricket and the origins of Federation Organisation". In Hilary Beckles (ed.), *An Area of Conquest: Popular Democracy and West Indies Cricket Supremacy*. Kingston: Ian Randle Publishers, 1994; also Christine Cummings, "The ideology of West Indies cricket". *Arena Review*, 14, 1, 1990.

11 Angus Wilkie, *Daily Nation* (Barbados), April 10, 1996.

12 Pamela Nicholson, the Minister of Sport in Trinidad and Tobago, made this point and went on to state that west Indies cricket does not belong to the West Indies Cricket Board but to the people, and that they should now stand up and speak out with respect to what is good for cricket. Cited in *Caribbean Cricket Quarterly* (CCR), Jan/March, 1996, p. 9.

13 See Wes Hall, "Manager's Report on the Tour to England, 1995", serialized in the Trinidad Guardian, December 8 and 12, 1995; on the issue of Lara's litigation with the WICB, see *Daily Nation* (Barbados), Dec. 5, 1995; see also Brian Lara, *Beating the Field: My Own Story*. London: Corgi, 1996, pp. 45, 64–5, 223–6.

14 See Tony Cozier on Lara, *CCR*, Jan/March, 1996, p. 7; Hayden Gill, "Not cricket", *Daily Nation* (Barbados), March 4, 2000; also the editorial for that day, "Carnival over cricket, Mr Lara?". The statement by Lara that cricket had ruined his life is recorded in manager Hall's tour report.

15 Ibid.

16 Cited in *The Barbados Advocate*, December 6, 1995.

17 All citations from *CCR*, Jan/March 1996, p. 8.

18 Tony Cozier, "West Indies: Cricket Board, Players face off today". *Daily Nation* (Barbados), November 4, 1998; Tony Becca, "South African Boss pledges full support to Tour". *Jamaica Gleaner*, November 5, 1998.

19 "Why Lara is a loser". *Sydney Morning Herald*, November 6, 1998; Christopher Martin-Jenkins, "West Indies dispute: case of dismiss in haste and repent at leisure". *Electronic Telegraph*, November 7, 1998.

20 Tim Hector, "On Lara and the Captaincy". Cited in the *Trinidad Express*, December, 10, 1997.

16

CATHY FREEMAN

The quest for Australian identity

Toni Bruce and Christopher Hallinan

> One thing I do know is that if Australia is the cool, happy-go-
> lucky and friendly country we all claim it to be, then Cathy
> Freeman's smile symbolises the personality, the strength and the
> beauty of its people in the most exquisite way.
> (John Laws, influential public commentator, 1997, p. 35)

In 1990, a young female runner became the first Aboriginal athlete to win an athletics gold medal at the Commonwealth Games when she helped her team to the 4 x 100m relay title. Four years later, aged 21, Cathy Freeman romanced Australia with a solo gold medal in the Commonwealth Games 400m. But it was her victory gesture that rocketed her to national fame and ignited a passion for "Cathy" which continues unabated.

Rather than the usual approach of waving the official Australian flag, Freeman took the groundbreaking step of first draping herself in the unmistakable yellow, red and black of the Aboriginal flag before also collecting the red, blue and white Australian flag for her traditional lap of honour around the stadium.

With that one action, conceived in the mind of a young Aboriginal woman born less than a decade after most Indigenous[1] people gained the right to vote, Freeman powerfully and visually demonstrated the joining of two key parts of Australia's psyche: the first inhabitants and the white settlers/invaders.[2] "Cathy Unites Nation" read one newspaper headline (McGregor, 1999, p. 170).

Freeman's victory lap irrevocably changed public perceptions of the Aboriginal flag. Rather than being associated with protest and political activism, Freeman linked the flag to nationalism and international success. Her actions, repeated when she also won the 200m, generated widespread discussion, even "controversy" (Given, 1995; Olympic hope, 1998, p. 2) and ensured that she and the Aboriginal flag would be forever linked in the minds of many Australians.

How much Australia has changed became clear in September 2000 when, following an opening ceremony featuring Indigenous culture, Freeman was chosen to light the Olympic cauldron on behalf of all Australians. When

Freeman later won the 400m gold medal, carried on a wave of national emotion and goodwill, the country not only expected but needed Freeman to carry both flags on her victory lap. Indeed, the 2000 Olympics cemented her place as perhaps the most potent symbol of Australia's desire for reconciliation between Indigenous and non-Indigenous peoples.

The rise of Cathy Freeman as national celebrity cannot be separated from the broader context in which Australia has struggled with the legacy of white colonization/settlement. Indeed, at the beginning of a new century, Australia finds itself facing a complex web of issues coalescing around the desire for a national identity that embraces both Indigenous people and the many waves of immigrants while retaining white power.

Past and present: race relations

Cathy Freeman, the successful athlete, appears far removed from Australia's well-documented history of brutality, dispossession and injustice towards its Indigenous people (Bourke *et al.*, 1998; Broome, 1994; Kane, 1997; McConnochie *et al.*, 1988; McQueen, 1974; Reynolds, 1996, 1998). Yet, as a member of a group of people that the government initially hoped "would solve racial problems by dying out" (Sargent, 1994, p. 200), she is intimately connected to it. Freeman's grandmother is part of the stolen generation: one of up to 100,000 children removed from their families between 1910 and 1970 to be raised in white-run institutions or fostered out to white families "for their own good" (ATSIC, 1999, p. 1; McGregor, 1999). Both of her parents grew up on missions – known for their harsh and rigid conditions – to which many Indigenous people were forcibly moved (McGregor, 1999; Meade, 1998).

In 1999, when Prime Minister John Howard finally acknowledged this history on behalf of the entire country with an expression of "deep and sincere regret," he tempered it by stating that most living Australians or their parents were not personally involved (Milsom, 1999, p. 9). However, the Aboriginal and Torres Strait Islander Commission argues that not one Aboriginal family is unaffected by the policy of removal which occurred in the name of assimilation and of which few white Australians were aware of until the mid-1990s (ATSIC, 1999).

It is only in the last forty years, assisted by government policies designed to restore to Aboriginal peoples "their lost power of self-determination" (Broome, 1994, p. 181), that Indigenous people have gained rights in law and recognition in the broader culture. They were denied the right to vote in Federal elections until 1962 and could not vote in all states until 1965. It was not until 1967 that all Aborigines were recognized as "equal" citizens and counted in a national census from which they had been excluded in 1901 (Hemming, 1998, p. 31).

It should be noted that *Aboriginal* is an identity largely constructed by whites which collapses a tremendous diversity of languages and geographically localized cultures into a single collective group (Hemming, 1998; Stokes,

1997). However, Indigenous people have used this non-Indigenous category and others like *justice* and *self-determination* to promote their own interests (ibid.). According to Stokes, "This is not just a matter of random individual resistance, nor uncritical consent to European ideas, but represents intelligent appraisal of viable strategies within different political contexts" (ibid., p. 170).

In the last decade of the twentieth century, Indigenous pressure led to several national inquiries that resulted in government – and broadly popular – moves towards a "reconciliation process" (Broome, 1994, p. 237), and finally allowed Aboriginal communities to register claims for land they had occupied continuously and from which they had previously been denied ownership. By 2000, in the face of the government's refusal to say "sorry", public frustration had grown to the point where more than 100,000 Australians marched in support of reconciliation.

It was from this fertile ground of symbolic and legislative battles over land rights, deaths in custody, the stolen generation, reconciliation, and in the face of appalling disparities in health and widespread racism, and that Cathy Freeman emerged as the new face of Australian athletics and, more recently, of Australia itself.

Sport, Aboriginality and national identity

... it is our sporting stars who are our greatest ambassadors, the people we hang our hats on, who make us proud, who we stay up half the night to cheer to victory on the other side of the world. Their success is vitally important to our psyche, they make us feel part of the big world and a big player in that world.

(Evans, 2000a, p. 37)

New settler societies such as Australia are constantly engaged in a highly visible process of nation formation in the face of "enormous problems articulating a commonality across competing forms of ethnicity and against a history of occupation and dispossession of the original inhabitants" (Bennett *et al.*, 1994, pp. 2–3). Further, the process of defining *Australia* or what it means to be *Australian* is an ongoing process full of change, contradictions, ambivalence and fundamental realignments (Fiske *et al.*, 1987; Turner, 1994; White, 1981).

In debates over the future of the nation, the main issue has not been whether or not nationalism is irrelevant but the extent to which Australia's identity will be anchored in an historically exclusive, narrow, hierarchical and white dominant vision, or one that is inclusive, multicultural, democratic and progressively hybridized.

Australians have generally bypassed the establishment of a national identity through constitutional change (such as freeing themselves from connections to Britain by becoming a republic, or by adopting a new flag). Instead, they have adopted popular cultural symbols as markers of nationalism. Constructing a sense of nation includes creating significant symbols both of common identity and of difference from others.

It is widely accepted that the media are a key institution through which the nation is constructed. For Turner, the media "constitute the primary processes through which discourses of nationalism are deployed and disseminated" (1994, pp. 145–6). Indeed, highly mediated images of Aboriginality and sport have become integral to an understanding of what it means to be Australian.

As Evans' quote above suggests, international sport is a key arena in which particular versions of nation are expressed (Cashman, 1995). The extensive media coverage of Australia's international sporting successes in 1999 and 2000 bears testament to the importance of sport in defining Australia's identity in relation to the rest of the world. Indeed, Rowe argues that sport "constitutes a cultural apparatus that can be speedily and regularly mobilized in the symbolic reconstruction of the nation" (1995, p. 136).

For a nation that is "slightly awkward about expressing a generalised patriotism" (Turner, 1994, p. 68), sport is one of the few arenas in which Australians publicly display patriotic symbols such as flags and songs (Cashman, 1995). Both the official Australian flag and national anthem come together as signs of nationalism and winning at international sporting events (Given, 1995). However, like all markers of national identity, the official flag and anthem are not uncontested. Emerging grassroots challenges to these historically dominant symbols of patriotism come from both sport and Indigenous culture. For example, the unofficial green and gold boxing kangaroo flag and Waltzing Matilda song are increasingly visible at major international sporting events. Freeman's displays of the Aboriginal flag to celebrate her successes have also generated widespread support perhaps indicating the growing importance of Aboriginality to establishing a unique Australian identity.

Australia has witnessed a boom in the generation of artistic images inspired or directly created by Indigenous peoples (Godwell, 1999). The use of Indigenous music, imagery and people in connection with international sporting events is growing. Indeed, the 2000 Olympic Games in Sydney drew heavily upon Indigenous imagery as the "one original Australian expression on an international stage" (ibid., p. 19). However, Godwell critiques the Olympic branding of Aborigines for representing Indigenous peoples as linked to the past and to history, thus challenging their existence in contemporary Australian society.

Although multiple and contradictory meanings of Aboriginality circulate in different domains of Australian culture such as sport or law and order (Fiske et al., 1987; Stokes, 1997), popular culture has increasingly appropriated symbols and individuals with Indigenous connections such as Uluru/Ayers Rock, musicians and media personalities such as Yothu Yindi and Ernie Dingo, and elite athletes like Cathy Freeman and Australian Rules footballer Michael Long (Lattas, 1997; Marcus, 1997; Turner, 1994).

Crossing both the Indigenous and sports worlds, Freeman may have become – as Rowe argues about sport in Australia – an "amplifier" of citizenship and national identity (1995, p. 102). For just as sport has shown an ability to bind together disparate communities (Cashman, 1995), Freeman's appeal appears to cross cultural, ethnic, gender, and other boundaries.

The embodiment of reconciliation

> Everyone wanted a part of this attractive personality, the smiling kid who made everyone feel good: when she addressed the prawns and champagne luncheons everybody could make-believe that all was well in the Aboriginal world.
>
> (Tatz, 1995, p. 293)

That Freeman has become a national celebrity is indisputable. Hurst claims "whether she likes it or not there is a sense of public investment in her as in all our national heroes" (1997a, p. 114). Much of Freeman's claim to fame is her status as a world champion athlete in a country where sport plays a vital role in the construction of national identity. However, it is the conjunction of Freeman's identities as internationally successful athlete and Indigenous Australian that appear to have catapulted her into a celebrity status that initially far outstripped her achievements (Harding, 1996; McGregor, 1999).

In 1990, so little was known about her that the official Australian Commonwealth Games team manual had "no details other than her name" (McGregor, 1999, p. 68). Yet her location as an indigenous athlete appears to have singled her out right from the start. Several months after the relay win, a team-mate criticized the imaginary barrier she saw being created to separate Freeman from the other three runners: "We shouldn't be separated into three white athletes and one Aboriginal ... We should all just be athletes because being black or white doesn't mean anything on the track" (ibid., p. 73).

However, by the mid-1990s, Freeman had notched up an impressive list of firsts: the first Australian to win back-to-back world track and field titles, the first female and second Australian to win any world track and field title, as well as the first Indigenous track and field athlete to participate in an Olympic Games or to win an Olympic medal. As a successful Indigenous person repre-senting Australia on the world stage, Freeman appears to embody the potential for reconciliation between white and Indigenous Australians.

Freeman's celebrity status in Australia extends well beyond the arena of sport. Aged only 24, she became the first Australian to be named both Young Australian (1991) and Australian of the Year (1998). She was voted a National Living Treasure in 1997, became one of four living Australians to have their portraits commissioned for the opening of the National Portrait Gallery in 1999, and was chosen to light the cauldron at the 2000 Olympic Games.

Hers is one of the most recognizable Aboriginal faces of the past decade. Her popularity is such that more Australians chose the 2000 Olympic Games 400m final as their first choice in the Olympic Games ticket ballot than any other event except the opening ceremony (Stephens, 1999). When the International Amateur Athletics Federation threatened to alter the athletics draw, an uproar ensued over possible changes to "Cathy's race" (Walker, 1999, p. 28). Media commentators proclaim her as "our Cathy" and the public's adoration has grown to the point where she now trains overseas for much of the year to escape the pressure (Hinds, 2000; No private life, 1998).

Yet how did Freeman rise to such celebrity status so quickly? It is likely that, at a time when Australia was being asked searching questions of its history of race relations, the young, attractive, and internationally successful Freeman emerged as a non-threatening Indigenous person with whom the entire country could identify. Even today, Freeman is not seen as a threat to the current structure although she is often asked to speak about Indigenous issues (Harding, 1996; Malakunas, 1998). "Despite the Aboriginal flag which she carries on significant occasions, she is not seen as an Aboriginal militant. Not for her the raised fist, the boycott or the strident protest" (McGregor, 1999, p. 346).

Instead media commentators suggest that Freeman has become an unexpected lightning rod for debates about race. "For reasons even seasoned commentators find difficult to explain, Freeman has become a very rare beast: a political activist who, without speaking, brings forth debate on serious issues and remains (almost) universally adored" (Overington, 1997, p. 32).

Freeman's determination to display her Aboriginality throughout her career (Hatch 1998) has won her the support and admiration of many Australians (Malakunas, 1998). When Freeman drapes herself in both the Aboriginal and Australian flags for a victory lap she becomes a powerful visual symbol of the reconciliation for which Australia is striving (Given, 1995; Rowe, 1995).

Yet this is not a spontaneous gesture on Freeman's part. She has always competed wearing the yellow, red and black of the flag, whether as a band in her hair or on her wrist, or in the colours on her running shoes. The flag is a yellow sun against a background of black, which represents the Aboriginal people, and red, which represents the earth, red ochre and the people's spiritual relationship with the land (Given, 1995). She first wore the Aboriginal flag as a statement of her identity, an identity that was not recognized in the official Australian flag.

By waiting for a moment of international success to display the Aboriginal flag, Freeman presented it in a completely new light (Given, 1995; Stephens, 1999). Given argues that "for most of white Australia, the ... Aboriginal flag had not been seen as a symbol of victory. When the colours had been seen at all, they had been at sites of defiance, conflict or physical squalor" (1995, p. 30). The rapidity of changes in attitudes towards the flag are indicated by the stark contrast between the positive responses to Freeman's wearing the flag in 1994 and 2000, and the Queensland government's response to Indigenous protesters at the 1982 Commonwealth Games.[3] First, the government instituted draconian laws that, in essence, gave police wide-ranging powers to control Aborigines wanting to protest. Then it characterized Indigenous people intent on using the Games to peacefully bring the foreign media's attention to the issue of land rights as drunken troublemakers (Given, 1995). Police surrounded protesters who draped the flag and banners over rails inside the sports stadium, again associating the flag with political action. Twelve years later, major changes in public awareness and support of Aboriginal rights meant that any controversy when Freeman first carried both flags was both limited and short-lived (Given, 1995; Olympic hope, 1998). By 2000, not only had the International Olympic Committee approved the flag to fly at Olympic Stadium as an official Australian flag, but Freeman was expected to carry it on her victory lap. The IOC, who saw the approval as "an important symbol for Australia's efforts at Aboriginal reconciliation" (Bita, 1999, p. 3) further aligned this powerful Indigenous symbol with national identity and supported Commonwealth Reconciliation Minister Philip Ruddock's earlier statements that "the flag was being recognised as being Australian" (Olympic hope, 1998, p. 2). However, it is unlikely that the Aboriginal flag would have gained this level of acceptance and recognition without Freeman's gestures associating it with winning and Australian success against the rest of the world.

As predicted, the 2000 Olympic Games proved a site of both contestation and celebration for Aboriginal Australia. Although some Aboriginal leaders discussed calling for a black boycott of the Games (Cathy told to, 1997), the eventual focus was on using the Olympics to draw world media attention to the living conditions and experiences of Indigenous people. For example, Aboriginal leader Noel Pearson stated, "We can't go into an international celebration pretending that we are not subject to constitutional discrimination, because we are" (Jopson, 1998, p. 14). However, in the lead up to the Olympics, Indigenous discussions about potential protests at the 2000 Olympic Games were invariably tempered by discussions of how to get tickets "when Cathy runs" (ibid.). Indigenous academic Tracey Bunda expressed a widespread view when she said there was no doubt that Aboriginal protesters would stop their activities to watch or listen to the 400m heats and finals (Bunda, 1999). Indeed, most of Australia came to a standstill as Freeman raced. "A nation's will drives Cathy to her destiny" read one headline after she won gold (Masters, 2000).

Freeman's popularity among Indigenous Australians can be tied to the integral role that sport plays in Aboriginal identity. Sport is "immensely important" (Cashman, 1995, p. 150) if not "essential" (Tatz, 1995, p. 297) to Aboriginal communities that see few other areas in which they can achieve success. Further, Tatz argues that it is sporting prowess rather than other aspects of culture that produce "such grudging respect as Australians accord Aborigines" (1995, p. 359).

Ideologically, white Australians embrace superstars like Freeman as representative of what all Aborigines could achieve if properly motivated (see Rowe, 1995) but the reality is that opportunities to excel in sport are considerably more limited for Indigenous athletes. Tatz strongly argues that Aboriginal athletes who succeed do so in spite of a system that provides facilities and opportunities far inferior to those available to most Australians. "Most do not have money, transport, equipment, arenas, instructors and access to organised competition" (1995, p. 297). Just like Freeman, many successful athletes have to leave home for places where training and competition are available (ibid., p. 355). At a 1990 media conference, Freeman herself identified structural discrimination as an issue for many Indigenous athletes, saying "A lot of my friends have the talent but lack the opportunity" (McGregor, 1999, p. 72).

As well as structural discrimination, overt racism impacts the experiences of high-achieving Aboriginal athletes (see Gardiner, 1997). Freeman reports that, early in her career, white Australians refused to get into a lift, sit or stand next to her because of her race (Connolly & McCabe, 1998, p. B3; Cathy's inside Running, 1998; Freeman eyes political, 1998). Others refused to queue to be served by a young Freeman working for Australia Post under the Olympic Jobs Program in 1992 (McGregor, 1999). Although Freeman faces double discrimination based on both race and gender (Cashman, 1995; Stell, 1991), she identifies racial stereotypes as having the most impact. Freeman has said that growing up, like many young Aborigines, she lacked self-confidence because of the prevailing stereotypes and attitudes towards Aboriginal people (Hatch, 1998).

A survey of newspaper and magazine articles over the past five years suggests that media representations of Freeman draw upon both race and gender stereotypes and that little may have changed in the thirty years since Aboriginal tennis star Evonne Goolagong Cawley was "patronised by both racist and sexist descriptions by a white male-controlled media" (Stell, 1991, p. 237).

Like black athletes from the USA and UK, Indigenous Australians are widely believed to possess different skills and qualities to non-Indigenous athletes (Hallinan et al., 1999). In general, media representations paint a picture of quick, instinctive, naturally talented, inventive athletes of flair and imagination who may also be unreliable, lacking discipline, unable to handle success and unsuitable for positions of responsibility (Cashman, 1995; Hallinan et al., 1999; Hallinan, 1991; Stoddart, 1986).

Freeman is often represented as a natural runner (Critchley & Walsh, 1998), who has the ability to relax and rise to the big events. Chisholm cites a psychologist who says Freeman has a "completely unaffected kind of relaxed natural way of being coupled with this incredibly fierce determination in competition ... You don't often get those two things in the same person: this joking, relaxed, devil-may-care attitude combined with an almost killer instinct" (1997, p. 25).

Although Freeman is often represented as a strong, tough, determined competitor with a fighting spirit who refuses to give up (Hurst, 1997c; Chisholm, 1997; Johnson, 1997), some descriptions play upon racial stereotypes of Indigenous people as childlike, lazy, unmotivated and lacking the drive to succeed (see Bourke, 1998). For example, Freeman has been described as needing constant shepherding because, among other things, "of her nature" (Evans, 1999b, p. 40). Some stories focus on her early avoidance of hard work, dislike of hard training and tendency to exert only the minimum effort necessary: "Doing only what she needed to win, as is her habit" (Jeffery, 1999, p. 1; McGregor, 1999). Early in her career, spectators made overtly racist comments about the likelihood that Freeman would "turn black" or "go walkabout" which meant she would "waste everyone's effort by walking away from her career before she had reached her potential" (ibid., p. 100).

In terms of gender, media coverage of Freeman shows the ambivalence, infantilization and focus on traditional images of femininity and female sexuality identified in Australian and international research (Duncan *et al.*, 1990; Kane and Greendorfer, 1994; Mikosza and Womensport Australia, 1997; Phillips, 1996). Thus, athletes like Freeman who are physically attractive and small in stature attract extensive media coverage. This tendency is most clearly displayed in a 1998 story in which Freeman, then aged in her mid-twenties, was described as a shy, charming, sweet, unaffected wisp of a girl (Critchley and Walsh, 1998).

Few stories miss the opportunity to emphasize Freeman's size: she is most often described as small, little or diminutive (e.g., Evans, 1997, 1998; 2000a; Hurst, 1997c; Payten, 1998). Much attention is paid to her smile and trademark giggle, along with her natural charm and bubbly personality (Harding, 1996; Critchley & Walsh, 1998). And, just as international research has found representations of female athletes to be marked by ambivalence, so too has media coverage of Freeman. Descriptions veer from strong-willed dominator, to helpless traumatized girl, sometimes in the same article.

Her personal life has always attracted intense interest (e.g., Chisholm, 1997; Hurst, 1997b). Several of the many stories on the trauma of her break up with long-time lover/manager Nick Bideau – in the same year she won her first 400m world title – speculated on how she would cope without his guidance. For example, Hurst asked whether her chances of success depended on whether "she is now able to interpret life other than through the filter held up by Bideau" (1997a, p. 114).

Given that she was only 16 when she won her first Commonwealth Games gold medal, it is not surprising that her career has been guided by others. However, the media has until recently represented her as being unable to take care of herself, and her success as being orchestrated by white Australians such as her former lover/manager Bideau, coach, and agent. Despite the increasingly positive media representations that have followed Freeman's continuing success, stereotypes reappear in coverage of any setback. For example, stories about the highly publicized management split between Bideau and Freeman a few months before the Olympics included quotes such as "The whole thing is going off the rails … She only gets one shot at the gold medal and it looks like it is slipping away" (Evans, 2000b, p. 81).

Interestingly, in a sports world dominated by commercialism, Freeman – now married to a Nike executive and whose sponsors include the multinational sports company – is seldom represented in the press as a Nike Athlete. Instead, perhaps because she competes primarily upon the world stage, she is Australian or Aboriginal Australian.

In the wake of the 2000 Olympics, where Freeman showed the ability to succeed under the weight of a nation's expectations, the ambivalence that has marked past representations may give way to more of the following: "No longer shamed by her colour or scared to stand up for herself, Freeman presents as a proud, strong, Aboriginal athlete very much aware of her place in the world and her ability to change its landscape" (Evans, 1999a, p. 26).

The white embrace of Cathy Freeman: an easy way out

> For me, Cathy represents an ambivalence. On one hand, she is the forerunner of a generation of young Aboriginal women who make it against the many hurdles confronting them – the racism, sexism, stereotyping; on the other hand, her very breaking out, her sprinting out, has made her the very convenient "sample of one", the attractive, sunny, achieving, sporting lass whose very presence cures the blight that is still so much part of racist Australia.
>
> (Tatz, 1995, p. 295)

It is likely, as McKay (1994, in Rowe, 1995) argues about black athletes in general, that positive media representations like those of Freeman serve to comfort white guilt about structural racial inequality. Indeed, the quote from John Laws which opens this chapter perhaps best expresses this desire for a comfortable way to embrace Aboriginality without having to confront the anger, pain, poverty and disenfranchisement of so many Indigenous people. In the words of Indigenous scholar Darren Godwell:

> To some extent, it's better for white than for black people to have Cathy Freeman running around ... It was the same with Lionel Rose in the 1960s and Evonne Goolagong in the 1970s. They made it easy for white people to say, well, things can't be too bad for Aborigines.
>
> (Overington, 1997, p. 32)

Freeman also contributes to this comfort with public statements that support the notion that success is available to all prepared to work for it. McGregor suggests that Freeman's statements are "guilt-freeing; the sort of tone that White Australia likes to hear" (1999, p. 83). As Young Australian of the Year, Freeman said, "It's so important for my people that we get up and make a future for ourselves ... The opportunities are there, I've proven it. I'm an example" (ibid., p. 82). Seven years later, as Australian of the Year, Freeman is quoted as saying, "I come from a humble background, and this award shows

Australians that if we truly, truly believe in ourselves and work hard, then great things are possible" (Malakunas, 1998, p. 5).

On a more positive note, what Freeman might offer is the chance to contemplate a hybrid Australian identity: one in which two forms of identity (Aboriginal and white Australian) retain their distinctiveness but in combination produce something startlingly new (Turner, 1994).

Freeman's popularity may in part be tied to her own hybridity: she is firmly planted in both the Indigenous and the white worlds. Overington claims "Freeman's people are black – her mother, her father, her siblings – but also white, like her lovers and friends and her stepfather" (1997, p. 32). Freeman's statement that she is a proud "Australian Aborigine: they are two in the same" expresses just such a sense of hybridity (Overington, 1997, p. 32).

Freeman, much like Michael Jordan, appears to have transcended language and cultural barriers to be as widely embraced within diverse Aboriginal communities as among white communities. Indeed, the overwhelming public support for Freeman may reflect the growing desire of many Australians for a nation that recognizes and values both Indigenous and non-Indigenous peoples. Yet often this desire is embodied only in a symbolic, rather than real, relationship with Indigenous peoples (Bruce, 2000). Embracing Freeman may be an easy way out for Australians who, without having to take any action, can believe: *We are not racist: We love Cathy.*

Acknowledgments

The authors acknowledge the assistance of University of Canberra graduate student Josh Whittington who gathered many of the newspaper articles on Cathy Freeman.

Notes

1　The term Indigenous is used throughout the chapter to include both Aboriginal and Torres Strait Islander peoples. Aborigine/Aboriginal is used to identify individuals or groups identified specifically as Aboriginal rather than Torres Strait Islander.
2　We abide by Graeme Turner's (1994) ideas that old identity symbols are bound up in accuracy issues but still have power and utility. In recognition of the history of the White Australia policies and their impact upon Indigenous Australians, we have used the term "white". We note that others have used terms such as "invader", "settler", "Anglo", Anglo-Celtic" and "European" to identify those non-Indigenous Australians who first colonized the continent and continue to wield economic and cultural power.
3　For a more extensive discussion of these events, see Given (1995).

Bibliography

ATSIC (1999) Issues: The stolen generation. Aboriginal and Torres Strait Islander Commission, December 2. [On-line]. Available: http://www.atsic.gov.au/issues/bringing_them_home/Default.asp

Bennett, T., Turner, G. and Volkerling, M. (1994) Introduction: post-colonial forma-tions. *Culture and Policy*, 6 (1), 1–5.

Bita, N. (1999) Blacks to fly their flag at Olympics. *The Weekend Australian*, October 2–3, p. 3.

Bourke, E. (1998) Images and realities. In C. Bourke, E. Bourke and B. Edwards (eds), *Aboriginal Australia* (2nd edn) (pp. 16–37). St Lucia, Queensland: University of Queensland Press.

Bourke, C., Bourke, E. and Edwards, B. (1998) *Aboriginal Australia* (2nd edn). St Lucia, Queensland: University of Queensland Press.

Broome, R. (1994) *Aboriginal Australians* (2nd edn). St Leonards: Sydney: Allen & Unwin.

Bruce, T. (2000) Cathy Freeman symbolizes the spirit of the Sydney Olympic Games. *The Canberra Times*, March 23, p. 21.

Bunda, T. (1999) Personal communication. Canberra, Australia, November 28.

Cashman, R. (1995) *Paradise of Sport: The Rise of Organised Sport in Australia*. Melbourne: Oxford University Press Australia.

Cathy told to boycott Games. (1997) *The Sun Herald.*, November 9, p. 1.

Cathy's inside running in matters of race. (1998) *The Australian*, November 20, p. 5.

Chisholm, C. (1997) Cathy's secret. *The Daily Telegraph*, August 9, p. 25.

Connolly, S. and McCabe, H. (1998) Cathy tells of race she can't win. *The Daily Tele-graph*, November 20, p. 5.

Critchley, C. and Walsh, B. (1998) Cathy Freeman in a different light. *The Daily Tele-graph*, July 18, p. 21.

Duncan, M.C., Messner, M.A. and Jensen, K. (1990) *Gender Stereotyping in Televised Sports*. Los Angeles: The Amateur Athletic Foundation of Los Angeles.

Evans, L. (1997) Cathy freewoman. *The Sydney Morning Herald*, March 7, p. 40.

—— (1998) Cathy's comeback. *The Sydney Morning Herald*, October 31, p. 54.

—— (1999a) Toughened Freeman heads back to business. *The Sydney Morning Herald*, January 25, p. 26.

—— (1999b) The club. *The Sydney Morning Herald*, February 11, p. 40.

—— (2000a) Freeman gets gong in photo-finish. *The Sydney Morning Herald*, January 1, p.37.

—— (2000b) Money, lawyers and love Freeman's recipe for catastrophe. *The Sydney Morning Herald*, June 17, p. 81.

Fiske, J., Hodge, B. and Turner, G. (1987) *Myths of Oz: Reading Australian Popular Culture*. St Leonards, NSW: Allen & Unwin.

Freeman eyes political run. (1998) *The Sydney Morning Herald*, November 20, p. 7.

Gardiner, G.S. (1997) Racism and football: The AFL's Racial and Religious Vilification Code in review. *Sporting Traditions*, 14, 3–25.

Given, J. (1995) Red, black, gold to Australia: Cathy Freeman and the flags. *Media Information Australia*, 75, February, 46–56.

Godwell, D.J. (1999) The Olympic branding of Aborigines: The 2000 Olympic Games and Australia's Indigenous peoples. Unpublished paper. Centre for Indigenous Natural and Cultural Resource Management, Northern Territory University.

Hallinan, C. (1991) Aborigines and positional segregation in Australian Rugby League, *International Review for the Sociology of Sport*, 26(2), 69–81.

Hallinan, C., Bruce, T. and Coram, S. (1999) Up front and beyond the centre line: Australian Aborigines in elite Australian Rules football. *International Review for the Sociology of Sport*, 34 (4), 369–83.

Harding, M. (1996) Race of her life. *Sports Weekly*, February 6, pp. 22–3.

Hatch, G. (1998) Love yourself to success. *The Sun Herald*, November 29, p. 33.

Hemming, S. (1998) Changing history: New images of Aboriginal history. In C. Bourke, E. Bourke and B. Edwards (eds), *Aboriginal Australia* (2nd edn) (pp. 16–37). St Lucia, Queensland: University of Queensland Press.

Hinds, R. (2000). Tinkering tailored to stop spies. *The Sydney Morning Herald*, June 13, p. 22.

Hurst, M. (1997a) Cathy learns the hard lessons. *The Daily Telegraph*, February 14, p. 114.

—— (1997b) Faltering Freeman hit by break-up. *The Daily Telegraph*, February 21, p. 102.

—— (1997c) Cathy's golden opportunity. *The Daily Telegraph*, May 28, p. 75.

—— (1999) Perec's dig at Freeman. *The Daily Telegraph*, August 28. [Online]. Available: http://www.sport.news.com.au/news/4341324.htm

Jeffery, N. (1999) Freeman needs bigger test than Italian meet. *The Australian*, July 12. [Online]. Available: http://www.theaustralian.com.au/masthead/theoz/state/4122538.htm

Johnson, L. (1997) Female of the championships. *Australian Runner and Athlete*, 17(4), September/ October, 30, 39.

Jopson, D. (1998) O'Donoghue holds boycott card. *The Sydney Morning Herald*, September 25, p. 14.

Kane, J. (1997) Racialism and democracy: the legacy of White Australia. In G. Stokes (ed.), *The Politics of Identity in Australia* (pp. 117–31). Melbourne: Cambridge University Press.

Kane, M.J. and Greendorfer, S.L. (1994) The media's role in accommodating and resisting stereotyped images of women in sport. In P.J. Creedon (ed.), *Women, Media and Sport: Challenging Gender Values* (pp. 28–44). Thousand Oaks, CA: Sage.

Lattas, A. (1997) Aborigines and contemporary Australian nationalism: primordiality and the cultural politics of otherness. In G. Cowlishaw and B. Morris (eds), *Race Matters* (pp. 223–58). Canberra: Aboriginal Studies Press.

Laws, J. (1997) Cathy helps keep the dream alive. *The Sunday Telegraph*, August 10, p. 35.

Masters, R. (2000) A nation's will drives Cathy to her destiny. *The Canberra Times*, September 26, p. 5.

McConnochie, K., Hollinsworth, D. and Pettman, J. (1988) *Race and Racism in Australia*. Wentworth Falls: Social Science Press.

McGregor, A. (1999) *Cathy Freeman: A Journey Just Begun*. Sydney: Random House.

McQueen, H. (1974) *Aborigines, Race and Racism*. Ringwood, Victoria: Penguin Books.

Magnay, J. (1997) Cathy and Kieren: 1000 days to 2000. *The Sydney Morning Herald*, December 15, p. 3.

Malakunas, K. (1998) We all can be great: Cathy's call to the nation. *The Daily Telegraph*, January 26, p. 5.

Marcus, J. (1997) The journey out to the centre: cultural appropriation of Ayers Rock. In G. Cowlishaw and B. Morris (eds) *Race Matters* (pp. 29–51). Canberra: Aboriginal Studies Press.

Meade, K. (1998) Cathy Freeman, island of despair's patron saint. *The Australian*, January 26, p. 4.

Mikosza, J. and Womensport Australia (1997) *Inching Forward: Newspaper Coverage and Portrayal of Women's Sport in Australia: A Quantitative and Qualitative Analysis 1996 and 1997*. Canberra: Womensport Australia.

Milsom, R. (1999) The fear of sorry. *Newcastle Herald*, August 30, p. 9.

No private life for a superstar. (1998) *The Sunday Telegraph*, March 1, p. 65.

Olympic hope for Aboriginal flag. (1998) *The Daily Telegraph*, October 26, p. 2.

Overington, C. (1997) Cathy the great. *The Sydney Morning Herald*, August 9, p. 32.

Payten, I. (1998) Freeman holds court. *The Daily Telegraph*, November 4, p. 65.

Phillips, M.G. (1996) *An Illusory Image: A Report on the Media Coverage and Portrayal of Women's Sport in Australia*. Canberra: Australian Sports Commission.

Reynolds, H. (1996) *Frontier: Aborigines, Settlers and Land*. Sydney: Allen & Unwin.

—— (1998) *This Whispering in Our Hearts*. Sydney: Allen & Unwin.

Rowe, D. (1995) *Popular Cultures: Rock Music, Sport and the Politics of Pleasure*. Thousand Oaks, CA: Sage.

Sargent, M. (1994) *The New Sociology for Australians* (3rd edn). Melbourne: Longman Australia.

Stell, M.K. (1991) *Half the Race: A History of Australian Women in Sport*. North Ryde, NSW: Angus & Robertson.

Stephens, T. (1999) Taking the weight. *The Sydney Morning Herald*, November 23, pp. 45–6.

Stoddart, B. (1986) *Saturday Afternoon Fever: Sport in Australian Culture*. North Ryde: Angus & Robertson.

Stokes, G. (1997) Citizenship and Aboriginality: Two conceptions of identity in Aboriginal political thought. In G. Stokes (ed.), *The Politics of Identity in Australia*. Cambridge: Cambridge University Press.

Tatz, C. (1995) *Obstacle Race: Aborigines in Sport*. Sydney: University of New South Wales Press.

Turner, G. (1994) *Making it National: Nationalism and Australian Popular Culture*. St. Leonards, Sydney: Allen & Unwin.

Walker, F. (1999) Battle over Cathy's race. *The Sun-Herald*, September 12, p. 28.

White, R. (1981) *Inventing Australia: Images and Identity 1688–1980*. Sydney: Allen & Unwin.

INDEX

Aboriginal Australians 258–9; identity
  257, 262–3; life chances 263–4;
  otherness 17; removal of children 258;
  rights 258
Aboriginal flag 257, 260, 262–3
Adams, Victoria 13, 138, 143–4, 147,
  148–9
Adidas 210–11
Advertising Age 77
affirmative action 12, 26, 70–1, 81–5, 96
African Americans: family 11, 37, 38;
  masculinity 11, 27, 29; 1936 Olympics
  218–19; as Other 43–4; physicality 25;
  sexuality 41–4; stereotypes 40–1, 44–5;
  Williams 12
African athletes 218, 224–8; *see also*
  Kenyan runners
Agassi, Andre: Canon 58–9, 60, 61–2,
  67n12; Donnay 60; Generation X 11,
  51, 58–63; image 59, 61–2; media 63;
  Mountain Dew 58, 64–5; Nike 58, 60;
  performance 60–1; reinvented 62–6,
  67–8n13; as slacker 11, 59–63
aggressiveness/humour 142
Aikens, E. 36–7
Air Jordan 22
amateurism 88–9, 234
American Dream 53, 65
American Tennis Association 88
Americanization: Canada 166–72, 175–6,
  179; ice hockey 181–2; Japan 197
Anderson, Elijah 99
Andrews, David L. 10–12, 22, 25, 32–3,
  166, 211
anti-affirmative action 76, 82
anti-colonialism 238, 243, 244
ape images 45, 48–9n4
appropriation of black runners 225–6

Araton, Harvey 63
Archetti, E. 132
Arcucci, D. 162
Argentina: football 14, 151, 154–5;
  national identity 14, 154; *pibe* 14, 132,
  154–60; *potrero* 14, 154–8; World Cup
  152–3
Arthur Ashe Stadium 87, 90
Asahi Shinbun 187, 191, 193, 195
Ashe, Arthur 78, 88, 89–90
assimilation: Australia 258; imperial 232,
  233
Association of Track and Field Statisticians
  225
Athletics Weekly 221–2, 223
Athletics World 225–6, 226
Australia: assimilation 258; hybridity 267;
  national identity 259–60, 261; new
  settler societies 259; popular culture
  260–1; postcolonialism 17; race
  relations 258–9; racism 264, 266, 267;
  reconciliation 258, 259, 261–3; sport
  263–4; *see also* Aboriginal Australians;
  Freeman; Indigenous peoples
L'Auto 218

Babyboomers 56–7, 67n10
Bailey, Donovan 180
Bale, John 15, 226, 227
Ball Park Franks advertisement 30
Bank, Dick 228
Barnes, John: nationality 109, 110; racial
  stereotyping 120n4; racism 112–13,
  120n3, 121n7; and Wright 102, 111
Barrett, L. 36–7, 38, 40
Barthes, Roland 124, 131–2
Base, B. 23
baseball: Japan 14–15, 187–8, 194,